A PS

AUTOBIOGRAPHY

BY

AMANDA T. JONES

1910

Contents

DEDICATION 1

INTRODUCTION 2

THE AUTHOR TO HER FRIENDS...4

CASTING THE NET 17

CHILDHOOD AND THE DUAL MIND 24

TO DREAM AND TO DESIRE 33

SUBJECTIVE VISIONS 41

MIND SUBMERGENCE AND PSYCHIC REVELATIONS....................48

A FLOWER OF PARADISE AND A SOUL IN SHADOW 59

A CHILD AND A PHYSICIAN...66

TELEPATHY, RAPPING AND WRITING......................................75

LOGIC AND SPIRIT-PERSONATION...84

PROPHECY FULFILLED 94

INDEPENDENT SIGHT AND KNOWLEDGE..............................100

PHANTASM AND REALITY 108

FRIENDS ON GUARD 119

WAYS OF PLEASANTNESS...128

PSYCHO-PHYSICS AND PSYCHOMETRY 141

PSYCHOMETRY AND SPIRIT-INFLUENCE 154

A HELPER IN MACEDONIA 171

RUE AND ROSEMARY 183

THE WAY OF A SPIRIT...199

TRANSITION 212

PREPARATION 229

ACCEPTANCE 243

WAYS AND MEANS...262

A SAFETY-CAGE..280

THE CRUSADE DOCUMENTS..295

AERIAL BRIDGES..323

MOUNTAIN PATHS..344

CREVASSES AND CANONS..361

VALLEYS AND PITFALLS 384

FOUNTAINS OF DESIRE 409

DEDICATION

To Prof. William James [known as the Father of modern psychiatry and brother of writer Henry James], who long ago proposed that I should prepare for publication a history of what I may venture to call my super-normal experiences, and who now adds: "You may remember how I encouraged you to write it," this faithful record is humbly and reverentially inscribed.

A. T. J.

Junction City, Kansas.

INTRODUCTION

I HAVE read these life experiences of Miss Amanda T. Jones with extraordinary interest. I do not speak for them as scientific evidence of the supernormal, where that method involves certification and corroboration for each incident, but I do speak for them as human experiences coming from a source that is entitled to have its testimony heard. Miss Jones is a well-known poetess in this country, having published several volumes of poems, including a collected edition in 1907. She has also been a successful inventor and practical business woman. These accomplishments have made her well enough known to make attention to her psychic experiences desirable. We can easily find objections to each and every incident taken alone, but the collective mass of them, though having only a record of memory, must have its interest for those who are seeking to justify investigation into such phenomena when they are verifiable and for those who are seeking confirmation of better attested ones.

I do not indorse the critical views of the book, though I enjoy the vigorous and satirical assaults made on certain views, and I am sure they will meet approval in some quarters where the duty to science is not as great as mine. But it is the mass of experiences told here that suggest the improbability that they are wholly without significance. The "Crusade Documents" are extraordinary incidents, considering their origin. One does not need to assume that they are what they purport to be,—though they may be all this,—but as an illustration of automatism, which is becoming better known all the time, they should receive the attention and attract the interest of science. Here the record is fairly good, and the phenomena are familiar to all of us who are interested in psychic research. Someday they will be a part of a collective whole bearing upon a larger conclusion, and the whole book, with its more apparently supernormal incidents, will add to the literature of human experiences tending more and more to widen the significance of human personality.

The trenchant and dramatic style of the author will make her autobiography much more readable than the usual scientific account, and those who have already familiarized themselves with the supernormal will recognize material which will help to throw light upon obscure portions of better attested facts, in as much as they are reported without that consciousness of their interest which comes from a study of the literature of the supernormal. The scientific aspect of these phenomena is much in need of having their quantity verified, and we may well value incidents which are unfortunately less evidential than we wish they were. But, in the absence of the desirable attestation, the story of an interesting life of unusual experiences may at least teach the scientific man, in the future, to catch them on the wing and protect them against the natural scepticism of a materialistic age.

JAMES H. HYSLOP.

New York, May, 1910.

THE AUTHOR TO HER FRIENDS

THEY who essay to write, hope to be understood; and they who write from irrefutable experience, may hope to be believed.

One says to you: "The Russian emperors are crowned in Moscow."

"By that same proof, which seems no proof at all," you tell your little son: "The Russian emperors are crowned in Moscow."

Another, no less reputable, says: "I have a spirit-friend who visits me." But as for that, "It so exceeds familiar forms of proof," you have (or think you have) a right to doubt.

And yet, in very truth, conscience requires of me some outward revelation of an inward life—made luminous by spirit-intercourse. If, then, you care to read, I ask you first to take me as a child whose known progenitors were "trained along the centuries to hound and hate a lie"; then follow on four years beyond my three-score years and ten, up to this present hour.

Thereafter, if you find it possible, declare: "Nothing is true! No emperor was ever crowned in Moscow. There is no Moscow,—neither any Russia. As for this woman, she—with all the rest who claim to know that there is life to come—may clash the cymbals, chanting after Deborah: 'Hear, O ye kings! Give ear, O, princes!' Not the less we know that Sisera* is dead. He lies within the tent." You give some prisoner a bunch of flowers:—forthwith he understands that somewhere out beyond, great fields are all in bloom. Even so I have—and all of us may have—some dim acquaintance with the spirit-world, whose people enter in (fair prison-visitors!) and so bestow their gifts. These I would fain transfer. But first I give my little story of descent and soul-inheritance, adding thereto a simple narrative of early life as printed in my latest book of verse—made up of former books and later poems. This was addressed to all my friends: pray let me count you in.

Commander of the Canaanite army of King Jabin of Hazor, who is mentioned in Judges 4-5 of the Hebrew Bible.

As to what follows, let it signify that I, a spirit, speak to you, who may be many spirits, out of the airy void, as spirits may, hoping that you will hear and understand.

INTRODUCTION TO "POEMS: 1854-1906"

Because you who have known me personally have given me true affection and you who, not having met me, have yet proved yourselves kind and dear, I am minded to preface this presumably final collection of my metrical writings (covering a period of fifty-two years), with a few notes which may, in your estimation, add to its value. Also, I have been so often solicited to give some account of myself for others to print, that I can scarcely avoid making use of this last opportunity for showing by what inheritance and through what impulses I was led to choose the poet's vocation. Whatever is autobiographical herein, closes with my nineteenth year. After that time the poems themselves continue the story, since, whatever their demerits, sincerity is nowhere lacking; and albeit my "singing robe" may not be a fabric to wonder at, I may at least claim that the spinning and weaving thereof were most carefully done.

Upon an elevated, horizontal grave-slab in Watertown, Mass., dated in Puritan times, you may read: "He Was a Painful Preacher." If anyone shall say of me two hundred years hence: "She Was a Painful Poet" what more could be desired?

Henry Jones, born on Greylock Mountain (then Saddleback), Mass., March, 1798, of early Welsh-Puritan English and Scotch-Irish ancestry, and Mary Alma Mott, born in Oriskany, N. Y., February, 1813, of Huguenot, English and (remotely) "North River Dutch" descent, were united in marriage July, 1828. They welcomed me—their fourth child, in East Bloomfield, Ontario County, N. Y., October 19, 1835. My mother and her eight children then living, welcomed the twelfth in Black Rock (North Buffalo, N. Y.) soon after my father's death in 1854. That this large family was well endowed with physical vitality appears from the fact that although four were removed by induced and accidental causes, two of the elder ones lived till quite lately, and the average age of the six who remain, including the youngest three, is at this date (March, 1908) sixty-four and one-half years.

5

My great-grandfather, Seth Jones, who inherited the upland farm first taken up by his ancestors about 1670, left home to serve two years in the Revolutionary Army. Among his seven mature sons (summed up by him as "forty-two feet of boys"), was one Seth, who—first being ordained as a Baptist Minister—puzzled his lone way, by much Biblical study, into Universalism,—then looked upon by most with feelings akin to horror. He drew after him several brothers, and sixty of his one hundred and eighty church members— "a third part of the stars of Heaven," my grandfather Isaac used to say. And indeed his biographer, the loved Stephen R. Smith, states that so great was his fervor and natural eloquence, Calvinists flocked to hear him; while in sermons of almost interminable length, but never wearisome, he won many over to the doctrine of Free Grace.'"

Especially did his intense belief in the "Prayer of Faith," produce a deep impression—partly due to this unquestioned fact: During a distressing drouth (I think near Sackett's Harbor, N. Y.), an assemblage of farmers in open field expressed, in his presence, utter hopelessness with regard to rain, saying that a single more day would ruin every crop. "If you would pray for rain with Faith, it would come," he said. "But we have no Faith. Will you not exercise it for us?" Whereupon he knelt down upon a stump and prayed mightily for three hours, while (it was related), copious showers fell from the eyes of his hearers. When he descended, the first great drops of a "glorious rain" were dashing down. At eighty-three he presided over a national Universalist convention.

A letter lately received from Mrs. A. C. Pierce, of Junction City, Kansas, giving me an account of her grandmother's conversion from Calvinism, and of the sermons of Seth Jones, adds: "They told me of his wonderful gift in prayer, and that, through his intercession during a dry time, the answer came in the visit of a copious rain. I heard the rain story many times during my youth, until it grew to be a part of Seth Jones to me."

I am proud to record that a stranger, who had been his parishioner in youth, once addressed me because of a marked facial resemblance to "Elder Jones." Nor was the likeness merely facial. In my eighth year, while, one morning, scurrying through the Lord's Prayer, an unvoiced message arrested me as a bolt: "Child! You are not praying! You are insulting God!" I slunk away, wholly ashamed. "Do you pray?" asked our Sunday School Superintendent of each deeply pious child soon after; but when my turn came, I alone answered "No!" I think the look in my mother's eyes meant approval. Both she and my father abhorred a lie.

Now, something had been lost across the way in a vacant house or its neglected garden, and my eagle-eyed mother, with four others, had made long and fruitless search. She stopped her spinning one day and her favorite song ("The Bower of Prayer"), to offer me a reward if I would find it. Such an easy thing to do! And there were beads in prospect. As I crossed the road, the impossibility of succeeding first occurred. Then every thought was merged in one intense desire to pray. Now I could ask—which I had never done in my life. I fell on my knees among the sunflowers, and seemed to myself going up, up, almost to the clouds, for my answer. It came: "Yes, Child! You shall have the key." It was in my hand within five minutes. That same key has since unlocked for me many heavy doors.

Several of my father's immediate family, including himself, were not only devout Methodists but were subject to experiences, such as would now be called "Psychic." Yet they were not anemiacs. I am inclined to refer certain tendencies of my own in that direction, chiefly to my father's mother, born Hannah Henry. Listening in 1856 to a rather noted blind revivalist (author of quaint religious books—"Wedlock and Padlock," for instance), who was liable to be swept away in veritable trances, a young man, uncommonly apt in the study of human nature, insisted that, despite my non-Methodism, "Blind Henry" and I were "temperamental counterparts." The preacher proved to be my father's first cousin. Now I have not a scrap of written authority to prove that Patrick Henry belonged to a branch of our family, but the great uncles, on some now forgotten authority, asserted it; and one's great uncles are to be revered.

My maternal grandmother, Naomi Daggett (Mott), of Pittstown on the Hudson, was the daughter of one who, acting as drum-major in

General Wolfe's army, displayed such fortitude under hardships and so distinguished himself by bravery at the battle of Quebec, that his superior officer presented him with his own sword, saying: "You have been a better and braver soldier than I." Alas and alas! His children had that same sword "melted, beaten, hammered or rolled" into—souvenir spoons! Another of Naomi Daggett's ancestors was that Mayhew, who was driven out from among the Puritans for liberality of religious teachings. He took up his abode in Martha's Vineyard Island.

Louis Mott and his son Josef (or it might have been Josef and his son Louis), being French Huguenots, fled to America and settled in Mount Pleasant, Hunterdon County, New Jersey. Dropping an aristocratic prefix, they fore-gathered with the Quakers. Ebenezer, a grandson of the elder Mott, greatly enhanced his wide influence in the society by marrying Sarah Collins, an English Quaker lady, who had celebrity, abroad and in America, as a "preacher" of singular sweetness and power. Both are memorialized in "The Lives of the Saints."

Each of their sons was given, on leaving home, sixteen Jos and thirty-two half Jos—a Jo (Spanish-Mexican, I think), being a gold piece that rated as worth sixteen dollars and a half, when a dollar was of much greater value than now. A spinster daughter inherited the Homestead property-—willed to that one who should remain a Quaker. So far as I know, this was the high-water mark of prosperity among all my progenitors.

Their son, my grandfather, John Mott, supposed himself to be a "Friend," until about thirty years of age, although he had lost his "birth-right" by marrying out of the Society. It came about, however, that owing to this following circumstance he became a fully accredited Revolutionary officer. One bitterly cold Sunday in December, 1776, John Mott was forced to defend his family (a wife and three children) from six marauding Hessian soldiers. They broke down the barricaded door with axes, but were without firearms, as was the case with my grandfather (unless, indeed, tongs and poker might be so classed). As a result three took to their heels, and the remaining three were cast out over the door-sill dead. One of the two little girls, hidden in the cellar, never forgot the tumult overhead—she living to be not much under a hundred.

The following morning John Mott went to General Washington's camp, near the Delaware, and received from Washington's "own hand" a lieutenant's commission, authorizing him to organize a company of recruits for the Continental Army. This he did at once, equipping them at his own expense; and thereafter spent all his possessions in the service of his country throughout five years and eight months, till conclusion of peace.

Be it noted that his "saintly" mother, after having been taken by him through camp, humbly confessed that the "carnal heart took pride and rejoiced in the protection of a son who was a tall and brave soldier." The son would never apply for a pension, although forced to support his third family (a wife and eight children, of whom my mother was the youngest) by learning and practising the tailor's trade—nor yet in a beggarly way, for he had apprentices. Hale and unbowed at seventy-seven, he died, as did Washington, of quinsy and mismanagement. Shortly before his death, his sons and others saw him crossing the Mohawk river on the string-pieces of a very long bridge in process of building, but none dared follow.

The fact that his name does not appear on pension rolls makes it difficult to obtain a complete record of his services. We know that he fought at Brandywine and at Germantown, and was much employed by Washington in secret service. He, himself, related to my mother (then a child of nine), the story of his pursuit and capture of a spy who was carrying important papers to the British. His older children stated that he never spoke of the three Hessians whom he was forced to kill, without tears, saying always that it seemed like murder. Yet after that, he fired with intent to kill, upon a Hessian soldier, who was flaying a live cow for meat, after a manner known to exist among his countrymen.

To digress: John Mott's second wife, Mrs. Mann, brought him a stepson, William, who became an eminent educator of Pennsylvania, a president of one of her universities for thirty years. In a letter to my mother, written in 1855, when he was very old, he gave the credit of his great success wholly to my grandfather, who

9

had wisely advised and generously assisted him; and he added that, mindful of what had been done for himself, he had, besides his own family, "brought up three boys who had become Governors of their respective states." Further to digress: The fact is beyond question that had it not been for his eminent son, William B. Mann, of Philadelphia, who controlled the Pennsylvania delegation to the Republican convention of 1860, William H. Seward would have been nominated for the Presidency instead of Abraham Lincoln. "We know not all the paths."

And yet more concerning John Mott! The country, after the war, was overrun with desperate men; and my grandfather was chosen County Sheriff, to hold them in restraint. It came about that a large family—even to a babe in the cradle—was murdered—plunder being the object—during his absence from home. Knowing nothing of this, he dreamed that he entered into an untraversed forest in his home neighborhood, noting his way carefully, and finally went down into a tangled dell where were two villainous looking men lying under cover. A third, young and prepossessing, sat wringing his hands. "Why are you doing that?" asked the dreamer, and was answered: "There is blood upon my hands. It is the blood of a lamb." Upon his return home the next afternoon he organized a search-party, caused the glen to be surrounded and arrested the three, who, in all particulars, answered to those of whom he had dreamed—save that the youngest one instantly rose and made full confession for all. As he had never before been engaged in villainy, and had been compelled by the others to drink to the point of frenzy, my grandfather labored hard to get his sentence commuted, although it was he who had, in distraction, killed the babe. Grieved that this man must die with the rest, the sheriff resigned his office and would never track another criminal.

I relate this incident because it permits me to say that the development of what may be called capacity for spiritual illumination seems to me a not unlikely result of those inner communings characteristic of Quaker worship. I suppose my mother to have drawn from this source a certain power of pre-vision in dreams, sometimes fore-showing even national events; as in 1832, I think, when she saw the whole land covered with tents, upon the largest of which she read: "In 186—there was war for liberty"—the last figure seeming to be blurred as if made up of several. Nor was I myself (since I am to be spoken of) left absolutely without inheritance of such a gift. As witness: "The Prophecy of the Dead" written when our apprehensions had been quieted by the declarations of Seward that the Rebellion would be over in ninety days. Leaving mother at 10:30 one morning, and merrily telling her I had promised to write a love-ballad, I crossed to a large school-house and shut myself in. Eight lines were written when I dropped the pencil. Then all the billows rolled over me......I wrung my hands, saying "I cannot write it!" But the law of utterance was inexorable. At noon I returned and read the poem to my mother. She heard it with a pale face, and said solemnly: "Amanda, you have been inspired!" I answered: "Mother, I have been inspired!" In July, 1862, I with others, expected to hear any day of the fall of Richmond. Again prophetic knowledge and utterance came—verified nearly three years later.

Love of country characterized our parents equally. Our father read aloud to us the history of the long struggle with as much evidence of emotion as he exhibited at "Family Prayers," or in his fervid church meetings. Our mother sang and recited to us innumerable revolutionary ballads, learned before her tenth year, of her father and half-brother, John, who had served through the war of 1812. The latter had enjoyed nothing more than slipping over into Canada, where he was well-known and certain to be called upon for entertainment, and singing those very songs—the fun lying in the certainty of arrest for "contempt of the King." Landed in jail, for form's sake probably, he made the ballads ring again till he was let out.

Our parents biased us politically, one as much as the other, though I think mother most thoroughly instructed us. At nine I hurrahed by the road-side, in a faint, scary way for Henry Clay, while the boys were singing: "Van! Van! Is a used-up man!"

Also I ardently believed in a protective tariff—having understood that "free trade" had virtually annihilated woolen manufacture—my father being master of the art. And when a long Whig procession trailed along before election, having a great band-wagon filled with young ladies all in white, to represent States (I forget how many), I laughed at the one lady in mourning following after with the flag: "Please let me in!" What, let Texas in to make another slave state? Not I! For sentiment I delighted in hearing my mother sing Whittier's "Yankee Girl."

When in later years, my mother, as a widow, was dependent upon our oldest sister (see "The Life Beautiful") and her sons, for support of herself and the younger ones, two of the three boys enlisted with her consent—one of whom did not return. My sister never complained of her added burdens. Patriotism was, in itself, a religion with us.

I had not—none of us had—our mother's phenomenal memory, but this is my earliest recollection: Before me, a few rods away, was a clear creek, beyond which rose a green hill. A red-faced and red-haired boy was pinching my right arm. I was not crying (and that was characteristic), but to avoid seeing his mocking face, I looked past him to a brown two story house, where I wanted to go, and all about me, so fixing the landscape indelibly upon my brain. I saw and recognized the place just fourteen years later, on my way to a country school I was to teach,—ignorant of the fact that for a single summer that house had been my home, I then being less than two years old. I grieve to say that the boy was in "State Prison" at twenty-five. My older brother had a still more remarkable memory of an event and conversation which took place when he was but eighteen months old. My parents imagined that a child of three, exceptionally vigorous, who could name all the letters of the alphabet after a single telling, was old enough to go to school. And, indeed, an older sister was in the highest reading class at five. After snowfall they kept me out till the time of mud. The first abiding affection I had outside of home was for a man who saw me astray in the middle of the road on my way to school, and, wading through, pulled me out of my shoes and carried them and me to the school-house door. As I never asked for help, the older ones had forgotten me. I was quite seven before I was promoted from the New Testament to the

"English Reader"—practically a high-school reading book, made up of master classics.

At three we were visited by my grandmother Mott, whose beautiful, white face filled me with wonder. A year or two later, I strayed from home, through a meadow where tall grass almost hindered movement, and came upon a Turk's cap lily. Perhaps I shall be as much amazed when I first open my eyes on the flowery wonders of Paradise, but I almost doubt it. I worshipped the flower, until at last a conviction fastened itself upon my mind that here was something that God had "just made!"

I was not quite six when imagination sprang into existence, the manner of which is related in "Coming Home."

Now, in those days, we country people were mainly dependent upon the weekly church paper and the "District School Library" for reading, outside of the Bible. Sunday School libraries hardly counted if Charlotte Elizabeth's pious books had achieved the honor of the Pope's malediction. (I used to wonder why they seemed so tame.) But books were more necessary than daily bread to our parents. They taught the older ones, including myself, to consider the religio-astronomical works of Thomas L. Dick, D. D., LL. D., with Milton, Pollock, Baxter and Bunyan, as almost biblical. My father was impressed with the idea that the Blest (his uncle Seth had shaken his faith in there being any perpetually ablest), would roam from star to star to learn of God, and perhaps find at last that "Central Sun," from which all glory and all law emanate. I liked my father's ideas better than my mother's, for each time that she convinced him of a literal resurrection of the body, from Scripture texts, something unconvinced him by another sunrise. I, too, remained as unbelieving.

But we had lighter reading: Frederica Bremer, Jane Austen, Maria Edgworth, Eliza Cook, and, best of all, Felicia Dorothea Hemans, whose passion flowers of poesy are unwithering.

Oh, but we had much more than this! I do not know how my mother had made such vast reapings in English literature. She left school at ten when her father died, and was much employed in spinning and the like until her marriage, five and a half years later. But large portions of Dryden, Pope, Campbell, Goldsmith, Scott, and many other poets, were seemingly as familiar to her as her own spelling book, whose chapter on orthography I heard her repeat in middle age. History, biography, romance, all had been gathered up as sheaves. She sprang surprises upon me even to the last of my stay with her—spiritual hymns, quaint "love and murder songs," ghostly old ballads. Not less, her own thoughts had swift and brilliant utterance, and her conversational powers were unusual.

During my ninth year came the great Millerite excitement, and nearly all the members of the Methodist Church we attended, were swept away. "The tenth day of the seventh month" was to be the great day of resurrection. With what pride I listened to my mother on that wild, last Sunday, when she arose in the midst of "Hallelujahs" and silenced them with a plain exposition of Scripture, gathering up text after text to prove the delusive nature of their expectations! Men and women looked at each other in dismay, while in a clear, controlled voice she summed up her arguments; and in the vestibule, one came to her sobbing: "Sister Jones, but for you I should have gone over the bay!"

Such poems as came in my way between six and nine retain their hold upon my memory yet. "Barbara Lewthwaite" gave me the heart-ache, and I never read this stanza of Bryant's without a tremor:

> "The stormy March has come at last,
> With wind and cloud and changing skies;
> I hear the rushing of the blast
> That through the snowy valley flies."

But I loved best of all that wonderful story of Lady Mary Campbell's dream, as related in verse by the family chaplain, beginning, "The moon had climbed the highest hill." I longed to believe it true, as I have since learned that it was. No ghost could have scared me—I loved the very thought of them!

I ought to have learned the meaning of grief when eight years old, through the death of little Mary (see "A Flower of Paradise"), but instead I lost myself in contemplation of some imagined glory hiding her from sight. In lower moods I planned how I would tell, when grown up, about her beauty and sweetness, and how, when exactly eight months old, she had with perfect distinctiveness repeated a sentence of thirteen words, shouted out by brother Bennie; and how God had wanted her—I was proud because He had wanted her. Three years later I sobbed violently over the coffin of a schoolmate; but it was not grief so much as a realization of her wonderful loveliness.

At thirteen, Sorrow took hold of me with might. A brother, but two years my senior, died in my presence, in school, of heart disease. The teacher, being frightened and incompetent, left me to take entire charge of removal, summoning physician and parents, and there could be no possibility of tears, grief was so vast. This was the "pure young lad" of the poem "Father." He was the most wonderful boy I ever knew. Endowed with the splendid intellect of our mother, as none of the others could claim to be, it had been sublimated by the refining fire of his malady into spirituality, so that I might well name him in another poem, "The Sun-Bright Boy." After this I was dull and morbid, finding little comfort save in study and in the singing of mournful hymns. It was, in a sense, well for me that at just fifteen I began teaching "all by my lone" in the backwoods; and rather strenuously, since boys of eighteen were among my pupils. Two years of alternate teaching and high-school attendance resulted in a failure of health, from which I never fully rallied.

"The Dead Pine" signalizes a partial emergence from a six years period of physical depression and distress, which had culminated in such an excessive weakness of the lungs that the ablest of physicians (Dr. Hubbard Foster, of Clifton Springs Water Cure—who, with Dr. Cordelia Green, undoubtedly saved my life) prohibited the writing of verse for all time. That poem concludes the volume entitled "Ulah"— 300 pages, copied, compiled and partly written a year later.

"Lost and Saved" marks the opening of a new era of thought and purpose, accompanied always by such severe mental labor as uncertain well-being would permit. I owe my increased length of days to the care and tenderness of many friends.

At this point I turn aside to say that but for Davis W. Clark, D. D., editor of "The Ladies' Repository," and afterward a bishop of the Methodist Church, I doubt if the gates of that sacred enclosure, where poets learn to sing, would ever have been opened for me; and, indeed, the little quarterly payments for verses contributed to that Magazine during six years, comprised nearly all my earnings. A merry letter which I wrote to him in 1853, denouncing a contributor for advising young poets to "stop," appeared in the Editor's Table as having "bubbled up into our face." Now my father firmly believed that I was to be a poet, and urged me to send something for publication, himself selecting the verse. During the three following months I heard him several times say in an undertone, "I wonder whether Dr. Clark will publish 'The Transplanted Flower.'" While I was standing by his bed—he slumbering toward Death—the magazine, containing the sorry little piece so named, was handed me; and to his unconscious soul, I said: "Father, I will be a poet if only for your sake."

Now why should I add more?

CASTING THE NET

THE REV. O. B. FROTHINGHAM, a devout and profound thinker and reasoner of the school of Liberal Theology, finally bade farewell to his devoted congregation and retired from those public ministrations which had made him eminent; announcing that he should never again ascend the pulpit until he should have attained a summit of spiritual experience as yet unknown to him. He said, not in these exact words indeed, but humbly and to this effect:

"I have made the various religions of the world my deepest study during many years. I perceive that however they seem to differ, all have had their origin in that inherent faculty which enables Man, environed by a visible universe, to divine an invisible one of incalculably greater moment. Confucian, Zoroastrian, Hebrew, Catholic, Greek and Protestant, all with one accord and by one common impulse, bow down before a symbolized or inwardly perceived Unseen; and all of these—nay even Barbarians and Savages, number among their multitudes fine souls, who in supremest moments, rise to supermundane heights or become conscious of the approach of supermundane beings.

"I have, moreover, held converse with men and women of many classes and creeds, whose self-revealments, indubitably sane and trustworthy, have convinced me that they know more than of what is beyond mere mortal ken. They have told me of inspired thoughts, of illuminating visions, of visits from departed friends. They have shown me that there is an inner, converting Power, which regenerates guilty souls. They have breathed holy atmospheres; and beyond all else, they have had ecstatic seasons of communion with One of ineffable Name and Nature, To discredit these would be to malign humanity; to scoff at Moses and Elias upon the mount of transfiguration; to shame the Christ, who talked with them; and to pronounce God, Himself, a liar and a cheat.

"A faculty that belongs to mankind belongs to me. Believing, to the core of my heart, in the verity of a spiritual universe, whose immortal inhabitants were once prisoners of mortality even as I, reason tells me that, in the distribution of heavenly gifts, I shall not be overlooked. There must come an hour when I shall no longer grope in twilight, but walk joyfully among men, blest with the infinite consolation of open sight.

"I await my special revelation. Meanwhile it becomes me to wait in silence."

—So Octavius B. Frothingham!—Not so Thomson Jay Hudson, Ph.D., LL. D., Author of "A SCIENTIFIC DEMONSTRATION OF THE FUTURE LIFE," "THE DIVINE PEDIGREE OF MAN," "THE LAW OF PSYCHIC PHENOMENA" and "THE EVOLUTION OF THE SOUL." Instead of reaching reverentially at the Lord's table for the Eucharistic bread and wine, he set himself, as a spiritual "Scientist," to formulate a "working hypothesis, universal in its application to all classes of Psychic Phenomena,—being conscious in a vague, general way, that the phenomenon of telepathy, if it could be proven to exist, must be a factor of supreme importance in any theory of causation."

After a time he chanced upon Mrs. Carpenter of Boston, whose "Psychic powers had been trained by her husband to a high state of proficiency." After "partially hypnotizing" her, he procured from a store nearby, a pack of "common playing cards" and with her eyes so sealed (mind you), "that it was a physical impossibility to open them," he "shuffled and drew." Not seeing the selected card himself, he held it up for others to see, until the lady had correctly named "half the pack," and was "exhausted." Twenty-six successes, and not one failure! But, in a series of tests, he found that if he were alone with any "percipient" and handed him or her a card without looking at it, the experiment always resulted in failure. "It was thus," he adds, "that I learned to doubt the existence of the faculty of clairvoyance, properly so called." "Clairvoyance," he explains, "is the power to see what is occurring at a distance, independently of the aid of telepathy from living persons." Moreover, after spending much time with other "percipients"—all partially or totally hypnotized—and conducting experiments upon a still loftier plane, he prognosticates, nay, he stoutly proclaims that telepathy between "living persons" may be made to explain all classes of psychic phenomena—defined as "the phenomena of the human soul."

"These," he tells us, "include Mesmerism, hypnotism, spiritism, demonology, mental therapeutics and a thousand other things which need not be mentioned," since he has "no intention of troubling" us with them. But one and all "must be studied just as the physical sciences are studied," viz: in the quoted words of Lord Bacon: "By observing or meditating on facts." Most conscientiously he studies them just that way.

Now, he surveys a very broad field and he picks up facts by hundreds,—by thousands, one might say. He observes, he meditates, he frames logical deductions, (he is nothing if not logical!); and it is all so plain! Through hypnotism we arrive at telepathy. Through telepathy we arrive at mental duality. Through mental duality we arrive at the relations between man, the finite, and God., the Infinite;—also we learn "a thousand other things." In fine, we know just where "we are at," for Dr. Hudson tells us. Let us absorb a little of his wisdom: i: "Man has two minds, the objective and the subjective."

2: "The objective mind is that of the ordinary waking consciousness."

3: "Each of these two minds is capable of independent action, and they are also capable of synchronous action. But, in the main, they possess independent powers and perform independent functions."

4: "The distinctive faculties of one pertain wholly to this life, those of the other are especially adapted to a higher plane of existence."

5: "The subjective mind is constantly amenable to control by suggestion."

6: "The subjective mind possesses the power of transmitting intelligence to other subjective minds otherwise than through the ordinary sensory channels."

7: "Telepathy is a power belonging exclusively to the subjective mind."

8: "Observable telepathic phenomena are never produced under other than abnormal conditions of the body and of the objective mind."

9: "The subjective mind, is the mind of the soul."

10: "The subjective mind or entity possesses physical power; that is, the power to make itself heard and felt and to move ponderable objects."

11: "Science has at last succeeded in unraveling the whole mystery of spiritistic phenomena, removing them from the domain of superstition, and demonstrating that all the manifestations, of whatever name or nature, proceed from the subjective minds of living persons."

12: "With a difference only of degree, therefore, we find in the soul of man every essential attribute of Omniscience, and every power of Omnipotence."

13: "Last, but by no means least in importance, we find the faculty of telepathy, which we must suppose to be a divine potential. Science pauses here and asks this question, which each must answer for himself: 'Does not the possession of this faculty involve the logical deduction, not only that it is the obvious means of communication in the future life, but that it is the ever open channel of communion with God through prayer; and not only that, but is it not the potential agency of divine inspiration?'"

Now, at last we arrive at Dr. Hudson's "working hypothesis,"—formulated "in strict accord with the inexorable laws of logic and scientific deduction!" As thus:

By means of hypnotism, our Psychic powers, which are, "divine potentials," may be "trained to a high degree of proficiency,"—even to the extent of being able truly to declare that someone present is looking at the knave of clubs. This demonstrates "wordless transference of thought,"—in one word telepathy; "the power that is obviously adapted to the uses of disembodied intelligences and no other." We may possibly hypnotize ourselves, but we can never know anything of the result—our objective minds being rendered imbecile by the process, for the time being. The proper way seems to be a hypnotization by someone else, who better knows how. He can "train" our "psychic powers," tell our subjective minds what to think, what to see, what to tell others, even how to discriminate between

20

spades and diamonds! Should he be very gracious indeed, he may "suggest" to our subjective minds that they communicate to our objective minds some special matter, so that, when the latter fairly emerge from idiocy, they "remember" that which, in fact, they never knew; and forthwith they work like bees constructing brain-cells in which to store up that mock remembrance, with others, safe from obliteration.

When we are hypnotized, our subjective minds become "disembodied intelligences," untroubled by any outward consciousness. We converse with each other, at will, by the law of telepathy—that "divine potential," which all subjective minds, incarnate, discarnate or half-way between, share with the Infinite. Such potency is ours, that we can transfer thoughts, all around the world, without the aid of sense-organs. *Telepathie a deux* is comparatively simple; but there are *telepathie a trois, telepathie a mille,* if you like! Oh, your messages may vibrate through a thousand, thousand minds, and, like the light from fixed stars, burn their way to recognition.

By means of telepathy God communicates with us through an "ever open channel." By telepathy He communicates with celestial intelligences or disembodied subjective minds. By telepathy they all communicate with Him and with each other. By telepathy we also communicate with God and with each other. All, all—finite and Infinite—possess this "divine potential," and control this divine law, or are controlled thereby.

But wait: What hinders disembodied souls, who exchange thoughts with God and with each other, from exchanging them also with us, who are their very kith and kin? They used to do so objectively and subjectively when they were greatly restrained by earthly conditions. Now they are set free. Nay, the mere waving of hypnotizing hands (not always, alas, overclean!), will disembody us for a season, and render us like unto them. Having, in common with us, "every essential attribute of Omniscience and every power of Omnipotence," why can they not tell us somewhat of all we yearn to know?

21

Well, because Dr. Thomson Jay Hudson has logically demonstrated that telepathy between "living persons" explains all "Psychic Phenomena" under the sun; and moreover—because!

At last we perceive the beautiful simplicity and consistency of this "inexorable" logician's "*working hypothesis!*"

O! Octavius Frothingham! You, who lifted dim eyes heavenward, and waited meekly the coming of that hour when it should be your turn to climb Mt. Sinai, where "out of the midst of the fire," God talks face to face with the sons of men, why did you not visit "some store nearby and procure a pack of common playing cards?"

Let us be just. Dr. Hudson has been a most conscientious, painstaking, patient and ardent investigator of hypnotic futilities. For our sakes, rather than for his own, he has worked his way through the narrowest possible crevices, into many an underground cavern of almost illimitable extent. He has warned us who have followed, against foot-entrapping fissures. He has called upon us to admire stalagmite and stalactite, as though they were floral wonders,—veritable roses of Sharon. He has discovered (or imagined) more than one bottomless pit. He has cast his nets into that river of the underworld men call the Styx, believing that those silent waters teem with life; and he has brought up, out of that darkness, a great number of little living fishes—all blind.

To change metaphors, he has not been measuring and estimating the human soul, but rather the long shadow it casts over earth, as it moves, at early dawn, along the mountain tops. Search his books through, and you will not find one record of an individual spiritual experience, known to one unhypnotized "living person."

"Of myself, this I saw!" "These words I verily heard."

"This matter I foreknew." "This holy fire that burns and hurts not, has been kindled in my heart by divine grace." So spake Savonarola, Martin Luther, Richard Baxter, John Bunyan, Philip Doddridge, Isaac Watts, Charles Wesley and Sarah Flower Adams. So speaks Eva Booth today; and so have spoken innumerable men and women who needed no hypnotic suggestions to make them believe that they were immortal,—so sweet and abundant are the springs of heavenly comfort that overflow the earth!

"After these things Jesus showed himself again to the disciples at the sea of Tiberias."

"Simon Peter saith unto them: "I go a-fishing." They say unto him, 'we also go with thee." They went forth, and entered into a ship immediately; and that night they caught nothing.

"But when the morning was now come, Jesus stood on the shore; but the disciples knew not that it was Jesus.

"Then Jesus saith unto them'. "Children, have ye any meat." They answered him, 'No.'

"And he said unto them'. 'Cast the net upon the right side of the ship, and ye shall find.' They cast therefore, and now they were not able to draw it for the multitude of fishes. Let us cast our nets upon the right side of the ship.

CHILDHOOD AND THE DUAL MIND

BEFORE I enter upon that intimate and most faithful narration of the experiences of an inner life, which my friends have a right to require of me, it may be well to mention a desire expressed by some few to the effect that much shall be interpolated or interfused, concerning my life "at large." Whenever it shall seem to me that exterior conditions or happenings, even remotely, may have led up to, or enhanced psychic agitation, I shall not hesitate to outline them, so that the severest reader may weigh their influence in the balance against ultimate effect. To go further would be to obtrude myself and degrade my thesis.

These stories of the soul, without regard to their relative consequence, will mainly be related in chronological order. Should many, even the most of them, seem trivial, it may be urged that trivialities, like protoplasmic molecules, make up the sum of that conscious life, which is kept in pulsation by inherent spiritual energy. It may be reverently said that the Infinite manifests infinity by moving among and operating upon, an infinite number of finite particles. If there be a seraph, the history of his conscious existence must include all that ever concerned him, from the quickening of a primordial cell, to his present supernal exaltation. Be sure that he has not attained seraphic potency through any dislodgment of slender capacities or annihilation of minute remembrances. He is the greater because of them.

Should a friend, long absent in foreign countries, stand before our door and knock, or ring a bell, to apprize us of his return, would we consider his act trivial? We would be triflers in truth, should we stand within, and hesitate to open, were we able to undo the locks.

And should another friend return from holy mountains—never trodden by mortal feet—and call to us from the shore, can we imagine that he would refuse again to break bread with us and give thanks? One of the most beautiful spirits that, to my knowledge, ever dwelt in mortal frame, went out after days of singing, shouting and bursts of holy rapture—aware not only of Divine favor, but of the visible approach of mere men and women "gone before," who

24

had shared with him the little interests and perplexities of daily human life. Nevertheless, when his loved earthly associates afterward gathered for fervent prayer, and one with another joyfully, tearfully said:—"I feel the presence of Brother Kendall."—"I am conscious that he is with us this moment,"—uprose his wife, Martha, answering them as with authority: "William C. Kendall is not here. He is with his God. He stands, night and day, before the great white Throne, singing:—'Alleluia! Worthy is the Lamb!'" She forgot that God, Himself, abides among men. It is said He is immanent in plasson and despises none of his protozoa.

Returning to my introductory chapter, and taking up that little story of the arrested prayer and the lost key, it seems to me that not all the tenuous reasonings of even a Dr. Hudson could web that experience over with hypnotism.

I had leaped from slumber at the call of appetite. I had but one distinct purpose. I must hurry to join those others at the breakfast table. It is in my mind that, while on my knees, rushing through the Lord's Prayer, I was hooking my dress. Before I could say, "For ever and ever," the bolt fell. "Child, you are not praying! You are insulting God!" I did not see, but my mind located above me the one who had sent down that stinging rebuke, causing my flesh to tremble and my cheek to burn with shame. A child, not eight years old—myself at least—could neither have constructed that sentence out of a vacant brain nor entertained the thought so embodied, without suggestion.

Was that stern rebuker just my own sublimized, subjective mind?—or the floating subjectivity of any "living person," by chance abroad and, by accident, within hearing?

There are hypotheses that no sane thinker can accept; and these are of them.

How then? Can it be supposed that any exalted person not "living"—mortally dead but spiritually quick—would take notice of a little girl's benighted, heathen soul? My long sainted great-grandmother, maybe, that noted Quaker "speaker" who stoutly strove to lead the "higher life" on earth, and who incited many others to follow her example; For was not I the child of her very son's very youngest daughter?

Quoth Thomson Jay Hudson:—"The question whether we shall retain our individuality in the future life, is, to most people the question of immortality itself. Manifestly the non-retention of personality would be the equivalent of annihilation."

Sarah Collins is therefore still an individual—an earth-remembering, infant-loving Mother. But what matters the identity—herself or any other? I had learned my first religious lesson: Speak when the Spirit prompts. At all other times keep silent in the presence of God.

Whether I addressed the Supreme Being as I knelt beneath the sun-flowers, praying child-wise: "Let me find the key!"

I hardly know. But I remember that, as I seemed, to rise heavenward in a confusing light, One—fully apprehended as an individual, albeit not seen—met me with the message: "Yes, Child! You shall have the key," and I sank back to the body, if indeed I had been absent. I can remember no other moment of my life when my mind was so emptied of all thought and so filled with all content.

I arose and went around to the western side of the house. The key, not being Janus-faced, would only lock and unlock from within; it was therefore necessary that we should enter by the window. Now, my mother had been given the privilege of using rooms for storage, on the sole condition that the key should not be lost;—and when did my mother ever fail to fulfill a trust? Under the window was a hard, bare, clay-and-gravel bank, thrown up to protect the cellar from cold; and it was my mother's theory that the four-inch piece of brass had slipped thereon, from the pocket of one climbing out. The search went on fully two weeks,—a search in which the three older children, my mother and even my father, took part. A hundred times, at least, sharp eyes had scanned that broad stone-hard bank; and now clear, young eyes scanned it once again. I turned away saying in a sing-song voice, "The key isn't here! The key isn't here!" I propped up the window and climbed in, walked once around the lower room, passed up stairs, walked part way around the upper room, and then, announcing to myself with happy satisfaction: "Now I will find the key!"—ran down, swiftly crossed to the window and leaped out. Before me, as I alighted, some four feet from the house and exactly in the middle of that barest of banks—impossible to be overlooked—there lay the key!

My amazed mother, by searching inquiry (we had but two neighbors), satisfied herself that none but ourselves had entered that deserted yard. But I, because of innocent shame, kept silence.

Saith Dr. Hudson: "The subjective mind or entity possesses physical power, that is, the power to make itself heard and felt and to move ponderable bodies."

And again: "The Phenomenon that presents the greatest interest in this connection, is that of levitation of ponderable bodies without physical contact or appliances. This I have repeatedly witnessed under the most exacting test conditions."

And yet further, mentioning Alfred Russell Wallace and Sir William Crookes: "Each of these eminent savants verified the physical phenomena of spiritism, especially telekinesis, by indubitable tests."

Well—but whose subjective mind met mine, half-way up the blue; and whose subjective mind levitated that ponderable brass?

But is it so indeed that "a spiritual energy, inherent in the souls of men, is competent to modify or set at naught the action of the physical forces of nature?"—that it may "neutralize a powerful current of electricity," "defy the law of combustion" and "defeat the law of gravitation?"

And have the greatest of living scientists demonstrated all this?— Sir William Crookes, Alfred Russell Wallace, and their collaborators Sergeant Edward W. Cox and Dr. Huggins, F. R. S., in whose presence the conclusive tests were made?—All these and many others, including Dr. Hudson?

Behold, then, my great uncle Seth Jones—noted expositor of faith in prayer! (See introductory chapter.) Mark him among those faithless farmers who could perceive no sign of coming rain either in

27

heaven above or on earth beneath. Listen while he advises them. "If but one of you would pray with faith, the rain would come," and again, "I have the faith." Watch him, for three long hours, kneeling upon that oaken stump. Mark his mighty strivings. Be melted to tears by his heaven-moving eloquence. See or not see, (for your eyes may be holden), that ascending spirit—all unmindful of the fleshly habitation. And fail not to understand how his ecstatic, cloud-compelling energy, answered his own prayer, offered in the Name and through the majesty of that Omniscient and Omnipotent One whom he addressed. Remember that there were many witnesses— plain, farming men—who lived long to testify how the great drops, falling on his upturned face, recalled him to outer consciousness; and how by jubilant increase, they poured and poured,

"While the rocks and the rills, While the vales and the hills," rejoiced in the plentitude of that "glorious rain!"

Now, once for all, let us talk a little about the "dual mind," discovered by means of an inexorably logical "*working hypothesis*" and demonstrated by the Psychical Researches of Thomson Jay Hudson.

"The distinctive faculties of the objective mind pertain wholly to this life. Taken in the aggregate they constitute pure intellect. When the brain dies the objective mind ceases to exist!

[Ergo; Mind—pure intellect—is destructible]

"It should always be remembered that the power of the subjective entity is the most potential force in nature, and, when intelligently directed, the most beneficent. But like every other power in nature, misdirected, its destructive force is equally potent."

"The subjective mind should never be allowed to usurp control of the dual mental organization. To believe in the reality of subjective visions is to give the subjective mind control of the dual mental organization; and to give it such control is for Reason to abdicate her throne. Its ultimate manifestation is insanity.

Ah! What shall we do throughout the æons of Eternity without our objective minds; All belief—"gross superstitions," all thought—

28

delirium! Naked, naked beings, more potential than gravity, more devastating than elemental fire!

Alas! I am no logician! When I read that "the moneron—the very lowest form of life—is endowed with Mind, and exhibits the essential attributes of Omniscience," I wonder which mind?

But one of the attributes of Deity would seem to be the power of appropriating a physical universe to spiritual uses. Does not He, the Infinite, make room for his disparted finites—our very selves—in plasmic cells? Are we not tenderly nurtured there with very matter, out of which we build us fleshly habitations?—and are they not consecrated temples, in which we stand to minister, or fall before that cloud whose glory fills the Holy Place? Eternally conscious of the outer, He, our Progenitor, holds fast His objective Mind forever and forever. Nothing of Him can die with any dying braincell. And always that "pure intellect," emanating from Him, goes on transferring its energy—Dr. Hudson tells us—"from a microscopic, unicellular organism, up through a thousand gradients, to the grand culmination of physical perfection," while all along the way, "is found the promise and potency of a human soul."

God associates us with Himself, from the first, endowing us with His power of appropriating the material to the necessities of the spiritual. Shall not we also retain our objective minds, with abundant means for recognizing and taking part in His outer Universe—though brain-cells die and scalpels demonstrate that no soul ever found lodgment therein?

Nay, will not both our minds, as one, inhabit finer bodies than these that are "sown in corruption?" Are there not incorruptible bodies of veritable substance, invisible to earth-dwellers? Have they not been elaborated from and within the visible, and may not they be subject to further refinement throughout the cycles of eternity, yet never lose their hold on the primeval world? Always a body, tangible to itself, however near to imponderability: always a spirit—finite particle of the Infinite; always an objective consciousness, mediating between the two; always an indomitable entity, more and more closely approximating to the Divine Essence, but never to be absorbed therein!

If we are not to be eternal associates of God, in his outwardness, how shall we find Him in His "Holy of Holies?" What shall hold firm our ladder of ascent?

Verily, I distrust my unbolstered subjective mind. Once it found its way out, and, being whirled back violently to its companion-mind, the latter caught the story, and built it into a special brain-cell from which it has not as yet been driven out. This was not long ago; that is to say, it was in the year 1881.

The experiences of a busy day may have impelled that mind to release itself from a tired body; and I admit, it may have carried something away as a drag, deterring it from creditable exhibition of its supposable superlative powers when released from domination of intellect.

I had installed my direct-feed oil-burner under a bothering old boiler that neither wood nor coal nor those other burners had induced to meet requirements. I fired up at sunrise, and—as the work in the yard had been much delayed—I sent the engineer to assist Mr. Brain at his brick-making, for the machine was running at very high speed and all hands were needed to dispose of the manufactured product. Naturally, I looked often at my pure white fire, for my eyes love brightness.

Now, this was close to Bradford, Pa., and, as afterwards appeared, an oil-well, one or two furlongs from us, had slackened its yield,— which could only be increased by means of a Roberts or Whitehead torpedo—taxable if used in the daytime. As for me, I went to sleep that night in Mr. Brain's brick mansion, occupying a very large chamber, well supplied with windows East, South and West.

I suppose thick walls were no hindrance to the escape of my essential self,—which after all may have gone out by any window. But somehow I was out of doors about mid-night, moving slowly about, not by walking upon the ground, but by floating in the air, upon the West side near the house. I glanced around casually, seeing things very well, particularly a large storage shed, never noticed before, but observed with interest on the following day. Meanwhile the night was illumined only by stars. Fixing my attention upon them as more attractive than baking furnaces and piles of finished brick, almost at once there flashed into sight among the constellations, a mighty portent. Extending to the zenith, its hilt near to the horizon, its blade, toward me, appeared a flaming sword, in color a vivid orange-crimson.

The essential self, as I apprehend, is incapable of fear or amazement. Emotions belong to that lower sphere of consciousness, which rounds out and completes that absolute entity, spoken of on earth as the human soul,—elsewhere known to be immortal. I was not afraid. I looked at the prodigy, tranquilly meditating, yet summoning whatever power I had of "inerrant deduction," (authoritatively declared to be a "divine potential" of the subjective mind), that I might solve that sublime mystery. And my subjective mind said unto me in almost these very words:

"It is many years since I believed in that legend of the Garden of Eden. I do not believe in it now, but if I were persuaded of its truth, I should say: 'This is the flaming sword which turned every way and kept out Adam and Eve. Yet surely that sword need not have reached to the very stars, in order to defend the tree of life from one trembling man and one weeping woman. Moreover, Cherubim could not have handled this weapon. None but an archangel could put forth a hand to grasp that hilt. He would need to be as high as heaven. Are there such majestic beings? and will the one chosen to wield that sword really appear?" I was striving to realize what he would do,—being filled with a reverent sense of his power,—when the blade descended without his aid. All flame, it swept downward with one instantaneous rush and smote the corner of the house—the South-west corner of my room. One might say, it drove me back to my blessed common sense, even before it struck. The force of the impact was that of a cutting blow, a million times multiplied. I awoke! Every pane of glass belonging to every window in my room, and as I plainly heard, many a pane far through the house, was falling in fragments to the floor. My every-day, wise and wholly sane objective mind, said to that half-demented wanderer: "Nitro-glycerine! Moonshiners!"

31

All this leisurely thinking, this unalarmed apprehension of celestial dynamics and heaven-high potentialities, this wonderful exhibition of "intuitional knowledge"—oh, yes! and this "inerrant deduction," may have gone on during the one instant when that eighty-pound torpedo, secreted under that furlong-away boiler, like a crouching giant, was straightening out its knees for a mighty spring; or it may have occupied the millionth part of a second after the act and before the sensible effect, that gouged out the earth and sent fragments—to the zenith, for aught I know, since but one was found anywhere in that vicinity.

I humbly acknowledge that the power of imagination possessed by my subjective mind, has not, as yet, wildly illumined my verse. But, oh, its "intuitive knowledge," its "essential perception," its ability to "reach all legitimate inferences with a marvelous cogency and power." Lo! its possession of these "divine potentials" cannot be denied; for hypnotists have tossed their arms about, "percipients" have slumbered, and all has been found out—by means of common playing-cards!

Now, Heaven forfend!—lest I be given over eternally to the exclusive control of my subjective mind! Let us trust and believe that when we pass from earth, our objective minds—"admitted to that equal sky"—like the Indian's "faithful dog," will bear us company.

TO DREAM AND TO DESIRE

NOT for an instant would I deny the law of telepathy, nor deride the minutest fact justly cited in evidence of its reality. If demonstrated to exist at all, it must be recognized, not as a mere local accidental force, but as a universal, eternal principle. Like the law of refraction, the law of gravitation, the law of elliptical orbits and the law of the ratio between the planetary periods and distances, it has its genesis in Mind.

As the vibrations of light are propagated through cosmic ether, so through some medium, sublimated beyond imagination, vibrates forever this illuminant of the soul. We hold up our telepathic rush-lights for guidance in dark places, we even kindle telepathic bon-fires, upon our hill-tops, for "Psychical Research" into crannies and crevices through which we cannot wedge ourselves unpinched. But let us remember that every star in the universe sends out sparks never wholly wasted through unmeasurable distances; also, that every spiritual being, embodied or disembodied (according to our manner of speech), every resident of Earth, of Mars, of every habitable world among all constellations, and every spirit that ever ascended therefrom, must perpetually contribute to life's perpetual effulgence.

If this be not true, there is no law of telepathy.

My mother's half-sister, Beulah Mott, born March 11, 1788, twenty-five years earlier than herself—at the age of two and a half, spent an entire morning playing by running water, pleased with the glittering pebbles underneath. Coming in at noon, she climbed her father's knee and said sweetly: "Daddy, I have seen God. He says he is coming for me at two o'clock." "No, no!" said my grandfather, thrilled with an instant's fear. "Daddy cannot lose his little Beulah; she is the light of his eyes." "But he will come!" she persisted; "He said he would." After dinner she climbed his knee again: "Daddy, God will come for me at two o'clock;" and, laying her head upon his breast, she fell asleep. Curiously disturbed, he said to his wife, Beulah: "Are not her cheeks over-red? Can she be ailing?" "She is only warm from playing in the sun," answered the mother. "Lay her in the bed-room, where it is cool." Twenty minutes before two, the child was laid away; twenty minutes after two the mother went in to look at her—and found her not! The promise had been fulfilled.

Now this from Dr. Hudson, (whom I must quote a little farther now and then): "Nothing can be positively known except the past and the present. It would require a miracle to give one absolutely, unconditioned knowledge of future events; for there is, there can be, no law of the mind that would make one to cognize that which does not exist."

Something seems to have gone wrong with that "working hypothesis." Here is one of its postulates. *With a difference only of degree, we find, in the soul of man, every essential attribute of Omniscience and every power of Omnipotence.*

The inference is inevitable: There is no law of the mind of God enabling Him to "cognize that which does not exist."

Beulah—loveliest of little ones—did not prophesy; but the being—finite we must presume—who presented himself in visible guise before her spiritual vision, first perceived a condition, then sent a radiant thought into the future, and took cognizance of one moment of time that—did not exist!

At long intervals, years lying between, my practical and logical-minded mother would say, "I had a prophetic dream last night;" and the future failed not to justify that statement. One of these dreams, frequently related by her, impressed my young mind the more because of the picture-creating effect of her recital.

"I dreamed that I was in Oriskany, standing by Mr. Bennett's gate, and looking over into his yard. I was surprised to see two fine trees growing near the house; I said, 'I never noticed those before.' They were beautiful trees, tall, slender, exactly alike in appearance—equally green and thrifty. As I stood admiring them, I discovered that both were on fire at the top. 'Now that,' I said, 'is out of Nature. Such a thing could not be. They are not real trees but symbols. What do they signify?' Then someone behind me answered:

'You are right. They are only symbols. Two young men, who are believed to be in perfect health, are just going into quick consumption and will die within two months.'"

In relating her dream the following day, my mother added:—"It can have but one meaning. Mr. Bennett's two sons—tall and handsome twins—were typified by the twin trees. They will die at the time predicted."

Not many months later, some chance traveler from the distant village of Oriskany dropped in and related, as a marvel, the swift progress of a consumption which had carried off Mr. Bennett's twin sons, within a few days of each other, and in less than two months after the date of my mother's dream.

Now it matters nothing to this argument concerning foreknowledge, whether Beulah's transcendent visitor or my mother's unseen interpreter of symbols, may have been the mind of any "living person" or of a soul released,—although it would seem that the latter would be better able to control and direct its "divine potentials." Someone was able to dart forward and take cognizance of a time non-existent save in the prescient Mind of Deity. Should this power belong to us, it will at times reveal itself,—a final proof above all proofs of our essential oneness with the Godhead, and consequent immortality.

If therefore I descend into the mind of childhood in search of this spiritual potency, and can but dream I find it there, I shall be justified in carrying on the quest well beyond my three score years and twelve.

It will be remembered that I was the junior, by two years, of a brother, who, at the age of fifteen, in the school-room, and in my presence, was snatched away by death. Shortly before my eleventh birthday, while as yet no human being was aware of his danger, I "fell on sleep" and this is what I dreamed:

Lester and I were walking, hand in hand, upon a lonely road. At my right, all the way along, ran the edge of a sheer precipice. At his left was a dense, dark forest. "Lester," I asked him, "why do you keep looking into that wood?" He answered: "Someone is there who has

35

followed me a long time. He is following me now. I can never escape from him. When he comes to take me I must go. He is not like anyone else—he is half white and half black."

"You shall not walk on that side of the road," I said. "Change places with me and then he will not see you." "I will change places," assented Lester, "because he is not following you. He does not want you now. You are safe."

So we walked on, tightly clasping hands, I, upon the forest side, intently looking into the deep shade and imagining I caught glimpses now and then of a black and white face, far back. After a time we emerged from this road, climbed a low hill and sat down where there was nothing to see but the fallen trunks of trees, mostly very old and mossy. Lester left me and walked among them, bending down as though looking for something underneath.

"What are you looking for?" I asked, vaguely troubled. He sighed deeply: "Poor Mary!"

"What is the matter with cousin Mary?"

"She is lying here, under these logs and she is quite dead. She had a very bad back and it made her suffer a great deal. She was sick all through, but she lived more than thirty years."

With this I burst into sobs,—a strange thing for me, though I but slept. So my brother came and sat down by me, putting his arm around me and saying tenderly: "Don't cry." "Let us go back," I urged; and, rising we returned along the lonely road. I, putting him at my left next to the precipice and clasping his hand very tightly, began looking again for that black and white one in the woods. Then "in the twinkling of an eye," my brother was snatched from me, and though I whirled about to save him, I caught but a single glimpse as he went down out of sight. Thereafter I walked on and on and on— save at whiles when I sank from weakness, but still crept on; until, after a lapse into unconsciousness, I seemed to be in my own home again. But I said, "I will not tell my mother." Nor did I, asleep or awake.

If it be true, as learned Psychists claim—as Dr. Hudson strongly avers—that the essential self in man has some means of discovering danger to the physical structure, and, without informing the lower or objective consciousness, is able to predict death or to protect from accident, something may be said here in support of that statement.

My brother, not yet thirteen years old, was delicate, but his lack of strength had as yet excited no alarm. In the deep sleep of midnight, his half-emergent spirit may have realized bodily peril and telepathically—if it must be so expressed—imparted disturbance to mine. Actual prophecy of certain and sudden death was thinly veiled under such similitudes as might suggest themselves to a childish mind, bent upon giving out unhappy tidings, with tender caution. A fine-spun theory, perhaps not wholly untenable. Nevertheless, what can be said of the interjected story of Cousin Mary? For in very truth, two years after my brother's death, a cruel fall resulted in such injury to the spine, that, although she left her bed after many weeks, she was never again well—and about thirty-seven years later, sank under a complication of diseases and so passed away.

Now, although I had been furnished with a key for unlocking Paradisal doors, I had not tried it in these three intervening years. I desired no gifts worth praying for. I had no task but study, and that was pastime; no occupation but the occasional building of a play-house, with Lester's help; no trouble but the hateful behavior to me of one pretty little girl, which he and not I, bitterly resented. Half the time I spent alone in roaming. When I was in a mood for prayer, it was usually below the "Twenty's" thirty-foot waterfall and beside a broad rock, printed I thought (but how could that be?), with the foot of some gigantic animal. There I thought of God and Heaven, and of angels who sometimes brought infants down at sunrise, and sometimes took them away, as they had taken our Mary Sophia; and I solemnly wanted to be good, and was aware that it would be hard work. Ah, me! It has been main hard!

After that we removed to Black Rock, a suburb of Buffalo, and I became my mother's household assistant. As for Lester, he begged so hard (at thirteen) to be put in the way of learning to be a doctor, that my parents took him to the ablest in Buffalo—Dr Bissell, whom they knew. Only an office boy, yet with a full medical library thrown open to him, he spent all his spare time in study. His patron, wondering at his mental grasp, said: "There is nothing that

Johnny may not read,"—calling the lad by that first name, which he had vainly besought us to use at home. After a year of this, Father and Mother were sent for, and Dr Bissell, in their presence, examined him, saying, with actual tears (for he loved the boy), "Johnny, I know that you will not be afraid of the truth. Maybe you will live a long time, but you may go at any moment." So Lester came home, laughed, whistled, played with the baby, returned to school, and only required that none of his brothers and sisters should be told.

When all was over, and I had dwelt in the shadow perhaps a year—in my sleep, like a night-blooming cereus, there opened out another dream.

This time I was walking across a very bare common, and I was alone. Presently, down a dark opening, I went underground. First I passed along a passage, dimly lighted from above. Then I entered a room, through a door which swung open to admit me. I stood all amazed, for there were flowers upon flowers, chiefly white, banked against the four walls, massed, with down-looking faces, upon the ceiling; and only the floor near me was without them. I had never seen a hothouse flower, but the forms of some of these I dimly remembered the next day. They might have been camelias, gloxinias, orchids or other exotics not unfamiliar to me now. I said: "How wonderful it is to see all these growing, without sunlight, underground!" And then, after my mother's way in dreams—I asked: "What can it mean?"

A voice behind me answered, clear as the ringing of a silver bell: "These are the flowers that you are going to plant."

I turned, passed out of the door, and on, into a dim open space. There I saw trees; not very many but of good size and tall. "This," I cried out, "is more wonderful still! Flowers might possibly be grown underground, but not trees, surely. What can this mean?" And the same voice interpreted: "These are the trees that you are going to plant."

Thereafter I was sensible of being comforted.

From the date of our removal to Black Rock, one desire had been stirring in secret. I wanted religion. Was I not old enough? Lester had united with the church at nine, and I well-remembered how he would rise in meeting and, in a low voice, humbly and reverently tell that he felt the presence of the Holy Spirit in his heart; and how grown men—class leaders—would say: "This boy shames us all, he has so clear a comprehension of the plan of salvation!" Poor boy!

I cared nothing for the deep theological works, more accessible to children then than now, which he read and re-read with avidity. I passed by even the histories which he drew from the not insignificant "upper village" library, although Willie and Bennie would lie awake for hours while he told them of great battles, how they were planned, and why they were won or lost;—till we thought the boy was born to be a soldier. Meantime—my Milton and Pollock days having burned themselves out—I thrilled to "The Red Fisherman" or dropped far below Praed and read "Fannie Campbell; the Female Pirate Captain," quite comfortably (not a drop of poison in it!).

And now, all that gone by, and I in training to be a teacher,—at thirteen I longed to be "saved." Not saved from Hell, for I was the child of my father, who strove to keep step with Methodists, yet doubted whether those eternal doors would ever close upon a lost soul; nor yet from sin, which did not weigh me down with "conviction," I think rather from myself. I was so tired of me, my heart seemed breaking. If God would only lift me up and love me, what law of His could I ever disobey? And I should be so white!

So, one night, when the church was crowded because the minister had announced that there would be revival services, I answered to the third and last invitation:

"Come ye sinners, poor and needy."

Hating the publicity, yet forced on by bitter need, shaken with uncontrollable sobs, I took my place to be prayed for,—the only "mourner" on the bench.

"Let us pray," said the would-be revivalist; "O, Lord, we have called upon dying sinners to come and partake of the riches of Thy grace,—but no one has come!" On went the prayer and still the voice affirmed, four times over: "No one has come." I was no longer weeping. I heard a sibilant utterance that broke in upon the sudden silence, after "Father Graham" had clutched the minister's arm and brought him to a stand-still. Then the raucous tones began again: "O, Lord, there has one little girl come, but we're afraid she doesn't know what she's come for."

With the "amen" of the benediction yet in my ears, I passed through the crowd, which seemed to divide itself before me, went home with speed, got into my bed, and, drawing the covering over my head, with the utmost vehemence possible to a whisperer, I— added to my vocabulary, a single, wicked word. Let it remain unwritten.

Now the three years that followed after, were as Pharaoh's lean kine; and there was famine in Egypt!

SUBJECTIVE VISIONS

FINDING our way as best we can throughout the secret chambers of this Mammoth Cave into which this supposed Psychist has led us, we come, at last, to the edge of its deepest pit,—that "bottomless pit" from which hands—indubitably friendly—have waved us away. Listen once again to wise and warning words, meant to set us trembling in the presence of appalling danger, and to urge us back to the safety of those halls where stalactites (in lieu of stars) fret the vaulted ceiling:—

"To believe in the reality of subjective visions, is to give the subjective mind control of the dual mental organization; and, to give the subjective mind such control, is for Reason to abdicate her throne.....The result, in its mildest form of manifestation, is a mind filled with the grossest superstition,—a mind, which, like the untutored mind of the savage, 'Sees God in clouds or hears Him in the wind.' Its ultimate form is insanity."

I once observed a stalwart Irishman, who was standing near a chance group of singers at a camp-meeting. With intent, uplifted eyes he had been joining in their melodious worship; but the rich baritone broke off, and I saw his face grow white and luminous as if a great light were shining thereon. In an instant, as though he had been struck backward by a mighty hand, he fell all his length upon the sward. Very soon he opened his eyes, uplifted himself and said, amazedly, with bated breath:—"I saw him."

Something very like this, happened to Saint Paul,—causing "Reason to abdicate her throne."

At this camp-meeting, now fifty-four years gone by, I saw that lovely-minded Abraham Castle, and heard him pleading with an insufferable dandy, who stroked his mustache, twirled his rattan cane, and sneered. "O, Henry, won't you come! won't you come!" and all the while his streaming eyes attested his unutterable love and sorrow. Now, when next day I saw him deep in trance,—being there myself to study Psychic Phenomena under an earlier name—I must needs keep near and gather all the story. Much I must omit, but this, at least, I may transcribe, without wronging the sense; all this and more, he told in open meeting, I listening with the rest.

"I was with my father! 'Abraham,' he said, 'I have something to show you. Look at this broad and shining sea. It seems to touch no shore but this. See this beautiful white ship lying at anchor, with all her sails set for the voyage; and watch the multitudes that come from all directions. They cross the gang-plank, they crowd the deck, but no matter how many come, there is always room.'

"What vessel is it, father, and to what port is it bound?"

"'It is a great ship built to carry souls over safely to the Heavenly shore. Question me further, my son?'"

"Father, will it be lawful to ask if my wife, Sarah, will be there?"

"It is lawful to ask. Sarah will be there."

"And Robert? And Mary? And Elizabeth? And Martin?"

"'They will be there.'"

"And O, Father, Father, Will Henry be there?"

"'My son, Henry will be there.'"

"'Abraham, have you nothing more to ask, before you go back.'"

"Father, God has called me to preach; but Sarah cannot consent. He has not called her to be the wife of an itinerant. I have no right to drag her with me; I cannot leave her behind. What shall I say to her, so that she may be willing to let me obey the call?"

"'My son, return to the body. Sarah is in the smallest tent of all. Find her; she is calling for you. She will tell you that you may go and preach.'"

Up rose Abraham Castle, trembling in every limb. Three men, by his request, and under his direction, went with him and sought out that little tent. Before they could lift the canvas they heard a voice:— "Praise the Lord! Do, someone, go and get Abraham! Where is Abraham?"—and as they drew him in, Sarah, newly emerged from her trance, cried out rapturously: "O, Abraham, you may go and preach now!"—And that was just what he had told them she would

42

say; to which they testified. Because of this, one more Evangelist, yielded himself to the control of his subjective mind, and in the Name of the Most High, went out to save the souls of men. Once again was illustrated that supreme danger which attends upon those who "believe in the reality of subjective visions."

At that very camp-meeting came "Happy John," bounding in among us as one immortally young—albeit, maybe, fifty. For twelve joyous years he had been kept in exaltation because of a subjective experience that had lifted him instantaneously and forever out of the gutters of the streets of Rochester, where he had long time wallowed. No one imagined that he was insane; but if to "see God in clouds and hear Him in the wind" be "grossest superstition," I fear he was no better than an "untutored savage." However, Dr. Hudson found God in the moneron; and I myself, at the tender age of four (little pagan) saw Him in a Turk's-cap lily.

My father, who married at thirty a girl not sixteen, never dreaming, perhaps, that she might not absorb his prejudices, three years later came home after a few weeks' absence, to find her all astray among the Methodists. He would not hold her back, but after he had gone with her to a number of meetings, he broke down and said: "Mary, we have been altogether happy; but now that you are going off with those wild Methodists, all sympathy between us is at an end. Our happiness is wrecked." Forth-right he went away into the woods where he remained fasting, nearly two days. Returning he found my mother upon her knees and fell down by her side. Instantly he was filled with an ineffable spiritual blessing, that caused him to "walk softly" all the days of his mortal life.

If this was not an actual "subjective vision," that kind came later, during a long search after "holiness of heart" in which my mother joined. Did the children of two so evidently under the control of the subjective mind, suffer by inheritance, live in "gross superstition," wander away into insanity?—absolutely, No!

On All Saints' Eve, October 31, 1517, Martin Luther nailed a paper to the door of a church in Wittenberg, on which ninety-five theses were written denouncing papal indulgences. That night, in his capital a hundred miles away, dreamed Frederick, Elector of

43

Saxony! He stood near the castle church in Wittenberg, and saw a monk writing upon the door. Now the quill wherewith the monk wrote was so long that its point reached to Rome and roused a lion crouching within the city; again, as he wrote, the point struck the tiara of Pope Leo, the tenth, so that it rocked upon his head and the cardinals all rushed to hold it steady, that it might not fall. The dreaming Frederick was appalled and would have hurried to arrest the monk and stop the movement of his pen; but, filling all the sky on a sudden, was an innumerable host of shining ones, who cried:— "Stop not the monk! His writing is of God" And because Frederick "believed in the reality of his subjective vision," Martin Luther was not murdered nor the great Reformation stemmed from sweeping clean the roads by which men travel to their God.

Let us re-write the script:—To give the objective mind control of the dual mental organization, is for Religion to abdicate her throne, Honor, Truth and Purity to perish by the way-side, blessed Charity to flee the haunts of men, rivers to run thick with innocent blood and ravage and rapine to devastate the Earth.

But as for my subjective mind, it began striving for its own. Teaching my second winter school at sixteen, I had become so much of a personage, that when I started afresh, and went to a Christian altar for prajers, in response to that solemn exhortation:—

"Come ye sinners poor and needy," shoutings welcomed my approach. I had no tears to shed,—was conscious of no griefs requiring alleviation. One chief thought was in my mind. I was a child of Eternity; I must enter upon my heritage. The shoutings moved me not at all. I am not a good Mesmeric subject; I have been tried and could not be made unconscious. The emotions, thrilling around me, did not thrill me. I was not to be hypnotized into the kingdom. The matter was altogether between God and myself.

Nevertheless I "went forward" as often as anyone in my school-district would take me all that four miles through the cold. I strove to avail myself of the "means of Grace." I was instructed that I must realize my exceeding sinfulness. I tried, but could not quite make a mountain of what seemed a mole-hill. Exhorters said I was in

44

danger of hell-fire. After a time—God taking no notice of me it seemed—I was too humbled to dispute that proposition. But, above all, I was to remember that Christ died to appease an offended God. I must rely upon him. There was no other way.

After some weeks, dismissing my scholars one night as usual, I locked myself within and said: "I will not leave till I am blest!"

Oh, I was a sinner! Over and over again, when I was little, I had falsified about my knitting work—ten times around instead of eight! Yet I had hated the lying! I summed up all the wickedness I could remember, and then mourned: "For these sins Christ died." Oh, the agony of trying to realize his sufferings! Worst of all, the injustice of it! Christ to endure all of that just because of me!

Hours passed on. My fire, built of rotten wood, was utterly out; the night was bitterly cold.

Some unseen power seemed to drive me away. I put on my things, went to my boarding-place, crept late to bed and—chilled into indifference—said: "I did not keep my vow.

I suppose I shall never be blest."

Nevertheless, I rode to church the following evening, and, because I must, went to the "mourners' bench" as before. I think the friends were a little tired of me, and I was more than a little tired of them. It was as if I were at some neutral point of polarization, where there is no light. So home again to my district.

I left the sleigh, ran into the house and passed through the warm family room and the cold parlor to my bed room. I had not even provided myself with a candle, intending to return at once. I took off my quilted hood and heavy cloak, laid them on the bed and paused a moment to say, hopelessly, but without any special poignancy of feeling: "There is nothing for me. There is something for everyone but me."

Instantly from above, I was answered: "There is something for you! "I fell upon my knees, lifted my blind eyes and waited. Nothing came. I arose and went into the parlor, moving forward toward the living-room beyond. And now with strong insistence, came the startling word: "There is something for you now!"

A little moon-light, filtering through the windows, showed me a chair, set between them. I crossed over and once more sank upon my knees.

In one second, through all my physical frame, it seemed there swept a rushing wind. It bore me out,—it left me standing beside my brother Lester. Two others, dimly discerned, as though they kept in shadow—tall men they seemed to be—stood on either hand. Upon Lester I centered my mind. There was no amazement, no perturbation. Neither of us, by word or gesture expressed any of that surface-joy in reunion that we mortals exhibit in greeting long-absent friends. We stood close together and I was content. Then, by a movement, he seemed to desire that I should look upward. This I did, not looking upon him further at that time. We were all rising through space. We were nearing the stars. They were no longer stars, but great, whirling suns, effulgent,—yet I was able to look upon them. I saw one far beyond all others in glory, and I said (remembering Dr. Thomas Dick's suggestion), "That may be the central sun, where God resides, and from which He governs His Universe. Yet He is also everywhere." And my soul was filled with a sense of the power and majesty of the Deity.

Lester, now on my left hand, who had at first seemed to be on the right, laid his hand upon my arm: "Sister"— speaking for the first time,—"Sister, look away to the left."

I turned, and, afar off, there was a great darkness. "That is Chaos," I thought, and wondered. Then I saw a sun, undiminished in splendor, not swerving from its orbit, roll in and utterly disappear. "It has become," I thought, "a part of Chaos. It does not exist. Was it ground to powder? It could not have been burned!" Then for the first time I thrilled as with fear: "If that is the way they are brought to an end, it will be so with our earth." And I imagined it rolling in.

Still intently looking, I saw the sun roll out, even more splendid than before, and still true to its orbit. And now did Lester say what, word for word, I have remembered to this day:—

"Sister, the law that keeps all these suns rolling in their places, governs them just as well when they are in the dark as when they are in the light. As no star can ever escape the influence of that law, so no soul can ever move so far away from God, that He will not surely draw it back into His marvelous light. And now, sister, as you go back to the body, remember this: Never believe anything of God that seems to you unjust."

There was nothing more, I had returned.

One, having had a stroke of catalepsy, never stirs—remains rigid. But I had fallen over upon the chair and my hands on either side touched the carpet. I arose, a little trembling, moved about and seemed to myself all enveloped in God's Love, one happy soul in a universe of happy souls.

Soon after, riding with my father on the way to my school, I said all I dared say: "Father, I have had a very wonderful, very beautiful experience."

Without questioning me, he answered: "Daughter, that is only the first flower of a tree that will be full of blossoms. There have been years of my life, when every day and all days I could have said, 'Peace is flowing as a river.'"

O, sweet, remembered prophecy fulfilled!

O, happy child, to have been so blest in daughterhood!

MIND SUBMERGENCE AND PSYCHIC REVELATIONS

PARDON me if I delay narration for the moment. I am aware that my experience will need a reconciling touch with some of you. No one as yet, I apprehend, has ventured quite so far as I am venturing in my revealments. Friends may naturally say: "A poet will unconsciously embellish here and there,—or, being old, forget to be exact." But Psychists claim that the subjective mind "never forgets;" and I have reason to be certain they are right.

A Psychic vision is an etching that cannot be effaced; nor can it be re-touched without the graving tool, which none of us possess. A Psychic message might reverberate down all the steeps of time, and not a word be altered by the echoes. If you pick a flower, why, there it is! You did not spread a leaf nor tint a petal. As for my floral offerings, you must take them as I give them, even though you cast them down as having little worth; there is no "art that, in their piedness, imitates great Nature."

When Harriet Martineau* (a power behind the people and the throne!) became an advocate of Mesmerism as a curative agency, ungrateful England laughed from Falmouth to the Tweed. She had been "prisoner to her couch" five years and had arisen by Mesmeric means, a healed and happy woman. What then? There was the more to laugh at, so they laughed the more. But she went further still, reporting as she went. In healing her sick waiting-maid, she came upon the fact that even a mind but little educated, being submerged, might manifest unlooked for attributes,—might for example, prophesy. She had not learned, or did not practise, those Mesmeric tricks that lecturers exhibit to make audiences laugh ("admission twenty cents"). The sleeper, half released, was left to find her own way through the dark, uninfluenced by "suggestion." It was not Harriet Martineau who prophesied, but just that simple girl, her waiting-maid!

*Martineau: 1802–1876) was an English social theorist and Whig writer, often cited as the first female sociologist.

48

And now the laugh became a jeer; mere criticism merged in persecution. The family her labors had enriched, denounced her openly. Her "liberal" brother—ablest of the Unitarians, did not forgive her to his dying day. She might have said with Mrs. Browning's penitent:

"God, over my head,

Must sweep in the wrath of His Judgment seas,

If He shall deal with me, sinning, but only indeed the same

And no gentler than these:" albeit she had not sinned. And I, who have not suffered persecution (since I am not great), feel the need of an appeal to courage while I propose to add my modicum of knowledge to her one discovery. Since her day—since my own in fact—there have been Scientists who have exalted truth,—Crookes, Myers, James, Hodgson, Hyslop and the rest. Wilson from a fossil bone could re-construct a bird; Huxley could show a man emergent from a plasmic cell; but these discern the man emergent from the flesh,—deathless as God Himself. I have not been their pupil;—much of my life has antedated theirs, and I have taken just what came to me with little thought of "Science" in the abstract. Do we think of oxygen and hydrogen when we are drinking at the rock of Horeb? The wonder is to me how Harriet Martineau could find the prophet in the sleeper, and fail to understand that only an immortal entity could have immortal sight. She thought she thought that Death "blows out" our individual lights—we being mere candles taken out of doors and caught in mighty winds! Yet all the time, no doubt, belief hid smiling in the shadow of that unbelief.

When Andrew Falconer's mother, by whose terrific creed her son had been "eleckit to damnation," saw him standing, saved and sane, before her dying eyes (so runs MacDonald's story), she laughed and sobbed aloud: "O, Lord! I knew it all the time!" Let us think of Harriet Martineau and Marian Evans Lewes (no less great, and equally at fault) as waking from the trance of Death with that same jubilant cry!

One of the attributes of God is self-existence,—"life inherent, underived." We are not "derived" from Him, but He inheres in us.

49

We have this attribute with all the rest. Eternal life would be eternal loneliness without the power of interchange between the self-existent. The Infinite, inherent in the finite, wins for Himself companionship, gives and receives, loves and is loved—moving within us to the end that we may love Him and may love each other, to our own perpetual aggrandizement; also to His delight. Herein is ample warrant for belief in spirit-intercourse!

Mere belief however is not operative. Each one of us must have a personal revelation. Little use to cry "Lo, here!" "Lo, there!" and hunt up "mediums,"—or follow hypnotizers!

Still it appears that Mesmerism, or its variant Hypnotism, is a sort of postern gate to this King's castle of the human soul. Not by any means the royal entrance;—it may give admission to the court-yard very likely—never to the throne-room or the citadel. But, to drop the metaphor, we may admit its therapeutic value; and if a mind, submerged, were let alone, not subject to "suggestion," who can tell upon what voyage of discovery it might embark? It has been claimed that should the Hypnotizer waive his privilege in favor of a "disembodied" spirit,—so giving him possession of the subject,—much could be revealed. Perhaps it may be so. Never having been a "subject" or an "agent," I have learned the most I know about the lesser hypnotism from the books of Dr. Thomson Hudson, which are much in vogue. No one is so popular as he among the masses; and he disputes the possibility, or actuality rather, of communion with the so-called Dead. Although he is certain of a "spirit-realm," he labors to expunge it from the reckoning. I am told that he succeeds so well in this, many have been made unbelievers in a future life, by his recorded investigations and opinions based upon discovered "psychic facts"—such as he chanced upon (poor stumbler!) as he ran,—bearing his pack of cards!

But note his attitude: He was convinced beforehand that his "hypothesis," already formulated (the "facts" not yet in evidence!) would disprove spirit-intercourse.

Now minds, submerged by his hypnotic influence, he states, were altogether "amenable to control" by his suggestion. Accordingly not one of them could see beyond his own dense atmosphere. They saw

50

what he required of them, if possible—whether the furniture in his far off library, or a king of clubs nearby! He made "percipients" do much drudgery for his behoof, and was delighted and amazed to find how much they knew—after they had been' told! They spoke their little pieces very well.

As for his "facts" no one denies them. They belong to lower Psychic states. From higher Psychic states his crass, cock-sure opinions shut him out completely.

Not the less, a fact is but one point in the continuous line that stretches either way, even to infinity. If it be a fact that one mind can approach another by this hypnotic road, that is but one of facts innumerable. That same route may be traveled by all souls, whether in Heaven above, on earth below, throughout the habitable stars, or in the nether hells.

But is this Hypnotism the only "Highway of the Lord?" Reason forbids the thought. When two friends meet upon the street, shake hands, converse by interchange of words, or glances which convey far more than words, or mind-pulsations which convey far more than either, we cannot say that one has hypnotized the other. Mental submergence is not necessary to celestial converse. If it were, what use? Nothing would be remembered. Obviously we have a right to see and hear and know and not forget, if there be any law permitting consciousness.

Which one of us is not aware at times, of spirit visitants,—being alone and dominated by the higher thought,—or even at our lowest, when we sink and need them most.

A spirit-mother passed through atmospheres so foul that I could scarcely breathe therein, who followed not long after. So standing all revealed before her errant daughter, and, calling her by that dear household name none in the place had ever learned, she said: "Arbie! What are you doing here?" And Arbie did not eat or sleep for many hours. So, when the door was open for escape, she caught my hand as one in desperate need, and came away—a soul sweet-saved forever. We cannot burrow in so deep that beatific souls will not descend and find us, first or last.

But this is the "domain of superstition," Hudson says. Well, be it so! Make haste and pull down every way-side cross, lest some poor wanderer kneel in hope of resurrection! But have a care! As Mrs. Browning cries:—

"Here's God down on us! What are you about?"

I have told you of an hour in early life when my own mind was in submergence—by no human means; then I became an entity disburdened of mortality. To claim that those who made me see, (invisible sleep-inducers), were the subjective minds of "living persons," acting independently of outward consciousness, would be illogical, beyond the wildest dream. To pretend that, I, myself, did hypnotize myself and practice on myself a spiritual fraud, would be to credit me with powers for wickedness akin to those of Milton's Lucifer.

Now they who caused the slumber, set me no slavish tasks, after the manner of our mortal hypnotists. They left me free to think my very thoughts. Mindful of tender hearts, two kept themselves aloof, that one who loved me—whom I knew and loved—might show to me how Infinite Mercy governs all. They brought me back, all faulty as before, yet saved from blind belief in daunting creeds. They left me at the foot of God's eternal hills, with roses in my hands and sunlight in my soul—looking up and pondering what rocky path to choose for my ascent.

Whenever, in these further revelations, I shall say: "I saw," let that be understood as a "subjective vision." When I shall say, "I was aware," that will imply subjective consciousness. To illustrate the latter phase: I entered once a

Boston depot, and found my mind confronted with a vivid thought of Dr. Alicia Carey, who during ten years had been remembered seldom if at all. The thought became a singular consciousness of her. I walked into the long sitting-room, with my eyes cast down, intent upon her personality. At the further end, I paused, looked up, reached out my hand and touched—Alicia Carey.

This is what it means to be "aware,"—quite different from telepathy or word-and-thought transference. She had been my physician before removing to a Southern state; I was still sensitive to her aura; and yet there was no interchange of thought till we shook hands and spoke. I was "aware"—not she.

My winter school of 1852 being ended, and my summer school late in beginning, I went a-visiting. First, I sought out Mrs. Lowell in Buffalo, with whom I had made my home, while at an "up-town" school. I found her lying upon her bed, all other furniture being gone, for it was moving-day. She presently said very sweetly: "I hear you have become a Methodist." I answered "No! I have experienced religion;" for I knew not how to answer otherwise. "And have you heard that we are Spiritualists?" "Yes; but what is it to be a Spiritualist?"

Mrs. Lowell—lately a consistent Baptist—was an intellectual woman of such dignity and moral worth, as well as grace of manner and beauty of appearance, that I revered and loved her most sincerely. I could not fail to give her words much weight. As a patient in Fredonia Water Cure, she had become convinced of spirit-intercourse by most unusual tests. I heard her story without disbelief, but finally I questioned: "Do you believe in Christ?" "He was Divine," she answered, "being filled with the Holy Spirit in full measure, as a man;—One with the Father by submission to His will. He wrought by inspiration; but can a mortal frame contain One who is Infinite and fills the Universe? Assuredly he was not God."

I arose to go. "I beg that you will visit me," she urged. "We are removing to a small brick cottage, Franklin Street. It stands a little back. You will see the number, 91, in gilt letters on the corner."

During a long walk that followed, I meditated deeply: "It seems to be my disposition to throw away beliefs. All my life I have heard that there's a personal devil; also that there's a hell. I believe in neither. But one must stop somewhere. I will stop right here. I will not doubt the Deity of Christ. If I should doubt, the next thing I might say would be perhaps: 'There is no God.' I will never visit Mrs. Lowell again. Much as I love her, I will cast her off, before I cast off Christ!"

Two weeks later, I set out to walk from Black Rock's lower village, up long Niagara Street, four miles to Main. That I could stray therefrom and lose my way, would have seemed unthinkable; and yet, absorbed in thought, I lost it. Looking up at last I found myself where I had never been before. Over and over I inquired my way and then forgot directions. Finally I gave up asking and just walked. At last I sat down on a raised sidewalk and declared: "I'll go no further. I'll step into some house and beg for leave to rest." I rose, opened a gate just at my hand, looked up, saw 91 upon the corner of a brick cottage, heard a cry of joy within, and while I stood poised for flight, was clasped by little Emma Lowell, who drew me on into the house.

Her mother rose to greet me, saying, "I am so glad you have come just at this moment. Here is Mrs. Warwick, whom I met for the first time last night! She is an excellent clairvoyant! Please listen to our talk."

I listened, conscious of antagonism, and mentally combatting every word that Mrs. Warwick uttered. But presently my mood softened, for I became "aware" of Lester, so close it seemed as though he might be heard to breathe. "Lester," I questioned mentally: "Do you want me to investigate Spiritualism? If so, communicate with me through Mrs. Warwick. Unless you do I will never look into it further;" and he answered, to my certain understanding: "Sister, you shall have a communication from me before you go."

I arose almost at once. "I shall lose the stage to Aurora, if I do not leave immediately, I am afraid."

"Lose it," said Mrs. Lowell; "stay and see if something cannot be obtained for you."

We sat down at a heavy, mahogany card-table, the square top of which folded double on hinges—I at the side, the two ladies at either end—sitting far back that I might see they used no lifting power. The table rose, rocked with violence, and settled over upon me. I said in my mind: "I do not want table-tippings." At once it lifted itself and sank back to its level, while Mrs. Warwick's hand began to move. We provided paper and pencil, and, with great rapidity, there was written a message beginning: "Dear Sister," and expressing in different words from those within my mind, a desire that I should

54

understand his happiness and believe that he could visit me. This was signed, "John."

Mrs. Lowell colored deeply: "That was not her brother's name." But I, laying the sheet again before Mrs. Warwick, asked mentally: "Why did you sign your name John?"

Instantly the answer came: "You know, Sister, I always preferred that name." I asked but one more question and that mentally: "Can I be influenced to write, in this way?" "I think you will, pretty soon"— written almost before I had formulated the words in my mind. I thought: "In that case I will investigate through no one but myself."

That evening my mother and I examined an old copybook, inscribed "The property of John Lester Jones;" and found that, letter by letter, the two scripts corresponded. Not that I believed because of that, but because I had been "aware" of him and of that telepathic message, received before the writing. I might doubt Mrs. Warwick, but not my brother "John."

Not long after this, I dreamed: One came to me, whom, in my sleep, I understood to be a "disembodied spirit." "Come out now," he said, taking me by the arm, "and look at the sun." I saw it, still high in the West, but less bright than it should be; and while I continued to gaze, it faded more and more. At last it rocked violently and dropped down out of sight. I fell upon my face crying (still in my mother's way!); "It is a symbol! What does it signify?" And I trembled and was greatly afraid. Then the one who had led me out, answered: "It signifies the death of your father. But inasmuch as you looked upon the sun sometime before it fell, his death will not be immediate." This dream is alluded to in the first stanza of "A Flower of Paradise"—written but four years ago, in order to record in verse a Psychic vision yet to be described in definite prose.

There was nothing whatever wrong with my father apparently. I had never known him to be sick. In view of what I have to relate, however, it seems necessary to state that at the age of twenty-one, he had been terribly wounded one "training day" in the village of Palmyra, N. Y.,—an accidental shot having driven a ramrod through his lungs, within one and one half inches of the heart and part way out under the shoulder blade. It seems pertinent to state that, some weeks earlier, that subjective mind of his would seem to have taken alarm; for he firmly resolved that should anything befall him, young Dr. McIntyre, with whom he had spoken but once, and no other, should be his physician. A good many practising doctors were on the ground and all concurred in saying that absolutely nothing could be done. Father called for McIntyre, (late from medical college and without one patient in the place): "I am not going to die," he declared, "and you are going to save me. This will make your fortune,"—which it literally did. Being resourceful, the young doctor drew blood until there was no color left, cleansed the wound by drawing a silk handkerchief through, and saw his patient sitting up in four weeks' time.

I am sorry to seem a little doleful at this point, but we are looking out for prophecies:—

A year and a half after that dream of the sun, this came: I dreamed that I was walking in a grave-yard and came upon an open grave, very old and sodden. "This seems to have been dug a long while," I commented. A voice from the void, as it seemed, answered: "It has been dug a great many years." I walked on, and began to observe the many graves around me. To my astonishment the one-time occupant of each lay upon the surface, smiling happily upon me, and beautiful of appearance. Each one put out a hand, from which I took a paper, written upon with a name. "These are all ancestors and relatives of my father and mother!" I said, and went on, wondering. I came again to that open grave. "Will this ever be filled?" I asked. The voice replied: "It will surely be filled." Again I wandered and looked upon the living, who had been dead. A third time I reached the empty grave. A heavy rain was pouring, in which I stood and meditated; then I questioned, with strong emphasis: "When will this grave be filled?" and the swift answer came: "In just three weeks."

I was very dull. It never entered into my waking thoughts that the grave which had been dug so many years had been waiting for my father all that time. I thought only of my mother, and was oppressed by a transient fear, howbeit (although the assertion may be doubted), I was not prone to superstition.

Eleven days later, it being Sabbath morning and my hands at leisure, there came to me, for the first time, a powerful impulse to test that opinion, which had seemed to be my brother Lester's, and learn, if possible, whether I could be "influenced" to write. I had been for six months at home, trying to recover from the effects of teaching a very difficult winter school and studying very hard during a summer's attendance at the Buffalo High School, but as I could not quite forego my books, I had fitted up a little room for study, arranging a shelf on a level with the arm of my rocking chair, for convenience in writing. I placed pencil and paper on this shelf, and sat down prepared to wait. A movement of my arm began at once. Names were written, intelligent answers were given to all my questions, and a request made that I should carefully test communications in order to become satisfied that they did not, unconsciously to myself, originate within my own mind. Very much pleased and interested, but without the least excitement, (composure has always characterized my subjective experiences), I obeyed, and sprang every trap I could devise upon this mysterious operating intelligence. For example: "Write the name of someone my mother knew in childhood, but of whom I have never heard her speak." This name I repeated later to my mother, (who knew nothing of what was going on), asking "Who was he?" She stared: "A man of that name lived near us when I was little. You could not have heard me speak of him, for he has not entered my mind, I suppose, for thirty years."

I had five sittings with—myself, or these invisible visitors, as you like, but by Tuesday noon was disposed to let the matter rest for a time, and, in fact, ceased thinking on the subject for some hours.

At four o'clock an uncontrollable impulse sent me up the stairs. I paused on the landing: "What am I to do?"

"Go to the window and look out." This message was wholly mental, but most forcible. I went to the window, looked out, and saw my father coming. Before there was time to infer anything from his appearance, came the second message: "He is very sick. He is coming home to die."

A few minutes later, I descended the stairs which led to the living-room, where my mother stood kneading biscuits for tea. She looked up, paused in her work, and said in a startled voice: "Amanda, are you sick; What makes you so pale?"

After a moment's pause, I said without preamble:—"Father is coming, and he is very sick. He is coming home to die."

I cannot say why she believed me, but she did. After a steadfast look into my eyes, she grew exceeding pale, as one who hears authoritative news. Then she turned and met him at the door. Although he said in all good faith: "I am not very sick," I think she had no hope. She, like myself, was sometimes made "aware."

Observe that none of these experiences, verging upon what the world calls "mediumship," could possibly have been induced by human hypnotism. No living person's mind willed me to turn aside from straight Niagara Street, or led me to the friend I had renounced. No "living person" could have taken on my brother's personality, and promised me a message from himself. No "living person," by telepathy or otherwise, could have induced the two prophetic dreams. Even if that were possible, the fact remains that some immortal mind fore-knew the coming death, and named the very day of burial three weeks before it came.

Prophecy—the Word that is with God, the attribute of angels,—our attribute as well! It is God's answer to the questioning cry of all humanity: "Is man immortal?" It is like the falling fire from Heaven that burned the sacrifice.

Let us be worshippers of God, and not of Baal.

A FLOWER OF PARADISE AND A SOUL IN SHADOW

I REJOICE that I am able to pour a sweeter draught for any who may choose to drink.

On the following morning (the physician having cheerfully concurred with father "A slight pneumonia,—no danger"), as soon as I had attended to my I went to my study. I may say that a few months earlier, three friends, with myself, had joined in a series of tests in order to discover the origin of that intelligence which, by tipping a small stand, as we pointed to the letters of the alphabet, spelled out coherent sentences. While we had not heard of any "subconscious" or "subjective" minds, (this was fifty-six years ago), we said it was highly probable that our "unconscious" minds had the power of controlling electrical currents, and were responsible for that display of physical energy and obvious mentality. Our theory, like a plowshare, cut rather deep furrows, and if it struck the root of any living tree, we very sensibly pulled it out and thrust it in further away. We never once talked of "spirits," wisely acting upon the principle of Timzeus in the Platonic Dialogues: "If we wish to acquire any real acquaintance with Astronomy, we shall let the heavenly bodies alone." Dr. Hudson himself, could hardly have improved upon our "working hypothesis," and I am quite sure he would have exulted in, at least, one striking example of *telepathie a trois*. "Who made you?" we asked the stand. "Orson W. Hammond." "That is a lie!" ejaculated our hostess from her distant seat by the fire. "No man of that name ever lived in Amherst, or anywhere else to my knowledge." But four times over the name "Orson W. Hammond" was spelled out with strong rockings. "Of whom were you bought?" I queried. "Of Henry Blake." "Right" said our hostess. When her husband came, we called out at once: "Who made this stand?" To which he replied: "I bought it before my marriage, of Henry Blake. He had just bought in all the stock of a man who went West and was never heard of again. That man made the stand. His name was "Orson W. Hammond." By common consent, we suspended our experiments forthwith. They had begun to tax our wits.

59

But now, as I shut my study door and sat down to think myself out of trouble, I reverted to our theory: "All this writing, which I seemed not to do myself, may have been the work of my 'unconscious mind.' If so, its power to delude is beyond calculation? Therefore, notwithstanding all the names of ancestors, relatives and others, which have been written—most of them strange to me although known to my mother it seems, should this one declaration that my father was coming home to die,' prove untrue, I will never again tamper with my unknown self. Yet I will, this once more, allow the writing to go on, and will not interpose my doubts."

I drew forward paper and pencil, being, by this time quite neutral-minded and non-resistant. This message followed: "The statement was true. Owing to conditions of which you are not aware, it was thought best to inform your mother at once. Give us an opportunity to prove that the tidings did not originate in your own mind. Put us to some test."

After a little study, I brought a large Bible and placed it on the shelf at my side. Then I said: "A spirit should be able to read print without the aid of mortal eyes. I will turn my face wholly away, and do you, whoever you are—turn the leaves of this Bible and put my finger upon some text which will tell of a death." With movements far more rapid than usual, my hand was made to whirl over the leaves. When my finger was held down firmly, I turned and read Gen. xxv. "Then Abraham gave up the ghost—and was gathered to his people.

"Again," I demanded, and again the finger pointed: Gen. xxxv. 29. "And Isaac gave up the ghost and died and was gathered to his people."

"Once more:" And the finger selected Gen. xlix. 33: "And when Jacob had made an end of commanding his sons, he gathered up his feet into the bed and yielded up the ghost, and was gathered unto his people."

Even then I would not be satisfied. Perhaps ten other texts were found to tell the same story; till, at last, all the leaves were flung over and my finger placed upon Rev xxii. 20. 11 He which testifieth these things saith:—Surely

I come quickly: Amen. Even so, come Lord Jesus."

And now the tempest fell. Long time convulsed with sobs, I gave way to what seemed unendurable grief. Not, I affirm, because of all this attestation, but because of an inner, invincible conviction. I also was a spirit, and I fore-knew.

At last the storm subsided. I said:—"I must be reconciled; I must be glad. He has earned his rest. But oh, if I could only see one thing that my father will see in Heaven!"

My thoughts drifted: "He will see little Mary; will she look as she used to look?" I tried to recall her face, but I was about eight when she died, and that memory was quite submerged. "He will see Lester," and I remembered his face perfectly—the broad white brow, the large gray eyes, the curling hair, the boyish beauty, and that pallor that prophesied of death. Other faces came, recalled without an effort. Weary of this, I rested my elbow upon the arm of my chair, closed my eyes and covered them with my hand.

Instantly, I saw light—white beyond all whiteness—undazzling, immaculate light! I said in my soul: "That is the light of Heaven. By that light my father will see." And it did not enter my mind that I, also, might see. Nevertheless, as though it were an ocean, there was presently an undulatory central movement as of one coming through from far away. Then appeared a child, slightly reclining, it seemed, upon a pale gray cloud, less effulgent than the light. I was enabled therefore to see with perfect clearness, the breast upon which my eyes first rested, then the floating robe, long, and diaphanous beyond human conception. Then I lifted my eyes and looked directly into hers. She had no earth-taught speech; there were no transmitted words. With celestial gravity her eyes met mine and I interpreted their meaning and intent. "Did you know me once and love me? Do you know me now?" My heart shook me with its leaping: "It is Mary! It is Mary!" Then she smiled! All her dimpled face smiled! and all those dimples I had known of old! Yet, from out those eyes of heavenly blue, angelic intelligence looked, forevermore denying infancy.

When the vision had dissolved in light, and the light itself had dissolved in ether, I arose and said in my thrice-happy soul: "I have seen one thing my father will see!" and I was content to have him pass away.

So back to common life and daily need. That afternoon—my father tranquilly asleep, the children out at play—my mother challenged me: "Why did you tell me that your father had come home to die?"

After a few minutes' delay for gathering courage, I replied: "Mother, I ought to tell you that I have become a writing medium."

She looked at me with evident contempt. But, presently, being fair-minded, she commanded: "Get a slate and pencil. If spirits can move your hand, they can read my mind. I will ask for one I used to know, and, should the name be written, I will ask another question. Should there be a false or inconsistent answer, showing that my thoughts are not known, that will end my investigation."

"Did you ask for your brother John, Mother; The name written is John Mott." "Very well! go on." "But now the writing says, 'I am your father.'" "That is the one I asked for," she admitted.

I had expected her to ask concerning father. Finding nothing in the writing that implied as much, I questioned: "Are these really answers to your thoughts?"

"They are," my mother said; but soon after put the decisive mental question: "Will Henry die of this attack?"

"So soon," was written forcibly, "that if you do not send to Buffalo for your daughters by tomorrow morning, they will never see him in the flesh again."

We laid the slate aside and it was many months before I wrote for her again. My sisters, being sent for, reached home Saturday evening. One day's delay would have prevented their arrival until Monday evening, when they would have been too late everyone knows that the happifying effect of some little attention from a

62

friend, or even a stranger, is often out of all proportion to a cause so slight. I did not seek for messages in those mournful days; but someone seemed to show me small, unlooked-for favors. For example: My much needed thimble could not be found. My moving hand reached for a pencil and instead of any matter of moment, wrote: "Your thimble is up-stairs, in a closet, on a shelf." This was incredible, for the closet had never been put to use. Yet there on the shelf stood my thimble, as though it had climbed there of its own accord! Lost in sorrowful thought, I was roused by another reach for my pencil: "Your cake is about to burn"—which I found to be the case. These momentary helps were strangely comforting.

On Sunday morning (my sisters attending to household affairs in my place), I went to my stud)7, simply for an hour of restful thought. Yet, when a writing movement was begun, I did not make resistance. Nothing at all like what was written then, apparently to relieve my weary mind, had I ever heard or read. This was the substance of the story:

"Corresponding with the light that illuminates the physical universe, there is a mind-light, which pervades all space. As a prism separates the colors of sun-light, the human brain separates mind-light. Each faculty has its location in the brain and each receives and absorbs that one refracted ray, which is necessary to stimulate its action. These rays, being again refracted, unite in a halo or aureole which surrounds every soul. Now, the mind-light is pure white, but its rays are unequally appropriated owing to the predominance of some faculties, which are either greater in themselves or more active than others. Consequently the re-united rays forming the aureole, cannot have the perfect whiteness of original mind-light. If one be strongly under the control of his conscience, he will be surrounded by a golden halo. If he be full of wrath, scarlet will appear. If benevolent feeling be in the ascendant, the color will be a lovely azure. If he reverence the Supreme Being, a clear silver will surround him. If the spiritual element overflow all others, there will be an atmosphere of soft rose. Should pure conjugal love inspire him, he will be encircled by a luminous, royal purple. Should he be given over to wickedness, his aureole will be dark and cloudy."

All this charmed me: "How does my uncle John Mott," (whom I had never seen), "appear to your eyes?" "A truthful spirit clad in gold." "And my Uncle Alanson Jones?" "One of good intentions, in pale gray." And I went no further then or afterwards. It seemed just a pretty story.

That afternoon, for the first time, the physician expressed a fear: "The crisis will come in three days," he said, "we will carry him over that with stimulants."

I went at once to my study. "I must be prepared. When will father die?" "A little before noon tomorrow." The next morning, after some hemorrhage, he sank into a state of lethargy. About nine, I was left in charge of him and stood a long time, it seemed, with my eyes fixed upon his face. I heard no one enter; but after a while turned and saw, sitting at the foot of the bed, regarding my father with a most sorrowful expression, one John McLaughlin—an Irish working-man, over whom my father had exercised strong influence, restraining him from drink. This word rushed in:

"Look at that man! He hasn't a week to live!"

The message did not startle me out of my abstraction; but I asked: "Am I to tell him?"

"No. It would do no good. He cannot emerge at once into a life of splendor and beauty, as your father will. He must take his chance! But he hasn't three days to live!" Now fully aroused, I trembled and left the room.

Twenty minutes before noon, my father breathed his last. Two days later, exactly three weeks from the date of my dream, we took our long, sad ride to the old Prospect Hill burying ground of Buffalo, and stood, in a pouring rain, to see the filling of that long-opened grave.

That night I slept most heavily. At last I dreamed that I looked out into a darkened space. There I saw John McLaughlin, with seven or eight other men, all very like himself. Before them stood a Catholic priest, draped in a long black robe. A scarlet cross extended from the neck to the hem of this robe, the arms of the cross reaching from shoulder to shoulder.

Out from among his companions, stepped John McLaughlin; and now he appeared draped in scarlet from head to foot. "That is the color of wrath," I thought. "He is fiercely angry." And that seemed strange, for he was a man of gentle disposition, willing to undergo any hardship for the sake of those he loved.

I heard him speak; and this is just what I heard him say: "You have lied to me all my life. But for your lies, I wouldn't have been here! I am taken away from my family. What will my wife do without me? Who will take care of my children? Tell me no more lies; tell me the truth: Where is Heaven? Where is Hell? Where is purgatory? Where do I belong? What will become of me? -Tell me the truth!—the Truth!"

The priest lifted his head as if to answer, then raised his right arm and hid his face behind the flowing sleeve. I seemed to pity him more than the other. I thought: "He did not mean to lie," and then I turned to hear what more the angry "penitent" might say. Just then my name, called loudly, broke my dream. "You must get up!" shouted Bennie: "It is eight o'clock. Mother wants you." A moment later he came running up the stairs again: "Say, John

McLaughlin is dead! He died last night at three o'clock!"

This was the physician's explanation of the sudden death: "Rigorous fasting during Lent, without cessation of labor."

And I believe that one, just gone before, who on earth had striven to keep this man from straying, may well have sought him out— foregoing all that glory, that John McLaughlin might tenderly be drawn from shadow into light.

Behold our holiest occupation in that holier life!

A CHILD AND A PHYSICIAN

THAT stern Scotch grand-dame of whom MacDonald tells us—handing the boys their portion at the table on plates so loaded that even boyhood scarcely could dispose of all that food, was wont to say severely: "Hey! Ye'll get na mair!"

With me a strong necessity for supermundane aid had come and gone. For long months after our immediate return to Buffalo, save once, I "gat na mair."

That once it happened I was in the church I knew so well, and recognizing friends I had not seen for years. Telepathic messages went flashing through my mind. "Emmeline will be in mourning for her father in a week."—"Ellen must wear mourning for *her* father in two months." I knew the prophecies were true (and so they proved), but I protested: "Spiritual gifts are much to be desired; but if this is one of them, I do not want it. Never tell me such a thing again!" And if it were a "gift" I lost it then and there!

Great pressures have been brought to bear upon me, as will, in part, appear; burdens have been imposed, such as no mortal could sustain, unaided from above; but always with my pre-consent and at my absolute desire. My rights, in no case, have been held in disrespect.

A weary summer followed. Mother very ill, the babe—born after father left—attacked with whooping-cough, and always close to death; three other children needing care; older sisters and younger brothers taxed with constant labor; myself racked with pain from spinal inflammation or, as afterwards pronounced, a general inflammation of the nerves, our neighbors more than whispering that I was "shirking work,"—I lived without companionship and grieved that none were helped because of me. The sole approach to what

I thought was "spirit-influence," was a persistent semi-daily exercise of hands and arms in bodily manipulation. That made me wonder, till I discovered benefit therefrom; and hurling medicines

66

out of the window, I instituted, by "suggestion" I imagine, a course of water-treatment well adapted to the case. So I began to mend.

One day it seemed "borne in" upon me, that I must leave my bed and seek to re-acquaint myself with Mrs. Collins, who, in former years, had followed mother's lead in working for their church. Sudden access of wealth had let her into wider social circles, in consequence of which her husband (fervent in his Methodism) and herself had been converted to my faith. Their daughter, Maria, three years my senior, had been my classmate, for I was rather well advanced in study, at thirteen. About that time she died, to the inconsolable grief of parents and a lover to whom she had pledged her troth, and from whom she had been separated by what seemed judicious opposition.

I walked a mile in misery. Then, quite worn out, I rang the bell. A little girl of eleven opened the door, but said: "I am all alone in the house,"—evidently expecting me to go at once. When I told my name she gave a little cry of pleasure: "Oh! come in! I have a splendid new piano on which no one has played, except myself; and I have had it for six weeks. I want to hear it, but my teacher lives up town, and I have only been to her twelve times. Your sister said that you should come and play for me as soon as you were well enough."

"I will, if you will let me rest a-while," I said; "but first sit down and let me hear your lessons."

"I only know two pieces," the child apologized. "The White Cockade" and "Irish Washerwoman." But she sat down and played them both several times over, one note to each hand, all her unoccupied fingers rigid with conscientious effort.

I took the stool in turn and played my little repertoire of waltzes, polkas and marches, she leaning upon the end of the piano, intently watching my hands. I had really played about all I knew and paused to chat awhile; but my hands went on of themselves, it seemed, so that I laughed and said:

They are being influenced"—not quite sure that she would understand. "Let them go on!" she cried, much interested, and began to make comments upon the melodies which were being played—very simple dancing tunes, quite new to me. In the middle of a sentence she stopped, and, looking up, I saw that her eyes were closed. She moved away into the center of the room and began to dance very gracefully. I learned later that she had never seen dancing, but her movements were charming. With my head turned over my shoulder, I paid no attention to the music, except to note that it answered very well and was without discords. "Make her dance the Spanish Fandango," I said in my mind; and the music changed, grew softer, sweeter, slower. Her poising figure, her lifted waving arms, her sylph-like undulations filled me with delight. After some time she pirouetted to the stool from which I sprang, took my place, struck the keys with practised hands, and played for me to dance! Not that I knew how, but someone did, it seemed. Of my own volition I could not have so exercised myself without much physical distress; and yet I was not harmed. All the while I kept turning my face her way that I might watch her nimble fingers, playing sweetly, rapidly and striking no false notes.

Then, I, too, paused beside the stool, from which she sprang in turn; and while I struck some final chords, she took her former place, opened her eyes and—finished her last sentence! Very evidently she knew nothing of all that had been taking place; and I refrained from telling her,—she was so very young.

This from Mrs. Collins, to whom I told the story: Two weeks before, her husband and herself, wishing to attend a "circle" and not willing to leave the child at home alone, had taken her along. Several children, with herself, were allowed to sit in the corner of the room on condition that their elders should not be disturbed by noise. But this child had floated forward, with closed eyes, and astonished all with her exquisite dancing. Finally she had crossed over to her mother, made a sweeping courtesy and asked: "Do you know who I am?" "I do not. Who are you?" "I am

Maria. Father and you would not let me go to dancing school when I begged so hard. You thought it would be wicked; but now I dance all I want to."

An argument of Dr. Hudson's—supposed to be unanswerable, is that alleged communicating spirits never tell what sort of lives they lead—what are their occupations and enjoyments. Perhaps they fear to shock our sensibilities. What! Dance? Laugh? Shout? Rejoice in liberty to breathe without restraint? someone has dared to say that God Himself has humor. How else, in fact, should such an "attribute" be ours? Dear, dear Maria: At sixteen, forbidden to dance, persuaded not to love;—Let us imagine her set free and full of sport!

We know from records that the "mediums" whom Dr. Hudson visited were hypnotized by mortals—himself or any other. Since their subjective minds were constantly amenable to suggestion, no doubt their hypnotizers could, had they so chosen, have put into those minds a thousand pretty tales about the future life. Perhaps they lacked imagination for it. Anyway it must have been far easier to—shuffle cards!

If anyone had hypnotized this dancing child, it must have been Maria; but she did tell—a little! and how much!

A woman whom I heard about ("Celestial Kite" they called her), "thought and knew, declared and testified" that if, upon a pre-appointed day, one hundred thousand persons would fly one hundred thousand kites, great power would be drawn down upon the sons of men. And really, if we want telepathic messages from the skies that way would answer just as well as any hypnotism, wherein a human mind supplants that of the sleeper.

The heavenly bodies up in space, will be reflected now and then in little valley-pools between our Everests and Chimborazos. Never mind! Pay no attention to them! Go on and study your astronomy by drawing diagrams! Or better, formulate hypotheses and logically prove there are no stars! at least that none can ever shine for us!

Of this we may be sure. A super-mundane being need not much concern himself with mortal hypnotizers and their "trained" percipients. He will come to us if we permit, by his own will and wish and in his chosen way. So let him come and answer for himself.

And if the "Dead" (we grossly call them so), can come, how can they come? One would not guess by intervention of a common hypnotist, a sort of lens for microscopic views of embryonic minds.

Light, by reflection, may be polarized till it is wholly quenched. What can these hypnotizers do for us but polarize our light? Push back the crystals; let us have the sun!

Come, then, O, living "dead," directly to our souls! By wireless telegraph, or telephone or telephote or blest telepathy! We want to read and hear and see and understand. Full well you know the way, and well you know our need! And if you make us fall asleep and dream of you, why, that is well; and if you let us keep awake and yet reveal yourselves, why, that is better still. Come every way or any way,—but come!

When autumn came, I sought out Mrs. Lowell, just to spend the day. "I shall not let you go tonight," she told me: "I've been hearing of your "laziness" and I intend to find out all about it."

"How will you find out?"

"By Dr. Jerry Carter, who will be here over night, or rather—Dr. Hedges;" and she told me something of that "dual personality." "You remember we became convinced of spirit-intercourse, three years ago,-while I was at Fredonia, in a Water-Cure. There we had frequent circles by consent of Dr. Brown—a very able man. This Jerry Carter was brought in to us because he had a way of falling into trances, not induced by Mesmerism. When in those trances, he was Dr. Hedges. To guard against all influence but his own, Dr. Hedges ordered the making of a horse-shoe magnet, to be held by Carter going into sleep—the only foreign aid allowed."

Mrs. Lowell then went on to tell me that the patients of the institution spread the story; and, though neither Dr. Brown nor the "medium" himself, nor any other within easy reach had ever heard of Dr. Hedges, word came from

See Appendix 11. far that there had been an excellent botanic doctor of that name; and more—some who had been his patients, came to see this Carter and identify his "influence." This was done beyond all cavil, so they said.

I only write affirmatively of the things I know; and here is what I realized myself.

70

Just after introduction to this Carter ("My friend—not very well!"), he took his horse-shoe magnet, sat him down, and laid the bar across its upturned ends. In a few moments he was deeply sleeping—not a quiver of the eye-lids. It seemed his very features changed. Expression moulds the face more than we fully apprehend, I think. He reached his arms to Mrs. Lowell, who removed the bar and spoke to him at once. She said to me: "He will not hear you; he hears nobody but that selected one who lifts the bar." So I took notes and held my peace.

Jeremiah Carter was a worthy man, a tailor, very ignorant. Some said he could not read. More awkward English, more desolate of Grammar, than his common talk, could hardly be imagined. His manners, not offensive, were wholly without polish.

Dr. Hedges was a gentleman. Courteous in deportment, scholarly in language, technical when speaking of diseases (which he seemed to read as one might read a primer) choosing botanic remedies, and carefully explaining to his patients all their properties, seeing past and present, yes, and future also within certain limits!—such, and more, appeared this Dr. Hedges.

When he had looked me through, it seemed, and stated what was seen, he said: "I must be absent for a time. I want her home-conditions." In that absence, Carter quivered constantly. Why did not Dr. Hedges search my mind for information? We were not en rapport for one reason, possibly. It seemed he could see better by himself.

"So many active ones, intent on necessary tasks," he said, "nothing to cheer and soothe. No one to blame, nor any hope of change. The child must suffer or be helped some other way. We'll try and help her somehow."

Although I had been ill at one time with lung fever, it had not been supposed that there was any special weakness of the lungs. This he detected, saying: "Just one heavy cold this winter would result in death. This I can save her from," and gave his remedies of simple herbs. "But there is more than this. There will be, by and bye, extreme convulsive action of the heart and lungs. As a physician of

71

the body, I declare she cannot live through that." He paused awhile: "I have superiors. They tell me she will live. But, after that, there will be hemorrhage. I know the body;—that must surely be the end." He paused again: "But my superiors tell me that she will not die because of that. I do not see how that can be, but they are wiser and I cannot doubt. They tell me they have chosen her; she will not be allowed to pass from earth till she is old. They tell me she has qualities that will make her yet a blessing to the world."

"I believe it!" ejaculated Mrs. Lowell; and I—breathed balm. For once my little gifts were magnified.

Now, having passed through all he had predicted, four years later, Rev. Rufus Cooley and his wife, my sister, sent me, as a last resort, to Clifton Springs, N. Y., where I was saved as by a miracle.

But pray, who hypnotized this Jeremiah Carter? From what "living person's" mind came all that knowledge and that power of prophecy? Long after I was told of Jerry Carter's marked development—the magnet laid aside and consciousness retained. I think he was not wronged by all that "influence." He who induced the sleep, well understood the law, and would not mis-apply it. He made it serve a purpose most beneficent, the while he did not fail to educate that long-neglected brain and greaten its capacity. He played no tricks with that subjective mind. He did not "train its powers to high proficiency" in reading others' thoughts, describing distant objects, telling the time of day, discerning dates of coins and just how many spades made black the card! Humble he was; although he knew far more than many a Psychist, let us say, he owned he had "superiors" and learned of them. Since always there is something to be learned, no doubt he went to school. They do this in the upper world, it seems.

As for myself, no loss of personality has been exacted. From that one blest experience in early life till now (fifty-eight years), I have not been deprived of my objective consciousness. If possible inheritance might count, it seems I might have been of finer mould. My father's sisters—two of them, at least, withdrawing at their stated hours for "secret prayer," were sometimes found entranced, by those who sought them, and were none the worse, it proved, for being touched "with that live coal from off the altar." I have heard that they were faithful wives and mothers—housewives capable and kind. Would that a certain niece of theirs had half their grace!

And yet I have a gift with which I would not part. A friend once named it "mental grip." Sickness has never shaken that firm hold, even near the gates of death, with any slight delirium. When "under influence," as we Psychists say, I have always known just what was being done with me, said through me or given me to say, and afterward, I have been able to analyze experience, and search for any trace of interference on my part. My readers will make full allowance for such cognizance throughout, and use it in fair argument, if so they choose.

But I may add that I long since discovered in myself (not that I am singular in this) two distinctive mental states. In one, origination leads the way. Intensity and energy of thought are dominant; also there is excitement—just enough to fan, and not blow out, the fire of composition. But in the other state there is tranquility (I speak now of the state conducive to control), and there is pleased attention, ready acceptance of what seems another's thought, even when opposed to mine. There may be mental effort on my part; if so, I am unconscious of it. When I said in my deep trance: "That may be the central sun," or "That is Chaos," those were my own thoughts, and were so recognized; but they were parallel with others not my own, and did not interfere, in any way, with that subjective vision.

These things were necessary to be said. It will be claimed that my own mind is much in evidence. I hope so—nay, I know so, in a sense. If spirits came, they found me seemingly alive, and did not slay me, first or last or ever! They had to deal with me before they dealt with others through me—as I well believe they did. I am very sure that educators on the heavenward side—however cramped by mortal personality—can give out more through us when we are wide awake than when we fall asleep. For we are spirits also, subject to the very laws that govern them. There must be interchange—they must descend or we must rise, to meet upon one plane. Perhaps we do not always know whose thought is uppermost, theirs or ours; for there must be commingling more or less. But that is better than hypnotic

73

sleep, induced by human hands, controlled by human wills, in which the soul goes dwindling off—the sport of cosmic winds, while ignorance directs.

The human brain is not a perfect substance for transmission; but, at least, it takes that "mind-light" in, distributes it and gives it out in halos, luminous more or less.

I am not saying with all this that "living persons" are not telepathic, each to each. I know they are. It needs no hypnotist to tell us that. Let us have done with such;—live out our little lives and think our daily thoughts, take in those messages that flit from mind to mind as homing doves; and if, from out the heavenly flocks of flying birds, one settle now and then, see that it be not slain of arrows at our feet by one who knows not larks.

This world's telepathy may fling its violets upon that wide and fertile field, the human consciousness. That world's telepathy enters like sun and rain to make the violets grow. "Earth is crammed with Heaven," writes Mrs. Browning, "And every common bush afire with God."

TELEPATHY, RAPPING AND WRITING

ANY supposed philosophy or scheme of thought that cuts man off from possible spirit-intercourse is neither sound nor safe. It makes of him an underling—a feebleminded thing, at best a creature of the earth and nothing more. He asks for light; it gives him glow-worms for illuminants; he longs for liberty; it locks him fast behind impenetrable walls; he asks for mountain-springs; it hands to him, through grated doors, some draught from wayside pools where common cattle drink; he dies for need of food; it thrusts within a mouldy crust or two, and bids him be content.

But "spirit-intercourse" includes that secret interchange of thought between these prisoners of flesh that certain teachers name telepathy,—a sort of tapping on the wall from cell to cell. I have some little knowledge of the code,—not very much. There is a blind intelligence at work behind the bars. I too have heard those knockings on the wall.

Once, riding on the Lake Shore Railroad, nearing Buffalo, a rosy little woman entered, sat down facing me and chatted volubly, in that sweet country fashion I have always loved! In this case it proved the basis of a sympathism. But presently, I settled back and, looking from the window, thought no more of her. A very tall pole caught and held my gaze, so that without a conscious thought, as we were rushing past, I turned my head and looked till it had disappeared. That instant a strong shock vibrated through me. I trembled, as in terror; thinking wildly: "There's an accident. Someone is killed!" Had such a wreckage really taken place, according to my wont I should have been quite cool. I had just time to ask myself: "Is this a premonition?" when the little lady laid her hand upon my knee. Looking round, I saw her pale and tremulous: "Did you observe that tall pole we just passed? Two years ago I rode on this same train, and right there, was an accident. Two men were killed. When I saw that pole again, I felt the shock all over, just as when it happened."

One friend, who had a way of calling on me frequently, never failed to let me know his purpose all unconsciously; but this I think was less by message than by vivid personality. His aura streamed my way and startled my attention. Some other few have had a like effect. Nor have I known myself deceived by any such perceptions. They are not imaginary.

Once I sent out a message. Some foreign element had made my habitat unbearable,—I must escape. Full of that sick distaste, I thought of two dear friends, Levi and Lydia Brown, with whom I often was a welcome guest. "Levi," I whispered forcefully: "No matter where you are or what you may be doing, leave all and come for me!" He, in a village sixteen miles from home, just turned his horses round into another road and whipped them well to reach me all the sooner. "You wanted me," he said, "and here I am!"

My youngest brother, Porter, one of our nation's martyrs at eighteen years of age, lay sinking in an army hospital two weeks before we were allowed to know. His nurses told my mother, who arrived the day before his death, that he was wont to call in sleep our several names—my own among the rest. I heard and I alone. This I have told in verse, with scrupulous fidelity.

One of those three who joined with me in testing the intelligence of that small stand that knew its maker's name, had, if I may express it so, a mental voltage, which I came to realize in later correspondence. I was young—by no means prone to over-estimate my influence, and it pleased me well to note that, while he wrote to me, his thoughts sped on and reached me in advance. I recognized in him a noble character—a friend, intensely loyal. But one night I awoke in deep distress. It seemed that I had found him in my sleep, and he was writing to me. Not his words but their intent, I knew, and strove to hinder. "Friend, it cannot be! Put down the pen." A moment later and the clock struck twelve. The letter came. "It is just midnight," were its opening words. Replying, I poured out the best I had, and that was much, but lacked the vital word. I hoped he was not deeply hurt, but said on Thursday noon: "I shall know how he feels at five o'clock." This I presently forgot. But just at five o'clock I seemed to rush away and stand beside him. He was saying: "I will wait five years."

Just five years afterward (Oct. 1860), I had a letter from him and he said: "I have a home in Kansas. May I come for you? But I must

76

tell you that, in any case, if there are battles I shall fight for 'bleeding Kansas.'"

Well I knew he would! With that strong frame, so tense with virile energy, that soul of honesty and indomitable courage, what else was there to do? And then I heard no more.

About Thanksgiving the next year, November (1861), I cannot give the date more accurately—I found him in my sleep, wounded and suffering and filled with thoughts of me. Never since then, till some few years ago, have I been any way aware of him. I had not felt that he must die and yet I longed to know. This world's telepathy was whispered in the void so far as I might apprehend; but I incline to think, had he passed on, he would have let me understand.

Only a year ago (being of late a Kansan) I visited Topeka, as the guest of our historical secretary, and, begging for a roster, found his name: "Enlisted Aug. 10, 1861. Wounded at Blue Lime, Nov. 24, 1861." Writing to the township where he had enlisted, I soon received a letter from his surviving brother, Carl, who, with his wife, wrote out the history of my honored friend. Twice wounded, many months a prisoner, once again a fighting "Jay-hawker," life packed with strange adventure long as his country needed him, then, rather late, a happy husband and a loving father—little wonder every thought of me was lost, and that full voltage turned aside through more important circuits.......

Forty-six years I waited for this proof!

Now I suppose that when we cross the Equatorial line and find another hemisphere, there will be many talks of olden times; and one will say: "I was aware of you that time you longed for me;" and one will laugh: "How well we loved each other! How our thoughts and sympathies went weaving in and out to make us happier, when we were far apart!" Another will acknowledge: "Mother, I was about to do a wicked thing, when suddenly it seemed I heard your voice within my inmost soul, beseeching Heaven for me; and I refrained. You prayed for me that very hour."

Let us be worthy such an attribute, made ours by Infinite Love! But how shall we be worthy save by exaltation?—lifting all we are, including that, into the spheres of thought wherein we meet all those who lived with us and loved us on this side of Death, and now, upon that side, turn round and love us on forever—even as spirits will.

An attribute grows with our growth, and strengthens with our strength. It cannot be cut off from what has been, nor shut from what may be.

I take up the dropped thread of my chronology.

During that winter (1854-5), being sometimes Mrs. Lowell's guest, I might have gone to that exclusive house held under guardianship by Mr. Stephen Albro (thirty-five years editor of the "Buffalo Republic"), who was at that time publishing "The Age of Progress"— quite the best expositor of my beliefs I ever read. Through Emma Brooks, a young girl of sixteen, one "Edgar Dayton" spelled out, rap on rap, fine, philosophical essays, which were published weekly. "Toe-joints" you say? I once heard raps fall on my mother's table fast and thick as drops of equinoctial rain; and, by request, they came down rhythmically, so that we sang our "Yankee Doodle" and our "Lilly Dale" in perfect time therewith; and all because an honest ignorant washer-woman, twenty-three, and mother of five children, laid her finger tips upon the wood. She had but ten toes, anyhow, with which to make a thousand raps a second; and beat them out in time.

Early in December (1854), someone rapped out a prophecy for Mr. Albro, which he made haste to publish—challenging his fellow editors to publish in their turn. They did so, merrily; but when fulfillment came, they had no space for comment. This was its purport: "In two months and a half the Russian Emperor Nicholas will die. The cause of death will not be given out, but there is one who will be greatly profited and leap at once to full authority under the new-made emperor." There followed intimation of a crime inducing death—but never to be proved.

When Edwin Lowell (brother of William Lowell, my friend's husband), was drawn in to help the "circle," one announced himself as "Fred"—a French musician. His rappings had to be translated; so an interpreter was hunted up, as I was told. However that may be, a good piano was procured, turned round—the key-board pushed against the wall—and, this being done, "King Edward did a selcouth," as the Saxon said. Emma stood at one end, and Edwin at the other, fingers on the rose-wood, while such force fell on the ivories—in broad daylight—that "music long and loud" resulted. My excellent and able teacher, Professor Robert Denton, told me the next year, that he had spent two years abroad and heard the finest masters, yet never had he realized till then what music might be made. "I never heard," he said, "such grand improvisations." This was confirmed long after to a friend of mine (Henry L. Kendall, Providence), by a most worthy clergyman, who had been favored with a special "circle." All that was daily talk at Mrs. Lowell's table, where no false things could be pronounced. But when I was invited also, something held me back. I chose, instead, to spend the only day I had at my disposal going to public "meetings"—caring very little then, as ever after, for material proofs. I am right glad that I decided so.

There was a hall where Spiritualists went in throngs, being yet in their "first love" as old time Methodists would say (and would the new time Methodists had half their fervency!). Imagine!—In the morning, lectures and reports from City circles, luncheon in the hall, circles till four o'clock, and, in the evening, something like a "love feast,"—speeches, testimonies, and reports again.

At least a dozen tables were brought in, there being one in place already beside which fifty might sit down, mayhap! My table held but eight. Across from me a lady sat, who closed her eyes at once and kept them closed throughout. Toward the last, (pencil and paper lying near) my hand began to write. A full page of foolscap was closely covered with a large round script. Nearly as I remember, it was an essay, half political, half philosophical. Then breaking off his theme, the writer added: "There will come a time when, through this one whose hand I move today I shall send out a prophecy." And this was signed "John Adams."

I kept this writing covered from the first, with my left hand. But after it was done, the sleeping lady opposite, not opening her eyes, said, pointing straight at me: "A sturdy looking spirit stands beside your chair. He has been writing with your hand. I watched him doing it. His name, he tells me, is John Adams." There fell a gavel on the chairman's desk: "The time is up. Report if anything has been received." A young man came and caught away my paper. It was not returned to me.

That evening three most solemn gentlemen announced that there had been a fine communication given that afternoon, through a young girl not more than sixteen (subject to correction by three years), whose mind was all "incapable" of so much thought. It had been signed "John Adams," and the three had spent some hours in trying to find that great man's signature. Their search had been rewarded; all could see how perfect the facsimile! And then the article was read aloud.

Efforts were made to find me afterward, for several weeks; but I appeared no more,—though often Mrs. Lowell's guest. I felt that none must clutch me; what I had to do was just to wait within my own environments and take whatever came. Near at home we met in little "circles" once a week or oftener, if I were well enough—three of us: Mrs. Haines, her daughter Mrs. Manley, and myself, with Mrs. Collins now and then (a relative of theirs), who had removed to Rochester. Much was to happen afterward because the one last mentioned learned to think, in those few times she met with us, that I had special gifts. At home I had my mother. She was not, would not be a Spiritualist, but said: "I know that Spirits influence you, for common sense has demonstrated that. Your mind or mine, might possibly do much of this, but both together could not do it all. That these are evil spirits is not credible; but if an evil spirit has the power to come, so has a good one, for the Lord is just. But I shall keep my old belief in Christ, the Son of God, whatever I let go. If these should contradict—what do they know about it more than I? They are in some intermediate state, I think, and reason for themselves. They may be honest as Tom Paine, who was the soul of honor; but may be just as wrong about the Bible. Their time of full revealment has not come—nor ours. We all await the final resurrection." Mother modified her creeds but meant to hold them fast. Meantime, as you have seen, she did not doubt the genuineness of my "mediumship."

So, learning of that writing at the hall, my mother said: "There may be something more to come. Sit down and let us ask." At once the name "John Adams" was repeated in the same old-fashioned hand—the straight line crossing "A." Nothing following, Mother said: "I cannot ask you questions as I would some other spirit, but I would like to have you grant one small request. Give us some little incident of your past life—the least will be sufficient for us." This was said aloud.

What followed was a dissertation upon immortality, based upon this incident:

"I stood beside the sea, and watched an eagle rise and soar aloft. He vanished in the sunshine; and I thought: 'An emblem of ambition! But shall the soul of man not rise and soar to heights no eagle ever reached?'"

My mother read the thesis studiously (about 400 words perhaps) and said: "You never wrote it. You have no such thoughts and words at your command." She had been brought up on Addison and Steele, Sam Johnson and those other fellows, and I felt she ought to know. I hated to write prose, and what I had attempted had not dignified me much in Mother's eyes—poor stuff!

One day, I think my Mother was not happy. Life was very stern to her, although she was the bravest of the brave.

"Get out your slate," she said, "and let me ask a single question mentally."

I looked up presently, a little puzzled. "Mother, Mrs. Collins' name is Sally—that means Sarah. Here is 'Sarah Collins' written. Can it be that she is dead?" I must ask again," said Mother. This was the response: "I am your grandmother." That name had not come up before, even in my thoughts. It had, as yet, no lodgment in my mind. Sarah Collins Mott (the Quakers often dropped her marriage name because of previous celebrity—as we say "Lucy Stone"), had passed from earth, supposedly, full twenty years before my mother's birth.

But sixty years of heaven had not divided her from mortal kith and kin.

At this my mother smiled, well pleased: "I asked, who was my guardian Spirit. I'll ask another mental question." My hand went moving round with no apparent purpose, so we talked and waited. Then "Such is Life," was written hurriedly and there we saw a perfect spider's web.

"I wanted her to warn me of my death some little time before," admitted Mother. "She has refused, but wishes me to understand that life is very frail. I must be always ready." Mother added audibly: "Spirit, I wish that you would represent Death with as fine a symbol."

The hand began again. This time we watched, but could not tell that there would be an anchor, till the flukes were drawn, the slate whirled round to bring them undermost, and this was written: "Such is death; an anchor to the weary soul and, to the sorrowing, rest."

"Please," asked my Mother, "draw a symbol now of your own choosing." A few lines brought to view a perfect flying dove. I feel obliged to say I could no more have drawn the bird than taken flight myself. Under it was written: "Such is Love," and, without picture, this was added: "The ostrich is an emblem of beauty and fleetness." At once with great celerity, faster than I could have written them, these simple verses followed:—

> "When from the frail body
> Thy spirit takes flight,
> And the anchor is cast,
> And past is the night.
> "Then may Love's gentle wings
> Bear thee hence and away,
> With the fleetness of light
> To the regions of day."

Then Mother said triumphantly: "You can write rather pretty verses, but to say so much in so few words, you never did. I fear you never will."

If anyone should read my "poems" of that early date, paraded in my full collection, "like broken tea-cups wisely kept for show," no doubt my Mother's judgment will be justified.

Anyway, she was undoubtedly the happier because of Sarah Collins' symbolism, and the tender summing up in those eight lines.

What better can a spirit do than comfort such a woman?

LOGIC AND SPIRIT-PERSONATION

THE ease with which a self-confessed Logician will refute what countless people know, is rather daunting to a lesser mind. As we have seen, because a "trained percipient," being duly hypnotized, could not contrive to see what none within her sphere of consciousness had seen, our Dr. Hudson "learned to doubt the faculty of clairvoyance, properly so called." To doubt, with him, is practically to arrive at certainty. "After the lapse of many years of patient observation" (he goes on), "I have yet to witness the first phenomenon that will have a tendency to convince me of the power of independent clairvoyance." And in all those years he had not once explored an independent mind! According to the law he has insisted on—the law of hypnotism,—his sleeping subjects followed his suggestions. Never once released, they saw subjectively what he could see objectively, or, stretching very far, what anyone in close alliance saw with his objective eyes. Therefore, he dares assert that the subjective mind is absolutely without vision of its own. All this by way of logic.

Well, I have seen a "trained" canary draw a cart, ring bells, fire off a little cannon, drag a wounded wing, drop dead, hop up and run away again as pert as pert! Mercy upon me, what a miracle he was! And yet, from first to last, he never sang a note. From this, most any child might learn—that no canary sings!

Each one of us has a subjective mind; so much is settled. "The subjective mind is a distinct entity. In other words it is the soul." It sees not of itself in spiritual independence, we infer, but borrows some objective mind to see with. Now that lesser mind, "pure intellect," will "perish when the body dies." Ah! what will the robin do then, poor thing? Is the scant soul worth saving after all?

"Behold He made us, and not we ourselves." We have His faculties and attributes with but a difference in degree. What are they? who may number them? or who shall say wherein is any lack?

Why, Dr. Hudson, verily! Through him we lost the gift of prophecy awhile ago: "There is no law of mind that will enable it to cognize that which does not yet exist." The Infinite is only infinite to this extent: He knows what was, what is, but not what yet shall be—more than we know ourselves. And now we lose the power of independent vision, save through objective eyes sure to be "darkened dust." Souls cannot see. The Infinite sees not at all except through perishable orbs—yours, mine, the bird's, the ant's,—those of the bat and moth that cannot bear the sun.

One needs to catch a breath. Without foresight, without immediate, present sight. All spirits—God's and our's—forever blind! What must we lose beside?

Communion of the saints it seems. That is to say there will be no telepathy between our world and theirs. We spiritists think we have proved it otherwise, but now observe how ignorant we are. This master of inevitable logic settles all. Hear him.

"The whole question hinges upon this problem: Can information, telepathically received by one person, be telepathically communicated by him to another? This is the crucial test. It is the last ditch of spiritism. If answered in the affirmative the spiritists will not have a leg to stand on—will not have a shred of valid evidence: their cause is forever lost."

Who answers "Yes?" Why Dr. Hudson's very self! Logician admirable! Able to reason out a soul for man (that neither prophesies, nor sees, nor answers if we call!) by reason of a shut-eyed woman, naming you whatever card you lift from out the pack—ace, deuce, or king of clubs.

Come, let's be logical! If Harry, speaking not, but having thoughts to spare, transfer a thought to Tom, and Tom to Dick—all being clad in tweed, then William—clothed in "white samite, mystic, wonderful," cannot transfer a thought to Tom or Dick or Harry, though his thoughts outnumber all the stars within the milky way.

And now we seem to hear the words reverberating, like De Quincy's "long farewells," throughout an infinite universe: "Our cause is lost!—forever lost!"—and yet again:

"Lost! Lost! forever Lost!"

O, Logic! Logic! turn your guns another way, nor slay us where we lie, deep sunk in our "last ditch!"

And yet I have so much to tell about my "mediumship" (if that is what to call it), that I must fortify your minds against belief beforehand, or you too may suppose we are not wholly "lost." I will not have you saying afterward: "She took us unaware." But now we find that Hudson has explained all that—if we had time to read and understand. Please read and understand; here are his very words:

"The so-called spirit-medium, in the trance condition, is simply self-hypnotized"........"Governed by all the laws pertaining to hypnotism"........"The objective mind is in abeyance and the subjective mind is in control"......"The subjective mind accepts as true every suggestion that is made to it," (Ah, dear, immortal idiot!)........"Tell the subject that he is a dog and he will act the part, firmly believing that he is a dog."

Must we go on through all the cycles of eternity, foreseeing nothing, seeing nothing, knowing nothing save what is told to us?— Some mischievous Mahatma drawing near and saying: "Friend, you are a dog, a cat, a parrot, or perhaps a wolf!" We shall have no defence, for we have lost our sole defender, that objective mind. We must believe all things that we are told in spirit-life: for Hudson tells us so.

However, take us in this life instead: One who is self-hypnotized, turns traitor to himself, and plays the very tricks professional hypnotizers play with their "percipients." If, of a certain loftiness, he tells himself he is a spirit—oh, any spirit!—Simeon or Socrates! And then he acts in character. How well he does it Dr. Hudson tells us of his own accord, designing to be wholly fair (for that is his design from first to last!):

"Mediums of unimpeachable character will personate the alleged spirit with marvelous fidelity to the known character of the spirit: voice, gestures, bearing and personal idiosyncrasies often so perfectly reproduced as to leave no doubt in the minds of witnesses of the identity of the alleged spirit; and this by mediums who have never been suspected of possessing any histrionic ability whatever, in their normal condition."

Self-hypnotism! Any hypnotism!—is there no escape? Must we go on forever, hag-ridden of this hypnotism?

But, meanwhile, let us figure out the case of Jeremiah Carter. At first he hypnotized himself and told his neighbors how to make a scientific horse-shoe magnet (poor, ignorant tailor that he was!), so that he could be more perfect in his art. Then he went roaming round to find someone to personate. He somehow got on track of Dr. Hedges, who had been "dead" so long his youngest patients were all turning grey. They had never heard of Carter; he had never heard of them. Nevertheless he found them out and ransacked all their minds to cull their memories of the "voice, the gestures, bearing, idiosyncrasies" and language of their old-time doctor. Then he found the old-time books of Dr. Hedges, caught his old-time thoughts and memories yet on the wing, came back and told himself (whom he had hypnotized), that he was Dr. Hedges. Taught himself good grammar, botany, therapeutics, technicals, fine manners and humility;—adding so much power of reasonable deduction as went far to prove himself a prophet; but he caught up himself, before he went too far, and owned that his "superiors" could see much farther. Now he prescribed for all the sick who came to him (a lot of them each day); then woke to outer consciousness, forgot all that he had done when he was fast asleep, and called himself plain Jerry Carter! Oh, wondrous Jerry Carter!

By such a roasted mammoth-ox, how small my truffled birds must seem! And yet they must be served.

Before the "writing" phase had passed, I called upon my friend Lavinia, a city teacher, whom I knew by correspondence chiefly. She introduced me to her mother—a pale and anxious lady, who was visiting the city, for a special purpose as it proved.

Lavinia's aunt and hostess, Mrs. McClevy, I had seen before and worshipped at a distance, in a young girl's way. Pretty soon the three withdrew themselves from me, and had a whispered conversation. Then Lavinia came, reluctantly, and said: "You have not told me, but your sister says you are a writing medium. Mother asks if you will write for her." "Certainly, if I can; but it must be on one condition: She must ask her questions mentally." I had a reasonable dread of interfering with "magnetic currents."

Something like a name was written once, and four times over. Mother and daughter took the paper and puzzled over it, but could make nothing out. "Let me try," Mrs. McClevy said, laying down her book and coming forward. She looked and burst out laughing, ran up-stairs, brought down a letter and showed the signature. Five exact facsimiles were on our little sheet. "What was your question, Julia?" Mrs. McClevy asked. "I wanted to be told what Doctor in the city would do me the most good, if I should visit him." The name was that of Dr. Warner—one of the very best—alive on earth, of course.

Dr. Warner did not write his name for us assuredly; whoever did, assumed his personality to that extent. It was not I; nor Mrs. Ayer, nor yet Lavinia. None of us had seen him. Mrs. McClevy had. Did her subjective mind find out the unuttered question from her sister's mind and forge the doctor's signature five times in answer? I do not know; but the advice was excellent. I naturally suppose a visiting spirit gave it, purposely in Dr. Warner's penmanship, to show us that he did not need our minds for guidance. I hand this filbert over to the Psychists. They may chance to crack it easily. I never did.

After some further mental questions, Mrs. Ayer said audibly: "I think of nothing else. But won't some spirit write me something on his own account!" She settled back not overlooking what was being written:—

"Dear Mrs. Ayer:—I cannot rest until I know you have forgiven me for what I did so long ago. I wronged you very much; will you forgive me? John Cone."

The lady read the words, and cried out in astonishment: "I never did forgive you, but I will, John Cone! I do forgive you!" which was very sweet of her, considering what the man had done, it proved. But when a search was instituted, it was found that "John Cone" was not "dead." However, when the writing came, he was lying in a state of coma during typhoid fever,—almost "dead."

Now, I must needs interpolate, at this point for convenience, that some years later, for a whole week through, each day the name of an old friend was given me, with written messages; I tested the intelligence, and am bound to say it seemed the very one it claimed to be. All that week (I learned after a year or so), that friend had been in lethargy so deep there was no outer consciousness observable; even breath was sometimes not perceptible.

Do these cases prove that "disembodied" spirits cannot come to us? I compassionate the wits of that Logician who will answer "Yes."

Although I knew, for my part, that visits from the liberated may be real, yet fearing to be over-credulous, about those days I set myself to reason them away, whenever possible. I had no instructors: Brown-Sequard and other notable physicists had not been heard of—by myself at least. But I did very well without them, on the whole. In place of what is called "telepathy," I said "mind influence" or "transmitted thoughts." I also said "unconscious mind," and fancied each of us endowed with highly subliminated magnetism, for effect on other spirits possibly, without our normal consciousness.

The writing phase passed gradually by, and I began to "personate,"—to act as though I were another than myself. Of course, I always knew that no one had displaced me in reality: but those I "personated," with a few exceptions, I had never seen or even heard of actually. You shall see what feats of logic I performed "all by my lone."

In our tripartite circles—Mrs. Haines, her daughter Mrs. Manley and myself—we had some chance to study that phenomenon.

One evening, I arose, walked round the table, growing tall and taller to my apprehension—quite majestic, full of dignity—and, in a masculine, recitative way, delivered a brief sermon—well worth hearing by the way. I announced myself as "Stephen Olin." Now Mrs. Haines, though she had never mentioned it to me, had seen that Stephen Olin, when she was a little girl and lived in

Massachusetts. I therefore formulated this hypothesis: Orilla Adams had an active brain; once seeing was enough. That psychic impress, left within her childish mind, did, after fifty years, emerge, take shape and six-foot personality, stand out and wave its hypnotizing hands above my head, control my mind—my halfmind anyway—fill up my brain with solid thoughts, and give them utterance through my throat and lips, with stately emphasis; and (that we might not think him Richard Baxter), did plainly tell us: "I was Stephen Olin."

As to the sermon, it had been delivered sometime, not in the hearing of Orilla Adams, but to some audience in that very State of Massachusetts! "Unconscious minds" caught up the ball and sent it rolling this way, that way, every way for fifty years, until it bounced among us, and from the brain of Mrs. Haines caromed away to mine.

All very satisfactory. And by the way, Orilla Adams was descended from old Samuel Adams and he was cousin-german to John Adams! So you see that name, those essays and the expressed intent of prophesying at a later date, might all have come from her! "Telepathy."—"The truth is far more wonderful," Hudson says, "than our wildest imaginings."—Just so!—I did not know her then, but that's no matter! Why be critical?

Once there was a spider caught from home in freshet-time. He took refuge on a cat-tail flag; but when he needed to cross over to dry land, there was no bridge. Being a logical spider, he formulated an hypothesis—a "working one!" Up and down he toiled, a-spinning threads and cutting each one off near to the water's surface. Came a friendly wind, caught up one of the threads and blew it over to a plant on land—whirled round and tied it fast. Easy solution!—the spider traveled over happily, and all was well!

Oh, these aerial threads that we must spin, to cross thereon and find a place for lodging webs and catching little flies!

We used to sit in a dim light and ponder, after singing the "Lord's Prayer," and "How Cheering the Thought"—till some slight thing would happen. One night my hand took up a pencil and traced out the name "Sophronia." I was aware, of course, what name was being written, at least the motion of the pencil brought it to my mind; but I said nothing of it, and in that semi-darkness could not even read. Then I began to "personate" Sophronia. I made-believe take down a lot of hair, combed it well, and parted it in many strands. Each one I curled with care, doing the right side first and thrusting through a phantom side comb, looped the curls together, and fastened them behind my ear. I spent some minutes at the tip, pulling and patting down, to cover it almost, but not entirely. The left strands were curled rapidly and put up without trouble.

Mrs. Haines, at my right hand, suddenly demanded: "Who are you?" Evidently the right ear was deaf. My head was turned around, the left hand curved over the left ear, and Mrs. Haines repeated: "Who are you?" Then

I was made to speak.

"I am Sophronia."

"When did I see you last?"

"She was a baby,"—pointing to Mrs. Manley.

Said Mrs. Haines: "Thirty years ago, Sophronia spent a week with me. I have not thought of her for twenty years. She was very proud, and spent much time curling her hair and prinking at the glass. She was deaf in her right ear, which had no lobe except a lower tip. I have seen her spend five minutes to make sure that the defect was hidden and the tip in sight."

You apprehend the matter:—An impression made upon my friend's objective consciousness and probably on her subjective mind, full thirty years before, took upon itself an actual entity, stepped out, came to my side, took up a pencil, wrote the name of her from whom the impression came; then went on, step by step, in sequence, doing what Sophronia used to do, failing to hear as she had failed to hear, answering with perfect truthfulness, naming aloud the very name and just how long ago it—the impression had been made! Sophronia was not there—She being in the "Spirit-realm" wherever that may be.

So many Psychic spiders!—How can a body tell? And after all, why play at being spider? Is not soul as much to be revered?

Please don't get tired! I want to tell about Aunt Peggy Hopkins.

Her impression had been made upon the mind of Mrs. Haines before Sophronia's I believe, in Rochester, N. Y. When I "personated" her (of whom I had never heard) my right hip was distorted badly. As I walked my right hand, flung behind me, jerked at every step; my left hand held straight out—to keep the balance I suppose—had fingers badly twisted, with the little one turned back. Then I sat down and made-believe to have around my knees a class of little children, pointing out the alphabet to them, and shouting lustily: "What's that? 'AH What's that? etc. All absolutely true to life.

Now old Aunt Peggy Hopkins had lived alone (near Mrs. Haines) in her small house, and would not live on charity; so the neighbors sent their five-year-olds to school, to give her livelihood and keep them out of mischief. She had education,—knew her a—b—c's—at least, and was intensely proud of "keepin' schule." All neighbors near-at-hand could hear her shout the alphabet—she wanted them to hear. She was a Methodist, and, strange as it may seem, was held in great esteem. Old "Father Fillmore," who had known her long, and whom I questioned closely, certainly revered her; and he was half-a-bishop—should have been a whole one. She had a way of doing unexpected things, explaining: "Faather told me to!" One night (be sure I have authority!) "Faather" came to her after she had gone to bed and said:—"Get up; I want you." So she dressed and waited till the order came:—"Go out of the city"—telling her what road to take—"I'll tell you where to stop." Two miles out or so, there was a hut. "Here is where I want you," 'Faather' said. "So she went up and knocked, although there was no light. Quite sure she heard a groaning, she went in and found a dying man. "I must go to hell," he said. The case was very urgent. There was no time to hunt a candle. Down she knelt and wrestled for the soul of that poor prodigal. At last he sighed: "God has forgiven me!" and so gave up the ghost.

Aunt Peggy found a neighbor, sent him over to the hut, and started home. At three o'clock, within the city limits, she was toiling onward, singing very loudly all for joy: "I'll praise my Maker with my breath." "A watch-man tackled me," she said. He took her to the guard-house—thought her drunk or crazy. However, she was so importunate, he sent at first-daylight, a message to that well-known Methodist whom she called her class-leader. He responded hurriedly and blamed the watch-man for arresting such a saintly woman. The officer apologized: "How was I to know she was religious?" She said: "Damn your soul!"

We must allow for spiritual reaction. I spoke that word myself, as you have guessed, by sheer necessity, after a strong religious impulse had been checked—and felt the better for it. So did she, no doubt.

PROPHECY FULFILLED

ONE who evinces full belief in the divine authority of Scripture and the Messiahship of Christ, observes that "if the spirits of the dead communicate with the living, Jesus was not aware of the fact." A venturesome assertion in the face of that recorded interview upon the mountain, when the Master's face "shone as the sun." Peter, James and John were there, we read, when Moses and Elias came in splendor—who had been "living persons," many hundred years before. Not only were those visiting spirits seen, but they were heard to speak. They "talked" with him, whose raiment had become "white as the light." And Peter said: "Lord, let us make three tabernacles." "While he yet spake" a voice was heard by all, that said to them in their familiar tongue: "This is my Beloved Son." But "they fell on their faces and were sore afraid." Now afterward, in that dark garden of Gethsemane, the record tells us: "There appeared an angel unto him from heaven, strengthening him." Was he aware of that? Did Jesus know?

"Logic is the science of correct thinking." "By observing and meditating on facts we demonstrate the truth." Me-thinks logicians should be "sore afraid" of overlooking facts in drawing their "inevitable conclusions" and framing for us "universal postulates." And how does Dr. Hudson know what Jesus knew or knew not, near two thousand years ago? If he were "not aware" before his crucifixion, he learned "the fact" thereafter; for he, himself, came back, was "seen of many," and "conversed" with them.

Can one suppose that Moses and Elias anyway demeaned themselves in visiting that mountain-top and holding converse with the meek and lowly one, who ate with publicans and sinners? Or yet in so bestowing grace of sight on simple fishermen? But had the foulest leper chanced that way, he too had heard and seen, and been as deeply blest: for these had once been men: they recognized their kind. Still we are told: "Jesus was not aware!"

Now they who think the loftiest soul in all the spirit-realm is not akin to us, are ignorant of LAW; and they who think he would not, if we needed him, acknowledge kinship, far or close at hand, by thought-communication or perchance by use of common speech, are ignorant of Love.

Happy am I to find one "postulate" put forth by this good friend of ours, with which I can agree! "Conditions prevailing in the spirit-realm"....."are not analogous to those of the physical world." Who ever thought they were? Do we say of the red rose and the white: "They are analogous?" We know they are homologous. They spring from roots identical in biologic structure. The processes that lead to individual development—to perfect flower and fruitage—are alike in all:—not similar but uniform.

Let it always be remembered we are spirits and live already in the "spirit realm." Emerson says: "The soul is not a function;" but we know the soul demands all functions for its constant use. It must see the visible universe here, and now, and ever after; it must see that universe we call invisible (but which is not so, even here, although its glories are to broaden on our vision more and more hereafter). The soul must hear bird songs and soughing winds and rolling tides as well as harmonies too fine for mortal ear. Material and spiritual are homologous, as roots and flowers of roses are. We shall not be denied a single one of all our senses, for we cannot be, without eternal loss. To see red clay is not the only use for eyes; but not to see red clay, not to be able to look back and see it through eternity, would signify disintegration and decay—prophetic of disaster on disaster, loss on loss, until the soul of man would all inevitably end in blank annihilation.

We three, who came together weekly, did not tease for messages or ask impertinent questions. We drew aside the curtain, as we could, and let come in whatever ray might pierce the clouds and demonstrate the stars. We were but feeble folk, not used to climbing mountains by ourselves—ready to stay below instead and pluck a flower or two or dip the cup in any wayside spring.

I had been deeply wounded, without apparent cause, by one for whom I had a strong affection. It had been her freak to call me "Nannie." This was the purport of a message, written, as it proved, a few weeks after her release from earth—of which I was not otherwise informed till two years afterward.

95

"Dear, dear Nannie! Now I know how much I hurt you and how well you loved me. Forgive me for I love you dearly. Mae."

The words knocked at my heart; and yet I tried explaining them away:—"Unconscious mind" and all that make-believe philosophy; the wisdom of the faithless, tapping as did Quarles upon a mimic globe:—"She's empty; hark she sounds!"—meantime the green earth solid underfoot!

One evening Mrs. Manley and myself were moved to write in alternation, each one walking round the table, pausing, writing, breaking off after three words or so, and yielding to the other, till the whole was written. We supposed the object was to prove another mind than ours, for my sake probably, since I was bent on disbelieving,—not the general facts of spirit intercourse, but each particular instance, till the proof seemed absolute. This was the message:—

"Sister:—Your mind is dark. You do not hope that any new and pleasant thing will come to you on earth. Something is coming very soon. Believe me, it will bring you life—health—happiness. Lester."

The message was not prophecy. No doubt the writer stated what he knew to be a fact; for brother and sister, at a distance, were secretly arranging for my stay at Clifton Springs, where, in those days, there was a "Water Cure" (now magnified into a "Sanitarium," immense in size—world-wide in reputation).

When I told my mother, she questioned sharply: "Well, do you believe it?" "Mother, no! Though Lester wrote it, he must be mistaken. No such happiness is possible."

"You are wicked," said my Mother, angrily. I must have been a trial in those days.

There was no doubt my health was failing steadily. Following that convulsive action of the heart and lungs, predicted four years earlier, slight daily hemorrhage had set in. The downward tendency was rapid. I was truly glad. Having let go the stimulus of desire to live, I would not even try. In that mood, I should assuredly have refused a kindness meant to save my life—as I had really done a year before.

The reading of a single poem—"The Frozen Goblet," by Thomas Buchanan Read—changed me effectually. Not a word have I forgotten after fifty years. For very gratitude, I must pay tribute to that poet-painter; for I owe to him more than I owe to any other of the world's sweet singers. The poem is made up of beautiful and novel phantasies, that carry underneath momentous thoughts. One whose "eyes were full of phantom light" proffered to the poet's longing soul the cup of dissolution.

So taught, I grew ashamed of wanting to ascend, while yet so poor of soul.... After a six months' stay at Clifton and a full year among the healing pines of Northern Michigan, I brought to Buffalo my earliest book of verse:—nothing to blush for,—let it be forgiven; and I am fain to own it started growth. My easy-writing times were gone. During that winter (1861) I wrote two poems—for I dare to call them so. Each cost me weeks of labor, though they were not long. I realized my calling as imperative.

More than six years had passed since one had prophesied that there would come a time when he would prophesy through me. The memory had been submerged, nor did it rise to consciousness till after the fulfillment.

At daybreak, April 12, in 1861, the first gun struck Fort Sumter. The following afternoon Anderson capitulated. Two days later came the call for soldiery, followed by Seward's optimistic declaration that trouble would subside "in ninety days." I was not anyway alarmed after that first strong shock. I said: "War is impossible!"

As I remember, it was but three mornings afterward, when I met David Gray, the poet-editor, who had been kind to me. He stopped me on the street:—"I have read your poem 'Morta.' It is beautiful, but you are off the track. You are growing ghostly. Such things do not reach the people. Give them ballads, love-songs—things that touch the heart. Go home and write a ballad."

"I will, and send it to you, if you'll agree to criticize it with severity."

"I'll tear it all in pieces! I'll lay it, a votive offering, on the altar of the gods, if you will only write it!"

97

Fresh from that stimulating interview I rode home, came in to Mother in a merry mood, announced my purpose, caught the school-room key from off the nail (vacation was in April), crossed the road, and climbed the stair to the wide session-room. Smiling, I jotted down my first eight lines; they were not even remembered after that.

I have been sometimes asked whether my poems come by inspiration—meaning "spirit influence." Assuredly not. Hard work produces them. Time and meditation are essential, with strenuous labor of revision. But on that day there was no meditation possible. What I did was done in ninety minutes only—from half past ten to twelve.

As once, nine years before, a rushing wind had swept through all my physical frame, so now a rolling wave surged through my brain. This time I lost no consciousness, though all my being rocked under the revelation. And here is what I wrote, unaltered by a syllable,—a single word transposed being the sole revision. A few days after, it was published in "The Buffalo Courier" and was copied widely—notably in the "Rebellion Record." It will be found in several verse-collections. No one seemed to doubt its truth when it appeared, but mother only knew the certain source.

When I had written: "Is the noon rising up from the sea?" my head was lifted and I looked in space above me, without the least remembrance or intent. Standing—not with effulgence—but in a twilight none too dim for seeing, there I saw John Adams!

I do not know that I had seen a picture of him, but I found one later after search. Let there be no mistaking me. I saw John Adams. There was an effluence or aura dimly discernible, not encircling him but streaming down from him to me. I had no time to keep on seeing; I had to snatch my words. When I had written four lines more, my anguish seemed intolerable. I rose and paced the long room up and down, wringing my hands and crying out aloud: "I cannot write it! Oh, I cannot write it!" But one was there who would not be denied. I think the next two lines were altogether his—I so rebelled against them. But after they were written I was aware of coming consolation. Perhaps the last two lines were also his. I wrote

98

them with a great and solemn joy, and I believe the prophecy will stand.

After the seven days' battle in 1862, I was strongly moved to write the poem "Richmond." My mood was optimistic. I thought, after such wholesale bloodshed, surely there would be quick capitulation. I was about to write that now the end was coming swiftly. Then without vision, I was once again and for the last time, made "aware" of my immortal friend. I think he did not dictate any word but "earthquake," which I resisted for a moment. Yet those terrific underground explosions at the last, will justify the word. At this point in the fourth stanza, I began to write as one inspired—yielding myself to that inspiring mind.

I am compelled to think that one who loved and served his country, helping her to win a place among the nations more than a century ago, loves her to-day—will love and serve her, long as principalities endure. John Adams lives!

INDEPENDENT SIGHT AND KNOWLEDGE

HAS the soul of man objective vision? A negative answer would go far toward nullifying immortality. Open the gate to one negation and all others enter in. We are here, primarily, to take possession of the physical universe,—to see, to hear, to touch, to taste, to smell. These functions are not grafts. They sprang to life in that deep soil where God inheres for transformation, quickening and endowment. They are His functions; He has made them ours. They are embedded in the plastidule; they are incorporate in Man, the microcosm. God is an Essence, resident in matter,—not in gross earth alone, but in the highest Heaven, where ultimate matter is beyond all vision save His own. We are essences in unison with Him,—finite in scope, but, in duration ever parallel with matter and Himself. Let us not fear to claim our rich inheritance.

But first we will be humble, asking one question only: Have our immortal souls the breadth of earthly vision? Can they see the lines of light that make up our chromatic spectrum? If they can, we must infer they carry vision lower than the red and higher than the violet. In their progressive life they must go on perpetually discerning further, clearer, this way, that way, never losing one bright line between—not even our narrow seven colors, which, with their gradations, are all the lights we see with natural eyes. Should this be true, we shall not miss one glory of the universe within our due degree. Not true—who knows but we may lose the whole?

So let us hold small things near to our purblind eyes, and find their very outlines as we may, to estimate dimensions closely as we can.

You will remember that I said one time, addressing a supposed discarnate Mind: "A spirit should be able to read print without the aid of mortal eyes;"—and how I turned my own away from seeing, while my right hand, under governance, selected texts of Scripture in a perfect sequence, each one answering to my inquiry: "Must my father die?" and all agreeing that the time had come when he had lain down for the final sleep. To have sought those texts myself, would have been most toilsome. I might have read the Bible half way through, and not have found them all. But there was no delay, there were no hesitations. Fast the leaves were turned and without error, texts were found and pointed out. If it were my sub-conscious mind (I being self-hypnotized), its power to read plain print without the use of mortal eyes was amply demonstrated by those many tests. But if my soul could see the so-called visible creation, then every soul can see! Subjective vision includes objective vision, as a photosphere includes a sun. Without a sun there were no photosphere; without a body there would be no soul. That which is breathed out in the act of death cannot be breathed away to nothingness. Far as archangels travel, we must suppose they still can see, at will, whatever shining orb gave each his birth. Nay, should one meet you, sometime in eternity, you would not need to say: "I came from that fair world where dwelt the perfect Man, who, after loving men, died on Golgotha and returned again." He would be first to speak: "Welcome, thou brother of the Christ! Pass on to greater glory!"

So of the loftier minds. But we too have the gift of spirit-vision, seeing small things first, because we are small ourselves.

You may remember, also, that when in Bradford, 1881, my very self slipped from its dormant body, I saw the common out-door serviceable things, which I had seen awake, and one I had not seen before, but went about to look for afterward, and did not fail to find.

This which I am minded to relate, I mentioned in "The Continent," I think in 1885—not giving all details.

A friend of mine, Elizabeth Graham, during the cholera year of 1849, bringing a pail of water from a neighbor's well, beheld a baby's coffin in the air. It rushed so swiftly toward her that she leaped aside lest it should strike her face. That night her baby was attacked with cholera and died before the dawn.

Again: Calling upon her in October, 1860, I found her sunk in deep depression. "I am going to lose another of my children," she averred. "How can you say so?" I demanded. "All three are well and happy."

"Yesterday," she told me, "passing through my parlor and glancing round, I saw upon two chairs, across the north-east corner, the coffin of a child;" and she related once again her vision of eleven years before. "That was prophetic; why not this?" I could not reason her belief away.

Upon the day that followed her recital, after a sickness of but half a day, Abby, her baby, died of virulent diphtheria. My mother and myself were with her when the sexton came, bringing the little coffin. He went alone into the parlor, coming out a little later to invite the mother in, lest she might disapprove of his arrangement. He had placed the coffin on a table set between the two West windows. After he had gone the half-distracted mother sobbed: "I knew that I should lose a child, for I was shown a coffin,—only not so small as this and not so placed. That one was in the further corner, set across two chairs."

On the way home my mother said: "It seems very strange Elizabeth does not understand! It was not Abby's coffin that she saw, but Martha's. She must lose another child, that's evident."

Three days later Martha had also died, and we were there again. Another sexton (the former having been objected to), drove up with Martha's coffin, entered the front door and parlor, remained a little while, and went away without a word. Soon after we went in to see what he had done in preparation for the funeral. On two chairs lay Martha's coffin, placed diagonally, in the north-east corner. Elizabeth cried out: "That is exactly what I saw."

Observe that, though there were to be two deaths, the first was not foreshown. Had Elizabeth been clear of comprehension as my mother, after Abby's death she might have thought: "The coffin that I saw was far too large for Abby.

Surely I must lose another child." She did not half perceive her vision's real significance—two deaths, instead of one.

It is for us to question: Whence did that prophecy come? We may assume hypotheses,—as many as we choose. This, for example:— Every soul has powers that may enable it to plunge, unaided and alone, into that vast black Erebus, contiguous to Hades. Among centrifugal and centripetal spiritual forces operating there, it may discern formations of dim shape, preparing to rise up to veritable reality on this world or another. There this inerrant soul may straightway find out something which is germane to itself, and lift that something prematurely, out of night and secrecy. After this, it may arrive at home, make known those foreseen certainties objectively, by symbol or phantasmal vision, or (more absolutely) by thought-and-word transference. This theory eliminates that superstition of a "spirit realm," where they abide who love us and who "hate the unreasoning awe that waves them off from possible communion" (as we spiritists have learned to think.) But say that we can visit Erebus in this life,—oh, the utter dreariness of those dread explorations we must make hereafter! Let us pray to be delivered from them, save as we may look their way for better measurement of our supernal heights.

But again (to tread more verdant ways and keep in touch with our humanity): Elizabeth was not a "trained percipient." Her mind persistently refused to be dislodged by any hypnotizer's will; nor had it shown itself "amenable to suggestion." She was not even imaginative; and although she mesmerized her sick step-mother frequently, to ease the suffering, she had not power to hold the sleeper's thoughts from wandering far away for "independent vision"—as it proved. So when her spirit-friends, (we have them, all of us!) foresaw affliction coming to her with a dreadful swiftness, and were fain by previous warning to relieve the sharpness of the shock, they could not reach her by the usual means. They gave her, not subjective knowledge, but objective sight—their sight, we must believe, as well as hers. As for their prophecy, it crowned the whole. They caught up things which did exist for composition of that prophetic picture. No doubt the coffin was already made; there was the room to which it must be brought; there were the chairs on which it must be placed; and there was Martha, playing in the sun with Rachel, by the currant bushes. The thing they pictured, with its sorrowful significance, was yet to be! From this, I dare to formulate the inference—applying it to spirits on the earth or spirits in the Empyrean; and to the Infinite Spirit, One and indivisible.

There is a law of Mind, enabling it to see what does not yet exist, but will exist hereafter.

Meantime a lower law permits the mind to see that which exists but is too far away for mortal vision, even without the intervention of a hypnotist or any other "living person" from the North pole to the South.

There are many yet among us who can recollect the great anxiety of Northern Unionists during the month (December, 1864,) when Sherman's army left Atlanta and struck across the State of Georgia to the sea. Not once my faith had wavered in that prophecy that our loved country should emerge from gates of death and "rule" its own beyond all peradventure. But I, too, suffered with the multitude, until it truly seemed the heart must break. During that month (I cannot give the date at this late day, but history will furnish it), I said one night in my first sleep: "I will go down and find the General!" and I was well aware of traveling. We have no chronoscope to measure intervals of time, minute as those that mark a spirit's flight, but consciously I fled, and toward the South. It was dark outside of Sherman's tent, but not completely dark. I lifted up the canvas (how could I do that?) and stepped within. I had never seen a picture of the general, nor a bust, nor even read a line describing him. In these days every daily keeps the faces of the notable before us, more or less distorted. In those days headlines flared continually: "No News from Sherman's Army!"

But he, himself, was not portrayed, save by his doughty deeds.

The General stood before me, not impressing me as physically great, but of commanding presence. Florid, rather spare in flesh, with that wide prominent forehead, and a face that somehow made a radiance for itself by which I saw it perfectly. His lips, I noticed, twitched as if with nervousness, but his whole frame was steady and alert. He wore two garments only; a white shirt and red flannel drawers. He was in the middle of his tent (and that was not a little one), standing sidewise to me, so that I saw his profile only, every line and feature well illuminated.

"General," I said, "how goes the battle?"

He did not turn his face, but answered audibly: "Hard fighting and almost a rout along our flank. The rebels drove us back. I have sent

104

on reinforcements, and now we are driving back the rebels. We are conquering—we shall conquer!" He spoke with fire and energy.

Not only did I see the General—as every picture I have seen of him and every bust has demonstrated, but I heard his voice! Can anyone suppose that voice, vibrating from the State of Georgia to Lake Erie, had reached my outer ear and roused its dormant hearing? I heard objectively, even as I saw objectively—quite independent of the mortal ear or eye.

When I told about my visit at the breakfast table, we remarked that "yesterday was Sunday," and made record of the date, which, by our earliest advices from the re-united forces at Savannah, we were fully able to confirm. Further than this: An article appeared in the Atlantic Monthly in the early eighties (I think in 1883), written by General A. C. McClurg, one of Sherman's bodyguard throughout that famous march. He says: "That Sunday's fighting has been under-estimated" or words to that effect. He writes the story out, of a most desperate struggle, ending in victory. Word came to General Sherman "at ten o'clock" that Sunday night, of a disaster near to rout. I quote: "Sherman leaped from his bed, ordered reinforcements sent, and stood for two hours in the middle of his tent, clad only in his shirt and flannel drawers, dictating and receiving his dispatches." On reading that account, I wrote at once to General McClurg (his house had published my third book—"A Prairie Idyll"), telling him my story, and laying stress upon the trivial fact that those same flannel drawers were "red." This he confirmed by letter, saying that account was wholly accurate. "You must have seen the General himself," he added.

About those days (I think in February, 1865), I had a dream or vision, which In no way indicates objective seeing on the part of my subjective mind. There was a mind that saw, but whether one terrestrial or celestial, let my readers answer as they will.

I lifted up my head, half-way aware that my poor bodily self was lying sound asleep. It seemed that I expected something from the East—I being actually near Angola, west of Buffalo. From far-away, I saw one coming rapidly through space and with a gradual upward movement, as though just leaving earth. He seemed a most majestic spirit, tall, and draped in sombre robes that swept below and seemed almost to touch the ground. He passed me, paused, turned back and, looking down upon me, said exactly this: "Three of the finest young men in Buffalo have just gone to Heaven in a fiery chariot!"—and then went on ascending! I awoke, and soon the clock struck three.

Telling this at breakfast, I remarked: "The language seems too common for a spirit, but I know there is a meaning. Time will make it clear." Not the faintest thought of what had really happened once occurred to me. In fact, The American Hotel had burned in Buffalo. Three wealthy prominent young men—volunteer firemen—working together most heroically, had, at half past two, been suffocated under falling walls. Every paper said that day—and even Angola's early telegraphic message said: "These were our finest young men." It seems a minor question: How could a spirit know just what was to be said a little later, when there had been time for thinking and reporting? I was told not many minutes after the event. The spirit did not state that they were crushed beneath the falling timbers, for he knew their veritable selves were not; being immortal they had merely "gone to Heaven in a fiery chariot."

Some weeks—I cannot say how long—before the final battles of the Rebellion, in my sleep I found myself upon an elevated porch, belonging to a house that I had never seen. I stood facing the South; the porch ran East and West. Seven or eight steps led up to it upon my left hand; on my right there was an open door and I was conscious of a family within. Evidently this was a farmer's home, for houses were not visible nearby. But all was recognizable, when, some four months later, I became a summer inmate of that very house. It would seem that I, in my sub-conscious roamings, had discovered it, and that I had been drawn by occult sympathy, although I had not even met one of the residents, nor heard of them. However that may be, after a time, in this my dream, I heard loud detonations from the far-off South, along a line indefinitely extended. I knew that battles were in progress which must be decisive, and that all was terrible, since even I, so far away, was almost deafened with the noise of cannonading.

Suddenly all was still. Then a great light burst out from the horizon all along, that streamed far up the sky, in white and dazzling splendor. Shouting: "Victory! Victory! Victory!" I ran along the porch and entered where I thought the others were. "Victory! Victory! O, come out and see!" No one responded. I ran back to look and wonder and exult. Then a curtain, black as blackest night, rolled down the whole wide South, and shut out all the glory from my vision—save a dazzling line along the horizon that proved it shining yet. Surely such a pall had never settled over victory before! I stood and sighed and sighed: "There is a great disaster! a great disaster!"

When awake I vainly wondered what enormous sorrow could befall us after all should have been gained. My thoughts not once approached the overwhelming truth.

Objective vision? Yes, so far as landscape went, and the plain country house that was to be my summer home;—By prophecy, objective hearing also, with subjective consciousness of most momentous happenings to come. I heard the sounds that were not, but would shock the world thereafter. I saw "the light that never was on land or sea."

But did I see and hear and partly comprehend without the aid of any sentinel-soul who "looked before and after," seeing inevitable battles, and fore-seeing, after triumph, that inevitable woe? Another or myself, it matters little; for the lowest soul ranks with the highest in possession of supernal powers.

In view of these and other Psychic facts within my knowledge, I venture to put forth two other "universal postulates." There is a law of Mind enabling it to be aware of sounds so far away that no vibration caused thereby can reach the mortal ear.

There is a law of Mind enabling it to hear sounds nonexistent, that will yet exist.

PHANTASM AND REALITY

HALLUCINATIONS are not Psychic facts. They no more illustrate a soul than fogs illuminate a sunrise. One who is Mesmerized is, for the time, infirm; his outward consciousness is dulled or nullified; the functions of the brain are interfered with or usurped. The subject may have visions illusive or "veridical" (fine words are like fine manners, worthy of adoption!),—but must we lean on such a crippled creature, while we seek the heights? We might as well ourselves, by drugs or drink or inhalation, upset or over-rule our faculties, and watch phantasmagoria,—"wondering at the gods that we must be" to have such luminous minds!

Happily I have escaped the hypnotizer and the drug dispenser. I have not even "brushed with extreme flounce" the borders of Hysteria. Still I have thought it wise to scan my least occult experience with questioning eyes, lest, by some juggle, falsity should take the place of truth. Twice, I decided on the instant: "This is phantasmal!" only to learn that it was something more.

One evening Levi, Lydia Brown and I were visiting by candle-light, because my head was paining me too much to bear a lamp. He, snuffing out the candle, left us for a minute in the dark. Into that darkness flashed an image of a child—a baby nine months old or thereabouts, and desperately sick. He was sitting up, but did not look at me nor manifest intelligence, as spirits do, and yet his face and attitude expressed an infinite patience. Strangest of all, his lips were swollen and rolled outward, almost past belief—indicative, I told my friends "of frightful inflammation all along the alimentary tract." I finished my description—very definite as to coloring, size and general features—then said, not waiting for a comment: "No such child could ever have existed.

He was created by a tortured brain. The vision cannot be accounted for by me, on any other theory."

Mrs. Brown, arising, left the room and presently came back with a daguerreotype. "Is that the child?" she asked. "No, but it much resembles him, only this child is well."

"This is George," she said, "when he was nine months old. We lost our oldest boy. Very few people know the fact; we never speak of him,—the trouble was too great for common talk. Unconsciously I caused his death. We had just built this house, and I was in a hurry to get settled in it. I painted all our inside wood-work, even to the floors, sometime before his birth. There are many rooms you know and he was poisoned thoroughly, though I escaped. It always seemed to me I was his murderer. Nothing could be more exact than your description. He lived nine months, and suffered horribly."

I am aware that "scientists" may claim I took this vision from a parent's mind where it had lodged some twenty years before. I do not think so. I have learned of possibilities outside of mere telepathy. Remember we are being photographed incessantly. Because of personal experience, I believe a power of vision lies within the brain that may be exercised without apparent eyes. Call it Psychometric sight or what you will; but I have little doubt I saw one of those radiographs the child had left behind. Being in a supersensitive condition, I perceived what had existed actually, and did not need to pluck the vision from another's mind. In truth the child had lived within that very room, and left his impress there.

The second time I called a vision nothing more than brain-creation, I was riding twenty miles across the hills of Cattaraugus Co., in my native state. The scenery was very beautiful and took up my attention every moment. As we were going down a long slope toward a lovely valley, all illumined with a noon-day sun, I saw (not with my mortal eyes, which were wide open—all intent on seeing, but from my frontal brain an inch or more above) a living, breathing woman! She was dressed untidily, in rather pretty calico, both her sleeves rolled to the elbows, neck-band open to reveal the throat, hooks-and-eyes down to the waist, half broken, and the belt awry. She stood beside a door that opened toward me, her left hand—lifted rather high—clutching the edge, her right hand resting on her hip. I took her in, even to the flying hair, with which her face was framed; and then I looked directly in her eyes. Large eyes, brown, bovine eyes, that looked in mine with curiosity, half-insolent, half-childish.

Then she blushed, simpered and dropped her head, slipped out behind the door as if ashamed to stay, and disappeared.

I said to my dear Margaret beside me: "How wonderful is the human brain! My own has just portrayed to me a woman who has no existence;—dressed her up in chocolate-colored calico, stamped with little roses; made her leer and simper just as though she were alive! What was she created out of, I should like to know? Certainly my brain created her."

Margaret McMaster, sensible and sane and little given to Psychic speculations, though wholly tolerant of mine, replied: "There may be such a woman. You may see her while you are visiting your friends."

Arriving at Horth's Corners, my companions stayed to dinner—leaving me for home at four o'clock. Mr. Howe said: "Please excuse me; I must help my wife clear off the table," and left me quite alone.

Very soon I heard the outer door being opened. Thinking he had returned, I said: "What! through already?" Then I turned about and saw that woman! Every item of her dress a reproduction of my vision—calico and broken hooks and rolled up sleeves and flying hair, in absolute similitude. Her left hand clutched the door, her right hand rested on her hip, and her brown, bovine eyes were looking into mine with impudent curiosity. She blushed, she simpered, dropped her head, slipped out behind the door and never showed herself to me again.

I ran out to the kitchen, crying: "Lyman! Sarah! I have seen a woman! tell me all about her!" I imagine they remember (for they both are living—somewhat older than myself). They said she had been all the morning hanging round, knowing I was expected and wanting to see a woman who had written books;—looking exactly as I said she looked, with just this difference: She had not stood within an open door in such an attitude as I described, nor acted as I stated. What I had seen was in futurity.

In fine, I saw the woman as she would be four hours afterward. Not hypnotism, nor telepathy, nor clairvoyance can explain that fact. I perceived what had not been, what was not, what was yet to be! The act, the attitude, the searching eyes that met my own, the

110

varying expressions and the shy escape, either my prophetic spirit saw, or some prophetic spirit made me see. It is not vitally important one way or another who foreknew. We are all "as like as like!"

What are phantasmal visions? How may we discriminate between them and reality?

One morning in my early life I walked a mile along a lonely road. A man caught up with me who jumped from side to side, talking of snakes!—being an inebriate with delirium tremens who had just escaped from durance.

I said: "Good morning! See how thick the dandelions are!" He stared about as though aroused from sleep. "Why, yes! You're fond of flowers; and so am I." They occupied his eyes from that time till we parted. The snakes were swallowed up in air, as flames would be from burning alcohol. They were phantasmal wholly, therefore they flickered out. That which originates in mind is not so evanescent.

A Boston lady—half a poet, fine as silk, a friend of mine at Clifton Water Cure in 1859—confided to me a momentous secret. Satan had come to her when she was twelve years old, in likeness of a serpent. He had stayed with her through nearly thirty years, and lately he had taken to whispering blasphemies. "And is he with you now?" I asked. "Not very near. You keep him back,—you don't believe in him." "Then if you stop believing, he will go." She smiled enchantingly: "You don't believe in him, my dear, because you are holy." And that was logic!—or dementia, if you see a difference.

Soon after that she died of brain-tuberculosis—dating back to childhood. One supposes that a serpent lurked in every tubercle. Yet, unavoidably one thinks of those "Subjective visions, whose ultimate manifestation is insanity." Now, n they were subjective, they must have followed her beyond the bounds of time; for the subjective mind lets nothing go, which it has seized upon.

This is inconceivable--unthinkable. So are all theories that minimize the soul. Spencer would say: "Therefore their opposite is truth."

These, then, are "universal postulates":

A spirit, being indestructible, is never subject to disease.

A spirit, being divine in essence, cannot justly be accused of sin, nor of proclivity to sin.

A spirit, being free, may traverse every path according to desire, from earth to holiest Heaven, from holiest Heaven to earth.

Meantime, there seems to be a simulacrum of the human soul, that has been called the "underself." This floats within the sphere where elemental force encounters thought;—where each of us becomes, as I have said in verse:—

Partaker with God in the infinite gain Of crush and fusion, passion and pain,

When Mind and flesh are blended;

When the jubilant Sons of the suns draw near To watch where a Spirit, through gulfs of fear,

Soars up—its conflict ended.

This mimic self, at times, is like a cloud surcharged with rain. It threatens, terrifies or blesses, answers its needful purpose, then loses that apparent entity. It is your mood—whatever that may be, your wraith, your dopple-ganger, your abysmal self—your medium of interchange when others visit you; your outward personality, your soul's interpreter—all these and more.

It sports in every tempest, rides on every billow, answers to every call. This is the self that makes obeisance to the hypnotizer, that "puts a girdle round about the earth in forty minutes. It is your faithful servant if you live aright. If not, it may become your wicked master.

He who said (or whose translator made him say): "The soul that sinneth, it shall surely die," could mean no other than this underling that we mistake for spirit. Within its realm all cruel creeds are shaped, and many mortals are obsessed by them. Voice answers voice: "Escape the wrath to come!" and they who warn us know not that the other name of wrath is Love. Here the seducer lurks, and murderers abide—defamers, hypocrites and usurers, who yet will slough iniquity and, having "peopled lowest Hell," will "angel highest Heaven!" Here Cowper toiled through floods of doubt and dread, calling himself a "Castaway." Yet martyrs here, ruling this underself, are not afraid of lions, nor of stake and fagot,—having learned the "mystery of godliness" and being certain of eternal life. Martin Luther here, and Bunyan, met phantasmal devils, thinking them realities, and had redoubtable battles with their underselves,— becoming spiritual giants, as we know. And here are those who are granted holy visions of celestial things (their underselves consenting), while others, standing near them, blindly wonder or deride. And here, as everywhere, the Deity is imminent for growth and consecration.

Much of all this is over-deep for us. Just now we are looking out for fantasies—having discerned that lower world wherein they "make believe." Sometimes the soul itself consents to them, as who should say: "There is a face behind this mask, and you may guess the visage, if you can."

Even an opium-slumberer will see the real at times, if clouds be not too black. The least reality is better than mere emptiness, we know. A friend of mine, deep-drugged and sleeping heavily, looked out, and saw a burglar wandering through the house. Last of all, he took a costly shawl, thrown down upon the parlor sofa, and slipped away with it. More to the purpose, she described him accurately next morning, and he was actually traced from her description, caught, and jailed for that as well as other burglaries.

De Quincy, in his opium-dreams, saw Oriental pageants, vast processionary multitudes, intent on idol-worship as it seemed. The poppies that betrayed him drew their potency from Eastern lands, trodden for many centuries by followers of Juggernaut, the terrible. Perhaps they wrought with him, so that his larger self had Psychometric visions—nothing less than radiographs of what had been, perhaps, a thousand years before. That would be no more wonderful to me than *telepathie a trois*, telekinesis, the mind of man "defeating gravitation," "neutralizing electricity," compelling fire to leave the face and hands unscorched while they were being bathed therein. And all this "scientists" have assented to, we have been told, so that we cannot murmur, if we would! By all means let us learn about Psychometry!

Agassiz, upon the brink of fever, so he tells us, spent a day or two assorting geologic specimens, and so absorbed their influence, or was so affected by their stored up energy (the word is not mis-used), that during sickness, all the places where they had been found were visible to him. Some of those places were not known to him by sight, but were identified thereafter. Mind did not originate those visions, more than the retina originates a landscape we are seeing. This also illustrates Psychometry; and I am Psychometric, as I mean to show you in another place.

Nothing of this was known to Fitz Hugh Ludlow's underself that ruled him without mercy for a time. Under hash-heesh [hashish], once he thought to scale the heaven of heavens; but dropped instead, and found himself within a senate chamber. All the senators—old women every one of them!—were knitting busily old women like themselves. Whenever one was "toed-off," up she sprang, snatched knitting needles, sat her down, a full-blown senator like all the rest, and went to knitting senators. Convulsed with laughter, Ludlow felt himself all ruffling up in stitches, and fled out and down—a-near to where they "smell the burning sulphur;"— was shut into an iron cell whose red-hot walls, contracting as a terrific vise, closed in upon him;—a terrible vise indeed!

And there you have phantasmal visions,—pathological, pathematic, neurasthenic—anything but Psychic! These diabolic brews are something heady:—Let us refresh ourselves with hippocras.

There is a higher atmosphere than this, where—even as winds and clouds—illusions and realities commingle, each with each. Rarely tempestuous, they come and go and leave sweet health behind them. Just a little flutter of your wings, and there you are! And there you have presentiments, telepathies, thrills of prophetic apprehension or delight. A wife pleads: "Let that man alone; he'll make you trouble;" and the husband laughs and answers: "Better not be fanciful, my dear:—the man's all right," then, later, wishes he had taken her advice. A mother says: "I feel a rush of happiness. My boy is surely coming home," and in he comes before the day is done.

Now somewhere thereabout, I get symbolic visions. How they originate, I do not know—whether in my mind or in another's, so transferred to mine.

They show me curiously what is about to happen. Though I get the sense of them at once, full half the time I must await the happening for a perfect understanding. Some of these are truly beautiful and wonderful to me; others (not many) are grotesque, absurd; but one and all have singular significance. The former I shall dwell upon in due connection; but to be wholly fair, I choose one now so foolish you will think I am reduced, as Alice was in Wonderland, almost to nothingness. Get out your microscopes and take a look at me.

I awoke at sunrise. Through or from my brain, I saw, beside my bed, a handsome—cow l Beneath her was a foaming pail of milk. I said: "Why, that must mean that I shall get the funds I need for my inventions!" Therefore I was glad! This was in New York, long time ago, at the old Laight Street Hygienic Home. After breakfast came a letter with a handsome check. I gave it to the clerk and said: "Please have it cashed and take out ninety dollars for my board." Next morning, I awoke again at sunrise, and there, close to my bed, stood that dejected cow!"—the brimming pail had vanished! someone said (inaudibly, you understand): "That is not a good cow." I answered mentally:

"It is." Another spoke, "It isn't a good cow!" "I know it is!" "And I say, it is not A replied a third. Then after pause: "Why, after all, it is a good cow! You were right."

Coming out from breakfast, I was accosted rather brusquely by Mr. Harvey: "Miss Jones, your check's not good.

Three banks have thrown it out." However, after I had telegraphed, I learned that, by mistake, the sender drew it on a bank from which he had just withdrawn his funds; and so my check was cashed that afternoon.

We needn't mind a little foolishness, since that belongs to infancy: What I object to is blank idiocy! A half-grown imbecile at Clifton, taking an electric bath, delighted her poor mother with a mental gleam. She said it "pinched." But I have met with those—not idiots—who felt no "pinch" from any spiritual dynamo; or if they felt it, would assure you positively that it was due to "summat wrong wi' their own inside."

Well, Dr. Hudson tried self-hypnotism once—the only personal experience he gives us; and to show that he was greater than he knew, I quote: "I caused myself to be securely blindfolded in presence of my family and two or three trustworthy friends, instructed them to draw a card from the pack, place it upon a table, face up, in full view of all but myself. I enjoined absolute silence, and requested them to gaze steadily upon the card and patiently await results. I determined not to yield to any mere mental impression, but to watch for a vision of the card itself."

With all those eyes concentered on that card and all those minds concentered on himself, according to his most insistent reasoning he should have seen—the card! He says instead: "The moment I approached the state of somnolency I began to see visions of self-illuminated objects floating in the dark before me. If, however, one seemed to be taking definite shape, it would instantly rouse me, and the vision would vanish. At length I mastered my curiosity sufficiently to enable me to hold the vision long enough to perceive its import. When that was accomplished I saw—not a card with its spots clearly defined, but a number of objects arranged in rows and resembling real diamonds. I was finally able to count them and there were ten; I ventured to name the ten of diamonds." This was correct and so he tried once more and rightly named the ace of hearts, but did not see the card. Aside from other proofs he had already, this personal experience "convinced" him of telepathy! Verily if I had been convinced of spirit-intercourse upon a proof so slight, to borrow Huxley's words, I should have merited "the inextinguishable laughter of the gods!"

Where was the telepathy? He did not see what others saw and tried to make him see. Each looker-on was saying to himself: "There lies the ten of diamonds"—just a common card! No one thought of jewels, each one kept his outward eye upon the card (face uppermost), and the "percipient" saw not, heard not, had no telepathic message:—just stood out alone in mental grandeur, had his "independent vision" and was satisfied; and "everyone applauded." "It was symbolical," he says. Possibly this may not be a Psychic seeing; but it seems to squint in that direction. I incline to think if he had put himself in "training" he might have realized clairvoyance—"properly so called"—as' I have done repeatedly.

This for example:—being fast asleep, without self-hypnotism. On my second visit to my good friends, Lyman C. and Sarah Howe, I found another bed had been set up within my sleeping room. The housekeeper, who occupied it, was solicitous lest I should be disturbed the night of July 4th—a ball being in progress at the tavern on the corner, twenty rods away; and so she shut both windows to keep out the noise, and drew down two green curtains to shut in our light. All our air came from the hall which had an eastern out-look. Next morning I was late at breakfast, and a little dull from heavy sleeping. Said my host: "Were you disturbed by what was going on?" "Not at all," I answered; "only just at daylight. Then a man was talking in the blacksmith's yard, and I looked out and saw him,—no one whom I knew. He was standing facing me, in a democrat wagon without seats. Then he wheeled and drove out, laughing and talking with the blacksmith. He drove up to the tavern steps and seven or eight young men came out, climbed in and stood up, holding by each other, while the man drove off and up the hill. The fellows had been drinking, judging by their looks." As I related this, I had no thought that it was just a dream. Horace, fourteen years of age, remarked: "I was up at early daylight and standing in the garden, so I saw it all. There's just one democrat-wagon in the place, and so our neighbor was called out of bed to take the young men to another tavern for another dance tonight. I counted seven of them—half drunk, I thought."

"When did you see all that?" my room-mate asked. "Just at daylight." "Well," she answered, "I awoke at three o'clock, and did not sleep until I rose at eight; and I can testify you never raised your head. And, if you had, there's not a window in the second story out of which you could have seen one thing you have described!" This was exactly true.

I remember that I lifted up my head and looked into the blacksmith's yard; the intervening wall I did not see, but even yet I can recall the features of the man who faced me from the democrat wagon. Horace saw what saw from a different point of view. If I had seen because he saw, the driver would have been in profile and the blacksmith's shop upon the East, instead of on the North. And what had I to do with Horace, anyway?

You think such dreams not worth considering? That's your— poor—little—think!

FRIENDS ON GUARD

THERE is nothing great or small," a poet sings; and since the Scientists have taken to weighing atoms (out-doing those astronomers who only weigh the suns), we may assume, at least, that there is nothing small. So borrowing your "Philosopher's scales," Jane Taylor, we'll "bowl the whole world and find it underweighs the least of all our Psychic facts. Let us go on relating them.

One autumn day in 1862 (save for some leaps ahead, we have got no further in our calendar), I was depressed and found I could not write a line of verse. That fact alone disheartened me. Just then, by rare revival of an art I had almost fancied lost, my hand was "influenced" to write. Could I have had my choice, something inspiring would have been revealed, to lift me into higher moods. Only this came, without a signature:

"Put on your things, go to Niagara Street, and take the horse-car. Ride to Main Street, then get off, go down upon the right hand side, and something pleasant will occur."

I followed the suggestion, though it seemed absurdly trivial. I thought so slightly of it, that I let the curious message slip from memory. Still, when the car stopped, as always, at Niagara and Main, in utter absent-mindedness, without a purpose, I got off and walked instinctively toward the lake, upon the right hand side.

Two or three blocks along, I met my friend Lavinia's brother, Major Ira Ayer—who, being wounded, was at home on furlough. He had known me eight years earlier when his friendly mother, thinking the country air would do me good, had sent for me, and I had been her guest. Detained in Buffalo for hospital care, he had sought me out, and I had made in at the grate" him tell me all he would about the seven days' lighting before Richmond. For recompense, I had dedicated to his regiment "The Battle of Gaines' Hill," which had appeared with illustration in *Frank Leslie's Weekly*—then a mammoth publication, read by every soldier, one might say.

The Major stopped me eagerly: "I am ordered to the front this morning, and must leave at three o'clock. Come to Aunt Sarah Lamb's with me. You know she is always glad to see you."

Well, that was pleasant, certainly; but when he brought me from her parlor table a handsome book of special value, inscribed already with my name, I found that pleasanter. Yet pleasantest of all was the delightful certainty that someone "disembodied" (if you choose to use the word), had tried to make my undeserving soul a little happier. I did not ask who wrote, for that was not my way. I did not even surmise; but it occurs to me, just now, that Ira's mother, knowing him to be a little troubled because he had no time to visit me, and bring the book as he intended, for his sake may have sent me after it. It had been her custom, I learned when I was honored with her hospitality, to "watch out" in the interests of others. Nothing was too small to think about or plan for, so it were helpful to her family.

No matter who, however! Notice: someone had calculated time with fine precision. Just so many minutes to get ready, just so many for the ride to Main Street, just so many on the Major's part to meet me just in season!

What can a spirit know about chronometers and horologes? Far more than you or I, it may be possible. It has been supposed that there are worlds invisible within those which to us are visible. If so, they are beauteous archetypes—we have a right perhaps to call them spirit-worlds. They are not supposed to be imponderable (we are weighing atoms now, you know), but fine enough to answer all the uses of a spirit who is not yet ready to soar out and ransack higher realms. These worlds are habitable to souls, dwelling in "spiritual bodies" as earth is habitable to souls dwelling in earthly bodies. That being so, they must revolve in unison with times and seasons, which, by God's decree, they have enforced upon their fellow-orbs.

Eternity is Time—without an end; and time is always measurable. Therefore our friends may have their silver-sounding clocks as well as we, keeping the self-same hours. That theory, could it subsist in fact, would bring our happy Dead so close to us, disseverance would seem imaginary.

"In my Father s House are many mansions. If it were not so, I would have told you."

City life being unfavorable to poetry, I Spent much of my time from 1861 to 1868 in Cattaraugus County and out among the farmers West of Buffalo some twenty miles or more. I made myself a little useful, teaching music here and there, and had my quiet rooms and pleasant haunts about the waterfalls or in the fields and orchards. Often dear friends would come and take possession of me for a visit, keeping me as long as I could stay. Some of these families (descended from the Quakers), called themselves "Progressive Friends." In April, 1862, a friend in Erie County solicited a visit. Her husband was an army officer and in his absence she was living with her widowed father—his other daughters being away at college. I had been a guest during the mother's life and I was cheered at thought of visiting again such dear, congenial friends—not Spiritualists by the way—who had thought enough of me to drive into the City purposely, and take me home with them. After supper, we gathered round the fireplace—my friend, her father and myself—and chatted merrily of former times. We did not speak of her who had been my hostess once, having already spoken quite enough; but she was in my mind from first to last. To me her personality had seemed compelling. Froude, in writing of the world's affairs, observes that women, more than men, have, on the whole peculiar "aptitude for sovereignty." This she exemplified at home, as mother, wife or hostess.

No one resisted her—assuredly not her husband. Loving greatly she was greatly loved and reverently obeyed.

But once—believing me to be a medium—she had caused me poignant suffering. Glad am I that I have never been one of those mediums at large! ("Pray for their souls all Christian gentlemen!") On the morning after my arrival, she had called her family together and, it being Sunday, had bidden them stay at home from church that we might hold a "circle"—quite without consulting me. I think her strong desire had overcome her conscience. She was a Methodist "dyed in the wool," as father used to say,—but evidently thought for once it might be pardoned if she leaned across the pale to smell her neighbor's flowers.

She carefully explained to me: "My first child died when he was two years old. I never yet have felt resigned. I want some proof that he can visit me. You are an invalid and ought not to be taxed; but you have only known our daughter and she has never mentioned him to you she says. I ask for nothing but his name."

I thought a child who had died at two, could hardly write his name; but trusted someone else might write it for him. Usually, in "automatic writing," the name had come before the message, so I had little doubt; and seven of us sat down to wait for it.

Now I know as well as you, my patient friends, that six minds, brought to bear on mine, all dwelling on that baby's name, might be one way of thrusting it upon my consciousness; though, please remember, just as many minds being brought to bear on Hudson's, could not make him see a single card, or even impress its name by telepathic means (and rather slender means they are, judging by my experience!). He guessed the "ten of diamonds" all by his underself,—or let us say by sheer subjective symbolism—evidence of mind on his part, not on theirs.

However, let that pass! A name was written in this case, almost immediately. I said in all sincerity: "Some man is writing whom perhaps you know. He calls himself Lowe Bradley.'" I said Low—as in the word allow.

The lady reached out for the sheet as hardly crediting the fact; then cried "My baby boy! My own Lowe-Bradley," using the long "o" Since the family name had not been written, it had not seemed to me a possible baby's name. Then up she rose and paced the room and wrung her hands and tossed her arms, reiterating many times: "Is my baby here? Satan can make himself appear an angel. Is he deceiving me? or is it really Lowe-Bradley; How can I ever know?"

Ah, sure enough! How could she? I had never seen that kind of thing before (imagine mother in hysteria!); I suffered deep distress.

But never think this violently loving mother was not sane, and even intellectual. Remember how John Wesley, whom she humbly followed, never scrupled to declare his faith in—I had almost said his knowledge of—a rampant, personal devil. Remember Cotton Mather, Jonathan Edwards, and a host of mighty spiritual warriors—verily their name is legion!—all contending with their underselves, and everyone instructing Christian souls like that of this dear, gifted lady, in the mysteries of demonology! Even I recall a time when it was hardly thought respectable not to believe in Satan!

Early Spiritualism had this element to deal with. For example: A worthy neighbor—Sally Doolittle—in 1852, became a "writing medium," much to the satisfaction of her household. But one day the name was written of a former friend, who had committed suicide. Trembling with apprehension, she yet contrived to ask: "Are you in hell?"

Getting no response, but getting a prodigious arm-ache (due to interrupted currents, if you please), what could she infer but that he was in hell? We may presume that if some old-time friend had come to her—not being "dead," of course,—she never would have thought to ask: "Have you just broken jail?" Even a spirit is entitled to civility. People did not always think of that "when was young"!

I am not forgetful of the title of my chapter, although I interject an object lesson. To return to that long dining room, where had been held that memorable circle years before; we three sat chatting by the fire till ten o'clock, as cheerful as we well could be with all those battle-echoes audible to soul if not to sense,—my brother William and Lavinia's husband both in line of battle! Till, at last, we spoke of sleep and Libbie brought the lamps.

I noticed her with favor. Just a "hired girl," but tall and handsome, with a dignity beyond her twenty years; very poor, I learned a little later,—her mother's main dependence. My hostess introduced her as an equal, though she herself was college-bred and passionately fond of Greek.

Well, Libbie brought the lamps, and I was led away.

"All these rooms were built since Mother died," my friend remarked and added sweetly: "This room is for you whenever you will come and occupy it." So she left me, comforted with friendship.

Observe: If we send out our radium-emanations, alpha rays or whatsoever—little "projectiles" that bombard the very walls about us—they may recoil and yet again recoil, bombarding all who come where we have been, till their kinetic energy is spent;—and when that may be who can guess? But these including walls had never held the mother of my friend. Not even a radiograph of her could flash out in the dark, confronting me with pallid face and anxious eyes to prove that she had lived.

No, I had not slept; I had not even begun to breathe a little slowly, before I was aware of her. Not in my room at first, but in the lower hall. She floated up—she did not climb the stairs. I noticed that, and yet I hardly dare to say I saw her. There was no self-illumination. Have you seen a friend by star-light? That was how it seemed. My door was closed against her, but she effected entrance easily, as though it were not there. She might have come as well some other way, no doubt, but she was yet conventional enough, it seemed, to choose the door. Tall as of old, and "slim and swift," in Charlotte Bronte's words, as any "Northern Streamer," in she came, paused at the foot, then passed around my bed and leaned above me. Never before nor since, in all my waking hours, did any spirit-form approach so near to sensible touch! I thought: "She breathes!"—I almost heard her breathe!

"You are needed in this house. I want you to exert an influence. Will you do for me whatever I may ask f"

Forty-seven years have passed and I have known of spirits many times. She is the only one that ever made me tremble. I answered: "I will do for you whatever you require, if it shall seem to me entirely right." Not that I doubted her integrity; but I must guard my own.

She turned away, went out, and seemed to sink along the stairway to the lower floor. She drew my consciousness along; whether I saw or did not see (in truth I hardly know), I followed every movement. "She has gone into a room that seems just under this—it must be there's a passage to it from the dining-room, not from the hall,"—'(it proved to be her daughter's room). "Now she is gliding through the passage, she is in the dining-room. She is entering an open door half-way along. I remember; there is the bed-room where I used to sleep. I must watch till she comes out."

Two or three hours perhaps went by. • I drowsed away at last, repeating: "She is in that bed-room still." I woke at early dawn and thought with certainty: "She is in that bed-room now!"

Presently I rose and dressed myself. "At least, I can escape," I said. "This is Sunday morning; and no one will be up so early. I shall have time to go and hunt for wild-flowers. The woods are close at hand." So I wrapped up well, slipped down the stairs, went, through the long room where we had supped, on tiptoe past the bed-room door. Impossible not to turn my head; for there my host stood, just within, hands clasped, and looking downward, deep in thought. He saw, and hurried out. "I am very glad to see you. Please sit down." He drew an easy chair for me and chose another for himself. "I want to talk with you. I have not slept a moment! My wife"—he paused and changed the form punctiliously, striving to be exact. "That is"—Mrs.——has been with me all night." Like a strong tree caught in a gale, his vigorous religious prejudice had bowed under his recognition of her potent presence.

Just here I ought, perhaps, to end the story, for if an "influence" came to me from her, thereafter, I "was not aware of it." Still, no one is left except myself to answer for a spirit's good intent; and having told so much because it seemed I must, I tell a little more because it seems I may. Both my host and hostess volunteered their confidence that day, from different motives, asking my advice and influence. I was neutral as an acid charged with alkali. Yet my neutrality was influence. It hindered action.

Quite within his rights, and not at all to his discredit, he had proffered marriage to—the "hired girl." And now he found, to his dismay, that her acceptance would disrupt his family. Children would stay away from home ("the worse for them!" I thought); and, save for Libbie, little would be left. He might retract, but there was manly honor—she must not even know that there was trouble brewing. Besides—what would you have? He really thought himself in love.

But Libbie had not yet accepted him. She had asked for time. She must consult her mother, twenty miles away—whose poverty afflicted her. Meantime my host had little doubt of her acceptance; neither had my kindly hostess, who recognized, with charity, "a great temptation." Libbie, herself, after some weeks, consulted me with secrecy. Was it her duty to accept the offer? It seemed her mother thought so,—and there were little sisters. And then I did, quite of my own volition I suppose, what seemed to me "entirely right." Not having so much aristocracy as might serve for stiffening of a paper napkin, I answered her in this wise: "Libbie, I believe in you. When you are ready to marry someone about your age (and half as good as you I hope), invite me to the wedding. Meantime your mother isn't going to starve and you're not going to live a lie! I have no respect for one who marries without love; but understand, to be a hired girl is altogether honorable."

Libbie rose up and laughed and kissed me. "I can earn enough to feed my mother, thank the Lord!"—so went quickly out and told her suitor "No." All the same she did not lose her "honorable" place within his house.

I said that spirit-wife and mother did not visit me again ,—there was no need. Not for her sake alone I did her service from afar,— aware that I was furthering her righteous purposes, though not by her immediate command. Let it be added that some two years later, he who had been her husband, married—to his children's satisfaction. I wish you would let me quote a sentence from Disraeli—I so admire the style: "So Peace descended upon that often-perplexed but always well-meaning roof."

About that underself! Do you suppose it will not be our faithful servant in the life to come? A little while, if we be terrible, it may be master, surely not for long. I have heard that spirits have been known to come mouthing profanities; but presently they slunk away ashamed. We need not be afraid of such; they cannot do us hurt; perhaps they come, out of those caverns where they breathe mephitic airs, that we may do them good; and they may learn from us, who roam in pleasant fields, to drink sweet waters trickling here and there among our violets.

But understand, such visitations are not Psychic in the higher sense. I have been told a man has lived with half his brain removed; but would he represent the MAN" "infinite in faculties," "in action like an angel," "in apprehension like a god?" Still less could any dominant underself—an infraspiritual pseudo-entity—stand in the place of an immortal soul.

The spirit-lady I have told you of, brought in to me, for Psycho-service, just that underself I had realized of old. By that I knew her perfectly. It was a personality that could not be mistaken. We are not spirits only—we are persons. We encompass all.

You think she was unblest, because unquiet? Surely not. Happy or sorrowful, inquietude belonged to her,—it was her special gift. No doubt she had her holy haunts, and beautiful associates, talking of holy things as she had always done—but with increase of knowledge and delight. Still, when dissension threatened to divide her husband from his children, what could she do but turn and seek her own? Once there, only by taking on the olden moods, could she effect her reconciling purpose. I felt her sharp anxiety, I recognized her force of will, her "aptitude for sovereignty" and, more than all, her unimpugnable love. She came as a strong wind, that blows through stagnant atmospheres, to pass and leave them sweet. Assuredly she was blest.

As for us, we learn our Psychic lessons: How shall we get wisdom otherwise? Certain it is these other-world revealments are not more foreign to humanity than seeds are foreign to the soil in which they germinate. They are the rarest inflorescence of our life. They are as cacti of the desert, lilies of the meadow, healing herbs along the mountain side, white orchids of the air.

We cannot force their blossoming time. If we have need of flowers we do not pull out plants to get at them; but we can "set the dibble in earth" to lift the roots and put them in our gardens.

And must you call them weeds?

WAYS OF PLEASANTNESS

IF all the revelations mortals have received from angels, "should be written everyone, I suppose the world itself could not contain the books that should be written." "The least of Psychic facts," I said—some pages back. We might say as well: "The least of cosmic stars:"—then train our telescopes upon them, and discover suns of girth immeasurable. What concerns a soul cannot be counted small; for is not any soul greater than every sun?

But say that we ourselves are small, no more than mere atomic germs of soul, late-quickened of the Lord and destined to celestial growth—not by accretion, but by perpetual forth-putting and inclusion. Now, physical atoms, it has been discovered (Svante Arrhenius, I read, has demonstrated this), may be so small that "particles of light," colliding with them, press them far beyond the pull of gravitation into ethereal space (and oh, to follow them along their luminous track!). There I suppose each one—being necessary to God's material (and spiritual) universe—is recognized as great. Let us call our revelations "particles of light," and if, at last, they press against us mightily and we go soaring off—so that we soar together (God takes care of that!), what more can we desire?

In April, 1862, while visiting my country friends, word came to me that a young girl, who was dying of consumption, wanted me to visit her. I found her lying in a pleasant parlor, so secluded you could hardly realize a world beyond the orchard. Only seventeen, her girlish loveliness defaced—and yet she had one beauty left. Her heavy curls were massed upon her breast that hardly stirred beneath their weight. In Robert Browning's words: "She had her great, gold hair!" But all her soul was quivering to escape, like an imprisoned bird.

"I have been told," she said, "that you're a medium. Will you tell me when I am going to die?"

"Dear child, I am just a common mortal. I could not tell you of myself."

"No, but you might get a spirit to tell you."

"But you can see that if we try to influence spirits, we are simply making it impossible for them to influence us."

"Yes, I see," she murmured patiently: "But you may be impressed to know. And, if you are, you'll tell me, will you not?"

So twice a day I visited sweet Mary Hard and twice a day she questioned: "Have you been impressed?"

One morning I sat down beside her and she did not ask her usual question, save with her asking eyes. I had heard of Mary's sister Frances, who had passed away two years before, a victim of the same disease. Now Frankie came, and satisfied the dying girl at last. She did not deeply influence me,—at least my eyes were open— usually (though I am always conscious), they are shut and sealed. Frankie said, in part: "We are all rejoicing, for the time is close at hand!"

"Not many days?" sighed Mary wistfully. "Not many hours!"—with such a voice you might have said she laughed! My voice, and yet not mine in sound or cadence: Frankie said the words.

Mary's eyes were wonderful. I never saw delight so manifest. I asked her aunt on leaving: "Do you think the time is near?" She shook her head. "There is no sign of it."

But six hours later I went in, and Mary only smiled. The brightness of her eyes astonished me. It seemed she would not close them,— bent on taking one last look. They did not cease to shine till someone closed them for her—not immediately. I saw the happy soul look through those windows after the "keepers of the house" had "trembled" and "the doors were shut."

It came about that Mary's guardians, George and Fondana Bundy, made very much of m®, and had me with them often—truly to my advantage, for their homestead-farm was consecrate to rest. And more than this: If ever spirits visit mortals, seeking recognition, spirits had visited these friends of mine, long years before I knew them. I was amazed to learn the depth of their experience, until I also learned how they excelled in all those gracious qualities St. Paul ascribes to Charity;—for such invite the blest.

Without the slightest prompting from the outer world, in 1849 they had emerged from Calvinistic mazes, and, in the sanctitude of home, had broken bread with angels. So it seemed to them, and so it seems to me. I could not see in them the least fanaticism, nor any trace of ignorant credulity. Having two children only, they—just working people!—had given homes to many, chiefly to Mrs. Bundy's father, mother, invalid sister Lucy, widowed brother and his three orphaned children. Of these the father and the widowed brother "died" before the others blossomed into Spiritualists.

Now when the father found he was to go, he called his children in and laid this charge upon them: "Never let your mother sleep beyond your hearing. You know she is liable to die of nightmare any night. Train yourselves to waken at the slightest sound. Spring to her side and grip her by the wrists, then shout with all your might, right in her ear: Nancy! That will bring her out, when nothing else can save her."

Permit a slight digression: Thirty-two years before that day—she being thirty at the time—Nancy Hard had lain some months close to the gates of death, with what the doctors called "brain fever." "I shall not come again" the last one said: "There is nothing more to do." A dear, old woman had been watching her, who, I am fain to think, became inspired (as once my mother was, when the last hope of saving brother Willie's life seemed gone!). It "came" to her, she said, what she must do. She gathered plantain leaves in haste, poured boiling water on them, and, often changing them, she kept that shrunken body wrapped in them three days:—a sort of Priessnitz pack, you understand, before great Priessnitz made his great discovery. I met her patient first when she was seventy-six, a little younger than myself, it seemed—I being twenty-seven! I played for her to dance one day. She took her steps, as Queen Elizabeth did—"high and disposedly!"

But ever after that recovery, from 1817 to 1849—she had, occasionally, dangerous nightmares; and please to let me tell you from her very lips what happened finally.

Not my experience, you suggest? No, but I made it mine.

"For she looked with such a look and she spake with such a tone,

That I almost received her heart into my own."

First, Lucy Hard became a writing medium. Notice that mediumship and invalidism may co-exist, as intellect and invalidism may,—not of necessity in either case. Lucy's mother looked askance. Dear lady! she was sixty-two, and bred a Presbyterian. She asked for no communications from her husband. He was safe in Heaven—and who could tell what Satan might pretend?

One day Dr and Mrs. Marvin (fellow-doctors) hurried in. They had built a Water-cure and wanted Lucy for a patient. Just then they wanted "Grandma Hard" to spend a night with them, while they were yet alone. Flattered and pleased—for they were virtual strangers—Grandma rode away. In the flurry, I am glad to say, nobody thought of nightmares. When bedtime came, her hostess led her through an upper hall, ten rooms away from all the family.

Early the following morning Lucy's father wrote a message to his daughters. Because of frequent hearing and an excellent memory, I am able to transcribe it practically word for word:

"Last night your mother had the nightmare. But for me she would have died. The blood had almost ceased to circulate around her heart. She saw me and she knows I saved her. Give yourselves no further trouble. She shall never have the nightmare after this, I promise you, long as she lives on earth!"

Grandma Hard came home that afternoon, seeming, as Mrs. Bundy told me, rather "flustered"—not her usual, quiet self. "We did not dare to show the writing," said her daughter. "First we let her tell her story, then we brought the message, and she read it. That ended all her opposition!"

Now, I shall tell just what had happened, in her very words, addressed to me—repeated many times.

"That night I had the nightmare worse than I ever had it in my life. I knew that I was dying. But my husband stepped up to the bed and gripped my wrists and shouted 'NANCY!' in my ear, with all his might. Then I came out of it; and then he said to me: 'Now, Nancy,

I've done this to prove that I am with you, and am able to take care of you as well as ever. But do not be afraid of nightmare after this. I promise you shall never have it while you live on earth."

To this account, for emphasis, she always added:—"Nobody need tell me it was not my husband; for it was! I saw him step up to the bed, and felt his hands grip both my wrists and heard him shout my name and heard just what he said. What's more I've never had the nightmare from that day to this, and that was fourteen years ago!" Nor did she have it ever afterward through seven added years.

Thirty-two years subject to dreadful nightmares—twenty-one years immune. She died at eighty-three.

What good can spirits do?—Well, by and bye, I shall begin to tell you.

Meantime, although in truth not my experience, I do not like to pass entirely by the case of Lucy Hard—substantiated by the statements of the Bundy family, her physicians, a Presbyterian deacon, and certain neighbors much averse to Spiritualism; also others, including Lucy's husband, whom she married some few months before her death.

From writing-mediumship she took to having trances; being at Mr. Bundy's, yet unmarried. Was she self hypnotized? Certainly there was no visible hypnotizer. Who says the mind lacks outward vision,—cannot see the physical universe save by suggestion? Lucy's outward, so-called natural eyes, were, in these trances, sealed from sight as though they had been put out. She roamed without attendance—hardly with attention. She never tripped, she never lost her way. She climbed the orchard trees and sat for hours among the

See Appendix III. branches (watched, at times, by curious neighbors)—then came in and said: "The trees give out a magnetism. Lucy is filled with it." "Lucy wants an apple. She is hungry; we must feed her. Down in the cellar in the farthest bin, close to the side, there is a red-streaked apple, largest and mellowest of them all." Down went sleeping Lucy in the dark, alone, and brought that chosen apple back. Being in Dr. Marvin's Water Cure, and having hemorrhage of the lungs, she said to him (this is exactly what he told me): "Lucy must be given Hamamelis!" "There is no such medicine," said Dr. Marvin; "I never heard of it." "You have a vial of it. Move your medicine bottles and you'll find it."

With not a bit of faith, except in Lucy, the bottles were removed, and—dropped behind them all—was found a little package, labeled under the wrapper, Hamamelis. Then Dr. Marvin had a memory of visiting Dr. Gray, a Homoeopath, of Buffalo, a year or two before, who had handed him the package, saying: "Here's a new remedy for hemorrhage—Hamamelis. Try it and report."

But previous to this, while under care at home before her marriage, Lucy, in trance, had said: "Lucy, when a baby, was given poisonous drugs by ignorant doctors, and greatly injured by them. Ever since, they have kept it up. Minerals are scattered through her body everywhere; the worst of these is sugar-of-lead. That is why she suffers so much pain. Lucy can't get well, but all this suffering must be stopped. The poisons must be driven out. We will begin on sugar-of-lead. First give her Homoeopathic doses of the poison for about two weeks. That will rouse those dormant particles into action. When that is done, have ready plates of strongly magnetized metal, and bind them on her feet. Leave us to do the rest." [Who were "us"?]

Aside from all the other testimony, I had the solemn affirmation of her brother Ezra—the Presbyterian deacon! He, himself, went out to Buffalo, had the plates or sheets made as directed, brought them home and bound them on her feet. "For three days Lucy lay asleep," he told me, "and did not speak nor move. When she awoke, I took away the sheets and found a full eighth-inch of coating on them. I took them back to Buffalo and had the coating scraped away and analyzed by scientific experts. They pronounced it absolutely sugar-of-lead."

Well, that's not half so unbelievable as *telepathie a trois*! Prove as clearly but a single case of thrice transferred telepathy, you'd make its advocates faint dead away from sheer astonishment!

Lucy was freed from pain thereafter; frail as a lily, but "happy all day long." Marrying Dr. Marvin's brother-in-law, her husband took her to the Water Cure to live. There, in her trances, she gave so much instruction to the Doctor, that, as he told me, he was greatly aided in his practice. "I learned from her" (these were his very words), "more than I ever learned from all my books."

After half a year or so of tranquil married life, Lucy fell asleep and did not waken. It was hard to understand that she had passed away. There was no sign of physical decay. They sent for many doctors, many tests were tried. All judged that she was dead. After a week—with yet no sign of perishing, no mortal odor—the neighbors sent in word that, if there were no funeral that day, a mob would come and force the burying. This was in Jerusalem Corners, eighteen miles from Buffalo, about the year of 1852.

"We buried her that day," Fondana Bundy said.

"Fearing the mob?" I asked.

"Oh, no! she came herself and told us not to keep the body any longer; it was dead."

I gasped! I had not "found so great faith—no, not in Israel!"

"How did she come?"

"She influenced Eugenia."

"How old was Genie then?"

"Only eleven. We were all amazed, the demonstration was so perfect. She told us things that Genie never heard about, and acted out herself completely. She said there was no other way to let us know; but Genie never was entranced again."

I came to know Eugenia very intimately, as a wife and mother,— singularly guileless, free of all pretense as a white rose! I would have staked my life upon her lightest word.

So I hark back at last and talk about myself. You understand that poetry, not mediumship, was my vocation. It was, in part at least, my livelihood. I had, besides, to think of battles and to write of them with vehemence of patriotism. Had I been ten thousand men, I think there would have been ten thousand soldiers more. All I could do, when physical weakness did not overcome, was just to suffer with my country and to serve her, if I might, with song. I had no thought of being turned aside by any "spirit-influence," nor did it interfere with me in any way. I did not seek for mediums, nor as a medium, let myself be sought. I did not bind myself to any Psychic service. Always I have known that to "consult the spirits" would be no more effectual, for me, than to consult the winds. When they have come to me, I have received them gladly: they have done me good and never any harm.

But I began to have, between my spells of study, a certain power to hand out little psychic gifts to those about me. I shall tell of these, to some extent. For instance:

Being a guest one time of Mrs. Bundy's (she was good enough to let me call her "Auntie"), she came into the sitting-room and sat down with a very tired look. Presently she said: "When I was young I had an aunt of whom I was very fond. Sometimes I am almost sure I feel her presence."

"Auntie," I said, a minute after, "there she stands beside your chair. She doesn't show her face; that seems to be behind a snowy veil. She's a slender lady, and she wears a white, three-cornered handkerchief around her shoulders, with the ends crossed in the front. She has on a fine white apron, and a wine-colored pressed-flannel dress."

"Auntie" sat up suddenly. "For all this world! That was what she always wore in winter—wine-colored pressed flannel! She used to spin the yarn herself and do the weaving, getting them to dye and press it at the factory. And she always wore that handkerchief and apron."

"Stop!" I said. "Don't speak her name! I think she is going to give it! Then I was bothered. Two names came at once—four syllables tumbling in together, hard to detach at first. "Auntie," I said, "I haven't got her name as yet; but someone else is here whose name was Achsah."

Auntie shook her head: "I never knew an Achsah."

"Well, never mind! That wasn't your aunt at any rate. Her name was Betsy."

"Why, for all this world! That was her name!" cried Auntie with delight.

Next day she chanced to speak about the first year of her married life: "George had a cousin who was in consumption. None of the relatives seemed willing she should stay with them. So Achsah came and lived with us a year until she died. We wanted her."

"Why, Auntie! you said you never knew an Achsah!"

"Oh, for all this world!"

Late in 1864, Levi and Lydia Brown called where I boarded, thinking they would like to know me. Two or three families met together at their house occasionally, as Quakers meet and "wait the moving of the spirit." I well remember that first evening, when they welcomed me to such a gathering. I was ready to be pleased with any evidence of spirit-visiting, and so were they. Naturally I have kept in mind the things that came to me rather than to the others. Sitting by Mrs. Brown, I said to her: "Some old friend of yours is here. Her name was Mary Mills."

"I never knew a Mary Mills."

"She says: 'Tell her I taught her how to make buttonholes.'"

And Mary Mills, the Quaker Seamstress, with just that foolish little message, brought to Lydia's mind—not herself alone, her name, her kindly act—but many a childish effort to be good, sit still and learn to sew; also there came a wonder: "Strange! After forty years to hear from Mary Mills again!"

And then another gave her name: "Surely I never heard of her!" Then there was thrust before my brain—my mind, or what you will—a grey silk bonnet, very old fashioned, with a scoop in front, a little three-inch cape,—the silk most beautifully shirred. An artist must have made it. This I described; and Mrs. Brown laughed out: "That was the first hat that I ever bought; that was the milliner's name of whom I bought it!" And back went memory to the spinning wheel that helped to earn the money that bought the shirred silk bonnet that had been so becoming to the pretty girl, thirty-five years before. I only wish that dear young face could have been shown to me under the scoop! I may as well say that I was very fond of Mrs. Lydia Brown.

Suppose that Lydia before this time had wandered (under pressure of some "particle of light") into celestial realms, and there had met the skillful milliner: What would they have talked of, first of all? The great illumination? The wonder of the "four-square City"— "pure gold, like unto clear glass?"—Not so! They would have chatted merrily, for at least one minute, about that grey-silk bonnet!

That evening there was present a little, pale, half-worn-out lady, whom I had never heard of—Mrs. Higley. Perhaps eighteen of these "Progressive Friends" (another name for Spiritualists), sat circling round the slightly darkened room, not holding hands, but all in sympathy. There passed before my vision (I think, as usual, my eyes were closed), a soldier in his uniform. Instead of looking at his face, my sight was fixed upon his hands. He held them out before him, curved as if to make a cup for drinking. He crossed to Mrs. Higley, stooped and laid upon her lap, a double-handful of whole hickory-nut meats! This I reported instantly. I do not know that I had heard her voice before; but now she said: "Yes, that is my son, Curtis. He was a soldier. He was starved at Andersonville." (Ah, these patient, patriot mothers!)

Then Mr. Hawley asked: "But what about the hickorynut meats?"

"Well, you see, we lived close to the woods in Michigan, and Curtis gathered nuts. We had barrels of them. I liked the old ones best; and Curtis, when a boy, would crack them out of doors until he had his double-handful of whole meats—he threw away the half-ones. Then he'd surprise me with them! He'd come in, just as he has this evening, and lay the double handful on my lap."

Curtis, the boy, did this: but not Curtis the soldier! Notice the difference. I did not see the loving boy—catching a glimpse of him through her! I saw the young man, in his uniform, who had died in

137

Andersonville! How could he better have suggested that he loved her still and would be glad to gratify her lightest wish?

"Such trivialities!" you mourn, "to come from spirits." Oh, yes! it might have been more wonderful to fall asleep before some hypnotist, he shuffling cards, selecting and inquiring: "What is this?"—You rightly answering: "The Jack of hearts!" But, by the way, the hypnotist himself would be a spirit; so would be you, the hypnotized! And yet you both would think your microscopic thoughts and solemnly reveal banalities! Why, even the ass could prophesy!—However, there's a difference.

Sometime in 1865, I think, being, as frequently, a guest of Mrs. Brown's, I gave her something finer.

There was no "circle," and, so far as I may know, her mind was dwelling on the common things of life, as mine was, I remember. Neither she nor Levi, who was present, had the slightest thought of hypnotizing me. I did not hypnotize myself;—and by the way, I do not think self hypnotism belongs to me or ever helped me to a Psychic fact! Even as a child I never "made believe;" and if I rocked rag-dolls they were not "babies"—they were calicoes, or "talloes" for an easier word. I made for me a crown of burdocks,—not to pretend I was a queen, but to be beautiful! (And how the scissors pulled and how the locks were yanked!)

Still further by the way, whoever is self-hypnotized? I have dwelt in Methodist camps and frequented "revival" meetings, where many prayed and sang and prayed again—some of them occasionally falling into trances. Ah, you knew they had a power upon them and a Pentecostal fire!—even though they gave no verbal testimony. Others just "made believe,"—did not deceive themselves nor anybody else. Try as they might, they could not fall asleep. If they shut their eyes, you could see their eyelids blinking or opening "on the sly." Sometimes (I hope but seldom), professional "mediums" also make believe!

I understand Hysteria very well. If it were in the moon, I'd know it—looking through a telescope. And catalepsy now: I have seen a cataleptic do the one thing over and over, in oblivion, that she was doing just before she went unconscious. Nobody called her self-hypnotized!

I know that one (incarnate or discarnate as you please), may Mesmerize another. I do not know (nor yet believe) that anyone may Mesmerize himself! That may be Psychic heresy. Perhaps the sun does move around the earth.

You speak of Fakirs—Yes, but they never make a farce of death, or sleep. They shut the eyes and shut the mouth and let themselves be buried decently. There is a law permitting life-suspension.

Among our human kind, cases of this deceptive sleep, more wonderful than death, are well attested. Some, learning this, have fabled that a frog may live, imbedded in the rocks, for many years, and, when released, may leap about again.

But mediums are neither frogs nor fakirs; and if they fall asleep, as though by hypnotism, I needs must think that spirits other than themselves have wrought such magic spells. But whether spirits in the flesh or out of it, the difference is not in principle, but in development. To rise from lower spheres to higher ones, is every medium's privilege. And hypnotizers that descend from heaven are much to be preferred to those who strike out from the lower plane.

What was I saying?—Well, I was not self hypnotized. My hostess and myself were sensibly conversing (likely as not about a bed-quilt pattern, I had just invented!), when suddenly I broke the thread of talk: "There stands a lovely girl within three feet of you! She is facing me, but turning and looking toward you, and smiling just a little. How she loves you!" In truth the tenderness of her regard was in itself a revelation! Do they love like that in Paradise? Sweetness and gentleness were with her—ladyhood and angelhood were all as one!

Impossible to describe; and yet description must be hazarded, or how could Lydia know? When she was gone I said: "She was not tall,—about your height I judge, or possibly my own. She was very handsome,—her forehead broad, her features all in harmony. There was no brilliant coloring; her face was calm and fair. You were lower down than she, and so her eyelids drooped a little. I did not see the color of her eyes, exactly, but they were large and soft and full of love. I judge that they were grey. Her hair was short and black, and very thick indeed. I never saw hair dressed like that before, although I think there was no other way to manage it. There were three rows of curls. The upper row began just at the parting on the top and overlapped the second row, which overlapped the third, making a mass of short thick curls all round her head. They were beautiful—they seemed to lend her dignity."

I did not tell her name; it was not given. I only added: "You have known her and you must have helped her; for she is full of gratitude."

"Yes," said Mrs. Brown, "she died of quick consumption several years ago. I went to see her often, and toward the last I stayed with her as much as possible. She was the sweetest girl I ever knew. Her name was Mary Henry."

The following day, without my being informed, "Willie" was sent away to get her picture. Mrs. Brown came rather carelessly, after his return, and handed me an open ambrotype-case. Imagine my delight! There I saw a triple crown of curls, a broad, sweet brow, a placid, gentle face, a tender, girlish dignity. All these I had seen—they showed the outward Mary Henry! A little hollowing of the cheeks (consumption being imminent), I had not seen. They had been rounded out—"there is no sickness there!" And super-added to the pictured loveliness, I had seen that which never could be seen by mortal eyes—the ineffable tenderness that proved her super-mortal! My super-mortal eyes, had looked in hers!

My share in this was greater than my friend's. She had but seen the living flesh and I had seen the living soul, in that celestial body that was like the natural one (enhanced in loveliness). I had seen the "dead"—alive again! And now I had the affirmation of the sun itself—ninety-three million miles removed—to demonstrate the fact! And I suppose the story of her visit was told by holy lips, in holy climes, among the happy folk who welcomed Mary back.

Behold, their ways are "ways of pleasantness" and all their "paths are peace!"

140

PSYCHO-PHYSICS AND PSYCHOMETRY

IN 1863, or thereabouts, Professor William Denton, Mrs. Denton, and Anna Denton Cridge, three scientific walking tourists, being much in need of rest, stopped at the Baldwin farm-house, not thirty miles from Buffalo, asking for entertainment. Charmed with their guests and greatly pleased to be instructed, their host and hostess urged them to remain as long as possible. Their book, "The Soul of Things," had recently been published, and their affairs permitted them to stay two months, I think, during which time they studied still that science they alone had fairly apprehended (one might say discovered)—the science of Psychometry.

Mr. and Mrs. Baldwin found me out about the first of June in 1865, and wanted me to teach their children music, making my home with them, and having for my study a lower room remote from noise and opening upon a pleasant grove. Verse-making racks the nerves, and city life upsets poetic moods; so such a chance for writing poems tranquilly was not to be refused. I was no lark, that I should carol on the wing. Theirs proved to be the house that I had found in one of those prophetic dreams, of which I have told you. Upon its elevated porch I had shouted "Victory!" then mourned: "There is a great disaster!" We have so many Psychic problems brought before us, that little puzzles similar to this, are scarcely worth considering.

I think these friends had not been told that I had, now and then, a Psychic vision or revealment; for it was understood among my intimates that others must not know. But Mr. Baldwin said almost at once: "You're a Psychometrist."

"Not that I know of," I replied: "What makes you think so?"

"When we were introduced, you gave me one deep look. You Psychometrized me. What did you find out?"

"Nothing at all. I only thought: 'That is a cruel man!' And now I see that you are full of kindness."

"Am I?" he questioned, ruefully: "I kicked a cow to death not long ago!"

141

Still he was kind; but oh, these underselves!—And notice how they interfere to make us harsh in judgment!

Psychometry lies next to obvious sciences, as ultra-violet lies next to visible colors. No mortal eye has actually seen that beauteous border of the rainbow; and yet it has been photographed. Denton divined a soul in rocks and shells, in fossils, nuggets, flies in amber—anything we call material; and his collaborating wife and sister saw, with Psychic eyes, the souls he had divined. He was in truth, the Psychophysicist—they the Psychometrists.

"I know not which is greater—no, not I."

The writer is aware that Psychometric facts which, in themselves, are indisputable, are subject to another and perhaps higher interpretation than that offered by Professor Denton, who first lifted them into recognition. Neither he nor his wife nor his sister had practical acquaintance with Spiritualistic phenomena at the time their book "The Soul of Things," appeared in print. It would not have been possible for them to refer the astonishing results obtained from their many Psychometric readings to the influence and inspiration of discarnate intelligences. As Dr. Buchanan's "sensitives" (who indeed had opened their way to discovery), readily perceived the nature of poisonous powders which they ignorantly held shut in their hands, by the sensations induced or the ideas conveyed thereby, so these pioneer Geologic-Psychometers naturally referred all their tremors, perceptions, visions, or thought-agitations to the article being Psychometrized.

Now since these various effects were evidently far greater than mere inert matter could be supposed to produce even by the most prolonged physical contact, these tireless investigators believed and proclaimed that a power or quality resides in every particle of matter—a certain sort of soul, which may be detected and clearly recognized by immortal souls or minds yet held in earthly environments.

This idea or belief is so nearly inconceivable that it will probably be repudiated by our ablest Psychists. And, in truth, one of those very "sensitives" which the President of the Cincinnati Medical

142

College discovered, seems to have indicated another source from which these so-called Psychometric impressions might be derived. For example: having been tested with human chirography instead of with life-destroying agents, he declared that the piece of writing which he held pressed against his forehead (in the manner adopted by later Psychometers), could have been executed by no man who had ever lived, save by Thomas Paine.

This specimen which (if I recollect aright), had been sent in under seal, proved to be, or rather purported to be, a vehement essay flung out by the spirit of Thomas Paine, through a "writing-medium."

Undoubtedly here is a vast field for exploration. Were Professor William Denton, his wife and sister correct in their interpretation of Psychometric facts? or must we refer them all to Psychic illuminations emanating from the spirit-world? But let it be always remembered that we, yet on earth, are also spirits possessed of all the inherent power of the highest archangel, and that we own all the faculties with which he is endowed! We are of the spirit-world; albeit so tethered to our little trees that when their foliage is browsed away, and we have grazed our circle of ground over, what is left to do?—unless indeed some visiting spirit may untie and lead us into fields of his own discovery? That is to say: He Psychometrizes us— not we ourselves; or he communicates and we but learn of him.

Let it be understood, that while the writer assumes the correctness of Professor Denton's explanation of Psychometric facts and applies it largely to those which lie within her personal experience, she is not putting herself forth as its discoverer, nor saying yet that any fact of them did not present itself to her entirely through the agency of disembodied spirits.

Does anyone remember (save myself), Dr. Buchanan's discovery of a differentiated, Psycho-physical magnetism? Not that he called it so, or called it anything, so far as I can recollect. Doubtless he had a name, if he had only mentioned it. Squire Shandy sent to have his son called "*Tris-megistus*," but the syllables got jumbled somehow, so the puzzled chaplain made it "Tristram" in the christening. Please pardon me for jumbling syllables, if I really must.

Buchanan's "Journal of Man," was meat and drink to me in 1855; and out of that I fish this rare philosophy—Psycho-magnetic, Psycho-electric... Oh, no matter! Christen it yourselves! Lo, here it is!

A powerful current circulates around the globe from pole to pole, electrifying positively or plus the masculine portion of humanity. A counter current flows from east to west, electrifying negatively or minus, the feminine portion of humanity. This theory, if correct, should have a thousand million proofs. Buchanan offered one; videlicet.

Suspend a slip of steel (scissors will do) by any common string some inches long. Be sure and hold the string yourself, and use the other hand to keep the one from wavering. Shove underneath a letter, or a lock of hair or shred of cloth—just anything you choose. Now if the article has been pervaded by a masculine aura—charged with masculine magnetism—the steel will vibrate, rock and feel its way, till—pendulum-like—you find it swinging North and South. If it has been pervaded by a feminine aura, your steel swings East and West. But mark the wonder of it! Lay two things together, one of the masculine influence, one of the feminine, your whirling steel will trace a pretty circle! Some of Buchanan's correspondents published articles confirming this, with evident delight. I may as well confess, I tested the device myself. It seemed as capable of self-propulsion as a ouija-board; but not so given to lying.

Maybe to get the best results you need to be a "sensitive," but sensitives are common—two men out of five, four women out of seven, I think, the college President said.

Whether this theory be demonstrable or otherwise, at least it partly falls in line with one indubitable truth. Because of our inherent spiritual life and inexhaustible energy, each one of us imparts a sort of soul to all the molecules within our "spheres of influence;" we pervade or charge them with our Psycho-physical magnetism, or whatsoever; we produce a force in them, which they continually discharge through "times and times and half-times;"— who can guess when all that borrowed force will be expended?

Let us discriminate: Spirit is Essence—one with Elohim the Ineffable. Soul is the instrument of spirit—an agent or transmitter—individual, personal, quick with intelligence! By means of soul, a spirit may impress itself on things—on molecules of things. They send back messages: Nothing is lost along the way. Because of this mysterious transmission, this eternal inter-play, no atom can exist without its modicum of soul. Spirit is self-existent;—soul is co-existent—eternally a servant, humbled yet how exalted!

But put aside pride of humanity: Have not all the beasts their "spheres of influence" also? Do they not impress themselves on matter? Perhaps the steel will swing because of them, even as because of us.

Nay! put the beasts aside and say that even molecules have tiny "spheres of influence." And now behold how Physicists flock in and prove the Psychists right. One radium particle will send out rays that travel many thousand miles a second. And, come to think of it, all atoms send out rays, and with terrific force at that. Why, now it is conceded that all the atoms in the universe are changing places, changing worlds or changing cosmic spheres; and, traveling so, they take their little souls along with them,—perhaps for some great summing up of infinite beneficence. If we impress ourselves on them unhappily, they turn again and rend us possibly;—at least, they pay us back a full equivalent. Let us beware of them.

People once believed there was a flying island; and many traveled far, hoping to catch a glimpse of it; but that aerial realm the Dentons found was not an Avalon,—it was a universe. Some idiot, (for the moment), blithely said their book was an "exhaustive treatise!" If they exhausted Psycho-physics and Psychometry so did Balboa—

"Silent upon a peak in Darien," exhaust the wide Pacific; so did Newton, letting a single ray into his darkened laboratory, exhaust the solar fires; so did St. John, who "saw a door opened in Heaven," exhaust all prophecy; and, turning back to atoms, so do we, who have our revelations (particles of light), exhaust supernal energy!

Do not think that, like Aurora Leigh, I "exaggerate a small thing with a great thing over-topping it." This Psychic realm (or is it super-physical), has many devious paths, but none approach an end. In sober truth, if a descending host from Heaven should visit there, not an archangel of them all could find a boundary. Are there not many universes—sphere enwrapping sphere, and each of infinite extent? Why not a Psycho-physical universe wherein Psychometrists may roam at will?

Minded, myself, to catch a glimpse of this miraculous realm, I took a sea-shell, polished for admiration, weighing an ounce or more, held it against my forehead, closed my outward eyes, and waited what might chance to come. I did not wait three seconds.

A headland thrust into the sea, two hundred feet in height, perhaps, stood up before my brain. It seemed the bulwark of a tropical island. This bluff or headland rounded out of sight upon my left. Its crest was green, but did not overhang with greenery; nor were there any trees in sight. One would long to climb, but could not, for the steepness of the cliff—which had no lodging place even for verdure.

Below the sea this headland shelved a little, outward and downward, making a shallow where the waves came rolling up in blue and silver ripples, outlined with crests of foam. All was radiance, yet nothing dazzled (no blazing noon can dazzle Psychometric eyes!). The scene was beautiful exceedingly, and did not disappear till I had seen its faintest line of loveliness, and noted how the waters danced in light and washed the glittering border of that impregnable rock.

My point of view was, seemingly, a hundred feet away therefrom, a vessel's height above the surface of the sea. Afterward I learned that first you see the recent; but continuing to look will take you further back. Atoms are like palimpsests; writing is superposed on writing, picture on picture, influence on influence.

Did I see a photograph imprinted on the shell as on a single surface? Or was every particle a surface, catching and holding fast the scene in its entirety? Either way, we seem to find that Nature has that perfect art none of our picturers have yet discovered—of photographing all the colors of the spectrum,—not by the slightest shade diminishing their splendor.

But again: How could a picture so minute, loom suddenly before my brain, full size, so that I said: "Here is a steep two hundred feet in height, and here a bordering sea—the waves are rolling in the sun?" Well, I suppose obliquity of incident rays, deciding angles of refraction, will account for that. ' I saw, not a mechanical picture, but the out-streaming light that, having made the picture, glanced away, with its diverging rays, to spread the whole before me,—great in size and wonderful for beauty.

A few hours afterward, I tried the shell again. There was the headland, there the sea, though I had somewhat changed my point of view; but all that lovely radiance had disappeared. The atmosphere was clear but grey. The verdure on the cliffs was hardly green. I noticed inequalities along the face that had not shown before. I thought: "That was the way it used to look, before the elements had made it smoother; may be a hundred years ago."

But now my mind was occupied by something underneath the waves; some small thing drifting very slowly in the undercurrent. I thought there might have been a heavy sea, in some late storm, that tore it from its place.

The water was not bright enough for perfect sight; I tried to see if it were not my shell, but failed; and so the vision passed.

By and by I took the pretty toy again. At once I saw the headland perfectly displayed in light, but there was change enough so that I said:—"This goes still further back in time." I was very near the rounded bluff upon the left, and suddenly I went down under water. There was such a shining sun that everything was visible, but only one thing fastened my attention,—a little mass of yellowish pulp. "It needs a house," I said: "It has to build itself a house; and will it take a century, I wonder?" For actual mind-influence, that softly palpitating nucleus, was more to me than cliff or sea or sun. I almost feared to be identified therewith. So I put down the shell in haste; and verily it was time! I could not lift my eyelids for at least a minute; they were far heavier than if I had been sleeping.

147

"The known facts of telepathy," one writes, "account for the phenomena of Psychometry." And this he illustrates quite in his usual happy, cock-sure way. "Draw a blank card from a package, hand it to a subject and suggest that it contains a picture of a person." "Nine times out of ten," the subject will perceive the picture. This perfectly explains the Dentons and "The Soul of Things." Being an "eminent geologist," Prof. Denton's mind was stored with pictures, which, by telepathy, he unconsciously transferred to his collaborators (otherwise hypnotic subjects).

This wiseacre says: "The explanation is exceptionally easy!" "Telepathy affords a perfect solution" There! Now you know!

You have all read "David Copperfield." Alas! Poor Mr. Dick! He wrote, and wrote and wrote! He would have been a great philosopher, but Charles the First had been beheaded and that gruesome head of his kept tumbling in among the sentences!—Just as telepathy tumbles about in this philosopher's books! Likewise that everlasting pack of cards!... Verily, after this manner, one could solve all mysteries of earth and hell and Heaven, with just a—euchre deck!

Peradventure, when I was moved to test Psychometry, Professor Denton was a long way off, King Charles had left his head in England, and my head was in America! Everybody on the farm was picking berries, probably, and I was all alone. I think we'll let telepathy go by.

"Do you know anything about this lovely shell?" I asked my host that evening. "I have Psychometrized it three times over."

"Nothing certain. I bought it for a tropical shell. What did you see?"

When I had told him he remarked: "I kept the Denton ladies well supplied with specimens, and I was present at the readings. They always told correctly, but they never told so much."

I suppose their words were not so many, but they saw more deeply. They discerned, at times, the forces that produced the specimen. I chiefly apprehended later influences. They were geologists and thought of primal happenings. I was a Spiritualist who dreamed of ultimates. One must allow for mental bias. Certainly, as scientists, they were far away beyond me. Still I had one advantage. When they began their tests, they had not known themselves for Psychics. When I began, twelve years of preparation lay behind me. I had been virtually trained in mediumship,—which I must think a higher state than Psychometric trance.

Naturally I was keen to make some further tests. So very soon when everyone was gone from home, except my pupils (seventeen and fifteen years of age), I said to them: "Let's have a real good time! Go hunt me up a specimen that you know about. Don't let me see it; don't say a word about it. Don't get it from the parlor table; bring it from somewhere out of all my sight and knowledge."

When they returned, bubbling with laughter, I commanded: "Victor, stand behind my chair and hold your specimen against my forehead. I refuse to touch it. Linda don't look at me! Both of you stop laughing. You mustn't speak or make a bit of noise. If I should see, I'll talk; I'll tell you everything that comes to me, foolish or wise;"—and I began almost immediately. This is virtually what I said:—

"I am in the woods. I am close beside a waterfall. I am standing by the upper verge. The stream is four feet wide, I judge; and, looking down, I think the little gorge is eight or ten feet deep. What a charming fall! How clear the water is!

"I am drawn away. I am going South; now I am hurrying West: Everything is wild—uncultivated! Just as it was before the white men settled here.

"I have reached the Mississippi. I am going down the river, only I am up in air. I look across over the tops of trees. Here and there, through openings on the left, I am seeing wandering Indians. There are some huts in sight; three or four Indians have come out of them and are straying off toward the North. I want to see those huts more clearly.

They are curiously constructed. But I am going very fast indeed! What great trees on either side! Something pulls me from the river. I am going into Texas.

"I am in a great, primeval forest. Here is a stream of silvery water, not more than twelve feet wide. Here is a waterfall. I stand upon the southern side, it seems, near to the verge. I look below. There is a fall of fifteen feet or so; the banks on either side nearby, are steep.

"I see an Indian girl down in the bed below. She is kneeling in the shallow water. She is prying something up. It seems to be hard work.

"No wonder! She is prying out a piece of flint. She throws it down upon a little pile the other side of her. She goes to work to pry another out. The streamlet's bed is altogether flint. Under the water, either way, there is nothing to be seen but flint.

"Across the water-fall from where I stand, I see an Indian coming. There seems to be a path made through the woods. There must be an Indian village out of sight. He comes close to the edge. I see him very plainly. He is young, but how he scowls! His face is most forbidding.

"Now he looks down and sees the Indian girl. She is looking up; she laughs. He keeps on scowling all the same,—really he looks ferocious!

"She catches up a piece of flint and throws it at him. It doesn't hit. She throws one piece after another. He only looks and scowls.

"Now she goes to work again. She pays no more attention to him. She keeps her head down, to make believe she has forgotten him.

"She begins to sing: I know her thoughts and I can understand her song, as well as though I knew her words.

"'No one cares for me. I am not wanted anywhere. Why should I stay where no one cares? I will go a long way off, toward the North. No one will know where I have gone. No one will miss me. I shall walk for many moons. I have heard of mountains that are very high. The snow is on them and it never melts. I will find a mountain. I will

150

climb; I will lie down in the snow. Then I shall die. No one will ever look for me. No one will care.'

"There! That is better. The Indian doesn't scowl; he almost smiles. He is not bad looking, after all. He leaps down. That is a long leap, but he thinks nothing of it. He comes and stands close by the girl. She won't look up. She goes on prying out a piece of flint. He looks down pleasantly.

"And now I see an old, old squaw—terribly old! I should think she might have lived a hundred and fifty years; and yet she walks alone and sees her way. She is coming along the path toward the waterfall. I think she is looking for the girl. She has the care of her, no doubt. She comes and stands just where the Indian stood. Now she is looking down. I wonder what she will say."

Just here Victor and Linda burst out laughing uncontrollably. The chaperone tickled them. "I see that I have made myself ridiculous," I said, "Take away that specimen. Give it to me! When my eyes are open I'll see just how ridiculous I have been."

Victor laid it in my hand. It was a large, flint arrowhead. I asked: "Where did you get it?"

"Linda picked it up, but I had seen it first. We were in the woods, close to the water-fall that you described at first."

"Was my description accurate?"

"Perfectly so."

"Where are the woods? I've never heard of any waterfall in Collins."

"Three or four miles away. People don't go there much."

To see so much and have so little confirmation!......Well, there was something further: About a year thereafter, I chanced to read a paragraph (going the rounds) to this effect:—"The question has been often asked and never answered: Where did the Indians get their arrow-heads?

At last the puzzle has been solved. Long streams have been discovered in the Texas forests, whose beds are solid flint. No doubt the Indian tribes, in their vicinity, were skilled in fashioning arrow-heads. It is believed they sent canoes far up the Mississippi and its tributaries to barter them for wampum. These arrow-heads could easily have been distributed further along the water-courses, so that any Indian, even at

See Appendix V. the seashore, might procure as many as he wanted. This seems to be a case of actual monopoly. Those Texas tribes must have been rich in wampum!"

Well, certainly there was the Alleghany River, rounding up not forty miles from where this arrow-head was found; but after all, somebody in the world had seen those Texas streams! So by telepathy........you see!... The explanation is "exceptionally easy!"...Still one "wants to know, you know!"

So we'll suppose that little cataract, first observed, was photographed upon the flint. There seems a little difficulty about the focus. I saw things up and down and roundabout. Still nature might not mind a little thing like that! Suppose we say telepathy, for once. The picture caught by Linda's brain or Victor's, was registered on mine. But why not see, instead, a later picture? Victor's bed-room for example, where the flint had lain upon a shelf, a year or so.

Furthermore, what drew me swiftly from the place they knew, to places they had never seen? What took me back in time through centuries of savagery? What mighty influence pulled me through the air above the Mississippi—turning me to Texas, and dropped me down, deep in the woods, beside that flint-paved stream? How was it that I saw three human beings, each one acting out consistently an individual life? And how about that pretty, girlish play, of tossing things that never hit? And that incomparable love-song—sweet as frozen nectar! One could swear it never came from out my dry-as-dust romanticism! Also its effect: To change a most ferocious face, to smooth away the savage frown, and make a smile seem possible.

Phantasms? Illusions? Pathematic symptoms? Brain created shams?

Percival Lowell, the Astronomer (and who today is more colossal?), perceives and states (howbeit rather whimsically), a simple Psychic truth, not more to be disputed than a mathematical law:

"An illusion could no more exhibit intrinsic change than a ghost could eat dinner without endangering his constitution. The mere fact that it is an illusion or optical product, renders it incapable of spontaneous variation."

But now you turn around and say: "That was self-hypnotism, which you repudiate!" Pardon me; I was in no sense hypnotized. I closed my outer eyes, having the gift of inner vision. I did not lock the door on any faculty. I was alert. I felt the flint upon my forehead,—was aware of every movement round me; I talked out what was in my mind as normally as you, who speak of bread-and-butter, picture-hats or fluctuations on the Stock Exchange.

Victor and Linda urged me: "Try the specimen once more." Doing so, a few hours afterward, I saw an Indian stealing through the woods, looking behind him warily. He was sorely wounded; blood was running from his side:—The arrow-head, perchance, had found its destined victim. ....I would not look again.

PSYCHOMETRY AND SPIRIT-INFLUENCE

PSYCHISTS, I cry you mercy. I am told that many of you "do not know Psychometry;" or rather that it lies unnamed, among your other gatherings not yet assorted out. Hence, I suppose, no Scientist would say or think at all, that every common happening records itself upon adjacent that human personality impresses its tremendous self upon a physical universe after its finite way,—as God, the Infinite, impresses all, Who is the Soul of all.

And yet, should that be true (all atoms being traced and over-traced with records of the past) there ought to be a Psychometric sense, enabling us to read;—an under faculty I grant, most imbecile to God's futurity, blind, deaf and unintelligent to all that is, but not to all that was. If one, as Thalaba, were "in the desert far from men," a pebble taken in the hand or pressed above the eyes might, through this under-faculty, inform the mind of what had fashioned it, what seas had worn it smooth, what heats had made its particles revolve— each one a mimic sun, and through what interchanges it had come to have a sort of soul, as Denton claims, and as I verily am prone to think.

But say it be not so: Say that I group my facts (indubitable facts!) about some meteor, dropped what time a blazing bolide burst in air, and make of that poor stone an altar to the gods that never were and are not meant to be! Why, laugh at will, my facts remain; deal with them how you please. Let the dead bolide rest, half-burned away, and take your cakes and oil to other shrines, less heathenish perchance.

And yet I pray you, do not misconceive nor minimize that which discoverers named "Psychometry." Give it what name you will, O, Scientist! "of learned length and thundering sound"—as "Rosa Rubiginosa," "Damascena," "Eglanteria;"—but let me pluck my rose.

Explain the Psychometric sense? Not I! And yet—Telepathy nor Hypnotism, nor both of them combined, account for it, more than uncertain whispers in the dark account for Milton's verse. But this is true: It stands Interpreter between the physical universe and souls that dwell therein, or have escaped therefrom. Perhaps—nay certainly!—discarnate spirits bring to us "indubitable facts;" but we are spirits, too, and may perceive those facts or kindred ones, without their aid. We, of the lower rank, are not detachable. We, too, belong to all the universes:—let us say the Physical, the Psychophysical, the Psychic, the Essential.

Each universe is infinitely great, and we are hardly more than infinitely small. That makes no vital difference; we have our share in all. We do not live on sufferance; we are necessary; nothing can get along without us. If it were possible for even one of us to be expunged—nay, for one physical atom to be so destroyed, where then would be infinity? An end to one least particle would prophesy, unerringly, the ultimate fate of all. Would God remain?

We seem to have achieved a certain greatness (after all we are very great!) because of having taken part in cosmic revolutions. We have from first to last, let us suppose, consorted with or battled with the very "souls of things." And are we not endowing molecules this very minute with the souls of us? If so, why should not they endow us in return?—so putting us in true possession, far as may be possible, of little secrets worthy to be spoken of throughout eternity: These, if they be at all, are Psycho-physical secrets—Psychometric mysteries—facts in any case.

Come, let us deal with facts!

Mrs. Denton, speaking Psychometrically, said, in effect:—"I see a lake of fire under the crust of earth." There is no lake of fire, but once there was. Her lesser seeings had been justified,—why not the greater? I must believe she saw—not looking downward through the solid rocks, but looking backward through the innumerable years, a new and partly molten world. "Not possible!" you asseverate? You do not know the claritude of Psycho-physical atmospheres, nor faintly guess the penetrating power of Psychometric eyes. I do suppose that, in the Psychic realm, when we are overweighed with light, we may, at any time, turn back and rest us in the luminous dimness of these underspheres—the Physical and Psycho-physical;— being glad to know and understand them better, because of long advancement through the spheres.

Frankie Marvin, dear and sweet, who never had been angry in her life, came visibly to me some ten days after she had passed away. In that last sickness she had been given some actual help through me. I think, because of that, she wished to let me know that all was well with her. She faintly smiled, uttered four words, then, with an upward movement, disappeared. "It is too sunny!" That was all; but oh, how dim it made the noon-tide seem!

Frankie had lived among the half-lights;—little wonder if the glory dazzled! Yes, we must have the shadows! Who shall say that even seraphs need not veil their eyes?

"Why do not spirits come to us more frequently?" Perhaps we could not bear it. Too much sun is wrong for tender plants. We need the darkness and the dew full half the time; and, for the other half, we hang our heads too much. Alas! We are none of us Helen Kellers,—having "sensibilities" so spirit-like they more than take the place of faculties.

Still, deprive yourself of outward vision, now and then, and see what comes of it!

Once I, myself, looked back, with Psychometric eyes, just a few thousand years,—any geologist might guess how far. I was very ignorant of Geology. I knew blue clay from marble, shale from quartz, and, seeing two specimens of rock, could tell which was the prettier; but I had never entered a museum, nor seen a re-constructed, pre-historic skeleton. If I had hypnotized myself in verity, and tried to cover up the bones of such a one with "too, too solid flesh," I should have made queer work of it.

Lewis Baldwin borrowed for me—himself in utter ignorance of its history—what the possessor thought a fossil bone; a fragment nearly half a foot in length. This young geologist was, in some degree, adept in judging specimens. I have said that Psychic visions cannot be obliterated; neither can the Psychometric. What you are made aware of, after this manner, is like a well-hung picture in a lighted gallery;—enter the door and when you look that way, you see the picture. I held the fossil bone against my forehead and this is virtually what I said:—

156

"Here is a deep and narrow gorge, I think among the Alleghany mountains;—I am almost sure of it. I stand below and look up, probably two hundred feet," it may be more. The sides are perpendicular. I see no place for climbing out. Here is the specimen, at the foot, close to the wall. I see the little hollow where it was embedded before some freshet washed it out. Another freshet, very likely, might have carried it away.

"Now, I am on the top. I see the gorge by looking down. I am standing near the edge. Here is a grassy level, very green. Here is a large boulder lying on it—almost uniform in shape but somewhat rough. It must be five feet high and five or six feet through. The sun is very bright. I wish I could see the landscape better, but the boulder interferes. It disappears, then comes right back again......... This is the fourth time I have seen that boulder! I am getting tired of it. It glitters here and there and gets before my eyes.

"What a singular sensation! I am in a void; I am sinking!—I am sinking very fast!—I keep on sinking—sinking! It is light, but I am seeing nothing, save the luminous space.

"I have found a watery plain. Once it was covered with the sea or some large lake, I fancy. It has been nearly drained, or lifted up above the water. This is what used to be thousands of years ago. I cannot even guess how many. Here is an animal standing knee-deep in the water. His head is down; he is evidently feeding. There are places that are full of weeds, and other places where the water lies in pools on beds that glitter. Either the sea once covered them and left small shells, or those I see belong to small freshwater shell-fish. Surely this creature cannot be eating shellfish, though he pokes about. He stands somewhat behind a clump of weeds; I cannot see his head entirely. Now I see! He feeds on weeds and grasses. He has tusks and a short trunk—much shorter than an elephant's trunk. He turns his head this way and that. He rakes in the long stems with his tusks and then gets hold of them with his trunk and pulls them out.

"His back is somewhat arched and slopes considerably toward the tail. Not a bison's hump exactly, yet if he had no trunk or tusks, I should think him like a bison. He is brown or leather color, but there are lighter spots that might be white if they were not so dirty. His

157

hair is very coarse, and thicker on the arch than lower down. He is not a terrible creature evidently, and not so very large! I have seen elephants that were larger. I should say he was just about the size of a big buffalo."

And then—as mother used to end her stories when we teased for more—"Just then I came away."

The gentleman who owned the fossil, getting this report, replied:— "I found it in the bed of a steep and narrow gorge, about two hundred feet in depth, among the Cumberland mountains. It was lying loose close to the wall from which it had been torn out probably by torrents. Some distance further down, I climbed up to the top. There was a green and level sward, on which a boulder lay, near to the edge. It was fully five feet high and five or six feet in diameter. I laid the fossil down beside it in a blazing sun, and chipped off specimens for half a day."

Four times I saw that picture of the boulder, manifestly printed on the fossil by photography, or radiography or what you choose to call it. It was an actual picture. How could I have seen it otherwise? Scientists who shut away the visible rays and conjure with the invisible, bring out similitudes that even outward eyes can recognize. Why not copy for us these that exist already? In that case we could see the pictures with our physical as well as with our Psychometric eyes. Here is a field that, by and by, may yield tremendous harvests.

As to the mastadons, they lived at any time it seems, from twenty thousand years ago, till almost recently. They frequented the swamps and watery places, where they fed on succulent weeds and where they were often mired and "perished miserably."

Their bones are found from Canada to Mexico. There are quantities at Big Bone Lick, Kentucky, not two hundred miles away from where my mastodon was buried. It must have taken Nature several thousand years to build him that Mausoleum.

Now will you please to note one point: Those human beings— Indians—whom, in the previous chapter, I took you back to see, were wraiths, no doubt, but they were genuine. They were not illusions. There is no pretense that they were spirits, or the souls of spirits or even the underselves of souls. Not one of them so much as looked at me—as actual spirits will. They were not physical realities: They were and are today and will be, I suppose forever, Psycho-physical facts. They are pictographs and registrations, aural influences and cosmic records,—proofs that God remembers!

And what became of that poor mastodon's modicum of soul, when the strong body sank in mire, to be entombed at last beneath the Cumberland Hills? Nothing will live eternally, which cannot grow eternally; but even a mastodon does not fulfil himself by going under "sooner than he would."

I have a mind to show again my marvelous littleness. During one of my happy visits at the Bundy farmhouse, I said at breakfast: "If I believed the way John Wesley did, that animals live hereafter, I should say I saw, last night, the spirit of a dog. I had just blown out my candle and laid down, when one of the largest dogs I ever saw, appeared and walked along before me, looking at me attentively. He stopped, turned round three times, so that I saw the whole of him, then sat down on his haunches and looked me steadily in the eyes with wonderful friendliness."

"What was his color?" Mr. Bundy asked.

"Quite dark but there were several clean white spots,—the small ones on the left side, but a very large one covered the right shoulder blade. It had two arms or prongs, one reaching forward toward the neck, one stretching up and back—considerably longer. He looked at me, as though he loved me."

"No doubt he did," said Mr. Bundy. He was no sentimentalist, but really his eyes were filled with tears. "That was our old dog. That white spot proves it, even if you had not described him otherwise. He was the largest dog I ever saw—the friendliest and the most intelligent. There was just one man he didn't like—a rather hypocritical man, but nothing worse. I would be far more glad to see that dog in spirit-life than to see many mortals I have known!"

I cannot quite let go Psychometry as yet; the less because the Psychometric insight is almost universal, whether recognized or not.

Helen Keller says:—"There are people who are color-blind, people who are tone-deaf. We should not condemn a musical composition on the testimony of an ear which cannot distinguish one chord from another, or judge a picture by the verdict of a color-blind critic."

Even so, though you may seem to lack this special gift, conceive that you are not authority, but do not doubt the faculty. I had to slip it under and forget about it, because a sharp pain in the forehead warned me that I could not work my brain that way and still keep writing verse—a proof that my own mind and not another's scrutinized the specimen. Revelation does not weary—study does.

Meantime, during one of my home visits—which were rather frequent—it chanced one of "The Nameless Club" (of which I had the happiness to be an honorary member), met me on the street, and told the others. So, being lavish of their courtesies, a goodly number—seven or eight—came down that evening to my mother's home, to do me special grace. All of these were notable. A few are living yet, who are noted men, because of noted work.

Not to talk poetry all the time, I said to them: "Gentlemen: there is a new Science—The Science of Psychometry." Only one of them had heard of it. They were not given to Psychic studies. I had withheld my personal experiences, not from cowardice but from a sense of incongruity.

Mr. Larned (the historian) challenged me: "You say you have the gift to some extent. Will you let us select a specimen, and will you venture to report without the slightest knowledge of its nature?"

I truly said that I would very gladly make the trial. Mr. Bryant (lawyer and city alderman) having been deputized, sent me next day, by special messenger, a little piece of battered brick—evidently very old. Nothing could have been more lacking in suggestion or, it proved, more puzzling as a test. No one but himself among the club had any knowledge of its history. I gave it several "readings," wrote them down in order and sent them, sealed, with the proviso: If the brick had come from any ruins of a fort by a large lake, or lengthened inlet from the sea, the document must be submitted to the Club:—otherwise burned and counted as a failure.

My keen and intellectual friends did not gainsay results, though there were doubtful points—some of them which were afterward made clear, while nothing was reported back to me as manifestly wrong. The document was not returned to me, but I suppose I used the following words with no material variation. In making several tests, I found my point of outlook little changed. These were the pictures and impressions:—such of them at least as float up in mind, forty-five years after the test was made.

I. "Here is a large lake, beautifully clear. Beside the shore a girl is standing and looking at a pleasure boat some little distance out—a sail boat large enough to carry several sails. She is a handsome girl, dressed in the latest style. I think this is a fashionable watering place."

II. "Here are the ruins of a fort. They are old. I see foundation walls of brick. They are built double, with quite a space between. The space is filled with stones and sand and gravel,—anything, it seems, that happened to be handy. Here is a large piece of fallen timber—a beam that had been used in building. It seems to have been thrown out, some way. It is broken and decayed, but very long."

III. "Looking up the lake upon the left, there are rolling hills. The scenery is very beautiful. Looking far ahead, I do not see the shore. Possibly this is an inlet or long arm of the sea; but I feel quite sure it is a lake."

IV. "I see some seven horsemen cantering up. They are dressed in uniform; they are a body-guard, apparently. General Washington is riding in the center. He cannot be mistaken. He is majestic."

V. "I see what may have happened earlier. Here is a weather-beaten vessel coming toward this end of the lake. It is drifting along slowly. It is a small vessel, but perhaps large for the time. It comes up to a landing on the right some distance off. It is made fast, or planks are laid. A lady is brought out on deck. She is seated in an arm-chair—something like a throne. Four men have taken up the chair. They are carrying it on their shoulders. The lady is richly dressed; she is being treated with the greatest reverence, as though

161

she were a queen. They are carrying her on shore. They are dressed in queer, old-fashioned clothes."

VI. "Now, I am in the fort. It is not yet destroyed; but there is fighting going on. I see nothing outside, and but little inside. I only see two guns. They are pointed toward the lake and one man has the charge of them. He manages them both. He is the spryest man I ever saw. He springs up to where he can look out; he leaps about; he sights the guns and fires. His energy is inexhaustible! Others may do their part, but he pays them no attention. He is all absorbed in fighting. He is dressed in corduroy clothes. I notice that the blouse is yoked along the shoulders, after an old

English fashion I have seen. He stops, he disappears—the fighting must be over."

VII. "Something terrible is happening. This is not fighting. Everywhere around, outside and in, there is terror. The air is full of it. It beats in like a wave. Every atom of this piece of brick is pulsing with it. I will not try to find out what it means. It is too horrible. I will never try this specimen again, I think; I cannot bear it."

In truth my nerves were shaken when I laid the brick aside. I trembled, not with fear, but as though in poignant sympathy with fear. Afterward, I handed the brick to Mrs. Dr. Marvin, who could see nothing only that it had crossed the sea. I tried it for a minute and felt that she was right. It had the influence of the sea about it. With that I ended my investigation.

This piece of brick was from the ruins of Fort William Henry on Lake George. It had been made in Holland. Mr. Bryant had himself removed it from the double walls I had described, while on his wedding tour a few weeks earlier. "Your description of the ruins," so he wrote, "was absolutely startling in its fidelity."

I suppose no tongue could ever tell the horrors of the massacre outside and in the fort after capitulation! But if all dreadful deeds are so recorded on every tiny atom within their scope, how will the guilty clamor for redemption! Have you read Gerald Massey's "Tale of Eternity?" Not a fancy sketch, but, as I chance to know, the record of an actual experience! It will show you how a spirit may be

162

compelled to stay below and look and keep on looking at the murderous act! That will be hell, in truth!—Till by and bye, the innocent rise up, confront the murderers, one by one, and seal their pardon with a holy kiss. So God enfolds them all.

You ask'(and very pertinently), did I never fail? Once only it was thought I failed, and lamentably at that! Mr. Bryant sent a broken piece of exquisite china-ware. I said the Pope had blessed it. I said the priests had handled it. I tried it several times and always saw a priest or two, bowing and genuflecting and lifting up the Host, or so it seemed. I said, further than that; it had been used in mummery—just mummery.

It had been dug up on the site of an old Jesuit Mission Station. Mr. Bryant, himself a member by adoption of a tribe not far from Buffalo, expected me, and wanted me, to see a lot of Indians. I didn't even see one—little—red—pappoose!

Mother said:—"Before you drop these tests, examine one small specimen for me; and brought it—wrapped in tissue paper.

"Mother, here is a long slope facing West and ending near the sea. It is not California; it is a foreign country. It is Japan. I feel its influence. There are no trees in sight, but any quantity of shrubs. Women and children are roaming round. They are picking leaves? This is tea!"

Mother laughed: "Uncolored Japan tea."

During that summer (1865), something momentous came to me. Just then it seemed a lovely incident—no more. In fact it placed me definitely under spirit-guardianship—not governance, but most beneficent supervision. I had been, I fear, a little insolent: "There must be no dictation, no imperative influence, no absolute control! Let others talk of spirit-guides; I am not guided, I am just befriended!"

There has been no tyranny on that side, no demand on this; but, since that summer of 1865, I have been a willing instrument. Otherwise I had not lived on earth these many years!

That old affliction, inflammation of the nerves, had pounced upon me as a tiger. I was a transient guest of Mrs. Brown's. Some other-where a wrong was being done to a sorry woman whom I, alone, was powerless to assist; and I had sent my friends away to set the matter right; so I was left in solitude. I sorrowed: "How Lydia will be troubled with me! This may last a long, long time, as once before. I see no remedy."

"Won't you come and help my sick sister?"

I turned and there was Porter, holding by the arm and leading in, a man but dimly seen. Our lovely boy—only last year a soldier! had brought to me an able spirit-doctor. Not for a moment did it occur to me that I should be relieved. I only thought: "How Porter loves me! How he always loved me!"

Mrs. Brown, but just returned, came hurrying in: "Can you get up and hear the story?" "I cannot even lift my head,"—and I forgot—I really forgot, my sweet experience! Very soon, as in a dream, I lifted up my head, arose and dressed. In torment still, I reached the open door. Mrs. Brown cried out: "Don't try to walk! I'll bring the rocking chair," and drew me to the dining-room. "Now talk!" I urged, "and tell me everything!"

She talked a full half hour—watching me furtively. I cried out suddenly, all amazed: "There is not a pain about me! Except for weakness, I am absolutely well."

She laughed: "I saw a change come over you. I knew the very minute you were helped!"—She knew a lot, did Mrs. Levi Brown!

When I claim the Psychometric state as ours—not "due to spirit influence" I do not mean that spirits may not use the faculty in us, as I admit they use our other faculties. One comes—heart full of love—and says: "I must be recognized." But should the spirit wear his new apparel, (mantle, toga, coronation-robe, or otherwise!), and you describe him so, his friends would shake their heads: "He always wore frock-coats, felt hats, black neck-ties"—and the like. And so the spirit catches up some picture of himself, dressed just that way, and lo, you! there's your friend! The Psychometric picture-book is always close at hand! Meanwhile he isn't cheating you. He says: "This is the way I used to look. I have changed since then!"

Ah, changed!—Did I not see Babe Mary—not in her olden garb, but all "transfigured," "shining," "exceeding white as snow?" Even as I have written heretofore:—

How sure is the peace of the undefiled!

As all my sins were a sealed book She looked on me as the seraphs look;

But the face where-through her spirit smiled, was the dimpled face of an earth-born child.

Just where to draw the line between the Psychic and the Psychometric, who can tell? Perhaps this final Psychometric story may reveal a blended state, or rather a suggestion of the soul that mediates and dwells between the two.

A gentleman whom I may designate, by actual title, as "The Squire," became enamored of "The Soul of Things." As a much greater man averred about telepathy, this other cock-sure gentleman declared about Psychometry: "All the phenomena of Spiritism can be explained thereby!" Between "The Squire," whom I had never seen, and Dr. Marvin, whom I knew (and heartily esteemed) there was a friendly feud.

"Bring me a good Psychometrist," the "Squire" exhorted, "Let me prove my case." "You'll prove the opposite!" Dr. Marvin vowed.

Now Lewis Baldwin was not over reticent about my Psychometric tests. Without my knowledge he reported them to Dr. Marvin, with a flourish!

I was flattered with an invitation from the Marvins to a New Year's dinner,—the more because, in ignorance of my whereabouts, messengers were sent out right and left to several families, all of whom were charged to find and bring me in. It was a case of "catch your hare, then cook him!" I was amazed and angry to be told at once: "We wanted you to give us Psychometric readings, for an important reason." I was in trouble with neuralgia and felt unequal even to common talk. After long resistance, I capitulated. "I'll try one specimen and only one, provided no one in the room knows anything about it and someone can be found and brought in afterward, to prove or disprove what I may have said."

I didn't like the "Squire." He rather boasted his Mesmeric powers at dinner. That made me take a "scunner."

Afterward the good folk sat awaiting. There was a specimen concealed in Mrs. Marvin's hand. "Turn the lights down low and hold it on my forehead," I commanded,—and straightway forged ahead.

"Here is a mountain top,—a little plat of green, bordered on one side by a bluff, some ten feet higher. There is a fine dry atmosphere, with vivid light. This is a state far West,—not touching the Pacific. I look across toward the West, and see a long clear lake some fifty miles away.

Looking down the mountain, I see a shaft, cut through in search of ore. Men are climbing up, and men are going down. Silver has been found in paying quantities. I see no mining works, nor any railroad. Everything is being done by hand. The men who are going down are carrying sacks slung on their shoulders, weighed with samples they are going to crush, down by a stream. I see this little specimen. It is silver ore. There is nothing more to tell." After this a gentleman was brought in and introduced as Dr. Marvin's patient. He testified—not knowing what I had said: "This is a piece of silver ore picked up by me upon the top of a mountain out in Idaho. Silver had just been found and men were flocking there to locate claims." Being interrogated, he described the plat of grass, the little bluff, the sunken shaft, the men with sacks. He had not seen the lake but knew there was one fifty miles away—not sure about the name. (The Coeur d'Alene, most likely.)

The "Squire," believing that the "hare" was caught, proposed himself to superintend the cooking. He had scarcely noticed me at dinner, very likely thinking I was some "fake medium." Now he asked:

"Have you tested writing by Psychometry?"

166

"No; and I never mean to! I hate the study of character. It is too demoralizing."

"I have a piece of writing for you."

"I must decline to try it. I have no such gift."

"I will lay it on your lap"—and did so in a lordly way. (Alas! Poor Mrs. "Squire!")

There was a dead silence. All the lights turned low, a roomful, mostly friends, waiting in expectation. Stifling my wrath I turned to Mrs. Manley, who was visiting me that week, and said: "Give me your hand. I want your magnetism."

Then to the "Squire:" "You will take the consequences. I have no power in this direction that I know of. Every foolish thing that I can conjure up, I'll tell you."

But under Mrs. Manley's calming spell, temper subsided. Never, at any time, had I so lost myself in visioning, as then after the first hot minute. Yet all the time I talked.

"I see part of a boat—the stern, close to a wharf."

"Iam seeing absolutely nothing. I am in a vacant space. I am going away from earth. I am going very fast and very far. I am near the planet Saturn. There are spirits here in space. They are moving about and signaling to each other. It seems they walk on nothing. They walk on space. These spirits look alike. They are all blonds. I should think they were all related.

"I was mistaken. They do not walk on nothing. They walk on spirit-landscapes. Everything looks blank before them and behind them, but for a little way around each one, I see what he is walking on. One is by a stream; another in a field.

"Perhaps they think the scenery, and so create it just by thinking. Maybe they think of scenes they used to know, and re-produce them so that they are real again. Or else the space is filled with spirit-landscapes of itself. That seems more reasonable; for now I see them everywhere.

"These spirits lived some time ago,—during our Revolutionary War. Some of them, I see, are Quakers.

"One Quaker lady dressed in soft gray silk is coming toward me. She sees me and she smiles—she even laughs. She makes me understand that she was noted as a good housekeeper. She takes a broom and makes pretence of sweeping. She stops and looks at me intently. She shakes her head; she is pointing downward.

"I am coming back; I am sinking very fast. Almost half the sky is hidden by the moon,—I see how rough it is. I only caught one glimpse.

"I am near the earth. Here is a bank of cloud. There is a young man walking on it with his head down—lost in thought. He is a thinker, but he doesn't think profoundly—he thinks abstractly. He tries to think out something;—how to make wrong things right; but he can't think of anything. He keeps his hands behind him, and he stoops a little. He is all absorbed in self. I do not see his face, and yet I know that he is young.

"A little way behind, and following him, there is an older man, who looks at him intently and almost hopelessly. He is the young man's father. He wants to get his son's attention, but he plods on patiently and won't intrude. He is a good man. He doesn't walk easily but he has no stoop, and he doesn't hang his head. He has sharp features, and a long sharp nose. He is not a blonde exactly, though very near it. His hair is light brown—not much gray, if any. I am very sorry for him. He wants to help his son, and yet can get no nearer. Something repels him.

"I am on the earth. Here is an emigrant train. Here is the young man whom I saw upon the bank of cloud. He is walking wearily beside the wagons. His back is turned,—I cannot see his face, but he is just the same. He walks on thinking—thinking; but the thinking does no good. It is not deep at all; it is all about himself.

"I am near a house. There are other houses—all of them are lately built. There is some peculiarity about their roofs,—I can't describe exactly. This is the house that I must enter. I go in at the front door, and climb the stairs. I turn into the nearest room—not a front room.

Here is that young man, lying on a sort of home-made lounge. And now I see his face distinctly. If he were old, he would look almost exactly like his father. He has the same sharp features, rather toned down, and the same light brown hair. He is young but he is dying of consumption. Nothing can save him. He hasn't long to live. He is in the last stage of the disease.

"A young girl sits beside him, sewing. She is rather curiously dressed,—in black, the neck half low. She attracts me, she is kind and gentle.

"The young man is dead. I am standing in a graveyard, though I see no grave but his. I am standing at the foot. There is a whitewashed head-board. If I could go around, I could read the name. It is useless—I can't stir; yet how I want to read that name!"

I ended. All of me was perfectly awake except my eyes. It seemed they never would unclose!

But presently the "Squire" was very flattering; he stood up straight before me, slender, tall and blonde, and told me many things about Psychometry;—for now, at last, he had met a real Psychometrist, and so was qualified to teach.

I thought: "You think abstractly, but you do not think profoundly." Then I discovered: "He looks like all those spirits whom I saw near Saturn."

But he was interrupted: "Are you not going to tell us what the writing was about. We think we ought to know." He hedged at first; but then he had a brother present, and a wife. They went the length and told us all there was to tell, whether or no! as soon as they were told by him what he had given me, for that they had not known.

His family had lived in Albany. James was his youngest brother. At twenty-three James had a wife and children. Then he fell into despondency. All the doctors said he had consumption. Only one held out a hope. He might perhaps be saved, if he should join an emigrant train and walk across the plains. Trains were being fitted out—there might be opportunity.

169

Having sixteen hundred dollars in the bank, without revealing his intentions, he drew out half, and took the boat from Albany to New York. He wrote one letter home—the one I had "Psychometrized." Two days later a neighbor saw him in New York and asked: "When are you going home?" He answered, rather ambiguously: "The boat starts in an hour." Nothing was ever heard of him thereafter. Detectives failed to find a murderer—policemen failed to find a murdered man. No one thought of emigrant trains. All thought him dead.

"But tell us about the spirits. Were they like your ancestors?" Here the "Squire's" brother intervened. "Just like them! She described our grand-mother, the Quaker lady, our father and our brother James correctly. And we are all blonds or very nearly so." The guests conferred one side. They all supposed that James had left his home to save his life and died—perhaps in Salt Lake City.

And I thought this: "May be that is true about the spirit landscapes."

A HELPER IN MACEDONIA

A FACT is not assailable. It is said of Deity: "With worms He can thresh mountains;" and that is true. But mountains are realities, not facts. Once you say: "This happened!" There is nothing more to add except: "Because this happened there were consequences." George Eliot would say: "It can never be altered. It remains unaltered to alter other things." Now, should I take my facts and build a structure with them, my building is entitled to respect. You are not justified in saying: "A silly house of cards! She has a clever knack of balancing them: but—puff—a single breath will blow them down!"

I said my brother brought a spirit-doctor, who afterward became a guardian. There came to me so many "facts" in proof of this, that I, perforce, must state a few of them. For if you stop to think of it, however people talk of guardian angels, very little faith in them is manifest.

After that New Year's dinner, Mr. and Mrs. Bundy's son Leroy came after me. He had been lately married, and Delia wanted music-lessons; moreover, I was pleased to hope, his mother wanted me. And anyway I had a three month's rest among them, varied with rhyming work; for I was busy shoring up my most ambitious—or at least, my very longest piece of verse. I pushed Psychometry one side; that was delight, not business. The Dentons, genuine scientists, spent, I was told, all they could gather up for several years, to demonstrate and make the world aware of Psychometric truth. That was not my calling. I had no mind to sacrifice so much as one Spenserian stanza just because of that. For, after all, if we must sacrifice, the most of us would choose the visible altar!—and on the mountain top, by preference. During those winter evenings, Leroy and Delia visited upstairs quite out of hearing; while Grandma Hard, George and Fondana Bundy and myself, took all the time we wanted, just for talk. But once our talk was interrupted curiously: Telling a funny story to entertain my friends, I had a mind to make it funnier; I—embellished it! Nobody had time to laugh. Right in our center someone gave a long, loud, whistling "Whew!"

171

We stared a moment; I was stricken dumb. Then Mrs. Bundy, who had a sense of humor, said: "Mother! What are you whistling for?"

Grandma (79 by this time), turned indignantly: "I didn't whistle; it was George."

"I haven't a tooth to whistle with," said George.

"Then it was Fondana."

"Mother, you know I never whistled in my life."

And then it came again, right in the center of the group; not quite so loud, but still a much astonished "Whew!" Confused, I said: "I wish that something else would come, as unexplainable." To tell the truth I was much ashamed. I inwardly resolved that all my life, I'd keep my funny stories well within the limit.

The door was open to the little kitchen. Just beyond that door a rattling noise began, much like the crumpling up of stiff brown paper, only many times exaggerated. It kept up, we estimated, full three minutes. All the doors, save that between the rooms, were closed. Not a living creature small as a mouse, was on the lower floor, beside ourselves. There was not even a paper curtain at the window, nor a scrap of paper visible, within that room.

Now, lest you think I have ignored the outer form of so-called Spiritualism too much, I frankly say that I believe a spirit caused the noises,—not for fun, but for an obvious purpose. The whistling showed intelligence and moral sense; power to rebuke and to enforce rebuke with repetition. And further, finding that my moral sense was quickened, I was granted "something more," to clinch the matter. Moreover, really, you know, the air within a tight-shut room could never whistle of itself. Ventriloquism? Not from within the house; nor from without, unless the very trees had learned the art.

I used to think that spirits of a lower order only, made such outward demonstrations. I am not so sure. There are good physicists in Heaven I dare suppose.

Nothing could be more plain and simple than the way in which my brother's friend began his ministrations. We were rather glum one evening. Mr. Bundy's eyes were troubling him, and Auntie had a painful rheumatism in her most serviceable right arm—our chief dependence practically.

One came and stood beside me, dimly seen as once before;—a well-built gentleman of fifty, whose hair was white. I saw no more and never saw him afterward. He never told of self but thrice—this night and twice again. He influenced me to speak and, I suppose, to personate himself. Always the voice he used was firm and masculine, his manner vigorous and his talk that of a cultured doctor, who had learned (chiefly in spirit-life we gathered) many truths not widely understood.

Speaking of me, he never said: "My medium;" he always said "My friend." During five years and more—long as I needed him—he made myself and others well aware of his most lovable personality.

This time he spoke to this effect: "My friend was very sick some months ago. Her brother called on me for aid. Now I have taken her in charge; I have her life to save." Having so introduced himself, he said to Mrs. Bundy: "Madam, I see that you are suffering. Before retiring, have your husband spend a half hour pouring hot water on your arm—as hot as may be borne. And you"—turning to Mr. Bundy, "will find relief from tea-leaves. Bind them wet upon your eyes and keep the bandage on till morning."

"But won't you tell us who you are?"

"Many years ago in Boston, I was known as Dr. Jonathan Andrews. Call me Dr. Andrews."

Once I asked an elderly Boston lady—a stranger met by chance near forty years ago—whether she had ever heard of Dr. Jonathan Andrews. She answered "Many times. He had been my mother's doctor and she used to say in every difficult case: 'If only Dr. Jonathan Andrews were alive, there might be hope.'"

This is no conclusive proof; howbeit I never sought for more.

Now, the next morning, both my friends were wholly cured. I suppose that gave them confidence; for when the spirit came that evening, they asked for further help:

173

"We are troubled about our son's wife, Delia. She was not well before her marriage. Two of her family had died, and she had taken care of them. We thought she only needed rest; but now we think there may be positive danger. If we call her down, will you examine and prescribe for her?"

"You need not call her down. I'll visit her and see what may be done."

Presently the spirit said: "Your daughter is in danger. She is in the first stage of consumption. She might be saved, but not by any common means, such as you have at hand."

While he paused, said Mr. Bundy: "There's a Dr. Dick who cures consumption, just at the beginning. We sent our nieces to him, but he sent them back within a week or two. He said they were too far gone. Could he save Delia do you think?"

"I don't know Dr. Dick; but I will search him out." Here let me state that I, myself, knew absolutely nothing about Dr. Dick, nor had Cordelia's actual danger fairly occurred to me.

"I'll tell you where to find him," Mr. Bundy said.

"Tell me in this way: Fix your mind upon the road and follow it in thought from here to there. I will go along; and you shall hear just what I think of him tomorrow night."

The following day I worried silently. To hand out Psychic gifts to friends was happifying, but having human life depend upon my mediumship was quite another matter. Till finally I begged of Auntie: "Don't have unbounded faith! You know that I am always conscious. Without the least intention, my mind might interfere. Whatever may be said to-night, remember you are the one to judge."

She only smiled: "You needn't be concerned. We have had mediums of our own." Why, so they had! How could I presume to follow Lucy Hard? Moreover, there was Frankie Hard—foredoomed to die in early life. When only seven years of age, I think, they set her down to play at picture-making. Quietly and long she seemed to play, then rose up sleepily and crossed the room to lay her slate on Auntie Bundy's knee—all written over with a message from her father (the father of the child). He had told things he wanted done. You may be sure they were attended to.

But afterward he wrote, through someone else I apprehend: "I shall not influence Frankie anymore. It would be unjust to her. She is too delicately constituted." That ended Frankie's mediumship, it seemed. My own was not so wonderful. I thought it wise to doubt. Moreover, I had yet to learn that Dr. Andrews had magnetic power. He gave, through me, just what he chose to give and not what I, or others, asked of him.

When evening came, we sat awaiting—they full of expectation, I dull and half-unwilling. Then just a little back of me one stood and reached an arm around, holding before my sight a perfect picture, eighteen inches long perhaps and actually framed! And, doing so, he said with emphasis: "Dr.—Dick's—House!"

I spoke without one doubtful tremor. "Mr. Bundy, Dr. Dick lives in a large, two-story house close by the road. There is a pump before it and a watering trough. The house has just one door in front, and, on each side of that, four windows. Taking both stories there are sixteen windows visible. Just at the right-hand corner, there's a gate through which you reach the back. A fence is just in line. The house is old, and not in good repair. It is what we used to call 'wood-colored,'—never painted. There is one clapboard missing high up, on the left. The roof slopes toward the road, and there is moss along the eaves in several places, and even higher up among the shingles."

Curiously enough, just then I saw what was not in the picture; rather, I lost the picture and looked away. I went on just the same: "Off on the left the scenery is beautiful. There are green meadows and a river. Across the river, a mile or two away, I judge, there is a large and handsome village. What village is it Mr. Bundy?"

"St. Catherine's in Canada. That is St. Catherine's River."

Why, so it is! I recognize the scene. We moved to Canada when I was nine years old, and crossed that river. I remember how the village looked so far away. We visited my father's cousin there. But certainly I never saw this house of Dr. Dick's."

"Well," said Mr. Bundy: "I have been there twice and if I stood this moment right before the house, I could not possibly describe it any better. It is very old; I saw the moss myself."

How did Dr. Andrews get that vivid picture and put it in a frame for me to see? Far finer than a photograph, for every shade of color had been reproduced. And here is something yet more wonderful:

The time was early March. There must have been Canadian snows on all those fertile meadows; yet they looked to me as fresh and green as if the time were summer. I had passed that way in March and afterward in October. It seems I might have caught the scene from Mr. Bundy's mind; for he had seen it looking just that way. But for the house itself, I am fain to think that Dr. Andrews showed me what he had actually seen; and, to be yet more definite, had framed the picture handsomely. Where did he get the frame?

Howbeit with such a double confirmation, I was well content, and then, and ever after, on occasion, I welcomed Dr. Andrews! This, in effect, is what he said:

"My friends, good evening to you all!—I have visited Dr. Dick. He pleased me very much,—a good man and an excellent physician. He has a method of his own; and for consumption, in its early stage, I know of none that equals it. I am at liberty to say that, in this one respect, he far surpasses any doctor in America. I recommend him to your daughter. Under his care, I promise her recovery."

Two of Delia's family had died of that disease, which once begun, had run a rapid course. The spirit-doctor's diagnosis was confirmed by Dr. Dick, under whose care she was immediately placed and soon was literally cured. I think she is living still.

As to this dire white-plague, whatever methods since have been approved, I think I ought to tell you more. For Dr. Dick, in saving many, after his toilsome manner, wore his life away, and I have never heard of its adoption by another. Being of a German school, he made much use of roots and herbs; but just you say "consumption"—off came his coat! And first he donned a pair of flannel mittens, with which he rubbed his patients, underneath their robes, with violence, for half an hour; then bathed and rubbed them thoroughly ten minutes in strong red pepper tea; then donned another pair of mittens and rubbed for twenty minutes longer. He skinned them now and then by chance, but this he deprecated; he "didn't wish to cruelize!" This every day and maybe twice a day, till the dread visitant fled in terror; for he never took a patient quite beyond that critical first stage. He never trusted to apprentices; people might knock at that dilapidated "tavern-stand" all day, but only ten at once were ever lodged therein; and when he died no doubt that hundreds lived because of him.

"Auntie" sent for me one time. Dr. Dick had come from Canada to roam the woods, guided by Mr. Bundy, in search of simples. I had congested lungs and functional disorder of the heart;—just on the point of breaking down completely, Dr. Marvin thought. I took a single "treatment." Half the night I dreamed of standing at the stake among the blazing fagots and suffering holy martyrdom. But when I came to breakfast, breathing like an infant, danger had disappeared. It seemed miraculous.

When Dr. Dick took Delia's case in hand, I had an urgent call from Mrs. Higley. Curtis, her son, who had starved at Andersonville, had someway set aside for her a little sum of money. If I would take that fund, go out to Buffalo, purchase an instrument, and stay six months with them instructing Nettie, she was persuaded Curtis would be greatly pleased. I had no doubt of it. I therefore did my final work upon "Atlantis," in the Higley farm-house, not a mile from Levi Brown's.

My brother-in-law, the Rev. Rufus Cooley, had lately settled in Wisconsin, and, being much beloved, had easily persuaded Mother and the rest to follow him, purchase a farm and learn to till the soil. I should have followed, but could not see my way just then to leave these country friends and Margaret McMaster (with whom I spent three summers first and last among the "Cattaraugus breakers"), nor yet that "Nameless Club" of Buffalo, whose members, even then, were sending in subscriptions for the book that was about to be. More than all these could realize, I was bound up in them. And so I stayed at Mr. Higley's farm-house half a year and spent six hours a day in mental labor.

177

Once a week, and sometimes in between, three families—the Higleys, Browns and Hawleys—with myself, had happy "circles." Thither every time came Dr. Jonathan Andrews. Not that he blocked the way of others. He was the soul of courtesy. He came, as any gentleman might, who means to spend an evening with his friends in pleasant conversation. Only at our desire, he led the way— instructed us and answered questions in philosophy. We were all engaged in scientific Psychical Research—he, the scientist, we, the investigators. He taught us Psychic laws, and more than once dipped into physics, even telling things I have seen announced since then as fresh discoveries. Sometimes he gave a message from another; that seemed to please him well. He loved the common folk and all their common ways.

One night he spoke of self. This was the manner of it: He was expounding something. I was listening, as usual. Meanwhile, I saw come in and cross the room, my Mrs. Manley's father, Mr. Haines. I had not known that he was dangerously sick, but he had passed away, it proved, two days before. Dr. Andrews paused, remained in silence for a little time, then said: "I wish to tell you something about my early life. My mother was a poor, hard-working widow. I was her only child. She owned a lonely little cottage by the sea; but, half a mile away, there was a summer boarding house, close to a little village. I was mother's errand boy, I carried back the work that she had done and brought new bundles home. I had a traffic of my own. The summer I was ten, I earned, for mother, thirty dollars, gathering clams and selling star-fish, shells and mosses, to the city ladies. I was intensely proud of that. But in the Autumn mother died. I suppose no boy could be more broken-hearted. They bound me out to a good farmer, who was kind; and really everyone was kind. But all the while I was unhappy. I had lost my mother. One day when I was twelve, I was allowed to swim with other boys and I was nearly drowned. With difficulty I was resuscitated; but there had been so great a shock, it made me dull for months. My mind lost balance; I grew dissatisfied, and chose to run away. I started out toward Boston. I had just eighteen dollars of my own. It seemed a fortune. People cared for me along the road, but when I reached the city, I was half worn out and very hungry. I bought a loaf of bread

178

over a bar, where men were drinking. Seeing that I had money, a smiling fellow offered me a drink of lemonade. I thought him very kind.

"At midnight, I awoke, sick and bewildered, lying in a doorway, deep in shadow. I rose and staggered on, thinking to find a tavern possibly. But when I looked I found that I had lost my money. So for hours I lay beside a wall and sobbed. There seemed no place for me in all the world."

Here I am compelled to pause. I cannot hope to reproduce the sweetness and simplicity with which he told the rest: How his mother came in visible presence; how she printed on his mind a street and number; how he sought the place and found a widow's home; and how she fed and kept him till her son came in, then led him forward, saying: "You need an office boy, and here he is!" And how he came at last to have an office of his own. Then in a few short sentences he paid a tribute to the mother and her son, that showed us something of the measureless depth of spirit-gratitude.

He ended: "I have told this for an especial reason. When you hear that a good boy with good intentions, has run away from home, remember this: He will not be allowed to go alone. He will not suffer serious harm. Some spirit will protect ."

The following day came Mrs. Bundy, saying mysteriously: "I have heard from Vineland." (In New Jersey—then Mrs. Manley's home). "Your friend is deep in trouble. She hopes, through you, to get a spirit-message; but I am not to tell you why."

"I know already that her father's gone," I said. "He came last evening."

"He was living when she wrote. Do try to tell her something!" I sat a little while in silence. Then I said: "I can see nothing but a vessel. I have no idea what it means."

Now the letter said: "My boy has run away; we think from sheer discouragement for lack of work." She doubtless might have added: "also because of grief"—he being very fond of Mr. Haines and knowing death was near.

Although his boys and girls, together with their boys and girls are kith and kin to me, I learned from him but yesterday, that first he went to sea.

We have our limitations. I was never used (but once) to seek and find a wanderer. This boy no letter could have intercepted. I had to be content with Dr. Andrews' message and the memory of a father, seven years in spirit life, who would not let him drift alone.

These be simple stories. You may conceive that spirits travel broader roads. No doubt they do, I have met them there myself and mean to tell about it. Meantime, along these narrow paths, I choose to show you first what gentle intimacy may be possible between ourselves and them. The greatest man will stoop to kiss his child. If we are children, not the less our elders in the other life, may find us lovable.

There was a yearly gathering of "Progressive Friends" at "Hemlock Hall" close to the Baldwin farm, that called in many thousands. "Speakers" near at home were always ready for the rostrum; others came from far. That year my Mrs. Brown was called upon to entertain a lady-lecturer from Baltimore, said to be held in high esteem. So, being diffident with strangers, she called on me to come and help her out with talk.

Our guest was rather elderly—fifty-seven she said. Though reticent, she drew me strongly, being a disciplined woman full of quiet dignity, very attractive also in appearance and of a gracious manner.

It chanced she feared an inability to speak because of cankered mouth. My Dr. Andrews had a way of proffering help, even on slight occasion. So, by telepathy, he named to me a remedy. Telling her this, she said: "I need more help than that; suppose we have a circle."

So four of us sat down, joined hands a moment, just for harmony, and presently the lady talked at ease with Dr. Andrews. Someway, I have no memory of what he said, although I heard of course. But all the while, after the first few sentences, I watched a beautiful young lady, walking to and fro, who seemed to me waiting her turn to speak. Dressed in perfect white, much like a bridal robe, she paced the floor from wall to wall along the further side, always upon the self-same line. She walked so swiftly that, as she turned about, her dress went floating out as in a wind. Will anyone be shocked? There were two flounces, deep and delicately traced with broidery—vine-like above, but heavier near the hem. I saw the very pattern—I seem to see it now; and there were similar effects about the neck and sleeves. And then I saw that all the time, whichever way she turned, she kept her eyes intently on the face of her whom she had come to see—her mother certainly. For, with a difference of years, the one was like the other, only more delicately made. An exquisite creature, verily alive!—

"A spirit, yet a woman, too."

At last she spoke;—she hurled her message forth as one might fling a rose.......Was it a rose?—I thought: "It may be sweet—I am not wholly sure;" and wondered whether I would dare deliver it.

But Dr. Andrews having spoken for himself then spoke for her: "Lady, you have a lovely daughter present. I hear her say: 'Tell mother to tell husband that I'm old enough for him now!' "

The mother rose and left the room. Mrs. Brown and I felt that we must not question her; but Mr. Brown was not so scrupulous. He asked on her return: "Did you understand the message?"

"You shall judge. I have a lovely daughter, who passed to spirit-life two years ago at twenty years of age. When she was just eighteen she loved and chose to marry a gentleman of sixty,—a worthy man and very intellectual. He and myself were strong Republicans and Spiritualists, as well as public lecturers. Our families were intensely orthodox and Southern sympathizers. I was compelled to leave my home because of that. My daughter clung to me. There was a storm of opposition to the marriage,—excused ostensibly by the difference in ages. 'She is too young for him!' was said a thousand times, I think. They all refused to visit her,—even her best-loved friends. She only lived two years. No words of mine can tell how much this message means to me."

But—old enough?---Spirits advance by leaps and bounds no doubt. After many years can we be sure of overtaking them?—Forbear the lower thought! "Depth pre-supposes height" says Frothingham. I add: Height pre-supposes depth!

BEHOLD then, Dr. Jonathan Andrews!—old and very old, if time in Spirit-life be measured by progression. He had passed away, we may conclude, no less than eighty years before he named his name, as I have said, and proffered services. He might have visited a myriad worthier; but one I loved had brought him,—he had chosen me! Perchance I was a little more in need than many, and rather more accessible; moreover one who could be used for helping others, if occasion served. He made occasion serve.

What he had seen in Spirit-life he did not come to tell. There must have been ineffable experiences, such as we, too, will have when we are "old enough." Yet still he chose to linger near a world

"That wants Love's color in the grey of Time."

We read that Christ appeared among his former friends—not clothed with light unbearable, but standing near, in olden guise, and gently asking: "Children, have ye any meat?" Peradventure, breaking bread with honeycomb and saying: "Come and dine."

How many ways this guest of mine had found that led to lowly homes, I cannot guess; but this I know: Not only did he comfort me but others near to me; and leaving me full use of all my mental powers, he shared with me a spirit's happiness in rendering aid. Twice, certainly, through me, he lengthened human life by many years. Howbeit, I, through him, am yet alive myself.

Having said that he must save my life, he watched me day by day as mortal doctors will, only with higher wisdom. Other physicians charged me not to write, which I was forced to do from inward pressure as from outward need. He never interposed his will against my chosen work. He aided me in each reaction, soothing irritated nerves in some mysterious way, as he had done when first he came; and there were chance prescriptions—new to me and strangely efficacious; with cheering promises or rather prophecies. I do not know that every spirit has the gift of prophecy; I know this spirit had.

Bear with me: The proofs I had of that identity were very many, the number I have given are very few. It seems I ought to add a number more, to make you understand more definitely how I came to have a vital trust,—saying at last to him (and to another after him): "Lead, and behold, I follow!"

During our frequent gatherings for spiritual service—"circles" you may call them—I noticed this: On my account this kind physician frankly gathered strength from others. Of course you understand the law. A minute's clasp of circling hands, a fine, magnetic circuit,—you, being the weaker, naturally receiving more than you are giving. While you retain that borrowed vigor, something may be returned in full equivalence to those who gave. But choose your comrades warily. We had a roomful—that is, eight or ten of us, with no discordant element,—clean lives, clear minds, calm judgment, Psychic aspirations. We answered very well.

All this enabled Dr. Andrews to personate himself the better, using weak lungs to reproduce the masculine voice, yet always leaving them a little stronger than before.

I noticed something further: Being our chosen lecturer, he often paused to lift my hand and look: After this, he might go on or stop abruptly, saying "Good-night!" beyond recall. It seemed a mannerism, till I perceived that he was judging by the aura (that odylic force, perhaps, "that still from female finger tips burns blue") how much was left of personal and borrowed vigor. Never once did he transgress the limit. Meantime, each was at liberty,—he to speak his thoughts, and I to think my own. Sometimes I disagreed with him at first, and had to be convinced by argument or explanation.

Once he chose to make us understand that light and music are correlative,—colors and sounds responding, each to each. This has since been demonstrated; but at the time, I half revolted. Not the less when he had finished his discourse, I seemed to be among the morning stars; and lo, they "sang together!"

Once, in effect, he said r "My friend supposes that the marriage-bond on earth, if holy, must involve eternal unity. That is to say: Love's ultimate perfection may exist where all is imperfection! That is not God's way! Marriage is holy when the highest self you recognize assents. Death may dissever even such a bond. I do not say it will."

"When Dr. Andrews talks to me," said Lydia Brown, "he answers even my thoughts. When I am all alone, I think of many things I want to ask. He picks them up, after I have forgotten them. Sometimes, I feel almost afraid, he knows so much, and yet I never was so happy in my life!" In truth he had a way of making people happier, right at home. How tolerant he was of human weaknesses! How tender were his human sympathies!

Does this imply continual presence? That cannot be imagined. They who are practiced in telepathy (as I am not) affirm that they can make themselves appear to others half a world away, and even converse with them. It may be so. Yet these are hampered with the flesh.

To come and go—what does that matter to a spirit? Less ponderable than light (though ponderable), is not the spiritual body yet more swift? From out their realm (wherever that may be), they who have left the earth long time ago, may, "in a moment, in the twinkling of an eye," return and make themselves appear to very common folk.

Nay! I conceive that one—not being omnipresent—who lived with men almost two thousand years ago, will answer every voice that cries to him in every wilderness: "Hear me and comfort—thou who art the Christ!"

Come, let us hear a little more about the Master's poor." One of them came to me one day, when I had dropped my pen from weariness,—a total stranger, landed at the door by some obliging farmer. You never would have guessed that she was "born to trouble as the sparks fly upward." Maybe instead she was born to conquer trouble. Certainly it had not conquered her. Sixty-five, and blithe and sociable—she did not speak of self except to say: "I am a Spiritualist";—which led me to suppose she wanted Psychic messages. That worried me; such favors come by inspiration, not by demand or even strong desire.

185

There came a better moment. Unmistakably my friend drew near and said: "I wish to talk with her, when you are willing." Ashamed not to be willing, I looked at her attentively, and presently I felt that she was lovable. I said: "Come here and take my hand. We'll have a circle, just we two alone."

Her soft, blue eyes were radiant. I closed my own and thought: "She has a sweet, old face!" But where or how she lived or whom she had to love and labor for, I knew no more than you.

Dr. Andrews always introduced himself to strangers with a certain ceremony; but now I noted reverence of manner and suddenly grew reverent myself. I thank my friend for this: Not only did he share with me his knowledge of disease, making me see clairvoyantly at times, the physical condition, but now and then he made me recognize some lustrous quality of soul. And here I saw an inner loveliness that shamed my late indifference.

There was no bodily disease, whatever, only a weariness, due to hard labor rather than to age. When he had given her due advice, instructing her how to conserve her energies and what to guard against, he said: "I shall be absent for a little while. I wish to find your home." During that absence, I perceived that all my frame was quivering as Jerry Carter's did, you may remember, when Dr. Hedges left him for a similar purpose. I noticed this at later dates, and thought it signified a slight relax of physical control, which probably was rather stronger than I realized.

It scarcely seemed a minute ere the trembling passed and he was there again. And now he seemed amazed: "You! You!—a woman past her three score years and bearing all those burdens! How many lean on you with all their weight? One, two, three, four, five, six! Infirm in mind and body, incompetent, sick, helpless, irresponsible! It seems too much! Too much! And yet I see no help,—no one can take your place; I cannot promise you a swift release. You are framed to last, and you will always live for others—not for self. Your patience, courage, fortitude and faith are wonderful. I honor you!

"I have but this advice to give: Be happy! I see in you a lovely trait. No matter what your troubles are, to see another pleased, even in the smallest way, will always make you glad."

Just here the little lady, for the first time, "spoke aloud in meeting": "Oh, yes! The other day a stranger stopped to smell my laylocks; it gave me lots of comfort!"

"But even less will make you happy. While you work, look here and there in search of beauty. Notice the shadow of a leaf, a butter-fly, a door-yard flower, a sunbeam darting through your window-vine, a shining drop of dew. See every rosy cloud at night and morning. When the rain is over, look for the rainbow. Even if you never turn your head something beautiful will pass before your eyes. When it comes, keep thinking of it. Make the pleasure last as long as possible."

"I will! Indeed I will! Thank you for telling me! I shall be happier all my life, because a spirit saw and understood!"

I also understood a little, at a later time. Her poor, old husband was insane, at home; her son had lost the power or lost the will to work; his fretful wife—who never left her bed—exacted wearying service. Three little children counted up the six; and all the household labor fell on her. Now, twelve years later, when I asked for her, they $aid: "She is always cheerful—always taking care of others. Age has made no difference." What need to tell her name? Is it not written in the "Book of Life?"

But why was nothing said about some great reward in future life? a crown, a harp of gold, a four-square City—every gate one pearl?

Love's highest recompense for work is—yet more work. Meantime the spirit gave her what she needed—something for here and now. Rewards are consequences; but "very present help in time of need," is better than to hear of Canaan's grapes—far-off, beyond the Jordan.

Another woman needed "present help." Certain friends appealed to me: "A poor man's wife has broken down. There seems no hope of saving her; and yet she must be saved if possible. There are nine children—the oldest but seventeen. What can her husband do without her?" Truly a pitiful case! Mr. and Mrs. Brown proposed that I should visit her with them and, peradventure, with another friend—invisible but very prone to help.

We found her sitting in her easy chair, directing house-hold work. One of the nine was absent—an intellectual wonder, people thought—working his way through school. You understood that Millard was beloved exceedingly. The eight remaining (one a year-old baby), were hustled out of sight. Only the husband stayed.

I said that Dr. Andrews made me see disease—that is to say the havoc that disease had made within the physical structure. Perhaps I should have said: "I saw it of myself, after he had induced the Psychic trance." I never saw it under other influence than his. He, as a doctor, looked for that. He doubtless took the lead; I, as a subject, followed.

Internal photographs, made by invisible rays, are not at all miraculous. No doubt still finer "particles of light" make perfect pictures meet for finer eyes. Psychometry, clairvoyance, astral-vision—call it what you will, there is an inner sight that pierces the opaque.

And so I saw a torpid frame, an ever lagging pulse, a tendency to physical destruction everywhere.

Dr. Andrews saw, it proved, that something might be done to keep the mother just a little longer where she was needed most. I think he spent a half hour talking to her husband, whom he installed, at once, as nurse and doctor. Diet and stimulating baths and rest and sleep, with herbal remedies,—he outlined all the scheme; so many things to do, so many not to do,—and, last of all a semi-daily, gentle flagellation!

The husband promised all—even to the flexible twigs; and then the Doctor turned to her:

"Dear Lady, all this care will bring about a marked improvement. Your friends will say that you are getting well. But you are very brave; it will not harm you in the least to know the actual truth."

188

"That is exactly what I want to know," the patient said with emphasis. "I am not afraid of Death."

"I see that you have many children. You have a certain time in which to plan for them, and there is much to do. I have the power to say how long that time will be. Do you desire to know?"

"Most certainly!"

"Two months! No more, no less."

"Thank you with all my heart. You have rendered me the greatest service. Now I can lay my plans, and I shall know just what I ought to do."

Well, so it was. We heard that she was getting well and working busily—setting her house in order, making and mending dresses, jackets and the like, just as a mother will. Oh, she was almost well!

Did Dr. Andrews know how, in that final week, Millard would hear "the bird's voice" calling him and rise up swiftly, going where he would? And how the bird would call a second time—the stricken mother rising up to follow?

Rue for sorrow—rosemary for sweet remembrance.

Her friends believed she might have lived much longer but for Millard's death.

One would think the Spirit must have known. "Two months no more, no less!"—even as it proved.

But now I hear you say: "Where were the doubters all this while? Why did you not convince a few of them?" You know that mediumship was not my personal calling. God speaks and we must hear and answer. After that, the angels possibly. And yet there were a few "of little faith" to whom the hand was reached, as, for example:

Alonzo Hawley tapped at my study-door one Sabbath afternoon. He said: "There is a family party at the gate—two wagons full. We have some distant cousins visiting us. The man is out of health. He says the doctors haven't done him any good, and we've persuaded him to come to you. He is not a Spiritualist—he never saw a medium and has a prejudice; but we've explained to him that you are not a medium for hire but only one of us, our dear and intimate friend; so he consents to come. He means to be as fair as maybe; and if your Spirit-doctor seem to understand the case, he'll follow all directions. Still he wants the strictest possible conditions. You are not even to look at him; and I have pledged myself to tell you nothing more."

"Very well," I answered: "Seat your family party in the parlor, and leave a vacant chair for me. When I am fully ready, I'll go in."

So I abased my eyes, went in, sat down and shut them instantly. Then Mr. Hawley said to Dr. Andrews: "someone is present, who would like advice." "You will bring the gentleman here," said Dr. Andrews, "and you will introduce him properly." His chair was far as possible from mine, and I suppose that he had meant to keep the distance. Still he came, a little slowly, as I thought, and Mr. Hawley gave the introduction. Dr. Andrews took his hand and said: "I am glad to meet you. Please sit down," then turned almost at once: "How many times within the last year have you most ardently wished that you were dead? *Just twelve times!*"

I heard a woman's voice cry out: "Oh no! You haven't wished that you were dead!"

Her husband answered, using Dr. Andrews words with bitter emphasis: "Just twelve times!"

He did not speak again, although the talk was long. I find it difficult to discriminate here, between the spoken words and what I realized. The spirit said that those "attacks" were chiefly due to his "inordinate ambition that he had taxed the brain almost beyond endurance, and borne the strain of "governing turbulent elements" as long as could be done without complete collapse. I understood that he had been a teacher, and I had a sense of multitude: "So many undeveloped minds!" I thought. "It must have been distracting!" Enough was spoken out to prove the spirit's actual knowledge, and yet there was a certain reticence. The gentleman said to Mr. Hawley afterwards: "If I had been alone with Dr. Andrews, he would have told me even more."

And truly, had the spirit plainly stated: "Sir, you have had twelve cataleptic fits within the year," that would have been to bruit abroad what he, through pride, had sedulously kept concealed. Albeit I was afterward allowed to know.

As for the remedies; rest from care and study, stringency in diet, constant recreation, persistent cheerfulness, were all enjoined; but to prevent "recurrence of attacks," one medicine must be depended on—a tea of white field-daisies.

One of the farmers present—Casper Clough—sang out; "Thank Heaven if the pesky things can be of any use!" None of us knew them as a medicine, but some years later in a Botanic Pharmacy in Providence, I asked for information. Books were hunted up, and white field-daisies found to be the one specific remedy for catalepsy.

This patient was a City High School principal, traveling through the long vacation for his health; but not as yet consenting to resign—as afterward he did.

Frankie Marvin's case was far more difficult—incurable in fact. For reasons not above plain common sense, I choose to tell the story; also, for Psychic reasons. If the latter tax credulity, I cry you mercy! I have no right to leave them out; and still I have a right to my apologetic word.

You being a medium,—whatever message comes to you alone, is not to be forgotten; nor any simple message given to you for others. But when a spirit personates himself, converses, answers questions, lectures, talks philosophy, you hear, as do the rest, remembering the sense and oftentimes the words, but not infallibly. And so it was with me. The Psychic trance (not the hypnotic), is characterized, as we have seen, by independent vision, independent thinking and no abnormal loss of memory. Whatever fixes my attention in the trance, as in my daily life, is kept a long time in the reach of recollection. What I forget is what I have not cared about.

Dr. Marvin (rarely equaled as a diagnost), drove up one autumn day to Mr. Brown's and called me out: "Our Frankie's very sick. Neither her mother nor myself can understand her symptoms. Auntie Bundy says you have a spirit-doctor. That is our only hope. If he can't save her, Frankie's got to die!"

I had talked with her but once; then I had seen that she was fine and intellectual. A teacher, barely twenty-five,—surely the world had need of her! I said in haste: "Frankie shall not die if she can possibly be saved through me."

So the next day, being the Sabbath (when it is "lawful to do well" and most convenient for a busy farmer), Mr. and Mrs. Brown and I went to "Jerusalem Corners," and found our temple in a sick girl's chamber—perhaps the very one whence Lucy Hard had slipped from sight, some fourteen years before.

We sat by Frankie's bed, holding her hands, excluding Dr and Mrs. Marvin, who were far too much perturbed to act as harmonizers. Both my assisting friends abounded, one might say, in Psycho-physical magnetism—always at my disposal in such a time of need; or rather at my guardian's disposal, peradventure. I think he paid them back in Psychic pleasure;—I paid in loving gratitude.

Leaning above the smiling girl, I closed my lids and found that it was given me to see with inner eyes—piercing through outward walls of flesh and bone—that which was no less physical within. First I perceived, scattered along the alimentary tract, as with a lavish hand, inert, metallic atoms. They might not have been visible to open vision, even through a microscopic lens; but there they were, and elsewhere—everywhere it seemed; no more to be removed than clinging dust blown in upon a wayside rose. I thought "Gunpowder looks like that." And then I saw the blood go traveling along the arteries, carrying its crimson through the heart and lungs, but growing paler toward the extremities, so that when it reached the feet there was no color left. Then Dr. Andrews courteously greeting Frankie, after his usual manner, took the matter up, describing just what I had seen as a condition, not as a disease. The mother said: "All that explains why I can never start a tinge on Frankie's feet by friction or by artificial heat,—even to the point of burning."

But Dr. Marvin urged: "I want to know the cause; and whether there is any possible cure."

Dr. Andrews turned to the tranquil girl: "I see that you are not afraid to face the truth."

"Oh, I must have the truth! I'm not an infant. Let me hear it all."

"That is your right." Then as one doctor counseling another courteously, he talked with Dr. Marvin.

I cannot with exactness, give the words, but this is what we fully comprehended. Each brain-cell is a battery which generates electro-vital or galvanic fluid, so giving out its current to unite with other currents and keep the human frame endowed with energy. Today the statement is familiar, but forty years ago it might have challenged doubt.

Over all these batteries presides the Sovereign Mind, apportioning to every faculty its task—differing from that of other faculties. Each has its definite location, its individual laboratory, its complement of cells. Let but a single faculty grow slack in effort, throughout the system everywhere there is a definite loss.

No particle of food or bodily provision can be appropriated till it is duly vitalized or charged magnetically or moved upon by one, at least, of these electric currents (unerringly selective). So, being energized, each atom springs along—not waiting to be dragged—and finds, should nothing intervene, its predetermined path and destined stopping place; or, being meant to keep afloat, will lend its force to all the rest. So here we have innumerable batteries, one united MIND made up of many lesser minds, each capable of thinking, willing, acting, generating power for mental contribution. So life and growth and health and God's humanity result.

This, for example: That faculty we call Combativeness, among its other offices must take in charge the inorganic particles of iron, electrifying them or giving them magnetic properties; then each one leaps along, hurrying—not hindering—the blood, encrimsoning it, sustaining life and beautifying flesh. Otherwise, not being duly vitalized, these molecules will drag, will drop wherever it may chance—infinitesimal, but menacing to life.

Now this dear, dying girl, who had combativeness enough to spur the intellect, had not enough to give resisting force.

193

The breath of wind that keeps your kites afloat, will not suffice to grind your necessary corn. All this and more, our kind physician made us understand,—saying at last of Frankie:

"That is why you have never seen her angry."

"Not once in all my life!" the mother testified.

Said Dr. Marvin: "This is what I have never found in all my books, and now I understand those baffling symptoms! But is there any hope?"

"There would be hope if there could come to her, at once, some unexpected, unimagined, overwhelming joy; something to capture every faculty. But that is not to be. And still, a little may be done. What I can do, I will. The rest I leave with you."

Just two hours after that, I sat at ease, observing Mrs. Brown, who flitted to and fro about her household work. Then, suddenly, beyond all thought or dream, I lifted up my eyes and saw a spirit. A veritable Arab, slender, brown and young and supple, one might think, as any desert panther. Turban and tunic white as drifted snow, sash vivid crimson, he needed but a flashing scimitar to seem embodied fire.

Right from the East and facing West, he paused and stood, and met my eyes with such a piercing gaze it seemed that he had never seen my like before. A Bedouin very likely—a slayer possibly, and yet if that were true, I think he had been "purged with hyssop." He seemed a son of Eli, clean before the Lord.

I quivered with desire to understand. So, when the "chores" were done, I called my friends! "I have had so wonderful a vision, that even soon as this, I want another interview with Dr. Andrews."

Now, (as at other times by inference) I learned that spirits lead a marvelous life. This one, I doubt not, might have said:

"I pass, like night, from land to land;
I have strange power of speech."

Instead he only said, right pleasantly: "Since I was with you last, I have been a traveler; I have journeyed to Arabia. Does that seem far

194

away! I found and brought along with me a young Arabian—a fine and worthy spirit.

"And yet, in earthly life, he was a very son of wrath,—ready to kill upon the slightest provocation. Now he is full of mercy! but he can never lose that fire and energy. The sinking girl is very low, but more than any spirit I have met, he has the power to rouse her into anger. Chis he is pledged to do. Under that stimulus she will rally for a time, but not for very long. It is not best to tell her parents, but I say to you that she will leave in two months and a half."

Does it seem incredible that even a spirit could calculate so closely, and speak of life and death with such a certainty? This spirit did, not once or twice alone, but when it must be done.

Next Sabbath-day we went to visit Frankie, and found her dressed and very much improved. "Tell her about the Arabian!" urged Mrs. Brown. When I had told it, Frankie said, with laughter: "You should have let me tell my story first. About the hour you name, I had a fit of temper;—more than a fit; it lasted just three days. I was brimful of ugliness. I said the most sarcastic things I could imagine. I don't see how my people bore it. I was unbearable. Mother can tell you all about it. A friend, whom I expected, came as soon as possible; and yet I taunted him: 'You have honored me by coming—rather late! My friends delayed the funeral; they thought perhaps you'd like to view the corpse.'" A sorry lover's welcome;—"top-full of direst cruelty!"

"It was very hard to bear," her mother said. "But then it gave us hope."

So Frankie left her bed, took pleasant rides, called in her special friends, stood up prettily in white and said "I will," went through a lengthened honey-moon, and sank away at the predicted time. After that, no doubt she had her unimagined, overwhelming joy; although she came and made her sweet complaint: "Too sunny!"

But is there not a sheltering Tree of Life, to cast soft shadows, meet for dazzled eyes?—not darkness: never that!

Our modern Israel's sweetest singer, Emma Lazarus, dictated on her dying day:

195

"It is blackest night between the stars,

And how is a soul to see?"

What right have we, who have learned that life and light are one, to let these wandering souls go down the road untaught and unconsoled?

I sometimes thought my guardian made his moods my own. Thinking his thoughts, Death seemed to me of little moment,—something indeed to be deferred as long as possible (that being a doctor's way), but not to be deplored. For those who lived and sorrowed, he showed abundant pity,—little for those who were about to die. One time, in talk, he let us know that every added hour on earth augments the life to come; so necessary is the physical foothold to the eternal traveler! Who, even imagining that, would be a suicide? After which he spoke of murderers of babes, and bitter expiation; also of compensating laws and life and growth, even for the least of these so robbed of human name and place.

It came my turn to ask a special favor. My sisters wrote, indefinitely, that mother's health was poor. They knew but little of that inner life of which my mother knew so much. For since she had elected to remain a Methodist, I thought to proselyte would be dishonorable, even had I the power. But now I asked of Dr. Andrews: "Will you visit mother and prescribe?"

There was no need to indicate the road (which I had never traveled); for she and I were so allied, that, not our sympathies alone, but our antagonisms kept us close in touch. My guardian went to see her;—so far as I can judge, I went myself. I had a singular triple consciousness. Not aware of going, yet I was perfectly aware of her, of him, of me;—even of my frame that quivered constantly,—who knows why? I leaned above my mother, searching the body through with Psychic, Psycho-physical or Psychometric eyes.

Chiefly I saw a much diseased, discolored liver, certain to poison all the springs of life, unless some magic remedies could interpose to cleanse. These were prescribed by Dr. Andrews, when he spoke at last, after his usual manner. You understand he gave me little, telepathic messages at times, but always spoke aloud when there was much to say. This time he told me how my mother suffered deep discouragement. He imitated her and sighed and said: "Oh, dear! Oh, dear! Oh, dear!" most piteously.

That was not like my proud, courageous mother. Yet, when I wrote the Psychic story home, my oldest sister (quite severely Methodistic) answered: "If you could hear her say, as we do constantly: 'Oh, dear! Oh, dear! Oh, dear!' you would realize how very sick she is!" And so the medicines were taken just as my guardian ordered, and health somewhat renewed. They were two botanic—old-fashioned liver remedies it proved. I used to wonder that a Boston doctor, practising so long before, had chiefly dealt in simples; but these belonged essentially to Eastern therapeutics. Partly traditional among the Puritans, partly adopted from the Indian tribes, the people valued them. Unhappy day when doctors threw them out!

Whether I went to see my mother or Dr. Andrews went alone— came back and made me see (as in a picture once before), Psychists, among themselves might differ. The fact remains—I saw! But that he went at least, I had a curious confirmation. One of my younger sisters wrote: "Mother has had a lovely dream; and she believes that it relates to you. She has been happier ever since."

Unknown to mother I was just about to publish my "Atlantis"— Poems of the war and other verse, intending to surprise her happily.

And now I thought: "If I could just be told what mother dreamed and write the story home, that ought to give them still more confidence." When next the spirit came he said: "It was a beautiful dream of flowers and light,—induced by me to make your mother cheerful." Nothing very definite it seemed, and yet I wrote the very words to her and asked her what they meant.

She answered through my sister: "This is what I dreamed: I stood within a garden, looking at a rare and singular plant. It had no leaves and but a single stem— tall, tapering and absolutely white. Right at the top were two large, wonderful, shining flowers—white without and white and lavender within. I asked: 'What is the name of this?' and someone answered: 'It is called the candle-plant,

197

because it gives out light.' I said: 'I want a slip of it. I want it in my garden. How shall I get the slip?' And I was answered: 'This is your garden; and the plant is yours!' Then I reasoned: 'A plant that gives out light must be a symbol. What does it symbolize?' and I was told."

Now what the symbol meant is not for me to say; but this I realized: Whoever made my mother happier had much enriched myself.

THE WAY OF A SPIRIT

AN occulist detects the faulty sight. The Psychist finds no flaw in spirit-eyes. They need no telescope to see far off,—across the earth or out among the stars; nor any magnifying lens to view the ultimate atom. Within their line of vision, nothing blurs the backward-looking sight; whatever came to light a million years ago, they see as well as that which happened yesterday, or happens on the instant, even while they gaze. "All this I steadfastly believe."

To me, the greatest wonder lies in this: How souls incarnated can ever be content with visual limitation when all the radiant universe is waiting to be seen.

Within my gallery of Psychic pictures—invisible to any save myself—hang, here and there, those that have borne invincibly the test of outward proof. I hold them not more genuine than others. On one and all alike is set the master-signature.

This faculty of seeing without the visual orbs, belongs to all mankind. Latent or evident, held in reserve for higher spheres, or active in the human life, this proof of immortality exists in every soul. If one perceives more readily than many, that argues no superiority—only, perhaps, a somewhat earlier development. The "plant that gives out light" springs white from every soil.

To be so sure, one must be fortified with facts. There have been times when I have seen from far (not being asleep in any sense, nor always with the eyelids closed), those who were living in the flesh but totally unknown to me; and afterward have met them face to face—color for color, line for line, wrinkle for wrinkle. That is living demonstration!

One of these incidents I have related. Trifling, inconsequent and even ludicrous, it had the element of prophecy, and so was dignified immeasurably. This one which follows, albeit not prophetic, has value, since it shows that spirits have a sense of fellowship, and sympathize with us in little troubles hardly to be thought afflictive.

Mr. Brown received a letter stating that his father—whose twentieth child was taking care of him—was in the act of death; and adding that a telegram should follow soon as he had breathed his last. So twice a day the son drove several miles to get the promised message, all in vain; till he was forced to let the matter drop.

One day his wife came down to visit Mrs. Higley, Nettie and myself; and after dinner Nettie urged: "You older ones can talk with Dr. Andrews—why not I?" And so we gathered for a little circle,—she also being given, at last, her bit of "bread with honey-comb." Before the spirit spoke, after I was aware of him, he turned my head around, requiring me to look away toward the East. I felt a vibratory motion first, and then I seemed to gaze through empty space, a long way off. "What is to see?" I wondered.

Now here is something strange. Nothing obstructs the Psychic sight. No dungeon walls could be so thick that such a vision could not pierce them through as they were thinnest ether,—and find, if so the soul desired, the squalid prisoner within. Even more strange: The prisoner, himself a solid fact, would start in view—a visible man in rags, and every rag as visible as he. It seems the soul elects to see or not to see, according to its will. Matter or spirit, either one or both, the eyes behold, and brook no interference.

And so I looked, or went, I know not which (with my companion consciously at hand), right through the intervening hills and through the plastered walls, without perceiving them, until I saw a very sick old man. I knew (impossible to say just how I knew!), that this was Levi's father.

Dressed in a clean white shirt, his rocking chair spread with a clean white quilt—brought round to wrap his knees, his arms upon the elbows, his eyes fixed steadily upon the floor,—he certainly was not a dying man.

And now observe: I saw the shell-work pattern stitched upon the quilt, as surely as I saw the man himself!—the square, strong face, the tuft of grizzled hair above the forehead (a little baldness either side), the slightly opened mouth, the pallid flesh, the listless attitude!—Such is the excellence of spirit sight.

Without the slightest doubt, I sent my re-assuring word to Mr. Brown: "Your father is alive, and convalescent!"

Nothing more was learned till eight weeks afterward. Then, taking tea alone with Mrs. Brown, I saw the outer door swing open and on the threshold stepped my sick, old man! I leaped up crying: "Here is Levi's father!" and ran to bring an easy chair. Doffing his hat, he sat him down therein, his arms upon the elbows, his eyes upon the floor—inert and pale, with slightly opened mouth, a tuft of hair—not altogether gray—crowning the grand, old head! Nothing was lacking but the invalid's dress and the white quilt brought round to hide the knees.

But let me add: I saw him no more clearly than I saw my scowling Texas Indian, my Englishman in corduroy who fired his guns, my mastodon that lived, we'll guess, five thousand years ago, my Quaker lady far away in space, who pointed me to earth, my old man walking on the clouds behind his wayward son, the son himself—a wan consumptive just about to die.

Time past erects no barrier before the Psychic eyes. Time present lets them rove at will,—ignoring all but that one thing the spirit means to see and that is never hidden! Time future laughs behind his blackest cloud to see what deathless orbs peer through!

And now some mis-believing friend might cry: "Look! How she tries to overlay with gold her carven-work of knops and flowers and foolish little stems!" Suppose I do: Are they not wrought in cedar—sweet and serviceable, cut for the Lord's own house?

Now since there is an infinite future latent in the Mind of God, why not a finite future latent in the mind of man?

One glimpse thereof establishes the truth. However narrow be the scope, our lives are drawn in one continuous line with that which never dies. Past, present, future—depth and height and ever widening vision, all are ours!

And so I linger for awhile to pluck these little road-side flowers of which I predicate perpetual bloom!—for verily, were nothing else in sight, a thistle-plant would demonstrate eternal energy! I interject what happened twelve years further on.

Letters had passed between a Manufacturing Company and myself concerning one of my inventions. By invitation, I was speeding toward Erie, Pennsylvania, for a personal interview.

Chancing to close my eyes for rest, I saw a gentleman approaching, ten feet or so away, and looking at a little card held up for scrutiny. Very pale he was and evidently sick. I had a clear three-quarter's view of a peculiar face that seemed a racial type. Fine, sensitive, strong yet non-assertive, pleasing yet puzzling,—evidently Jewish, though not a common Jewish face by any means; withal so young I felt astonishment, even while I said: "Why, that is Charles Jarecki!" I had supposed him old.

Some six hours later, at the Company's Office, I handed in my card and asked to see the President. I was told: "His brother, Charles, has written all the letters. He is dangerously sick to-day and can't be seen." A boy ran in announcing: "Mr. Charles is better. He is up and dressed." "In that case, call and send him in your card. His wife can tell you when to call again."

Exceedingly prosaic! I went that evening: In walked Charles Jarecki, holding up my card, and giving me, at first, a clear, three-quarter's view of that same pallid face that I had seen eight hours before,—kind, fine, attractive, young, and stamped with honor's signet,—a Poland-Jewish face that I am glad to let you see among my Psychic pictures!

Here is the absolute fact: A man not seen before, appeared to me exactly as he would appear, when I should see him eight hours afterward.

But at the very instant of the seeing, the man was in the throes of Cholera Morbus! The time between was short, but what of that? One such prevision came to me, in fact, three months, at least, before fulfilment—absolute as this! I apprehend that greater souls have looked through many centuries to come and prophesied momentous happenings. Did not Isaiah live? And John, the Revelator?

So back to my Progressive Friends, whom I was soon to leave: My book, at last, was in the printer's hands, and I was much in need of physical restoration. Consulting Dr. Hubbard Foster, (removed to

Buffalo) he ordered me away to Dr. Green, who, with himself, had saved me nine years earlier; and straightway wrote to her that she must take me in, though every room she had were doubly occupied.

Much averse to giving trouble, I wrote to Dr. Green that I should stop along the way, seven miles above Castile, till, somewhere in her crowded Water-Cure, there might be found a vacant corner. What happened at the stopping place, is what I choose to tell.

Near Warsaw lived a gentleman and lady whom I had met but twice. First, at a Hemlock Hall convention, during which the lady shared my room, and somehow seized upon me as a source of comfort—socially, not otherwise. My mediumistic possibilities were in abeyance for a time—not to be spoken of to strangers. The following year, these people came again and sought me out with such affection, I was deeply moved. Said Mary, Queen of Scots: "I have been much beloved." And I may say as well: "I have been much befriended!"

Learning from Mr. Brown that Psychic messages were often given out by me, among my intimates, this lady asked, with hesitation, whether I thought she also might be favored. It afterward appeared that she had lost a son (somewhat estranged after her second marriage), from whom she longed to hear. She supposed he had been shot in battle and buried on the field. She did not speak of this; but seeing her anxiety though I was ill, I took her hand and waited, hoping some small revelation might content the lady. Nothing came from Dr. Andrews, in the usual way; but some young soldier—name unknown—informed her that the one she wished to know about was fighting Indians. He amplified the statement by giving us, in a sort of head-long way, the story of a recent skirmish, and how the soldier fought while "dodging bullets."

But since he did not say out-right: "This one you wish to hear from is your son," the lady seemed bewildered: "I can't imagine what is meant! My boy was killed almost two years ago."

But, very like Prof. Lowell's "ghost" who, "could not eat a dinner without endangering his constitution," this son of hers considered as a ghost, had gone much further and ruined his entirely, by entering the regular army and fighting Indians merrily, without sufficient grace to let his mother know. This last he did soon after; and finding from his letter that all had been correctly told through me, these McWithys would not be denied, but wrote persistently that I must visit them as soon as possible.

Behold me, therefore, just arrived one Saturday afternoon, my bonnet not yet off! And verily my hostess saying in a breath: "I am rejoiced to see you! You have come just in the nick of time! I have a girl—almost a daughter, though she works for me—who is full of trouble. She has been crying all day long—I mustn't tell you why. I have promised her a circle. She knows about my son, and she'll believe whatever she is told. I'm sure you will help her willingly."

"I would if that were possible," I said. "But I am very sick. I think no spirit could make any use of such a tired brain."

"Oh, well! We'll have our supper first, and talk about the circle afterward. I know you can't refuse."

Not very cheerful—being waited on at table by a girl of singular beauty—nineteen possibly—whose tears "ran down like rivers;" nor happifying to be followed to the sitting room and made to understand that Undine's very soul might trickle off in that salt-water, unless, in some mysterious way, myself could lock those lacrymal canals! I grew so sympathetic, that I said, at last: "I see no hope of being influenced by a spirit to tell you what you wish to know. It comes to me that someone whom you love has gone away and you're afraid he'll not come back. If so, get me a lock of hair or something he has worn. I'll try Psychometry."

According to a reasonable theory, Psychometry concerns the past alone. Still I had once Psychometrized a letter that seemed to push me on long past the time of writing, (howbeit probably a spirit made me see in that case what the letter never could have shown.) I laid the lock of hair against my aching forehead and shut my eyes and waited wearily.

Not very long: A rescuing hand drew down my own and I was made aware of Dr. Andrews.

I think we did not go away in search of anyone. We looked—I looked, undoubtedly because he chose to have me see—a long way off. I saw a man, dressed in rough clothing, wearing a black fur cap, sitting upon the steps of a back porch belonging to a house built in the woods. With his left hand he used a ramrod—cleaning out his gun. A sinewy frame, long legs, brown hair, a partial profile visible above the chin, but nothing that would certainly identify the man above all other men. I understood that he had just been hurt and how he had been hurt; but all the rest was left to be revealed by someone else. What I saw, the spirit usually left for me to tell; what was beyond my knowledge he explained.

Now—holding out the lock of hair—said Dr. Andrews, in a jocular way, as one might pacify a foolish child: "Well!—It takes women to worry! The head from which this hair was cut is supposed to be all right! In fact, I have just seen the man, himself. I found him in the back-woods, several hundred miles from here.

"In firing off his gun, it had recoiled, so his right shoulder is considerably injured—not very seriously. Now he is cleaning out the barrel, meaning to fire again. You know he cannot write; but, if he could, there'd be no way of sending off a letter. Heavy rains have made the roads impassable. He can't come back, because he can't get out. Now, please to be content! He'll be here just three weeks from Wednesday—not a day before!"

While this was being said, I saw an elderly lady dressed in white—most fair and sweet, with glistening silver hair. She held a year-old babe, a very beautiful child,—earthly enough, you might have thought, to cling about its mother's neck; and there the mother sat before me, heart and soul intent on what the spirit promised. This I fully understood.

Therewith he added: "To convince you more, here is your grandmother with a message for you. She says: 'Tell her the boy is well and happy. I am taking care of him.'" When I was all myself again, I described the lady and the child minutely to the girl, so that she laughed for pleasure, recognizing both. But when I told about the man, she seemed a little troubled: "He hasn't got a black fur cap." "But what does all this mean?" I asked my hostess. "You introduce me to a girl who must have been a mother years ago—though certainly not twenty. And where's her husband? Why did she imagine he was never coming back?"

"It means that she was once betrayed—a child of just fifteen. I took her in, and I have kept her ever since. Before her baby died, Mr. McWithy hired an Irishman, a really worthy fellow, though he cannot read. He fell in love with her at once; but fearing to be drafted (though he had come from Ireland but a little while before), he ran away and hid—he never told us where. After a year he came, and they were married very happily. He has gone to get his chest of tools and other properties but promised to return this very day. She lost all hope this morning, believing he had gone forever—just as the other went."

There really is nothing more to add but this: "Three weeks from Wednesday" in walked the husband, wearing his black fur cap; explaining also that the roads, in Northern Michigan backwoods, had been so deluged by the rains, not even an ox-team could drag the wagons through; and furthermore in firing off his gun, one day, it had recoiled and hurt his shoulder rather badly; and being closely questioned he named the time and place: "On a back porch, three weeks ago last Saturday, in the afternoon."

Will anyone presume to say that this was all illusion? Or peradventure hypnotism?—self-hypnotism?—telepathy? Or anything but what it claimed to be,—a spirit cheering us with spirit-intercourse? And, by the way, what is telepathy but spirit-intercourse?

Or, be the fact admitted: Was it anyway worthwhile to come from "Beulah Land," merely to tell a nervous woman not to worry. In very truth a woman's grief may sometimes work incalculable harm; and anyway, were Christ again on earth, would he not stoop to soothe a crying babe?

You have read those nursery tales, that tell of mothers coming back to save their little ones from cruelties? If nothing I have written yet appeals to you, please do not turn away this moment. That which has made me happier for more than forty years, should have some little interest for kindly folk like you.

When I had said "Good-bye" to Dr. Green (physician, saint,— almost without a peer!), I slipped again, with better health, into the heart of things—the pleasant home of Mrs. Levi Brown.

One Sunday afternoon, without an invitation, there came to us an unseen guest. He spoke through me, and said that he was Levi's brother, William Brown, a sailor. To prove his calling, as it seemed, he did some personating, tried to be—or was—uncouth, and used a little sailor-slang; then laughed and said: "Good-bye!"

Mr. Brown remarked: "I never had a brother William. I had a brother who enlisted in the Navy under the name of "William Brown," and always kept the name. We never called him so at home." He said no more, waiting, perhaps, some further demonstration.

The sailor came again that evening, still without request. This time I saw him, but I only scrutinized a woman he was leading in—who made herself appear as she had been on earth—some forty years of age, quite worn away with sickness, anxious-eyed and sorely troubled—one who needed help.

I said to Mr. Brown: "Your brother's here and he has brought his wife."

"She was alive when last I heard from her. How does she look?"

"Slender and pale, brown-eyed, brown-haired, and very thin. She looks like Mrs. Higley; just that type of woman."

"Yes, that is true. You couldn't have described her better."

Now at this point my Dr. Andrews intervened, interpreting, as now and then he did. About these days, he seldom came, fearful, I think, of taxing me too much. The instrument was very weak, but here was ample reason for its use, and very urgent need.

He said: "This woman is unhappy. She tells me she has left a daughter twelve years old, alone and friendless—miserable—forlorn.

She wishes you to find the child and rescue her. Your brother asks you to adopt her as a daughter."

"Most gladly! Where can she be found? We don't know where the mother lived, nor where she died. Two years ago, we had a letter. We answered it, but never heard again."

"There is one way to find the child and only one. Write to the Post-master of the place from which you had the letter. Tell him to use all diligence in seeking her. He will succeed."

"What is his name?" asked Mr. Brown.

"That doesn't signify. Do as I tell you; write to the Post-master. There is no other possible way of finding her. Let there be no delay. The case is very urgent. The child is utterly desolate—utterly desolate!"

After a pause the spirit said in a low voice, once again, as though in deepest pity: "Utterly desolate!"

How was it with the child? The agent spent two weeks in diligent inquiry and active search. He traced her to a cabin in the woods, vacated by the owners for a house three miles away. But they had left behind an aged mother, bedridden, deaf and blind and witless, leaving the little girl to take sole care of her. This she had done for many months most faithfully, not seeing any human being save the son, who came just twice a week to leave provisions—driving off without so much as going in to view that living death. "Friendless," "alone" and "utterly desolate!"

Mr. Brown had written: "Notify my brother when she is found," and to the brother: "When you are notified, please go out and get our niece, and send her here, at my expense."

The brother answered: "She belongs to me as much as she belongs to you. We have had her for a week and cannot give her up. She is ours, we have adopted her."

What good can spirits do? I told you once that by and bye I should begin to tell;—and I have just begun.

Allow one more narration before I pass along to traverse broader fields. After a summer spent with Margaret among the Cattaraugus hills and breakers, where the water-falls went sliding over to find the creeks below (upon a farm more dear to me than any place on earth), I found myself the inmate of a Buffalo Air-Cure, that had just been opened. There during seven months, I spent two hours each day, with others, in a tank lighted with plate-glass windows, breathing and living in a more than doubled atmosphere.

"Your heart is tired to death!" said Dr. Foster. "Nothing else can save you." And, by the way, that compressed air-bath cured my Margaret's niece, who had consumption in the second stage and whom the greatest New York specialist condemned to speedy death. But I besought her to submit the case to Dr. Foster, who agreed with Dr. Flint, but thought her savable by compressed air. She lived thereafter twenty years!—albeit with half a lung destroyed! yet not an invalid—a working farmer's wife and happy mother. And I— "heart tired to death" at thirty-one—behold me seventy-four and writing still!

And yet this remedy, that should have saved a hundred thousand lives in forty years, is used, I think, to-day in but one Sanitarium— that of Clifton Springs! What are the doctors doing?

But for the narrative: Dr. Mary Bryant Burdick tapped at my door and introduced a lady barely thirty-five, with brilliant eyes and burning cheeks. "Please let her stay with you awhile; her room is cold."

This Mrs. Lydia H—-(I am not authorized to give her name in full), sat down and chatted pleasantly for half an hour, not even mentioning that she was miserably sick. Then, in a little pause, I was aware of Dr. Andrews, saying urgently: "I wish to help this woman"

"Do you belong to any church?" I asked.

"I am a Free-Will Baptist."

"Have you ever known a medium-one who is controlled by spirits?"

"I never have."

"I am obliged to tell you that I am one myself. Just now a spirit-doctor came and said: 'I wish to help this woman.' Are you willing he should try?"

"I'm past all possible help, the doctors say."

"Don't tell me what they say, nor anything about your case. Just answer this: May Dr. Andrews (that used to be the spirit's name) take up your case through me. He wants to do you good and I believe he can."

Her face was one delight: "And will you come to me tomorrow?"

"At any hour you name."

I had fore-gathered happily with Dr. Mary Burdick. So far as I can recollect, she was the only one in Buffalo, who ever heard me speak of Dr. Andrews. She came to me and said: "This Mrs. H. ... whom Doctors have pronounced incurable, appeals to us. There's nothing we can do, except to let her take an air-bath now and then. I'm not a Spiritualist but I believe you really are clairvoyant. Please see what you can do."

"Meantime," I said: "Don't tell me anything about what ails her. Dr. Andrews told me yesterday he wished to help the woman, and I agreed to visit her today."

So, with no other medical authority, I went to see the lady week by week and let my friend conduct her back to life. He said, at once: "Consumption of the nerves." He showed how they refused to carry, from the over-active brain, those vital currents generated for the body's need; and how the death of particles before their time had clogged the tissues, so that there had been one monstrous tumor (happily removed); and there had been paralysis; now there were frequent swoonings—not because of heart-disease, as other doctors said—but due to causes quite removable.

How then? Oh, first a change of diet; pea-meal to feed the nerves and artichokes (I never knew for what); but here's the one and only remedy:

210

Hot foot and leg baths to the knees, no less than forty minutes long, three times a week, in very strong herb-tea!

"There are certain wholesome herbs," he said, "that housewives used to stow away for use in time of sickness." He named a number, among them "yarrow, tansy, cat-nip, motherwort, valerian and penny-royal." "These are live herbs," he told us; "they are stored with healing properties and, rightly used, they have the power to quicken life. This bath, for you, means physical revolution; you will be very sick three weeks, and after that will follow gradual recovery. I do not promise perfect health, but in a year you'll say that you are well."

All this was realized. Whatever stored-up energy these many herbs possessed ran through her frame, quickened her circulation, set all her flesh a-prickle, made her nerves alive. The miracle, it seemed, had verily come to pass. So the lady lived, and so she said before the year was ended: "I am well!"

Now eight years after that I met her in Chicago. There had been a loss of home and means; there had been a painful bodily injury; but she had risen up from that to earn her living. She was teaching elocution and giving public recitations.

"Why, how is this?" I asked. "I never knew you were an elocutionist."

"I never was, till I had lost my home, and then a spirit came and taught me, so that I could live."

I cannot tell you how it was; but when I heard her exercise her gift, I thought: "Whoever taught her understood his art!"

TRANSITION

THAT which is spoken of as mediumship, is not miraculous. Even the so-called Psychic trance is not abnormal—much less supernatural. It comes by natural law, as birth and sleep and death must come, not otherwise. That is to say: All laws are natural. At least, can you conceive of one without a physical basis? Or any, obviously operative here, that has no reach beyond?

God does not disunite His peopled worlds—the spirit-world and this. They pass for two and yet are altogether one. I apprehend there is no law or force or element, which does not bear direct or indirect relation to the human frame and its immortal guest. What though the incarnate soul is soon to be a soul escaped and on the wing? Even so it cannot be released from law, but only from "the bondage of the law." That which we strive against is that which binds. Spirit with law eternally accords.

But what is law? A gentleman near eighty years of age, devout and philanthropic, challenged me! "Do you believe that God will answer prayer? We know that He has made His laws. They are inflexible; they govern all alike; there is no preference. It is not possible that He should make a special law to meet a special case. He could not if He would. Why should He think of us at all? That is not necessary; He has made His laws!"

"But you mistake," I said. "God never made a law,—He is law." That was not much to say but this resulted: Half a year later, I, being far away and uninformed, was deep in midnight sleep;—should you prefer, we'll say in Psychic trance. I saw him coming slowly toward me, smiling all the way, and looking at me just as I had seen him look when he was planning some beneficence (which I shall tell about most likely, further on). Close by, he gave a happy laugh, as though his cup of joy were running over; then said, in just his old, incisive way: "Miss Jones, you were about right. God is Law!" And then he passed along, still looking back and smiling, till I awoke, and, for a fleeting instant, knew that he was there. Not yet three days in spirit life,—I think he well believed that God can answer prayer.

If then we speak with angels, whether in sleep or trance, or by a happy flow and interflow of thoughts and words, we speak by natural law. Perhaps, a little earlier than yourself, one whom you call a medium has recognized a spirit world;—Oh, not his world alone, but yours and mine,—the world of all mankind! One world with this—one school with ours,—its classes more advanced no doubt, but not beyond our reach!

If I could meet you, face to face, your hand would clasp my own with no more certainty than soul would answer soul. You, who are reading this, to me are virtually disembodied. I do not see you, hear you, touch you in a physical sense. I am aware of you. I dare to think you are aware of me. Where is the miracle?

But say that in the natural way (as one prepares to dress for any banquet) I step from out this work-a-day attire of mortal flesh and come to you in gala dress (such as my means afford—not very lustrous, reasonably white)—why should you fear to have me as your guest? Why refuse me place at table when you serve your costly cates and delicates, your melons, grapes and honey? Even a crust with vinegar—should that be all—if shared, would give a sense of fellowship. Suppose I find you starving? At least may I not whisper in your ear and quote from Holy Writ: "Whoever perished, being innocent?" or urge, with tenderness: "Rejoice, and eat and drink; it is the gift of God?"

Let no one think that Psychic powers are accidents. All human tribes and races have one parentage, one homogenesis. No single soul can have a super-added faculty or miss an attribute. If then I claim to be a "medium" myself, I claim no less for you.

Beyond all else, there is an ultimate sense of spirit-contact with the Infinite. As though God would not have us join His merrymakers till we have burned our rags and taken from His very hands new dress and garniture. We know that this re-generating touch, sooner or later comes to every soul, whether it be a habitant of flesh or "hidden in the cloud." Have we not seen Ben Hogan—vilest of the vile—spring from the slough upon the instant, going forth to be for many years a true Evangelist? Have we not known a Harry Orchard—dipped in blood near to the drowning point—stand out

213

and call on God and men to make him clean through swift and shameful death?

Still you object: "Since Infinite Grace can do so much, what need of finite spirits trooping in? Keep to the higher level."

No less, the fact remains: Our one Redeemer deigns to make us co-associates in His redemptive work. Spirit-ministration, spirit-recognition, spirit-intercourse—these are our great prerogatives. Through finite love, we come to apprehend the Infinite.

Witness this: A man I knew in New York City, 1875, had been a delegate from Ireland to the Fenians—welcomed with jubilation, dined and wined till swept quite off his feet with hospitality. How then? His friends far off, his boon companions near—who was to intervene? Besides, what Irish gentleman would brook an interference?

Now, after I had known him long—he walking all that time "the straight and narrow path"—he came and told me what had so converted him.

Deep in the night "a spirit passed before his face"—nay, there were two, his father and his mother! They came and stood beside his bed, and spoke in common necessary words! "Son, stop this drinking. It will end in death. Go now and hide where none of these will find you. Be obedient."

"I never disobeyed them while they lived," he said. "How could I disobey them now?" And so, by wise direction, he had found a place of refuge—half-hotel, half-sanitarium (Laight Street Water Cure), and, to our wonder, took a far-off parlor corner, not speaking word to any; till, putting by distrust, we spoke to him and made him one of us. So there he stayed, went always to his morning mass, and, by and bye, went safely out and started honest business. "To everyone his way"—even though he be a disembodied spirit.

"Must we believe," you cry, "that any man, fresh from his cups, could have a Psychic vision? Are spirit-visits quite so cheap and common?"

"Well, for that matter, sunshine, which with babe or drunkard "pricks the eyelids wide," is altogether cheap. Sin as we may, "the ineffable light comes up." But do illusions pass before the eyes by twos, take on familiar forms and faces, pause, open lips and speak, say vital words, advise, command, convert? Pray do you think hallucinations lead to godliness?

Meantime, with your permission coming back to self;—my double atmospheres that have a way of quieting the heart by doing half its work, ransacking lungs and burning out impurities, detecting every shrunken plasmic cell and forcing them to seek for nutrients, had brought that mind of me down to a lower level. Physically weak yet renovated past the danger point, that "mental grip" relaxed. "I dare not eat enough," a hungry working-woman said when given a plenteous meal, "lest I should get the habit." The mortal part of me had got the habit. It took whatever vital energy a brain could generate'. It starved the poet—if so be there was a poet. As for the mediumship, that fared no better; it became much like a wilted flower—past further bloom.

When, after some few added weeks among the healing pines, I came to Mother's house in June of 1868, I seemed a very useless creature. Not that she wanted me to be of use; I trust that she was glad to have me back on any terms; and yet I felt my disability too much to be content. Why, even she—so ill a year or two before—took comfort with the hoe and sometimes kept herself full half the day a-field, trimming her flower-beds afterward; and if I begged: "Come, let me shell the peas!" she smiled and said: "This is the way I rest!" Nothing for me to do but eat and sleep and roam the woods, and gain a little every day, through very idleness.

Was that, indeed, "the whole of life to live?" Was it not rather "all of death to die?"

And now it seemed that whomsoever God might choose for almoner, I was the one left out. No one at hand who needed ministration, no one asking for a Psychic gift, poetic fervor fled— perhaps forever, baffled with hindrances, pushed back from climbing, tossed aside from doing good, the very gates of Heaven shut fast against my touch;—what was there left to do?

Not far to seek was this, my underself,—turning away from evident mercies, starving before a well-spread feast because the sweets were lacking, "choosing darkness rather than the light!" Let it be said there was one saving grace; my grief was not paraded. Not even my mother guessed that "climbing sorrow." At least, I spared her that.

There came a day when every burden I had ever borne, like forest fagots bound in one enormous bundle, seemed laid upon me once again; and, no less real to Psychic sense, the many years to come were there already, each bringing burdens doubly bound,—too great for soul to bear. I saw my sisters ride away to church, caught up my hat, fled to the woods, and sank full length upon the sward—prone at the feet of God. I was not used to violent emotions; but now my knees were water; I drank the "cup of trembling." Save for one childish instant, I had never known the touch of fear; but now, more terrible than all besides, my underself, come uppermost, had made me sore afraid. I cowered before the dreadful years to be.

At worst, I had no fear of God; I fled to Him for help. I called upon Him, heart and soul and voice. Here was a wrong that He alone could right. I had been called to serve, yet I was thrust aside. I had striven long and not without result, but now I was forbidden; earth itself would have no more of me. Once in the spirit-world, I might return, as others had, and reach out helping hands. I called on God to give me service there—not leave me idle here! I clamored, "Take me now! This very hour. This coming moment! I have a right to work! Take me where there is work to do. It is my right! It is my right!"

Then I was silent. He to whom I spake was just. I waited for the Word.

Lying face down upon the grass—my earthly vision sealed—let no one say I had not other eyes. I saw—not far above, nor heralded with splendor—one who moved as though he would have passed, then paused and turned and looked below,—looked in my very eyes. I knew him—not because of pictured semblances, though they are somewhat like—but in my inmost soul I knew him for the MAN of men, whom nations call the Christ. Once I said that he would hear and make reply, whatever desert wanderer called on him for help. I had not named his name—I had not thought of him; but he was there.

Was ever human face so stern? Were ever human eyes so tender?

Words there were none,—neither my own nor those which men had used two thousand years ago; and yet so long he gazed, with such a mastery of thought and sense, I felt and understood what words could never breathe.

He was aware of me in all my spiritual squalor, yet he loved. He made me know that still he held the memory of Life's immeasurable anguish, Love's immeasurable grief; and, more than that, the poignant memory of many men and women tossed to feed the lions, torn upon the rack or ringed about with fire—to whom the Spirit ministered of old; also, I was aware of souls, yet living in the flesh, who to the uttermost were sacrificing self, because of holy love.

Before all these my little sorrow was like a flake of snow that melts in fervent heat. Then it was given me to understand that I must follow them as one far off; that even I was chosen both for service and for sacrifice; nor must I make complaint. Therewith the vision passed.

I saw no others, yet I knew of them and how they said above me: "Let her be content." I rose—not glad but not rebellious—leaned against an oak and sighed: "Nothing remains save resignation! but, oh, the long, dark years to come! How shall I bear the burden of the years?"

"Go home now, and in First Corinthians, read the third verse of the second chapter!"

So came the message. What was this to be? I had no memory, nor felt in haste to know. I looked away toward my pleasant home and sighed again: "How shall I bear the burden of the years?" But when I rose at last, the message came again:

"Remember now! First Corinthians, second and third."

Notice: These words were not a repetition. The challenge to remember, the little transposition, proved them not an echo. So I returned; and finding all at home, gave them a hurried greeting, sought a testament and slipped away to read:

"And I was with you in weakness and in fear and in much trembling."

Since then, through forty years and more, I have not been afraid of "height nor depth nor any other creature."

And now another June had come. Meantime I had been stirred, as poets are, so Mrs. Browning says:

"With Spring's delicious trouble in the ground,—Tormented by the quickened blood of roots,

And softly pricked by golden crocus-sheaves."

That is to say, my thoughts began to blossom into rhymes. Aside from other work I wrote "One night"—a Psychic poem, rather long, (published in Scribner's Monthly, 1873) and realized that I was done with battle themes and still might hope to help a sweeter choristry.

About those days I had a dream that set me wondering. This I choose to tell, because, if I have judged aright, it proves that "living persons"—oh, you know the jargon!—men and women, in the flesh, can roam in sleep, can visit friends, foresee what waits for these, and symbolize, as by some miracle, conditions yet to be. There is no proof at hand that I, myself, have ever done the like. I prize the more this proof that others have.

I dreamed that I was in a great unfinished building, having many rooms whose low partitions did not reach the ceilings. There was no litter, all was swept and clean; and someway I was made to know that work was laid aside till I should come with means to finish all. How this could ever be I had no power to guess.

So roaming round, within an upper story, I came upon a wide palatial flight of stairs; and, looking down, I saw below and waiting for me, Mrs. Lydia Brown.

"Come down," she said. "There's something I must show you."

So I ran down, and after we had cast our arms around each other, still holding fast, she drew me to a dusky room and to a window curtained heavily. Then, lifting up the curtain, and dropping it behind us, so that we could see outside, she said: "Look up into the sky."

When I had looked, higher than any mountain top, but not too high for sight, I saw a group of three,—a man, a child, a woman. The man who seemed to be a farmer, was sitting tranquilly, reading his weekly paper one would say; the child was leaning on his knee, reading a smaller paper; the woman, on the further side, stood facing me and leaning on them both.

I said: "How very strange that is! Why do they read their papers in the sky? Is that where they belong?"

She answered: "You are looking only at the man and little girl. See if you know the woman."

"Why, yes!" I said, astonished; "that is myself!"

She answered: "That is you! But keep on looking at yourself! There's something more to see."

Now, by and bye, across the face of me, there came a startling change. It was the very face of one about to die—one in the grasp of death; ghastly and fixed—expressionless, save for the eyes that still were open, gazing far through space. I looked and wondered,— saying to my friend, but not in fear: "Why, surely this is death!" Then a white shaft of light streamed from the East and shone upon my face, that changed and presently became the face of one who was about to live. But still I leaned upon the child. And so my dream went by.

Soon after this, before the first of August, 1869, one day as I was wandering in the woods in half poetic, half religious mood (what is poetry if not religion?), I was aware once more of Dr. Andrews. This was not unusual;—it often seemed he came and looked and went away as soon as recognized. But now he had a definite purpose—he had come for speech.

Now, understand, those messages we call the telepathic, seem like accidental flashes out of some dark lantern may be—nothing to rely upon for steady guidance; but always when this spirit-friend (or other spirit-friends), had much to say, my voice was used and there was personation, just as much when I was all alone, as when my dear "Progressive Friends" were listening with myself.

I cannot give his words except approximately, but this is what they meant. He said that it was time for me to know I had been chosen for a special work, already under weigh. He said: "A great work utterly unlike what you have ever done." He spoke at length without defining it, but giving me to understand that it would call for life-long service, taxing brain and body, far beyond what seemed a possible limit. He said: "It is not ready for you yet,—you are not ready. When the time is ripe you will be called upon."

"I shall obey," my thoughts replied, "at any sacrifice; but what is it to be?"

"Nothing you can imagine; nothing you could understand. You would refuse belief. Even now you almost doubt; but did I ever tell you anything—even in prophecy—that was not true?"

"You never did. Must I appear in public?"

"Not as a lecturer. What you have to do is deeper, broader, more effectual for good."

"You know," I said, in thought, "how I desire to be a poet. Am I to sacrifice my art?"

"Not for a thousand worlds!"

I would not doubt; and yet—was ever faith so tried? He said: "Until you altogether trust, I will not come again." Nor did he during two full weeks, and then (one of the rarest happenings in life for me) I burst out sobbing: "Dr. Andrews; I believe!" With that he came at once: "First, it is necessary you should go away from home. You will be wanted in Chicago. Make your preparations."

I had in mind that funds would be required. This thought he answered, saying: "All you need will come." And so it proved, for certain sums yet due on book accounts, but given up as hopeless, drifted in till I was well supplied. And so I made me ready for departure, much to Mother's wonder.

I suppose spirits make use of common means to any worthy end, much as we mortals do. However, that may be, I wrote soon after this to Rev. J. M. Peebles, publisher of "Spiritual Songs" (including one of mine), suggesting that as he was going to Trebizond, there might be something I could do, perhaps, to fill his place in the United States.

H. N. F. Lewis, of Chicago, proprietor of a popular farmer's paper called "The Western Rural" wrote to me very soon, saying that Dr. Peebles recommended me, believing I was competent to act as editor of "The Universe." Would I come down and try?

A single number had been issued; this I chanced to see. It really seemed just what it claimed to be: "A paper in the interests of reform." So it was meant to be, and had a corps of notable contributors—while it lived; but oftentimes reformers have astigmatism—rays of light running in parallels belike, not coming to a focus on the retina; so nothing shows to them exactly as it is. I ought to say that just before I went, my faithful friend gave counsel quite sufficient; and, for more perfect guidance, described the person and the character of one with whom I had to deal. He sent me well prepared.

"The Universe?" Well, hardly that; not even a sun nor yet a morning star. We'll say a comet—not devoid of light, but carrying a train that might have blurred a star or two; only, like Biela's comet, it somehow lacked a stable nucleus. It rather blazed awhile, but truth to tell, I had the handling of so many manuscripts of somewhat doubtful import (which I edited severely), that I was ill at ease, and sought release. But in a month or two it whisked away to glorify New York. I did not follow. It was proposed and urged that I should be one of the nuclei (Biela's comet split, you recollect), and have my name emblazoned on the train: "And such a chance to make yourself a reputation," one philosopher said, "you'll never have again." I never did.

So, being duly meek, I begged of Mr. Lewis: "Put me on *The Western Rural*, make me co-associate with Mr. Glen (who did the heavy work). So there I verily stood and leaned upon the farmer;

yes, and on the child since half my work was for the young, who seemed to like it well.

Not having any startling salary, as you may guess, I more than doubled cash by writing from dictation after office-hours; till by and bye I struck! and, after that, was fairly paid, and rather prosperous. My stock—is that the word?—was booming. Why, now indeed, my wish to help at home, it seemed, might be fulfilled! But when the June was near at hand, a sister wrote that mother's health had broken down.

Well, there were compressed air-baths to be had. I wrote to Buffalo at once, engaged a room for her, and hurried home. "You've always had your way," I told her (mindful of shelling peas!) "and now my turn has come."

"You are doing right," said Dr. Andrews. "Nothing can save her life, but there's a little help for her; and I must let you know there is no other way to reach your Work." And that was prophecy!

And, oh, but she was sick! I sent her, under proper care; and round about her flocked her friends of old (as well they might! for who but she had helped their sick for many years? And who but they could feel such gratitude?) And so she stayed four months.

Meantime, the thought of her (likely to die at any moment, so the doctors said) was like a weight of lead. There came a "heated term"—air hot almost as when Chicago burned—and there was naught to do but struggle on, with every thought-pulse beating to the tune of "Mother"—always "Mother!" One evening Dr. Andrews came and chided me: "Throw off this deep depression; it pulls you down and does no good to her. You have one duty to yourself. Be cheerful! Get on the right side; and (lifting up the voice with emphasis) "get on r The Bright Side"

"Do you mean The Bright Side'—Mr. Alden's paper? Am I to leave the *Rural*?"

"That is what I mean."

You have all heard of John B. Alden. But for him the most of you had never heard of me. I had sent a contribution. After that he had a way of dropping in to see me now and then—a boy you understand, not twenty-two, and with a little young folks weekly all his own and rightly named "The Bright Side." Once he had said: "Suppose you come to me." "I can't in honor. When I struck I got my terms. I mustn't run away."

Now my employer had a pretty scheme for issuing a 11 Young Folks' Rural"—I being there on hand to do the work. It's "get and have," you know; that's natural! Next day he called me to the desk, all smiles: "What will you do for me on the new paper?"—"A great deal if you pay me for it; nothing unless you do."

Robert Browning talks about fulgurant eyes; I saw the flash of them: "Then you can Go!"

"I will;" and went to put my desk in order.

Presently he came: "Why don't you quarrel?"

"Oh, I haven't time! Come, let me show you all these pigeon-holes."

"You won't quarrel!" Really he wanted nothing but a fighting chance, to make concession. The greater need for haste. And yet I liked the man. In one day more "The Bright Side" lay upon his desk, announcing me as editor. So now in truth I leaned upon the child.

Just one month's work—one month's essential drill, Essential? Yes, for that young publisher, of all whom I have known, best understood what children ought to have. And so I worked and learned;—I learned of him.

Then down I went in sickness just as a streamlet, over a precipice, loses the last resistance. If I had stayed upon "The Western Rural" that would have ended all.

Now I have given you to understand that Jonathan Andrews (friend and spirit-doctor, not ashamed to bear a common name) stayed with me, first and last, till he had saved my life. Nothing, as yet, has made this evident, and so I beg for leave to open wide the sick room—let you see how very great a task was his to do.

This "heated term," I spoke of, burned out many a life, and all the nurses in Chicago were at work already—none was left for me. So Mr. Alden took my editorial place, in spite of other strenuous labor; also he took his sister Lydia's place (cashier and keeper of accounts) and sent her up to have the care of me; also he brought the best of doctors, and came in twice a day himself, to "cheer me up." John and Lydia, to me, were certainly God's ministers of Grace."

Meantime, within my soul, I talked with Dr. Andrews: "But is this all the work you promised me? It seems not even you can save my life."

Even my worn-out brain had still some power of Psychic apprehension. This is what he made me see: Almost innumerable lines, like telegraphic wires, coming from many distances and so converging, center-wise, in me. He said: "These are magnetic currents. I am directing them to you. They come from every friend who loves you. I use their magnetism for you." This he had done in part before, as you remember; but now it seemed a miracle. Still I believed; and for the moment knew I should be saved,—but afterward forgot.

You think this meant delirium? Well, I admit, (and make the most of it). I did not sleep nor even doze for fourteen days and nights. Do people sleep upon the rack? And this was nothing less. Still I was not delirious.

On the fifth day I only spoke in whispers. Miss Alden, (who was with me every hour) came with a second dose of medicine ("swash and sugar-water," say the Allopaths!) This I refused: "Don't give me that. It's quinine. The doctor promised not to give me quinine; but I perceive the effect."

Distressed, she pleaded: "Do you realize that you are going down as fast as possible? I see but little hope. I dare not take the least responsibility. Please trust the doctor."

"Very well," I said, "I'll take the medicine; but it will cost me dear." And I suppose that not again in life nor in the "act and article of death," shall I endure such mortal agony as followed soon. There came an ocean-surge of pain that rolled through every brain-cell, tore and dragged and spent its force, subsided, ebbed away, and left me helpless as the dead; then rose again, and sank and rose—oh, well, let that suffice!

About the fourth recurrence, tossed on the top-most wave, I found the strength to speak. I thought "Death is no matter, but delirium would be too dreadful," so I said to Lydia (holding both my hands): "Don't let me cry! Hold fast! Don't let me cry!" "No, No!" she said, and hid her face lest I should see the tears;—not soon enough; I saw them and they helped! Then—pain just lessening a little, voice not wholly gone as yet—my spirit-doctor found some thought-stuff left, made me aware of him and told me what to do!

I said, obeying him: "Go, get those grapes, press out the juice, bring half a goblet full, and give me every drop." Through half-shut eyes I had no power to open wide, I watched my nurse beside the window, haloed with girlish beauty (soon to be angelic), crushing the fruit I had refused before, in haste to fill the glass.

Just as the surge was rolling in once more, she came. If Christ himself had said: "Be still!" not sooner had the flood rolled back! It never rose again; but there I lay speechless, day after day, just looking out and breathing—hardly more; till finally I whispered once again.

That day they brought my Mother. I saw her, through the partly open door, push back the two who would have aided her and enter— arms out-spread. I thought of mother-birds and almost laughed.

I had been praying for the power to speak aloud, and did so with delight. She gave me one long look and said, after her whimsical way: "Your voice is down in China! Let me do the talking." You should have heard her entertaining me! All the time she thought: "My daughter'll die before myself;" and all the time I thought: "I'll go before and welcome her!"

You see, I somehow lost all thought of life with work, and work with sacrifice. The spirit world was near; and all I had to do, it seemed (remembering that hymn of Mrs.

Stowe's), was just "To swoon to that from this A Moreover, had a spirit made me understand how all that mountain yet was looming large, the calm that saved me would have broken up; whereas I lay as one already half in Heaven, and so was kept on earth.

I hate to tell what seems incredible,—well, no, I love to tell; but just this once I'll give you leave to doubt—oh, not the facts! but that propulsive force that brought the facts about. Judge for yourselves if it were latent energy in me (just at the door of death), or Psycho-physical power of someone else, that pulled me back, at last.

This was the way of it: The day my mother came I had a chill that lasted several hours. That being Sunday, I announced to brother (Rev. Rufus Cooley), who had come with flowers and benefits,— himself a benediction!—"I'm going back with you on Thursday morning."

A listening woman tip-toed to the doctor. "She is delirious. She says she'll leave the city Thursday morning." The doctor laughed aloud: "Delirious!—not much! And if she says she'll leave on Thursday morning, she will g°-"

But when he came on Monday morning I was sinking steadily,— had lost the power to whisper, or even lift a hand. He pondered deeply, then he urged: Will you consent to take that medicine again? There is no other way but that." He charged my brother strictly: "Give her three doses only,—the last at four o'clock. More would be dangerous."

Well, brother had been very sick before he came; and going off to sleep for half an hour—by special grace he slept the whole night through. I also (for the first time), fell asleep. And this is what I dreamed:

A large and florid gentleman stood beside my bed, closely regarding me. I thought: "He is a spirit-doctor; he is full of spirit power." Were I to see his like in actual or outward life, I would be sure to say: "That man abounds in magnetism. His lightest touch must needs electrify." He leaned across and said exactly this:

"You are preparing to have a long hard chill tomorrow. If that should be you cannot leave Chicago Thursday morning. Unless you leave that day you'll die." He gripped me by the shoulder: "Get up. I'll help you. Go to the table, get that medicine, bring it back and take a spoonful now and every half hour through the night."

I dreamed he lifted me and that I walked on air—dreamed that I got the tumbler, brought it back, and took the medicine, then set it on the chair beside my bed. Just as I set it down, I woke—my hand still on the glass. I felt that grip upon my shoulder still, and thinking: "That is how he helped me," sank down instantly, and slept.

How many times he came I did not count. I only know I saw him come, over and over, not awaking me, but saying briskly: "It is time to take your medicine," and every time I partly rose, reached out and took it, never waking till the spoon was dropping in the glass.

Next morning Dr. Davies said: "Why, this is wonderful! This is a favorable change indeed!" Well I could talk, and so I told the story. Be sure he did not sneer.

So Thursday morning Brother Rufus took me in his arms and carried me from carriage-bed to railroad-couch,—in Mrs. Browning's words:

"A mere, mere woman, a mere flaccid nerve,
A kerchief left out all night in the rain."

He took me—not to mother's house but to his own, my sister Emily's; and though I sank and sank, always that blessed grape-juice brought me back.

Two weeks from that return brother and sister left me in the care of neighbors and went to Mother's funeral. I think she too was there; but after all was done, within an hour or so, she came to me. I saw her perfectly. She leaned and looked with searching eyes—those great, grey eyes that always had been wonderful for telling thoughts!

"I have been told that you are better. That is hearsay. I have come to see, myself."

I laughed a little—full of pleasure: "Well, you see I'm better?"

227

She shook her head, leaned closer, seemed to look me through, then nodded, just a little: "But you are pitifully weak. Still you are gaining." So she went away. Mother was apt to know.

A week or two thereafter, at home among my other sisters, I learned to walk anew. And very soon there came a call from Buffalo: "We need you in the Air-cure, to help us out with Hygienic writings—come as soon as possible." And Mr. Alden wrote: "Your name is on 'The Bright Side still, and there is room for anything you write."

The light was shining on me from the East, and still I leaned upon the Child! I went to Buffalo.

PREPARATION

SOME wise astronomer (not Newton, nor La Place nor Schiaparelli and not Professor Lowell!) has ventured to presume—almost assert—there is no other world than ours inhabited. Also he lets us know that if there were, the fact to man (one man, at least) would be "humiliating." Belike he dreads an over-populated spirit-universe—fears to be jostled, hates to jostle others. We must allow, if every orb of size should, after cooling, prove to be a nursery for infant souls, preparing them to soar by billions into ether, even Gautama Buddha (wonderful at computation!) could not count those emigrating throngs. Still, space is infinite; and though, as Solomon avers, "There is no end to all the people, even of all that have been before them—they also that come after," no one need lack for room.

Peace be to that astronomer! Come, let us draw a circle in the sky, around some constellation (Ursa Major, say) and give him all the void enclosed in that periphery, for sacro-sanctitude. Thence he shall look abroad on whirling nebulae, horrific comets, vast areas of fire where burned out stars, encountering, blaze anew, suns multitudinous and never-terminating milky-ways—all, save for one small world, proofs of an infinite futility. So let him worship God,—or, by default, himself! Meanwhile the rest of us will find, each one, his vantage-coign, according to his worth.

At worst, we know that this dear place of our nativity has sent, is sending, and for a million years or so will keep on sending, souls from out the crush to populate the spheres.

And some are souls of babes in need of growth that must not be defrauded of the lower life (meant for aggrandizement). Needs be, they wait a season, close to the teeming earth, and learn to know the scent of all her flowers, the taste of all her fruits; aye, lay their heads, unseen, upon the mother's breast, and clasp their arms around the father's neck,—so gathering magnetic life and sustenance, till they are babes no more. But after that they pass.

229

And some are worthy souls of men and women, strong for human life and love, not having had their dues. They also stay awhile to get what more they need of Psychophysical power and amplitude; and this they use for helping other souls—those who are liberated like themselves, or those yet wearing bonds. Nor will they turn away from sinful ones, for whose redemption God would have them serve.

And some are old and very old. They need no more from earth, but love it well, and loiter—looking sweetly down on human kind, if possibly some child may want them still. They presently are wrapped about with loving arms, and so pass onward, turning back with smiles and looking up with wonder.

Moreover, since these loitering super-mortals are ours in fellowship (and will be ours forever) inevitable law compels an interchange. Often we think their thoughts, and take them all unconsciously for guidance—so escaping snares. Often they urge us into recognition, having inducing power. And this they do, not to our deprivation (after that manner of the hypnotist), but to our great enlightenment. So, many times we know; and now and then we see—nor yet by accident.

We do not see them wholly as they are (save by unusual grace); but rather as they were, with added radiance.

It seems to be agreed that the ethereal body (called by St. Paul, the "spiritual body") endows these gross integuments with all the elements that quicken them for life. This it does, at the behest of Spirit—essential, indiscernible—much as the sculptor's hand that shapes the clay, obeys the sculptor's mind;—only to grander purposes. And so we see with earthly eyes the earthly substance, but with clairvoyant eyes (not supernatural) the soul itself moving in god-like grace.

We speak of aural atmosphere, odylic force, and luminant effluence! Are they not all as one? Not soul;—perhaps its wraith, less bright yet visible;—some shining over-dress, woven of brain and body, where Mind—immortal weaver—stands directing all. Something very like the veil that Moses wore when Israel dared not look. Is not this outer radiance the spirit-body's doffing robe, worn in the tiring-room before the rich attire comes in for first appearance—splendid, refulgent—while the audience waits?

Now, as the mortal waste attending age goes on, and brain-cells one by one forego electric work, do not those weaving threads attenuate? Not to be wholly done away with when the death ensues (for they are partly spun of Psychic stuff), are they not sure to cling awhile and float between our eyes and each dear face we long to see once more? I think so. Change is ever gradual from mortal birth to death. Why not from mortal death and spirit-birth to higher states where veils are dropped away?

My mother, Nathan Haines and Henry Kendall came to me, as I have said, within three days after the final sleep. All had the look of age before they passed,—all had it afterward, though fined and vivified. Three days in spirit-life are not enough it seems for change of vestiture. But, oh, to see them now!

My Margaret's brother, Gordon—faithfulest of friends!—was more than eighty years of age before he crossed the great divide. Long out of sight and hearing, I had not learned that he was gone, when three years after that, I saw him coming, almost with a rush as might a happy boy. So holding out his hand (I being plunged that hour in deep distress), he cried: "How are you?" with an audible voice!—so absolutely Gordon's dear and cordial self, he could not be mistaken for another. Yet he was ruddy, blithe and young of face as any man of thirty—brimming with human life and prone to human laughter.

Suppose that I had seen him three years earlier—withdrawn indeed from flesh, but veiled as I have said; trust me, he had not seemed so charged with all the elements that make alive.

And yet I had a friend—pardon!—I have a friend, loved then and now unspeakably—who came almost at once, in singular beauty. Still she lacked.... This was the way of it.

For half her earthly life—passing at fifty years—she bore that morphine-cross, bound on against her will by one she loved (physician, husband, woefully misled) and by the time he passed away, the cords had cut so deep the very flesh had overgrown them—there was no escape. She strained against them to the uttermost, yielded, and struggled once again—almost had torn them out when Azreal touched her;—she was free indeed. Then all my heart rejoiced! But oh, the mortal waste! Youth, beauty, culture, intellect, poetic fervor, sweet vivacity and social dignity—so crucified! And oh, the place of skulls!

After the funeral, being very tired, I dropped upon my couch and closed my eyes. There was no time for sleep!

I saw a spirit enter, pass before me swiftly, turn and pass again and so recede. First I saw that she was clad in silver, that she wore a silver crown whose upward points were shaped like laurel-leaves; and round her, as she moved, there waved a faintly visible silver veil. And next I saw Augusta's very self—changed back to loveliness, but not, as yet, made radiant like one in rosy youth. I did not think of her (and that seems strange), until she passed the second time and faced me, waving recognition. She had but this to say, and said it humbly as in self confession: "Not yet worthy of the gold! "No doubt she wears it now.

Freddie, a babe of two, had seen me but a day and night before his glad escape; and being made to know that I was "Auntie," had let his great eyes follow me about and laid his head upon my breast in absolute trust. After the burial, when I would have slept, someone took up the child and set him down before me, saying: "Look at your Auntie!"

Then once again his great eyes met my own. The waste those four sick months had wrought had left no visible trace. A little pale he was, as one just waked from sleep in cooling shade; but rounded cheek and frownless brow, and lips that seemed about to smile, all told of sweet release from suffering. It seemed as though some soft magnetic touch had charged the babe with vigor, so that he had wakened, reached out hands, and been forever comforted. And yet, I think that very night he must have sought his mother's knee and clasped her round and gone to sleep again, to draw from her what even angels could not all supply.

Twice only I have seen my father—once a year or so before my mother left (he told me she was soon to go), and once when she was gone; but how he looked. I'll let my spirit-guardian tell. Before I fairly walked again, after the sickness I have told you of, this friend most kindly said: "I wish to make you happier by telling how your mother learned that she had entered life."

"She woke from that deep sleep in which she passed, and saw your father looking down upon her tenderly. She mused, not being wholly conscious: 'Henry looks just as young as on the day I married him. Soon it began to seem that many years had passed since then; and wondering but not yet comprehending, still she mused: 'Why, Henry looks as young as on the day I married him!' The wonder grew: 'Why Henry looks as young!—and then she rose up suddenly, and understood."

I also saw him young, though not so blest as she, and far away from Heaven.

Now, I suppose that when we enter spirit-life, each one is made to understand, according to his need. My oldest sister—wonderful for daily sacrifice—awoke, so I was told, upon a bed of flowers. My brother William, nearly fifty years a joyful Methodist, who uttered praises to his dying hour, soon afterward came back and said to me: "It is all glory! glory!" I asked: "And have you seen Permelia?" "Yes, but not at first. I saw the glory—nothing but the glory!"

Something like this the one who came to tell me "God is Law" revealed to me thereafter. He was first aware of light—soft, white, ineffable. Knowing, by remembrance of a dying hour, that he was in "the spirit," he moved on, well content, thinking: "If there were nothing here but light, that would suffice for happiness." Then, looking down, he saw that he was walking on the grass, and felt an added thrill of joy: "Green grass and sunshine!—who could ask for more? Do I deserve so much?" And then a lovely child came toward him, reaching out her arms. At first he did not know that he had ever seen her, but looking closer he discerned the face of one whom he had loved. With that she smiled and let him see that she was fully grown, though for his recognition she had made herself appear as much a child as when she left the earth. Sunshine, green grass and one to meet him—even so the eternal years of God began.

Dr. Philip Doddridge, whose books, men say "next to the Bible lead to godliness," whose hymns the people love (though not so charged with sweetness as those of William Cowper, Charles Wesley and the immortal Isaac Watts), tells in his diary that it seemed he also went to Heaven. He dreamed (I write from recollection) that an angel came and said: "Come, let me show you what awaits the Blest."

This angel led him to a spacious court near to a gate. Here all was beauty, light and harmony; while, from afar, came in rejoicing multitudes—cleansed after judgment—full of such delight as holy souls on earth are prone to hope for, to imagine, greatly to desire, but not to realize.

Now when the angel came again, he asked: "And are you satisfied? Is this what you have thought of Heaven?" The dreamer answered: "No! For it is written: 'Eye hath not seen, nor ear heard, neither have entered into the heart of man, the things which God hath prepared for them that love Him.' But nothing here is past my own imagination. Heaven must be more than this."

Thereat the angel smiled and led him to the gate and opened it and drew him in beyond. When they returned the dreamer brought no memory back, except a swooning sense of things unutterable.

It well may seem that those who visit us have not yet passed the Court. But who shall say the gate that lets the white elect go in, will not unclose at any touch of theirs to let them come again,—not for revealments, but to aid in God's redemptive work? Did not the Christ come back?

I have but one thing more to tell you after this manner, for if the veil be lifted, by but a millimeter's breadth, spirits must do the lifting. Otherwise we wait and ponder, staring at the blank.

But first there is a small, importunate self to speak of, not by any means because of merit, but from necessity.

Psychic experiences, as I have said, are like to flowers, whose roots are deep in earth. Now, in transplanting them, you cannot shake away the soil. Forgive! I speak of clay and sun and shower only because I must. Without all these there would have been no flowers.

My story led you, lately, to the Compressed Air-Cure, where I had once been saved from failure of the heart; and now, after excessive use of strength, I needed saving—well, from the whole of me! I may as well observe that fully eighteen months I stood upon the edge of things and buffeted the winds that would have blown me over.

While in Chicago, near to death, I had been told by one not in the flesh, that I might have to live for many years; and I had answered: "Since I am called to live, I'll want to live." And this strong word had followed: "It shall be made worth your while!"

Was there, in truth, a work for me to do? Where? When?—I would not look nor ask. This one enormous work of keeping me alive was all the mountain I could think of climbing. Verily, I did not climb alone.

So several weeks after my mother's passing, early in November, 1870, I was there in Buffalo, once more—trimming up some hygienic books for print, sending scraps to fill "The Bright Side" (leaning on the child)—and privileged to use its utmost space, so far as in me lay, for coming cash. Good Mr. Alden gave me many an alias from necessity; but stories bore my name and seemed acceptable. By his advice, in time, "The Interior" turned its juvenile department over to be filled by me; also "The Little Corporallet me in. Even in two months I had paid my money-debts in full and still had something left. Just then the Cure, not being properly sustained, was closed. This seemed calamitous.

And so the New Year found me once again with my "Progressive Friends." But since I would not, could not go a-visiting, I hid myself in Mrs. Hawley's far-off, upper chamber, and wrote and wrote that I might earn the wherewithal to go to Clifton Springs and pay for further air-baths. Not having sail enough to catch a favoring wind, I made all haste to get my skiff to shore by tugging at the oars.

The fund accumulated slowly. Mr. Alden wrote that he had offered fifty gold dollars as a prize for the best young folks' story. He was not to be the judge, and therefore thought it right that I should try among the rest, although accounted editor. He urged me: "Send a story to the judges under a pseudonym." Now, fifty dollars gold (there being a premium) would speed me on at once. But when I tried to bring my thoughts to bear, they failed me utterly. I had a vacuous brain; I stood and sharpened pencils, blank of mind. Just then a spirit spoke out with as much effect as though the voice were audible to sense: "Write about Mattie's cloak."

At once two lines from Drake's inimitable "Culprit Fay" flashed into memory:

'T was tied with threads of dawning gold, And buttoned with a sparkling star."

—"Sang Mattie's mother"—on I went, and in a minute had my theme in hand. So in two days, I sent away my "Fairy Arrows"— afterward a booklet largely circulated among the little folk—under my pseudonym of "Anna Man-ley." Was it not well done—the helping me to earn that golden prize? Let us hope that no one needed it so much as I.

One night my friends requested me to join a "circle." I think each felt the "moving of the spirit;" but speech was not for me. Encumbering thoughts must first be shifted off before you climb the smallest Psychic height. I dropped them for the hour and set my feet beside the mountain cedars, just above the clouds (that is, by simile!) So I had visions.

First I saw myself.... Not as a mere reflection in a mirror, but as an actual woman, frail and pallid, motionless, erect. And then I saw descend and rest upon my head a veritable landscape—like a lengthened island,—green with plants and trees. Within my soul, I said: "That typifies the burden I must bear—the work I have been promised. Spirits, it seems you ask too much. I shall be crushed." I trembled; yet I said (nor felt a fear): "Even so, I will accept the work."

But then I saw a curious thing! Strong silver cables, thick as those wires that run beneath the sea, looped under either end; and when I looked above, strong hands were grasping them—white hands, set close together, far as I could see. The island, so sustained, was resting on my head, but still I stood erect. And so the vision passed.

Straightway I saw my father—first descending, then pausing but a little way above and looking on me most paternally. When I had known him as a little girl, the blueness of his eyes, the whiteness of his temples, the vivid rose of temperance on either cheek, had made him look like this, albeit not so young. Yet he was altogether as a man might be, if he could carry perfect youth on through a century nor miss one deep experience. And then his spirit spoke to mine—not in the speech that he had learned beyond the gate, but in the words we use on earth, who talk of common things.

"Daughter, why do you think so much of dollars? Do not be troubled. They are waiting for you. By and be there will be many dollars needed. Trust and they will come. Someday there'll be an avalanche of dollars. Do your work:—trust, and remember."

And am I rich today? In dollars, no; in values, yes. And when the work came, means to do the work were not withheld; some little avalanches fell—one great one, which was turned aside by God's protecting rock to save my work and me from burial. And I am old, but suns are shining. You, if not myself, I trust, will hear that avalanche. Concerning all these matters I have yet to write.

Come, then and let us hasten! Yet delay a moment; and, after that another moment. First, please observe a pale, unhappy woman entering my study—much to my surprise. She had avoided me, had been uncivil—others had remarked:—a pity too; for Dr. Andrews, who had even now been helping two or three, might well have helped her also, as I thought. She had three little girls to mother, and she was very ill.

She sat down hopelessly, and said with visible trembling:

"I have come to beg your pardon. Spirits have said I must. I've put it off through pride; but now they tell me some great good will come to me from you, and I shall have no right to take the good, unless I make confession." So she told her story. Just a tinge of natural jealousy, or such a matter—adverse talk, but nothing worth considering.

237

"Come," I said. "You meant no harm at all. There's nothing to forgive. Meantime you're sick. Let Dr. Andrews tell you what to do. You mustn't die and leave those little girls."

I tell this partly by the way of showing what wide eyes a spirit has for observation, what swift hands for succor, what abundant interest in little matters,—the coin a woman loses, let us say, even the broom that brings the coin to light. Moreover, if this mother needed me, I also, at a later season, needed her.

Well, we were both astonished when Dr. Andrews said: "Make ready. When my friend goes to that Sanitarium, you are going with her."

"Impossible!" she almost sobbed. "We're very, very poor."

"Oh, you will have the money! You are going!"

I said to her: "This spirit never told me anything that was not true. He has the gift of prophecy. Do just as I am doing; make up your dresses, and be quick about it." So I wrote for terms to Clifton— room for me and special rates for Mrs. Huntington.

Within a week or such a time, one who had lately bought a farm came to the lady's husband: "I find a little corner of your land juts into mine. It's of no use to you, and since I want to straighten out my line, I'll purchase it and pay a hundred dollars." So the bargain closed.

Seventeen dollars weekly for myself, and seven for Deborah. I, with my fifty dollars (fifty-six), the prize for "Fairy Arrows," also with other funds—had all my pencils sharp for earning more;—and Deborah had cash enough to last three months. So we arranged to go together as the spirit said. (How could he know about the strip of land?).

See Appendix XIV.

More than we guessed, there was great need for both of us to hurry.

That "one thing more" I promised you, to show how life begins a-new, when turbid dreams are past, I dare not leave untold.

Three families and I, as formerly, met at the house of Levi Brown for one last service. Lydia and I had spent two days in visiting, and she had calmed me, as she always did in some magnetic way; so my receptive powers were at their best. It seemed that others also were aware of "ministering spirits." One of them—Alonzo Hawley—was moved to utterance on my account, and cheered me with a symbol, whose far prophetic meaning time has fully verified. Symbols, in my experience (presumably in that of others) enter very largely into Psychic life. They are not phantasms, not chimeras; they are not realities, nor facts nor prototypes of facts; but they are sure predictions. Or rather, let us call them searchlights, flashing far ahead and kindling into view those drifting mysteries we call "events to come." My mother often dreamed in symbols, and I to some extent. About these days they came as Psychic visions—every normal faculty awake;—and never yet has one of these been proven nought.

That night our circle had no word from Dr. Andrews, although I thought him present. He had begun to "wear away" I seemed to understand; for when he came to help the sick he did not tell so much of physical ailment as of its cause—obscure, remote, within the realm of soul; yet if he had not told me just what course to take at Clifton Springs, there would have been no help. The obligation he had taken on himself was well fulfilled before he passed beyond. This time he may have brought another spirit with him; I am confident he made it possible for me to see and hear and even personate the one who came.

I saw, by lifting up my "seeing eyes," a spirit—let us say a gentleman, clad in a plain, straight coat, holding a heavy cane in his left hand, as though to leave the right hand free for action. He wore no hat, and yet I did not see his face distinctly, it seemed because his head was thrown a little back, I being too far down. I saw the person very well—upright in carriage, compact of build and dignified of mien—one who would set his feet down true in walking and keep the straightest line. I waited, all expectancy; and then down fell his name:

"Isaac T. Hopper"

239

My thoughts ran here and there to find a clue. I knew the name. Had I not heard my father speak of him with reverence? What was he? Quaker? Abolitionist? "Underground" Philanthropist? Some such impression lingered, but not a definite fact was held in memory. And all I ever learned of him since then, is folded up in one small incident: I leave the rest with you.

In 1875, a friend beside the sea (I living in New York), requested me to get a servant for her, out of "The Isaac T. Hopper Home for Inebriate Women." I found the institution—old, obscure, but still effective. The man whose name it bore had builded it, fully endowed it, governed it in life, and left it to be owned, maintained and governed by his daughter during her life. After her death, I do not know what was to happen;—she was yet alive. I saw her through an open door, presiding at a weekly meeting,—a single lady, eighty years of age, placid, erect and dignified. Could I have touched her hand and whispered in her ear, would I have told this story I am writing out for you? Yes, if God had given me grace, and she had given me hearing.

I did not see him after he had told his name. He did not move away—he disappeared. A spirit, exercising energy to gain control of brain and hold a medium's thoughts, must keep himself from sight— or I have found it so. He lets you see some other spirit maybe, (he seeing first), but you and he are almost one. You think, if not in perfect unison, at least in correspondence, so that your lines of thought are parallel. It is not meant that they should interfere. In opening the gates of speech your hand and his must be upon the lever. I know not how to say it otherwise.

This spirit gave me thoughts and used my vocal instruments for utterance—producing, not my voice nor that of Dr. Andrews, but his own presumably. All his thoughts I well remember,—many of his words: I will not claim perfect transmission of the latter, phrase by phrase, but nothing shall be warped.

He said: "Friends, I desire to give you for a lesson, my first experience after I knew that I had passed through death.

240

"I found myself walking upon a narrow road, cut through a mighty forest. The light was very dim. I heard no voice of bird nor tread of beast; but I was not alone. Two walked beside me—one on either hand. They did not speak to me nor did I turn to them. I walked on, thinking deeply: How was this different from earth, save by immensity and lack of light? I looked above; tall trees were meeting so that I could not see the sky. I thought that I would counsel with the two, and turned to speak. I had not seen them go, but they were gone. And now I was alone. It seemed that it was terrible to be alone; but still I walked communing with myself.

"This is not Heaven, neither is it Hell. It has no name I think but Solitude. Since I exist, all other men exist after the body's death; but no one meets me. Each perhaps must walk alone as I am doing;— will it be forever?

"To be alone forever! If there be nothing more than this, there cannot be a God. Then what remains but infinite despair? Is there a God?

"After a time I issued from the forest. I had reached the sea. I saw no shore save that on which I walked, and yet I could not stop. I went on through the waters, walking till I had passed the surf. Then billows rolled against me—they compassed me about, the depths were under me. I toiled, and sank and rose and sank (with inward striving no less bitter), asking: 'Is there any God?' Under the surges, deep within my heart, I found the answer: Faith cried out:

'There is a God. O, God, deliver me!'

"I rose; then far across the sea I saw an angel coming,—glorious and swift. He lifted me from out the waters, laid me on his breast, and smiled and whispered: 'Son, the trial hour is over. Be at peace.'

"Oh, he was very strong; he seemed to soar up some amazing height! But now I heard my name called out, and called again, till many voices caught the cry—voices of multitudes.

"'Isaac T. Hopper comes! Isaac T. Hopper comes!' I heard them all rejoicing: He is coming! He has come!

241

And now the angel paused beside a temple: 'Enter, Son, he said: 'And be once more alone.'

"I entered and the door behind me closed. Was this a temple? Rather, a spacious picture-gallery. I moved about with wonder. What meant these pictures?—who had painted them? I looked at one: This was a picture of myself, giving a loaf of bread to a pale, hungry woman. I looked again: Here was a negro boy, my hand upon his head. And here and there and everywhere along the walls were pictures of myself bestowing benefits. Faces that I had seen, mourners whom I had comforted, toilers whom I had aided, children whom I had blessed, widows whom I had fed, black men whom I had lifted up;—and always I, myself, pictured in act of doing good.

"At last, I could endure no more. I cried aloud: 'Unworthy! I am too unworthy! Let me pass!' I reached an open door and so escaped.

"There were the multitudes! They closed me round; they called my name; they held me fast; they gave me greeting. All with one heart and all with one accord, they talked of me and loved me.

"Friends, there are sweet rewards. Good Night."

ACCEPTANCE

LATE one evening near the end of February, 1871, two patients entered Clifton Sanitarium and were assigned to separate rooms. One of these—myself, of course,—before the breakfast hour went hunting up the other; and there lay Deborah, like a withered lily! I cried out:—"What on earth's the matter!"

She answered faintly: "I haven't slept an hour. Someone has occupied this room, whose mind was black as night. The air is full of him,—he must have magnetized the very walls! I don't know whether he's alive or dead, but this is where he lived. The man was terrible!"

I hurried off to find a doctor. Fortunately the one I found had Psychic understanding. I pleaded: "Don't be prejudiced; she's desperately nervous—Not in the least insane."

"Oh, she's in the right of it!" said Dr. Prince. "We'll move her out at once."

One year before, a man had come and occupied that room, who meant to kill himself. This he had done in time; but all that year, save for the last few days, he chiefly sat alone and brooded over thoughts of death. How should he do the thing? and where? and when? and what would happen afterward? He kept a diary, and every night, before retiring, wrote therein his dreadful meditations. Finally, he went behind the house and shot himself. And so his room was vacant. Deborah was the next.

It seems I did not go too far that time I wrote: "If we send out our radium-emanations—little projectiles that bombard the very walls about us, they may recoil and yet again recoil, bombarding all who come where we have been." Nor, when I grew repetitive, declaring once again: "We are endowing molecules this very minute with the souls of us." "We produce a force in them which they continually discharge through times and times and half-times; who can tell when all that borrowed energy will be expended?" Remember also, how a shard of brick, concerning which I had no knowledge, became, to Psychometric sense, a thing of horror. More than a hundred years ago, implacable cruelty, frantic resistance, immitigable despair had registered themselves in every atom,—so confronting me till I could bear no more.

Come, let us all be good!

And now I wonder whether dead, black worlds, colliding—"the heavens rolled together as a scroll," "mountains and islands moved from out their places"—will not fuse and burn and dissipate and re-unite, all fined and purified before the sight of God; with nothing left for Psychometric eyes to see, or souls to grieve about.

From re-constructed planets to re-constructed bodies—that's not so very far. Our Dr. Prince declared I must not even imagine that I could write—and live. I wrote—how otherwise? My spirit-guardian had said: "Make haste! There is a new condition, too obscure to be detected by a common doctor, but sure to culminate in death save for a single remedy. Whatever may ensue, see that you take the air-baths." This I did, in spite of protest, walking in with others each alternate day and being drawn away in sick chair two hours later—helpless as a babe. Wholly obedient was I—to Dr. Jonathan Andrews!

And so about the first of May this dear physician came and said: speaking through me, after his usual manner: "The danger I have told you of is over. You are turning back to life. But three weeks more and you will realize that you are certain to be saved. Then I shall come and say, 'Farewell.' My friend, I am going away from earth and its vicinity. We hear of wonderful conditions on the planet Mars. Many spirits have been there and have returned to tell us. We have formed a company to visit Mars and be instructed, before we pass to other worlds—also inhabited. You will not know of me after I go, until you, too, shall leave the earth; but I shall know of you."

This was six years before Schiaparelli saw those complex, geometric lines on Mars that could but signify intelligence. Professor Percival Lowell was sixteen years of age. One year before that great discovery, he was a graduate of Harvard; and now, at fifty-three, he looms before our lifted eyes—the one astronomer whose deep researches give us cause to think and hope and ardently believe that people dwell on Mars. And, by the way, were not my Psychometric vision dimmed with age, I'd borrow one of those hundred thousand photographs and maybe see a little for myself—not through a telescope!

When Dr. Andrews came at the appointed time he said: "I go; but you will not be left alone. Another guardian comes. Since you are chosen for a special work, there will be many spirits ready to give you aid. When one shall come and speak through you as I am speaking now, saying: My name was Theodore Parker,' you may understand that you have touched your work. Promise me that you will never lose your faith."

"I promise you that I will never lose my faith."

Therewith he said: "Farewell."

Now, since that day I have not read diseases through Psychic eyes, nor proffered remedies by inspiration or in Psychic trance, nor yet exhibited, in Psychic trance, the manner, gestures, voice or personality of Dr. Jonathan Andrews. He found me on the road to mortal death. He led me from the "vale of Achor" through the "door of hope," to pluck the very hearts of things from out the good, green earth. I live thereon because of him. God speed him on from world to world, from sun to sun, from "companies" of happy spirit-friends to spirit-multitudes and archangelic hosts, whose "Alleluias!"—as "the voice of many waters"—all shall hear at last.

No less through many years, as I would have you see and understand, discarnate souls, always with my consent, have on occasion, led me where they would.

West of the Sanitarium at Clifton Springs there used to be a pleasant wood; and there, in May, were flowers—spring beauties, wind-flowers, violets a-plenty. Thither I went one day and, being moved in heart, was passionate in prayer: "*Show me my work! Master, I want my work!*"

After an hour of this, perhaps, the answer came: "It shall be shown to you this Summer." I was well content.

Before this time our Dr. Henry Foster sent me a kindly message: "No more bills for you." I went to him in hope of compromise, for it had pleased me from the first to say: "A worker must not be a beggar. If I am truly chosen, I shall be sustained and not humiliated." "This is your home for twenty years," said Dr. Foster (who had some memory of me—a patient twelve years earlier). "But no," I said. "I'll only take the air-baths as a gift. I've just engaged a room outside." So it was settled.

Now, on the rise of ground we called a hill, Mrs. Francisco had a desolate front yard, and on account of editorial favors, I had a lot of seeds. In those days there was dearth of flowers at Clifton. I planned for many floral gifts to invalids, and planted all my mother's favorites in memory of her.

You will have seen that I am not exactly "Patience on a monument and when I found the made-up soil was poor and plants were slow to start, I fretted inwardly. Meantime a drouth had come. Through sixty days we had no rain. My work-boy taxed the cistern, taxed the well, till both went dry, then went about to beg for water, very scantly given. Half one blazing week we lived without the dew. Impatience got within the bones of me.

Ah, Mother knew that faith and readiness to serve were not enough! That which I lacked she gave; or otherwise the mountainous obstacles, the strong rebuffs, the weary waiting-times, the plunderous attacks, had never been out-lived. Her plant has blossomed long.

When William Collins found himself possessed, quite suddenly, of rather ample means, he presently removed from Buffalo to Rochester and made investments somewhat hastily. Before affairs were well adjusted, I think in 1856, he passed away, leaving his widow sole executor. With other properties, he had acquired a thousand acres lying within the "Tonawanda Reservation,"—a strip of land extending Eastward from Niagara River, fifty miles or so, and slow of settlement because of tamarack swamps.

About a decade later, Mrs. Collins—a strong-willed lady of distinguished character and quite commanding presence—needing to get some real-estate cleared from incumbrances—proposed to sell this tract, which seemed to be of little value. Armed with a note of introduction, she went to Jonathan Watson—called just then "The Oil King." Before she had disclosed her business, Mr. Watson's lovely wife came in, was introduced, excused herself at once and turned to leave. She turned again before the door was reached—eyes closed in Psychic trance—and said: "I see your husband standing close beside your chair. He says: 'Don't sell the land!

It's very valuable. Have it investigated. There are healing waters beneath of singular virtue. Spirits want them brought to light, and used to help the sick and benefit the world. There are other values, chiefly oil and minerals, but they will never be discovered till spirits have their wish. Don't sell the land!'"

Mrs. Watson—Libbie Lowe—at fourteen years of age, began to be an "inspirational speaker"—most attractive then, and always, among "Progressive Friends" or Spiritualists. I, who have seen her, heard her, even dined with her, pronounce her wholly to be honored. No one could point to her and say: "Behold a charlatan!"

Down fell the blessed rain! And so I picked my flowers at Clifton, carried them about among the sick, wrote little stories, bathed in air and basked in sunshine, hardly noting that the summer days had drifted into August—that final month when, out of darkness, I must lift the hand and "touch" my very work. Pansies, Nasturtiums, and the like, absorbed me. Memory was quite submerged.

Some early day that month, there came a spirit-message:—You've heard the wires along the telegraph lines and know the ring of them, what time the wind is blowing? And did you ever doubt your ears?— That is the way with spirit-messages.

"Write to your cousin Julie Beach at Albion, and say that you will be with her on Saturday afternoon."

Delightful! Cousin Gilbert's widow was a poet—a truer one than I, though little known. I loved her well. The thought of seeing her was most inspiring. I took the pen—and paused: "Spirits, you know, as well as I, that all this coming winter, I must be a patient in the Sanitarium. I cannot bear exposure to the cold. You know that I must earn the needed money in advance. Now, if I go to Albion, there's a week for visiting, a week for broken health, a serial story cast aside, and nothing added to the little fund I have; much money spent, and only pleasure realized. No, I must stay at home."

Next morning in a sort of whirl, I caught my pen and Wrote: "Dear Cousin Julie: You may expect me Saturday afternoon;" and all within three minutes I saw my letter drop into the bag, last thing of all. The carrier started off—I started after: "I must get it back!" and on a sudden realized that this was more than simple impulse. What did the spirits want?

I said to Julie: "Dear, I have a mission. I've got to stay till I discover it." With that we laughed together.

Next day my cousin Lafa Beach, whom I had never seen, came up from Rochester; and, two days after that, came Mrs. Collins—lost to sight and knowledge since 1863. She said: "I chanced to meet your cousin Lafa Beach this morning. He told me you were here. I have come up purposely to see you. I have a cabin-home in Barre, eight miles out from Albion; and here's my carriage at the door to take you there. In fact I own some mineral springs and hope to have a Cure. Come out and see."

"Impossible!" I cried; then stopped and broke off suddenly: "Why, that is what I've come for!"

And God had led me by a cobweb thread.

That evening Mrs. Collins told me this: She had obeyed her spirit-husband, speaking through Libbie Lowe; had kept her tract of land, disposed of other holdings and bought six hundred acres more! (Behold the faith of her!) Not having funds, she had arranged with Jeremiah Eighmie (a man of three-score years, at least), a sort of partnership—just on what terms she thought not best to say, or so it seemed. He was a gentleman of means and leisure, living in Roselle, New Jersey;—like herself an ardent Spiritualist. Both of them—not thinking they were mediums themselves, consulted with the best they knew. All these agreed that oil and minerals might be found, after sufficient perseverance.

248

One result had been attained, as prophesied by Mrs. Watson. There were two abundant springs of mineral water. One of them was truly wonderful it seemed. Just pump for twenty minutes on a pocket-knife and it became a magnet, strong enough to hold a nail suspended,—I forget how long!

So, for two years, the country people round-about had drunk the Yuh Heh waters (Indian name for life) and had dyspepsia cured and heart-complaint and rheumatism and scrofulous swellings and other little troubles. Therefore

Mr. Eighmie ("Hand of Providence," said Mary Collins), had built a Cure—but what to do with it or how to get it started right, nobody seemed to know, and spirits hadn't told.

Mrs. Collins said: "I think the help will come through you." Far from agreeing fully, I added to my diary that night: "She tells the biggest stories! Seems to depend on mediums and now depends on me. That's not the proper way to manage business."

To tell the simple truth I had but little faith in mineral waters. I believed in blazing suns and blowing winds and double atmospheres and Graham-water gems and grape-juice, you remember. Still there was Libbie Lowe; something I must believe!

So the next morning we sat down together, not holding hands in manner of a circle; never again, so far as I remember, did I depend on borrowed magnetism! someone came and spoke in business fashion, saying: "Get your medical indorsement first. Take a sample of the water down to Dr. Foster. He will believe in it, and order it for patients. That will be of use. He will do more than that even financially, but he is not the one whom we have chosen to carry out our purposes. That one will not be known until the time is ripe."

Not for an instant did I think or dream that I might be the one.

Mrs. Collins brought to me that morning a bit of rock taken from near the surface of the second well, where work was going on in search of oil. The depth already reached was sixteen hundred feet, and nothing had been found except another mineral spring, not specially magnetic and having coarser qualities than had the Yuh

Heh water. "I think you must be Psychometric. Won't you test this specimen and see what lies below?" (So pleaded Mrs. Collins.)

Professor Denton, so I had been told, had found one obstacle to scientific application of the faculty he named Psychometry. Neither his wife nor sister—wonderfully accurate in many ways—could measure distances. In looking downward, they, and others he had found, who had the sight, could note the different strata all in order but could not state their relative depth. I think the fault was in the natural aptitude for measurement. It happens that I have this one mechanical gift in marked degree, but Psychometrically had never put the talent to an absolute test. Now in this case, I followed where the drill had been and so described each stratum as I passed along: "This silvery looking streak is six feet thick; this darker one is twenty feet:" I ended saying: "Here the drill has stopped. I cannot see an inch below. I get the sense of oil far down; I cannot go in search of it."

Mrs. Collins brought me bottles, each containing drillings numbered in order of the finding. All of these I recognized at once and all were labeled: "six feet"; "twenty feet"—or what the depth had been. They proved me right so far as I had stated. Others might see far more than I, just as the Dentons did, yet lack a little this discriminating power. Only a few, I think, out of a multitude, have proved themselves safe guides in digging wells.

I had but little chance to rest; having been brought there for a definite purpose that must be fulfilled. And so, that afternoon, another spirit came. I remember how the mood fell on me; how the outer world went drifting out of mind, the while I had a sense of peace and harmony and very gentle influence—though firm and strong. It followed that we had a sermon full of priestly benediction. I know not how it was with Mrs. Collins; as for me my heart was melting in me. It seemed that I was called anew to sacrifice, to serve, to render all and suffer all, if so the Master willed. When this was ended: "Tell us who you are," said Mrs. Collins.

"My name," he said was "Theodore Parker." And then I understood that I had "touched" my work.

250

Mrs. Collins, always obedient to what she thought was spiritual counsel, went, as my guest, to Clifton, was introduced by me to Dr. Foster, who instantly proposed to test the waters thoroughly, and gave her ample orders. This cheered her greatly: "You will come again," she urged.

"Why, no!" I answered her. "I went because I had been told to go. So far as I can see there's nothing more for me to do; and I must write again with all my might, to pay for losing time as well as strength." "Not so," a spirit said, speaking aloud through me; "We have more work for her to do. Expect her in about three weeks."

In ample time another message came: "Write to Mrs. Collins to meet you Wednesday afternoon at Albion." So I made bold to call on Dr. Foster: "Have you any word to send?" "Why, yes," he said! "the gentleman she spoke of, who has furnished means, is not, I judge, a suitable man to take in charge a healing work, like this. Tell her if she can honorably disengage herself from partnership, I can advise her better what to do; and I can be of further use, no doubt." While we were riding out from Albion to Barre, Mrs. Collins talked of Mr. Eighmie gratefully and spoke of his ability in finding mines, but said that he was slow to apprehend the needs of general business. She felt that he was not the one to have the management of Yuh Heh Springs, and thought him indisposed to furnish funds for launching out successfully. Still he had his right of partial ownership which could not be ignored.

Perhaps through sympathy, inducing thought-transference, it chanced I saw him in a Psychic manner, and told her so at once. I thought his features slightly Jewish—a racial likeness much accentuated by a patriarchal beard. Upon arriving she got me all her photographs, thinking that his would be among the rest. Not finding it, I seized upon a lady's picture: "This looks almost exactly like him only for the beard." She answered: "That's his daughter, Mrs. Carpenter; they're very much alike."

Next morning Mrs. Collins, rather vacantly inquired of me—who couldn't know of course: "Who are those men outside in conversation?" Looking out, I answered: "One of them is Mr. Eighmie."

Mrs. Collins introduced him to me, relating this about the seeing; on which he said: "Look at me very closely.

Did you see me exactly as I am?" "Why no! I saw you looking ten years younger." He had a subtle mind: After a little thought he gave his own interpretation: "That signifies that I shall prove to be a better man than other people think me; better than I have thought myself to be."

After a talk with Mrs. Collins, by themselves, he came and talked to me—she being present: "I suppose you know what our Agreements are?"

"She says you have a sort of partnership. I haven't learned the terms."

"I didn't wish to pre-possess her mind," said Mrs. Collins. "I knew her long ago. It always seemed to me she was an excellent medium; and now I must believe that spirits sent her here for some especial purpose. I left it all with them."

"Well, spirits impressed me yesterday, to leave my home and come to make a final settlement. And now it seems they've sent a medium here to meet me. I suppose they know that you and I could never fix it up alone. I'll trust their messenger so far as this: If they have anything to say through her, I'll hear it; but after that I claim the right to do exactly as I please. They want more money very likely; but I'm not going to furnish it, unless I choose."

He turned to me again: "Now I shall tell, myself, what our Agreements are. Mrs. Collins owns this tract of wood and swamp; she wanted to investigate the land but hadn't means. I had the money but I would not put a dollar into it. I lent it on security and hold the mortgages to make.it good. I'm to have half of what we get by drilling. We share and share alike. So I own half the springs, of course; and now it seems she wants to manage them alone. That isn't fair."

"Well, speaking as a woman—not as a business woman nor as a medium—it seems to me that you're a sort of Shy-lock. She is risking all her property and you are risking nothing. That is not 'share and share alike' by any means. If you, as well as she, believed that spirits told the truth and there were actual values, why not prove your faith by works and risk as much as she? Suppose you keep the mortgages, receive the interest, even foreclose them when the time expires unless she pays them off. Meantime give up the springs to her. That isn't your Agreement, but it's fair."

"Now, look here! These waters will be celebrated all the world around. I shall be celebrated. When people talk about the Yuh Heh Springs, they'll say that spirits first discovered them and Jeremiah Eighmie put his money in and got them. I want my share of credit"

"That would be wholly fair if you had risked your money."

"I tell you that I never meant to put a dollar into it! But since the spirits brought me here and brought you here to meet me, let them tell, through you, exactly what they want. I'm not obliged to let them govern me, but let them talk. I'll listen anyhow."

Here was an "underself." But I had yet to learn that back of it—not far removed—there reigned a soul as true and pure and generous as any I have known. This soul demanded guidance. Who was I that I should utter foolish words, and render judgment? Let the spirits speak!

You will have seen that God has blessed me with an accurate and retentive memory. It is not a drag-net seizing all and letting nothing go; but whatsoever Mind has made its own, is never quite forgotten. My poems, having cost me thought, are still a part of me. And so with Psychic visions—sometimes with lengthened Psychic messages; and here is one that never has escaped from durance. Mind has held it fast.

We heard a parable. No one forgets a parable entirely. Thought for thought, if not quite word for word, this was the little story, told to Mr. Eighmie, told to Mrs. Collins, and, with intention, told, as well, to me.

"There was once a king who had immense possessions. These included many fertile provinces, though dotted here and there with desert places, much in need of water. Two of these barren tracts lay very near each other. It chanced the king, in journeying to and fro within his kingdom, crossed them both. In each he saw a trickling fountain sending out a tiny rivulet, soon to be lost among the sands. Now where the springs came out and where the rivulets ran, were lovely flowers; but all beside was bare."

"So, having perfect sight, the king looked far below and saw two plenteous rivers striving to push their way between the rocks, finding no adequate vent. Each of these had lifting power; each forced a way through narrow crevices, and, out of all their flowing waters, sent one thread of silver up to make the desert bloom.

"When, afterward, the king was seated on his throne to judge the people, straightway he commanded: 'Let my servants go and open wide those crevices. Let them enlarge the fountains, giving both those rivers room to pass, and make my deserts green.'

"Therefore the willing servants came and brought their drills and toiled, as faithful servants will, through many weary days.

"Beneath one spring, there lay the solid granite! And it was hard to pierce. Point by point, slow inch by inch, the steel went cutting through to reach the stream below. And now but one more blow is needed; Will the waters flow?

"Under the other spring there lay the quick-sand! Not so deep—easy to pierce, but liable to sink and fill the well and block the tools anew. Here was much delay through need of building walls to shut away the sand. Yet now there's but a single blow to strike: And will the waters flow?

"And if they rise from underneath the granite, that barren soil above will bloom in beauty, where the children walk. And if they rise from underneath the quicksand, that desert will be rich with grain and give the children food.

"If either one, or both, refuse to flow and make the deserts rich, then will the waters force their way through rifts and secret caves until they reach the under seas and lose themselves in salt. But who shall tell the king?"

There was long silence when the story ended: "Well," said Mr. Eighmie (always quick of apprehension), "this is evident. Both Mrs. Collins and myself must sacrifice." He looked as though the thought delighted him.

And yet I listened half that Thursday afternoon, not uttering a word myself, the while these dissident partners strove to reach a point of settlement.

What was she offering? To get all needed funds from other sources, start the Cure, bottle and sell the waters, bear the sole responsibility of all and—share and share alike!

All that but angered him, it seemed. Being appealed to as an "underself" was not quite what he wanted.

I began to see the force and meaning of the parable—not understood at first. Here, firm as very granite, for two full years this woman had denied herself the sweets of home, the dear companionship of children, the social lift, the means of rest and peace in happy neighborhoods, and fixed her lone abode next to a swamp, with not a house in sight. And all to satisfy her spirit-husband, bring to light those healing waters talked about by spirits;—also incidentally, with Mr. Eighmie's help, to get their oil and minerals, and "share and share alike." Had not this woman sacrificed enough? Why should she offer more? You've heard that roots of trees will penetrate the metamorphic rocks and pick the feldspar out for means of growth? Just so this work had fastened on her, rooted in her, made demands of her; and it was slow of growth. A hundred years to build an oak, five centuries to lift a giant pine and five times five to root and rear a Calaveras monarch! This woman's faith was greater far than mine, for I, to some extent, was made to see, while she was left to grope.

So, painfully she groped her way along that day to reach a business "settlement;" till Mr. Eighmie flung himself away from conference:— "Come, let the spirits talk!"

This time we listened to a searching sermon—I cannot say from whom; but, when it ended, I, at least,—it seemed the others also— had felt the sudden warmth of altar-fires. The morning and the evening made the first of days; and there were four of them. We hear it took but six to make a world.

Now on the second day—so quick the shifting sands—three times this Jeremiah Eighmie said: "We two can never settle this alone. We'll listen to the spirits." Therefore we heard three sermons more, and each more sweet and searching than the last, leaving a longer silence; after which we went our separate ways.

Well, on the third of all these days the sands were slipping still. And then the preacher spoke of things both old and new, of things that make for loss, and those that make for everlasting gain. And I remember how he said to Mr.

Eighmie: "Keep in harmony with all above you; so doing, you shall live till you are very old." Not threatening him in any wise, but giving him to understand that life engenders life and all its elements are of the spirit—nothing of the flesh.

But after dinner I was left alone; one partner busy in the distant kitchen, the other tramping off to supervise the drillers, who had just begun to guess that oil was possible. So there I sat at ease, as women will, and tranquilized myself with sewing-work. In truth I have a certain art that makes for health and sanity. Right in the midst of what induces worry—even invites despair, I push distressing thoughts away and leave myself a safe, sweet space for happy meditation. And so it was this day and hour, or I had never known what followed—never told to you what I am forced to tell, or leave all records blank someone drew near and swept my eyelids down so that my soul could see. There was a blaze of softened light that filled all space around; and on the lift of land—Southward, between the swamp and road—I saw an edifice. It seemed an Institution—not a dwelling house—built all of brick, and wide, high, and "set four-square to all the winds that blow." One said:

"This is a home for abandoned women,—a House of Reform."

It disappeared, but still the light remained. Then it returned but in that instant "fifty years" had passed; and all around it lay a peaceful, prosperous village. First the "Home" and after that, so many other homes.

"As it will be! Promise bodily healing and you may save these lost ones!"

Then first I understood, what afterward was proven, that Yuh Heh Springs surpassed all other waters known, in curative effects. I rushed away, and in my private room fell down upon my knees, crying aloud: "My Master, let me be of use. O, give me strength to help!"

"It shall be yours to help!"

Behold at last a work! Behold a chosen and accepted servant! So the new life began.

When it was eventide and still the discontent between the two prevailed, there was an instantaneous response to Mr. Eighmie's call. This time we had a plain and practical discourse about the Yuh Heh Springs; their singular virtue, their abundant flow, their money-making value. Here was a means of just enrichment,—let them be used for that. But use them also for beneficence. Here let the Charitable come and build their many Homes. And one shall be for destitute and worthy sick; and one shall be for worn-out laborers, who need a time of rest; and one shall be for city children, pale inheritors of tainted blood; and one shall be for miserable, straying women, wanting to be saved.

Just here the speaker paused and said to Mr. Eighmie: "Something shall -be granted you before all others. We have already shown our friend, in vision, a great Reformatory yet to be,—an Institution for the help of fallen women. If you desire, it may be yours to lay the corner-stone; and, doing this, your name shall be revered

After these talks none of us ever spoke of them. No words of mine can tell how deep was their effect,—at least on me.

Still, on the Sabbath morning, Mrs. Collins said to Mr. Eighmie: "Come, let us settle something finally. What terms do you desire?" And Mr. Eighmie would not make concessions, would not accept concessions! Nothing pleased him. I think if she had sacrificed her all, he would have spurned the offering. "I want to hear from spirits!" So he had ended every conference before, and so he ended this.

Then for one blessed space of time some "minister of grace" addressed us. All earthly thoughts were swept away, I think from other minds as well as mine. I seemed to breathe a holy atmosphere. I had a consciousness of boundless good and inexhaustible mercy. Nothing was said of justice; no listener could think of any "wrath to come," only of everlasting righteousness and infinite peace. Whoever spoke had been within the inner court and learned that Law is Love.

I rose up when the sermon ended—rose and fled from out the "cabin-home" into the sunshine, over the corduroy road that led to Yuh Heh Springs; and there, above the healing waters, sat me down, full to the lips with blessing.

"Master, here I am! Do with me even as Thou wilt." How could I ask for more than mere acceptance? How dared I ask for that?

Yet, then and there, beyond all merit first or last—even to the hour of death, was granted me reward. From overhead, a hand of perfect whiteness reached below and on my forehead wrote four words, for endless benediction:

"Recreant to no trust A

Oh, long and difficult and sometimes terrible, has been my chosen road; yet to this very day I have not lost my faith.

Sunset was near at hand that Sunday afternoon when three of us sat down to hear the final word. Mercy and peace and love had been accorded us. The "servants of the king" had waited. Here indeed were fountains in the desert; underneath were rivers. One more blow to penetrate the granite; one more blow beneath the sand, walled back from choking up the shaft: But would the waters flow?

Now one stood up among us,—causing me to stand—and used my brain and voice, with my consent, to render judgment, even as one who had authority. Yet he announced himself as would a common mortal, chosen to interpose between two disputants, being accounted wise.

258

"I shall adjudicate between this woman and this man. My name is J. R. Evelyn. I was once a Judge in Liverpool. I am competent in law.

"Sir: I have read a contract, signed and sealed, which gives to you, upon condition, half the oil and half the minerals that may be found within a tract of land to which this woman has the right of property. Nothing is said of water. You have both inferred and understood that there is mutual ownership of Mineral Springs. Sir, not a reputable law-court in the world would give you title to a single drop.

"To whom do they belong? By common law the title vests in her; the Springs belong to her exclusively. But is not something due in equity to those who first discovered them? Neither this woman nor yourself can claim to be discoverers. Spirits discovered them. This she believes and you believe. Because of such belief upon her part, she caused them to be sought for, and, by sacrifice, permitted you to find. All that you have spent in bringing them to light must be, in time, refunded, with interest and even a little usury. What she has sacrificed must be, at last, made good. Spirits will see that she is well rewarded. When all has been repaid, there should in truth be equal ownership between possessors and discoverers. They I share and share alike.' Can you suppose spirits would leave their happy places, sink themselves below the common soil and search out healing elements, only to foster greed? So let the Springs be used for righteous gain. But spirits have an equitable claim. They have their holy purposes. Outcasts must be reclaimed; the sick must be restored; the little ones must be regenerated; the fevered, halt and suffering be lifted up. Who dare deny our rights?"

So much I have reported, thought for thought, and almost word for word; since, after all, these were but common words and common thoughts, such as will keep afloat in any common mind. Further I cannot go, except to say that every word which we had heard before, in parable and sermon—even in practical discourse— was brought to mind, in swift review and sequence. One might have said: "Here is a web of gold, and every thread was spun for us before this weaver took them up and made them all as one." I doubt if I

259

shall ever hear on earth such master eloquence again. Lawyer and advocate and judge—with none to say him nay!

There had been a sunset. When I looked I saw that night had come. We sat in darkness; no one moved or spoke. Till, being made to understand, I said to Mrs. Collins: "Will you bring a lamp? and will you bring pen, ink and paper?" After that my hand was moved to write two documents meant to be signed and witnessed.

[Copied from Jeremiah Eighmie's papers, Jan. 21, 1909, by B. F. Carpenter, 65 Orchard St., Summit, New Jersey,—he being joint executor with J. C. Eighmie, of that estate—including Yuh Heh Springs, whose heirs will "gladly" see the script fulfilled.]

"The well of healing waters first discovered through the joint efforts of myself and Mrs. S. A. Collins, upon land which she is legally entitled to, I freely acknowledge is free from all pecuniary claim except such as she may hold before she willingly resigns it in favor of the great healing work for which it is designed."

"I hereby promise, on receiving the above signature to the above acknowledgment, to resign all my rights to the water as soon as Mr. Eighmie is paid for his expenditure in finding it and for his labor and expenditure in building and putting up a Cure thereby and when I also am remunerated properly. I resign then my claim on the healing water as soon as it is secured from debt to others and myself. By 'resignation' I mean that the whole proceeds of the water shall be used in the service of God and the world."

Out of my line of vision Jeremiah Eighmie sat, until I read the papers out. Then up he rose and came—smiling as one who enters Heaven—and sat him down and signed his worthy name.

When Mrs. Collins also signed, he said: "Now this is most important. Let the spirit write these papers twice again, and we will sign them over—one for each of us. So that was done.

He would have meant no more if he had said: "Now let us make three tabernacles": and I, for one, knew that a "bright cloud" hung above and overshadowed us.

Whoever saw that "underself" again? Not I; it seems not anyone. So Jeremiah Eighmie passed away—sane, smiling, happy, when his time had come twenty-four years later—he being eighty-five. One writes to me: "Great numbers have been grateful for his ministrations. Numerous and marvelous healings were performed through him. His life was like a poem, his face an index of angelic indwelling." So "Father Eighmie" walks in spirit-paths, and who shall call him old?

As for my share, early in 1873 this Jeremiah Eighmie, having at heart the thought of that fore-shown Reformatory, put forth his "Hand of Providence" and laid its corner stone! Long be his name revered!

And first of all, honored be Sarah Collins! Who is like to her for trust, obedience, granite-like endurance, patience, energy, indomitable will?

Remember, but for her I had not found my work.

WAYS AND MEANS

SAID Jeremiah Eighmie: "Spirits sent you here on my account. I am the better for it. I ought to pay your traveling expenses."

I laughed: "Not for the world! They sent me here as much on my account as yours." So we shook hands and parted;—he to send the drillers back to Titusville, until a more convenient time, and I to write for bread. I looked at my depleted purse, and estimated: "Within two months, there'll be cold weather. Then I must go back into the Sanitarium and stay five months, at least; but after that I'm safe. So there's a lot to earn!"

Some spirit interposed: "You need to gather strength before your work begins; and rest is necessary. Do not depend on writing. That will soon be stopped."

My work! I realized that when it did begin, I'd have to stand up like a caryatid—not to sustain entablatures, but "floating islands" maybe. Still, I thought of silver cables—grasped and held by spirit-hands to keep the weight from crushing. So I meditated!

"Spirits, I cannot undertake that work and yet sustain myself. I'll ask for stronger proof. If, when my earnings stop, as you predict, I find myself provided for by spirit-power, and not as though I were a beggar, I will bear whatever spiritual burden God and you impose. But work should have a certain dignity. I have striven so hard for independence, I must not be humiliated. See to that and you shall have my confidence, my trust, my glad obedience." Just so we settled it.

I am no visionist in daily life. Nothing vague invites me. But I had seen a vision that appealed to me most poignantly. It might be realized. To make it actual was beautiful to think about, and terrible to undertake. I would not move a step without invincible conviction. I knew, by simple common sense, that one might travel all the world around, asking for means to build, endow and carry on a Home for fallen and repentant women, upon so grand a scale, and never gather up enough to build one martyr's tomb. I thought of Emma

Hardinge, honored and loved in England and America, who wore the long years out in fruitless supplication. I had no mind to follow after her on such a barren road.

About those days I could not choose but pray. Like James Montgomery I felt:

> "The motion of a hidden fire
> That trembles in the breast."

Whatever else was uppermost in mind, when this same fire incited me to ask, all thoughts, all aspirations became resolved into one single utterance: "O, make me ready for my work!" I spoke of this to none; my secret was already shared by three, who dwelt in flesh, and they but little guessed how all-compelling it would prove to be, even from that day to this.

Meantime I hunted up a cheaper room, and took the pen again. Spite of some idle weeks, there was a little overplus of young folk's matter in Chicago, waiting to be published. Rather freakishly, it seemed, I sent two stories otherwhere, each worth perhaps five dollars. To my astonishment, one editor (Moore, of the "Rural New Yorker ") sent me twenty dollars in lieu of five—a freak on his part also. Even while I read his lovely letter, great Chicago burned! My over-plus and all my income-sources blew away in smoke. My idle weeks had been no more than wasted time, if I had stayed at home and cared for self.

And now I thought the time had verily come for exercise of faith: "If I am chosen, I shall be provided for. I shall not be required to earn the money. I shall go back into the Sanitarium whenever that is best. I shall not be dependent on its charities to any great extent. Let spirits look to that! Meantime, I'll work for Deborah Hunting-ton. She needs another course of treatment."

So I furbished up some bits of knowledge held in memory (faithful custodian!) and wrote a lecture on Old British Customs, dating back five hundred years or so. Out of a coterie of six, we called a "reading class," I chose two clergymen—Rawlinson and Dickinson—to intercede for me with Dr. Foster: "Please let her read a lecture in the chapel at a price, to bring back Mrs. Huntington." "Next week," he said, "but tell her not to wait for that; send for her friend, at once."

I thought it well to trust. And yet, to trust, one must be lifted up. It seemed to me that I was all one prayer. I have known good souls who prayed to spirits. Even that may be a sort of exaltation—better than Buddha-worship let us say; for grace is often handed down through spirits—if we but stand in line. Yet is the Infinite not inaccessible: A prajer that recognizes Him, lifts up the one who prays. This way we reach those higher atmospheres where they abide who have not quite removed themselves from earth, but know the way to Heaven. There they abound in faith, and shall not we?

Now, faith is not belief, for that is often wrong, and faith is always right. Nothing is prayer, that is not justified by faith,—which, in its turn, is justified by inspiration. Prayer is not clamor, petulant demand, importunate desire; nor mere petition, howsoever earnest; nor sad complaint; nor urgent call for pity and relief—unless, indeed, an inward pressure come that cannot be resisted. God never urges us to pray, unless He means to give. But if we urge ourselves; that is another matter. I learned my lesson well in childhood. When it is given you to ask, rejoice! And, if it be not given, stand and wait—

"A-tremble for your turn of greeting words."

Be certain it will come. Suppose God verily chooses to reveal Himself through spirits—Moses and Elias, anyone who stands beside the open sepulchre and says with happy smiles: "Lo, Christ is risen—also Lazarus!" What then?

Must you turn back from His rejoicing messengers—whiter than whitest wool—because they wear no serge?

Let me report a thing from Dr. Henry Foster. He had his Wednesday evening chapel-meetings; and once he told us of an answered prayer. This was the way of it:

I think in 1858 (the year before I went to Clifton first), his health broke down. This was the more alarming because his family had known consumption. Drifting in that direction, he knew, and others knew, that, in default of speedy rescue, he must die and leave his work undone. Now, of that work he said, long afterward: "I thoroughly believe that God had planned this institution long before I lived ... .And so he finally chose me, and others with me, to develop what you see. My motto has been that of Paul: This one thing I do.'"

Believing so, even at that early date, he found himself brought face to face with death, and under every probability that "this one thing" must fail.

He said, substantially: "I left the Water Cure in care of others, and went to California. As it is with all who have been greatly over-taxed, no sooner was the strain relieved than strength began to fail. I found that I was sinking steadily. I judged, as a physician, that there was little hope. Week by week, I kept on going down!—down!—down!

"I left the coast, and tried the mountains. One afternoon I took my gun, and climbed till strength had., failed. Then I sat down upon a stone, and thought the matter over. There seemed no possible help. I said: 'It seems God's will that I should die!'

"'Now pray!' I heard the voice, and laid my gun aside. Then I knelt down and prayed that I might still be spared to carry on my work; and, while I prayed, I saw my chapel far away in Clifton Water Cure. I saw it filled with patients whom I knew; and they were all upon their knees, praying for my recovery. That moment I had perfect faith that God would hear and answer. Our prayers went up together—theirs and mine. I knew that they prevailed. There came to me a marvelous out-pouring of the Spirit. I rejoiced with 'joy unspeakable.' God showed me, then and there, that he had many years in store for me. I knew that I should live, and that my work should live long after me.

"When I arose, I thought with wonder: 'This is not the usual night for prayer at Clifton. There must have been a special meeting called to pray for me.' And then I wondered more: 'Why should they call a meeting in the afternoon? This is the hour for baths.' Then I remembered difference of time. So I took out my watch and it was four o'clock—but eight o'clock at home.

"Friends wrote to me and named that very evening, giving me the date. They said: 'We called a special Meeting in the chapel to pray for your recovery. We prayed with faith. We felt that God was with us.'"

When Henry Foster's eighty years on earth were ended, he had left a means for doing good almost unparalleled. And now I think there is a temple picture-gallery in Heaven, vast and high, whose walls portray himself as benefactor, with those he benefited,—for him and them to visit as they will; (I entering with the rest).

"Bring us indubitable proof," Prof. Huxley cries, "that God will answer prayer." The proof, great Scientist, is in the heart of man, and in his daily life!

I need just now to write of little happenings too small to dwell upon, save for their ultimate effect. Whatever sways a life, even as a far-off moon will sway the sea, or as a casual vacuum in air will start a hurricane, or any spark light up a house-hold fire to keep the babes alive, is worth considering. Be very patient; read my trivialities.

In all my life I had not prayed for dollars; but now I wanted more for Mrs. Huntington,—twenty-five, at least. I told our "reading class" (all comfortably poor and reasonably sick) that I had prayed for that amount; that I had prayed with faith; that it was coming soon. So I left off asking. Never tease!

Not less, one morning, early, I undertook to reach conclusions for myself. "I cannot ask for money. I have enough to pay my way till Tuesday; then, if no more should come, there'd be enough to take me far as Lydia Brown; no doubt there'd be some way to reach my sister's farm. There

I could stay as long as life should last—six months perhaps, or possibly a year. This then should be my epitaph: "Recreant to every Trust!" Lord, let it not be so.

I fell upon my knees: "Provide for me: lengthen my life. Give me my work. Help me to save the lost. Through weakness, pain and strife and anguish, let the promise be fulfilled. First make me worthy of my work; then give me every burden soul and flesh can bear. Provide for me; Now show me what to do!"

I know Who sent the answer. I did not know the messenger. "Go back into the Sanitarium."

"I cannot pay my way."

"How much will you require?"

"If I can have but thirty dollars more, I'll trust for all the rest."

"It shall be yours."

I rose from supplication: "I have one story, sent to

'Home and Health" and so accepted. That will be five dollars. Twenty-five must come from spirits—after they have brought the twenty-five for Deborah Huntington." Nor did I have a doubt.

So I sat down to breakfast, perfectly content. Olive McCune burst in—ablest of all the doctors, after Dr. Foster: "I hurried up to tell you; Dr. Cullis and his wife, who founded the Consumptives' Home in Boston, doing it by faith, will tell us all about it in the chapel. Don't be late! We meet at half past eight."

I hadn't been in chapel since my lecture—hard on weak lungs and nerves; but now I went, of course. When we were breaking up to leave, an elderly and pleasant lady whom I had never noticed (one of a thousand patients) came and said: "My name is Mrs. Rathbone. I heard your lecture, every word of it, though I am hard of hearing. Just paying for admission did not seem enough. Some poor, sick woman needed help, I understood. May I increase the fund? Were the receipts sufficient?"

"Well, I wanted more."

"Please call on me. I leave tomorrow morning."

I slipped aside to tell Miss Phillips—leader of our little reading class. Everybody knew Miss Phillips; virtually founder of the library, useful in many ways to Dr. Foster. Let me stop to say that she was twenty years confined to bed and couch—walking the halls a little on occasion. Not the less, some two years after that, as a direct result of taking many air-baths, she walked, through sloppy snow, two miles, to spend a day with me, did not lie down a moment—then walked back, and never fared the worse!

When I greeted Mrs. Rathbone in her room, she had her gift-envelope ready; but first I chose to visit. We talked an hour, as women will, for very love of it, and then I took her benefaction, kissed her and went away—to tell Miss Phillips. "Here's an answered prayer! Twenty-five dollars all for Deborah Huntington!" Can you imagine just how rich I felt?

Miss Phillips left her couch to say to Mrs. Rathbone: "You are greatly honored. God has used you as a means of answering prayer." So told the little story.

"I want to know Miss Jones. It seems she lives by faith. Ask her to write to me. Ask her to visit me in Albany."

That night I had a happy dream. It seemed that brother Lester came and handed me a bunch of pinks. "These I have picked for you," he said, "and there are more of them. Come see the root."

We walked together till I saw the plant, set thick with ruby-colored flowers. "These are all for you," said Lester.

"What do they signify?"

He answered: "Woman's love."

One sees heredity in this. Mother and I alike, in sleep, were sometimes taught by symbols. Each alike would ask: "What does this signify?" In every case these dreams were prophecies.

Miss Phillips handed me, next day, a sealed envelope. I said: "When I shall open this, we'll find what I was promised yesterday—twenty-five dollars for myself. Did Mrs. Rathbone send it? May I write and thank her?"

"She wants to hear from you. Here is another gift from her; a costly dress that she has never worn but once. Being in black, she has no use for it herself."

"Oh, me! Accordion-pleated flounces—half-a-dozen! I'll have to rip them off."

Said Rev. Rawlinson: "In your case, Heaven approves of flounces; that is clear." Quaker and Puritan—oh, well! I left them on.

Now, being safely in the Sanitarium, something puzzled me. "I owe eight dollars, sixty cents; but have I any right to pay my debts out of this little fund, meant for another use? Spirits have said they would provide for me. Am I to trust or doubt? I said that I would trust; so let me keep my word."

Just a week later I awoke at daylight and caught a Psychic message, flitting in, much like a homing dove. Oh, nothing very lofty,—only this!

"Ask for ten dollars this morning to pay your debts."

What? Was I called upon to pray for money? I got down to the level of it! I said: "Dear Master, send ten dollars, so I can pay my debts;" and this with absolute faith—the "substance of things hoped for, the evidence of things not seen." I had the "evidence" that moment, the "substance" in an hour. There was a letter waiting for me, that had no signature—post-marked Chicago, writing unfamiliar:

"Dear Lady: Please accept this little tribute from one who appreciates virtue and admires talent." It held ten dollars—one dollar, forty cents too much.

I wrote to Mr. Alden: "Are you responsible for this?

(Poor fellow, all burned out!) He wrote: "A lady called whom I had never seen. She said that she had never met you, but had been impressed for several days to send you money. She asked if you were in necessity. I told her I Yes,' and gave her your address. She would not leave her name."

Twice, after that, this unknown lady sent her "little tribute," saying, finally, that she was near to death. Each time her letter found me in emergency, and met an instant want. Now I suppose that she had climbed some Psychic mountain, half-way Heavenward, and caught the sense of me far off—or otherwise, a spirit prompted her. Who knows?

One day two gentlemen called together. One Doctor or Professor Fish—a guest of William Livingston Browne, who lived four miles away from Clifton,—the other, Mr. Browne himself.

The former, a geologist who lectured widely, knew of me, and having chanced to learn my whereabouts (I don't know how), desired to be acquainted. The other merely came through courtesy.

Some few days later Mr. Browne appeared: "Our

Shortsville people wish to hear you lecture." He named a moderate price, and gave a necessary invitation: Mrs.

Browne would gladly entertain me. Only to earn a trifle, I accepted. That was all the lure.

O, Deborah Huntington!—pale, proud petitioner for needless pardon! When spirits told you some "great good" would come to you through me, how would we both have wondered to be told what yet would come to me because of you!

Once, twice, three times that winter, by kind solicitation, I was the guest of Mrs. Hattie Browne. Most quiet lady, veritable artist—self-supporting, self-effacing wife and mother! To what shall I compare her? Let us say a still deep-shadowed lake within a forest, fed by hidden springs; and far off, in the happy meadows, herbs innumerable had their share of it. [Would there had been more sun!]

Her husband—let us wait awhile. I have no doubt far-seeing spirits chose him. I justify their choice.

Our tonic air-bath patients (shut in lighted tanks two hours together) grew to be good comrades. Ladies, clergymen and doctors made quite a happiness of getting well. Dr. Von Von Rosa (modestly he chose to drop the Vons), about that time received a legacy from Germany. He and his estimable wife,—not needing it,—thought well to give it all away in small instalments, making a lingering luxury of kindness. Someway they thought of me.

Before my little fund was quite expended, Dr. Foster met me: "God wants you to live; that's very evident! Dr. Rosa wants to pay your treatment for a month. I want to pay for it another month!"—and straightway Mr. Linton sent me to a better room. Dear No. 17! I wonder if some later occupant was ever so aware of angel ministrations, as I through five full months in No. 17. "Behold the Tabernacle of God is with men." Always I had the sense of unseen friends; I seemed to be at foot of Jacob's ladder;—little it mattered if the stone was hard.

Was I in need of actual earthly gifts? Twelve times within six months, means came to me, it seemed by spirit-intervention,—in every case foretold, in every case unlooked-for otherwise.

On Christmas Eve I took my diary, and wrote: "I have two gifts for Deborah; none for other friends. What do I need myself? Some handkerchiefs—a water-proof suit—a serviceable dress." This had been the compact: What I should actually need would be provided; so I formulated my necessities. You've heard that Spiritualism leads to lunacy. I never met a lunatic of my belief—albeit there may be such. Pronounce me one, if so it please you.

Miss Phillips met me at the air-tank, Christmas morning, with pocket-handkerchiefs a-plenty; also a rose-pink tie (I hope to wear rose pink in Heaven now and then—perhaps celestial blue. Why always dress in white?)

Straightway I floated up the stairs to show my gifts to Deborah, who loved me best of any. On the way a telepathic message like a meteor shot down—almost with detonation—unmistakable!

"Ten dollars will be brought to you this morning. Take it and buy a water-proof suit."

Now this I told to Deborah at once, to comfort her; and going to my room (a caller being in possession) said: "Miss Orr, I promised you should hear my next prophetic message before the prophecy should come to pass:"—so told the story over. I was so full of it, had you been there, you would have heard it also.

Next minute someone knocked. There stood Miss Shat-tuck holding out ten dollars!—Actually laughing—she, who suffered morning, noon and night till she had lost the art? "My sister-in-law

271

has sent you this," she said and went away in haste. Miss Orr stood voicing wonder for a moment, then wisely followed her. For me, I said in haste: "Don't send the dress! Don't send the dress!" Then dropped upon my knees, lost in a sense of greatness interclosing all our littleness. And, presently, being still upon my knees—how shall I tell it adequately?—Mother came: She stood so near—(J partly seeing her)—she seemed to press against me,—as palpable to soul, as flesh is palpable to flesh!

Now why expect from spirit visitants ineffable revelations?—"whirlwinds" and "clouds" and "living creatures"—like to "burning coals" and wheels with rings "set full of eyes," their work the "colour of a beryl." Let them be altogether human. This was my very mother!—not Saint Ann, nor "blessedest Saint Lucy." One who remembered, loved, forgave, as earthly mothers will. Once I had wounded her with accusation, and she had spared rebuke; but now the words that I had spoken then, her words brought back to memory in all their cruelty—and yet forevermore condoned.

"Mother, I think that you don't like to see me well-dressed." That had been my word.

"Daughter, I got you that money; You see I do like to see you well dressed!" That was her word, after so many years!

"Oh, blame of Love!—Sweeter than other's praise."

That afternoon I sought Miss Shattuck: "I did not know you had a sister here. How did she come to send me such a gift?"

Well, it is worth the telling. Two months earlier, having a special cause for fear, she promised secretly: "If I am saved, I'll give the Lord ten dollars." So, being freed from apprehension, she found herself indebted, not knowing how to pay. Once she decided: "I'll give it to the foreign Missions," but then an "inner voice" had counseled: "Give it to someone in the House." I think this lady was a Presbyterian; but what of that? Whoever spoke, she heard!

Miss Shattock said: "I chanced to speak of you. I groaned as usual: 'Oh, if I only had her faith!'"

"Who is Miss Jones?"

"A friend who earned her living writing children's stories. Since Chicago burned, she's lived on faith. God sends her all she needs."

"Go down to Mr. Linton. Draw ten dollars; take them to your friend." That was the way of it.

This gift, on one side pre-determined, on the other preassigned and prophesied, makes evident how close they are whom we have called our dead!—how potent to assist!

When the two added months had passed, amply provided for by personal gifts (not household charity), two or three more were needed. I would not stay a day beyond the limit. In Dr. Foster's absence, I packed my trunks and sent them to the attic, bade good-bye to Deborah Huntington, gave up my key and went, as pre-arranged, to visit Hattie Browne. Frankly I put the spirits to a final test. If, without any movement on my part, means for a further stay, up to the limit of necessity should be provided, that would confirm the whole. Thenceforward I should be irrevocably pledged! It was a solemn covenant.

And so I watched my silent Mrs. Browne lay on her pigments, paint her lovely landscapes (not for art alone, though that was much), and set myself to interview the children—very shy of speech. Also I hearkened to her husband patiently, the while he talked of general wrongs and individual rights—vaguely, as people will who never have been wronged appreciably. All other hours, when free to be alone, and not asleep, I wrestled for my faith.

"Promise me that you will never lose your faith" said Dr. Andrews. How could I hope to meet him far a-field, unless I kept my word? But, infinitely more, how could I hope to "wear away" from earth as he had done, if those I might have lifted up were left to crawl below? I dared not lose my faith.

When I had settled into perfect trust, there came a definite assurance: "What you need will come. A little tomorrow. After three days enough."

Next day an unsigned letter came from Clifton Village: "Trust in the Lord and do good, and verily thou shalt be fed." The would-be

273

thief who tore it open in the mail-car, had not the heart to steal my precious dollar. Perhaps the judge, who sentenced him to Sing Sing for the like, had been more lenient, if he had known of this.

"After three days," I went to Clifton. Passing by the

Cure, not meaning to go in, I heard my name called from an open window. Mr. Linton met me in the hall. Some said he never owned that he believed in God; but now he took my hand (hurting it not a little) and looked at me intently! "God is good to you! Last night a gentleman and lady prepaid your treatment for the next three months. They've gone away,—you are not even allowed to know their names. You're ordered back at once. You'll find your trunk in No. 17."

Ah, well! You guess the riddle? Dr and Mrs. Von Von Rosa! Not for a little fortune would I leave off the Vons!

This followed next: I sought an interview with Dr.

Henry Foster: "I have an offer—very pressing—from Chicago. Some wealthy men propose to start a family paper--I to be the editor. They'll give me thirty dollars weekly—they'll even hold the place for me two or three months till I am well enough. What would result in case I should accept?

"Possibly you'd live two years; not more than that. When you go down next time, nothing on earth can save you."

"Dr. Foster, when I told you on the first of January, up at Yuh Heh Springs, that I had seen a vision, I did not fully know that God had chosen me, above all others, to make that vision real. It had been promised me that I should "help;" I must do more than that. And now, I know that God had chosen me. I dare not die. I have this work to do."

Dr. Foster looked far-off in silence: Then he said: "have more faith in Yuh Heh Mineral Springs than in all other mineral and magnetic springs combined; and I have tested all!'

Dr. Hubbard Foster (visiting at Clifton) came to talk with me. He said, to my delight: "You are doing good. You are advocating air-baths. Patients have asked me whether you are right. I tell them all to trust your judgment first and last; it fully equals mine." Now, Dr. Hubbard was the chief apostle. He had unlocked the doors and let that system in among the other systems—far as prohibiting patentees allowed; not very far. Alas, how people will be dosed! Moreover, think of it! Shut and bolted in two hours! They found it terrifying. Suppose the thing blew up?

More to my immediate purpose, Dr. Hubbard said: "My brother Henry tells me you were the means of introducing him to Mrs. Collins, who owns Magnetic Springs. He's tested them six months, and says no other waters equal them. Strangest of all, he finds they have the cleansing power of mercury without its ill effects. God knows how such a remedy is needed! Once introduced, the world has you to thank as well as Mrs. Collins."

My vision and the words that followed—this was confirmation past dispute! I held my peace. Much as I loved and honored Dr. Hubbard Foster (who long before had proved himself a friend inestimable,) I would not speak again till doors were opened. God must point the way.

I used to sleep in air bath, waking with all my senses clarified,— the Psychic with the rest. And so it came about one day in early April that I awoke and saw what proved to have for me momentous meaning. There stood, within my reach, a large and very heavy wooden cross—unlovely yet illuminated of itself, as though from inner light.

I thought: "Now I am called upon for sacrifice. It must be someone in the house has need of me,—not Deborah; others have taken charge of her," (that was a marvelous place for benefactions) "who then can it be?" And, being in the way of sacrifice, I cast my thoughts about to no avail. After a day or two when nothing came of this, I let it pass from mind.

Then, all at once, like a strong heat from some wide conflagration, came a singular fervor, in which my futile wonderings were shriveled up. I dare suppose this was no mood of mine save under inspiration. Did not my spirit-doctor say another spirit-guardian would come? I was aware of him as I had been before of Dr. Andrews. I knew his very name.

And now I saw by perfect Psychic memory, that home for hapless women, shown to me before;—built out of bricks, made wide and high and

"Set four-square to all the winds that blow."

Straightway, I took my long-neglected pencils, sat me down and strove to be an architect. "Here is the facade, here the porch for entrance, over that the granite, carved with Mother's name—"The Mary Alma Homestead";—here shall run the halls, this way and that; here will be the reading-room well lined with books, and here a recreation-gallery hung with many pictures. This dining-room will glow with many flowers, this chapel thrill with organ melodies; and every little private room will be a sanctuary for some converted soul.

"Founded and built and well endowed:—write down a million dollars; write, 'not begged—provided" Who shall provide the money? That is for me to do.

"And now,—behold my Work!

"But after that, must be a Home for children, brought from profligate haunts and scenes of drunkenness. If this were mine to build, since father had a mighty love for children, that stone above the door should bear his name: '"The Henry Homestead.'" Even in the Heaven of Heavens, that thought would make him glad.

"But further still—let future generations see to all! The state shall drain the swamps; and ail around shall lie the berry-fields, the market-gardens, orchards, nurseries, floral beds and basket willow groves. Out in the sun and delving in the ground, those who have come from city hells, shall fit themselves to people Paradise. And all shall earn and none shall beg; till after 'fifty years' the second vision of the thriving village shall prove itself a glad reality. And men shall know that spirits dwell with men, for blessing, not for hurt."

All of this I dwelt upon with ecstacy; then I awoke from dreams. "Now let me demonstrate my faith. So I announced the work, as mine, not publicly but to a chosen few. I wrote to David Gray—poet

276

and editor, who had a singular faith in me as one called and elected to the poet's office; I said that I must utterly resign my personal ambition; what he had prophesied for me could never come to pass. I wrote to Mrs. Hester Poole, one of the founders of

"Sorosis." I wrote to my Progressive Friends;—to one who posed as a philanthropist;—to certain literary intimates,—• lastly to kith and kin. And then I told our "Reading Class"—five faithful Methodists,— (they never breathed a doubt.)

All had the self-same story; I had seen a vision;—I never hid that light under a bushel! I said that God had chosen me—I must obey,— must cause that vision to be verified.

David Gray grieved for the vanished poet: "And yet," he said: "You have no choice. You will succeed if there are miracles. God speed you on! Here is my contribution."

Mrs. Poole replied: "Come to New York. You shall be introduced to many wealthy women!" I have talked with one or two already. We think your work is glorious!" My corpulent philanthropist rebuked: "Such work is not for single women ... Very unbecoming" Progressive Friends believed! My kith and kin proclaimed no unbelief. No one had scoffed but one big man,—a camel laden heavily. Alas, the needle's eye!

Somewhere (perhaps Leigh Hunt imagined it), there is a story of an Eleusinian candidate, who, that he might behold the goddesses Demeter and Persephone, walked, well sustained, upon a bridge of air. And this did I, what time the hour arrived.

Meantime I faced the unsubstantial bridge and paused: Let Faith declare herself. Six days I spent in prayer. All the first day I talked about my weakness. That little nugget, health, mined out of shifting sands, I hammered like a very smith to prove its almost nothingness: "Behold," I said,

"how slight a thing is this!" I made myself appear the one most inconsiderable creature in the universe. "Yet here I am! Make use of me, or pass me by; but let the work be done."

When it was time to sleep someone drew near and said:—
"Ephesians: Sixth and tenth." When I had found the place, I read:
"Be strong in the Lord and in the power of

His might."—"Well, if the strength be His," I laughed, "what more
is needed?"—So I slept that night like any child.

Yet, soon as I awoke next morning, there was a fiercer lion close at
hand: "I cannot speak about this work of mine unless I tell my
vision—not to my friends alone, in secrecy, but to a scoffing world. I
must even stand, as one upon a rocky eminence—a mountain crag (I
so imagined it) and call aloud: 'Look up to me! breathe the higher
atmosphere. Spirits are my companions. God has appointed me to
be his prophet. Here I build an altar; here I sacrifice.'

"How dare I vaunt myself before the world—set up advertisements
like any spiritual charlatan—declare myself inspired? I am no better
than my fellows—no more to be revered. Who will believe my
words? Who will not scorn my work?"

And yet I sank upon my knees at last: "Lord, even so, if that shall
be Thy will."

Now in all scripture, searched with diligence through many days,
what one of us could chance upon a text equal to this, my need? And
yet the text was found; and not, I do aver, by any thought or
knowledge of my own:—

"*Read the last verse of the Book of Habakkuk.*" So I sought and
read: "*The Lord is my strength, and He will make my feet like
hind's feet, and He will make me to stand upon mine high places.*"
And I was glad again.

Next day I fell into another pit, and after that another, and
another. Three nights just such a braided rope, flung down, had
pulled me out; never the words of any text, always the place of it, the
book, the chapter and the verse,—contenting me with proof
invincible.

Last day of all the days, I had but one thing left to say: "Lord,
choose a greater woman; let her lead and let me follow. I cannot
spare my work—I want my work, but dignity and grace and power

and mental breadth and business talent all are lacking. There could not be a feebler instrument; give me the second place."

That was the hardest day of all; but, at the end of it, a final message came—an ultimate command: "Your lesson tonight is in Ezra." I thought to find the book among the lesser prophets (lacking the sense of place); Confused I said: "There is no book of Ezra." "Yes,—Your lesson is in Ezra. The fourth verse of the tenth chapter."

When I had read the text I said: "I'll ask no further proof. This is enough! *Arise; for this matter belongeth unto thee. We also will be with thee. Be of good courage and do it*

A SAFETY-CAGE

THE first of May had come. With yet a ld of strength to gain, my health was r well assured; and my physician thought no further remedy was needed: a draught, three times a day, during weeks, from Yuh Heh Springs. Only a wine glass full—that doesn't sound like much; and yet triple glasses sent me off to sleep beyond all precedent;—ten hours at night and four or five hours more out in the open, lying on heaps of rubble! Even ardor died away; I sank in waves of rest. I do profess myself an advocate of that magnetic water. I do believe that spirits first discovered it, perceived its unexampled virtue, brought illuminating thoughts to bear on spirits resident in flesh, and gently moved on human wills, to cause an exploration, bringing them to light.

Against my early prejudice, I, who would never tamper with the drugs of pharmacy beyond innocuous herbs, now find myself believing to the full in Nature's vital currents—• poured out with prodigality from that deep well. Beside it, I received my chrism of consecration! Well may I believe.

When Dr. Jonathan Andrews said another spirit-guardian would take his place with me, I do suppose he knew the very way of it. All along the path, his hand had led me on through shadowy places, beside the perilous abysses, over "frail and air-suspended bridges"— even to the very pass through which another hand should guide me into open fields. There I must sow, that others after me might reap. There was no place for me among discarnate souls till this should be fulfilled.

Behold then J. R. Evelyn—erstwhile a judge in Liverpool! This he said—this I believed. He never gave the date—nor spoke of former days when he was one with men and learned their vital needs. When the physician left, the lawyer came—to me an arbiter of destiny; to you, I trust, a friend. That is for you to choose.

While I was Mrs. Collins' guest during the month of May (1872) he came to me one day in homely fashion as to speech, keeping himself—the disembodied spirit—undiscerned. He had not come, he

280

never came, to make exhibit of himself, save as a human soul with human sympathies and interests. And this is literally what he said: "My friend, I ask your patience; I am about to shut you close within a small white tower. You will not even see a door for exit. When I shall set you free, then you may travel any way by any vehicle, save only upward, by balloon."

No saying could have seemed more blind to me. I had not long to wait. Come if you like and learn the mystery of the "small white tower." Escape from it with me and walk on many roads thereafter; but notice how aerial vehicles, that lured, were swept away, and I still left to walk on solid earth—a toilsome path, but safe.

Before I left the Springs a letter came from William L. and Mrs. Hattie Browne. "Come to our house; consider this your home, till you are called away."

These friends believed in spirit-intercourse, but not, I judge, wholly from personal experience,—rather from apprehension—all the more to be relied upon because of spontaneity. They wanted spirit visits; no doubt they hoped for such through me; but both were truly hospitable, being not rich, except in qualities.

Please let me speak in tropes. You've seen a silver mountain-brook drop suddenly from sight between the intercluding rocks. When you have peered far down, you've caught faint glimpses of a glimmering pool—its water silenced, deep in shadow;—Oh, the coolness! Oh, the peace! If not the peace, at least, the quietude! But all the time you understood that little channels here or there would somewhere deepen—rills would slip away at last, with infinite pleasure of escape and feed a thousand flowers. So dwelt, in shade, this little family! And so I dwelt with them. There was a small, white tower—a viewless, Psychic prison, shut in between the rocks (you see I think in tropes:) Be Psychometric, friends: look deep through thirty-seven years, let vision pierce the walls: Mayhap you'll see another than myself, set there to judge whatever needed judgment beyond the doorless walls. But speaking outwardly, I certainly was not alone: A mother, hushed, indeed, but not the less fulfilling every task,— housewife and governess and artist; three studious children—minds alert, but voices rarely heard as songs of winter birds; a father—not unlike the circling walls that kept all ruffling winds away, and—yes!—the noise of thrushes.

None of these five had aptitude for fluent speech, nor yet for ready writing. If either were required as being telepathic—foreign to myself—here was no source at hand; unless, indeed, by way of spirit-visitation. As for Mr. Browne, he had his fixed ideas. Loco-motors move on iron rails, and cannot be deflected without catastrophe. No doubt of estimable traits himself—he had a deep distrust of world-moralities. His children must not go alone beyond the gate; so they were taught at home. He had two patents, both unfarmed, through dread, it seemed, of partnership. If he had any plans for rectifying things—save by enforced division possibly, he never gave them utterance within my hearing.

I need to say these things in view of what must follow. You have a right to know who shared with me that "small, white tower" that seemed to have no door; also to study out, each for yourself, this problem, viz.: Whether that which came originated with myself or with the other five (the youngest barely eight), or with a higher source, as I believe.

Accounting for my vagrant personality throughout those fifteen weeks, I spent my mornings half the time, at least, in simply earning money. This I was at liberty to do. There was a serial story (Icelandic, I remember) written for the "Family Paper there were scraps for Mr. Alden; also I gained through him, a poet's prize for "Apple-Blossoms"—printed with decorations. I saw that poem after twenty years, among collected "Masterpieces";—the only piece of verse, I ever wrote, save one, that would not stay in memory!—an atmosphere, a fragrance, very little else! Oh, certainly, if there were any stress or strain of thought among the six of us, must be counted out!

The second night Judge Evelyn came,—strong voiced, emphatic, courteous withal, but like a man acquainted with the world, who has affairs, who thinks of earthly things and never talks of Heaven; upright,—perhaps severe, but not unmerciful; a man who never talks of love—yet loves.

When he had greeted us, he said: "I wish, with your permission, to give a series of discourses on Social Jurisprudence." (I thought: "What does he mean?") Then for the first and only time, it seemed he took a fact out of my store of knowledge, and made full use of it to illustrate some purpose of his own—not yet to be revealed. "For how," I thought, "could any Judge from Liverpool, who lived long time ago, know anything about a mechanism late invented?" However that might be, instead of opening up his chosen subject, he waived it for the evening and gave us first a parable—or rather as it seemed, an illustration in advance, prefiguring some ultimate intent, impossible for us to guess. He said:

"There is a mine not yet explored. I have myself discovered it. This mine is for the common people. It is rich in gold. No one can ever get possession of the whole; but each may search therein, pick out its particles of ore, and so, without defrauding any, be himself, to some extent, enriched.

"Now, every mine should have a Safety-Cage. Men step within, are carried down and brought above, without endangering life. These cages operate by means of cables, very durable—and yet they sometimes break. If that should happen, still the cage will not be wrecked, for underneath it is equipped with two steel arms, that when the fall begins, by automatic action, leap from rest, strike out and cut their way into the solid wall on either hand and so uphold the whole.

"Not only have I sought and found a mine, I have prepared an ample Safety-Cage; and all who choose may step therein and be conveyed below. The young and old, the rich and poor will be alike invited; but none shall bring from out the mine more than his rightful share."

The spirit turned to Mr. Browne: "Friend, you are near at hand and I invite you first; and yet I warn you in advance. I have prepared the Cage, I have attached the cable; but, understand, the shaft is not yet smooth. If there be any sharp and ragged rock of selfishness, not broken down, and worn away, that rock will cut the rope. The Cage will start to fall; but on its way to wreckage, two arms will swing from underneath, imbed themselves in rock, and hold it fast. They are the strong, steel arms of Law! However long the time of waiting, nothing shall harm the Safety-Cage,—and no one shall exhaust the mine."

Now, after that, he added certain trenchant words—a perfect proof to me, in later times, of preternatural knowledge;—a divination and a prophecy. These were personal to one among us; I do not write them down.

As for the lectures they were many,—never very long I judged, but very frequent. Begun in early June—I think we had the last in middle August,—at least before the close. Not always formal, never quite familiar, they dealt exclusively with social life, social activities and social righteousness. The spirit never talked of Heaven; he never crossed the line between this world and that. He taught us what is due to each and all from each and all. "Wrong must be followed by retraction," that is the mercy of the law;—retraction satisfies; but always, right must rule. He showed the home, a very resting place for faith and love and beautiful desire; he made the neighborhood a larger home, with gates that open out upon the world,—itself the greater home. He took us through the little market places, made us count our pennies, showed the essential rightfulness of trade, the holiness of equal interchange. Honesty became to us an all-embracing atmosphere—a breathing-space, boundless as Heaven, and glorified with light.

Once, speaking of benevolence, he turned to Mr. Browne, propounding this: "Suppose you saw two men near to each other, but not in reach of any save yourself. Suppose that one of these were wholly destitute—were actually starving—the other rich, well-fed and well-content, bearing a purse of gold. Would you be justified in snatching at the purse and, taking forcible possession, bestowing it upon the dying man?"

"Most certainly, I should!"

Half-shocked, and half in doubt, I waited the reply. Would I could write it word by word, and not by way of partial paraphrase! and yet I give the sense.

"Not so my friend. There is no man who is not moved to pity—wait but long enough. Meantime, extortion kills benevolent desire. The one whose body dies because of hunger, needs but common food. That is a transient evil,—death merges into life. But he whose greed withholds what love would grant, has far the greater need. He starves his deathless soul—forever dwarfed from what it would have been, had that one act of kindness helped to make it great. See that you hinder not the rich man's right to give! Stand back and let him have his opportunity."

During these talks, I was aware of mental growth. The field was new to me; at least, I had not entered it before with one who knew what weeds to pull, what wholesome plants to leave; and I was being taught. You know that I was looking out for news from Heaven; he gave us news of earth. We realized the strong necessity for human traffic, mutual enterprise and manual labor; for righteous brotherhoods, uniting rich and poor; for laws impeccable, and love that makes for peace.

But now I think of it, this lecturer never talked of spirit-visitation. He came, and that sufficed. I never saw him come. I knew that he was there when thought surged in and speech made haste to follow, when voice and action took on personality, and I—who seemed to speak—had nothing left to do but listen and be glad; and also, by the further fact, that what he uttered came far short of what he made me know, or dimly recognize. I was aware of brain-illumination. A mind was brought to bear on mine that, like a spiritual magnet, gave me qualities I had not owned, but never since have altogether lost.

Maybe I had a natural distaste for business. Certainly I had no mercantile forbears. They fought or preached or farmed, built bridges, manufactured cloth, and one of them, I'm told, almost achieved perpetual motion! But now I learned respect for bargainers—little admired before. For when Judge Evelyn passed from principles to practicalities, nothing, as I have shown, seemed quite too small to dwell upon. We learned to know what "Social Jurisprudence" means,—not merely abstract Right, but Right applied,—what one man has a right to from his fellows, and what he owes to them. Each for himself with others, all for each and all.

We'll say an artist—one like Vereshtchagin—sets out, by your desire, to paint a mighty picture. First you get an atmospheric space (hardly a sky) for sea-escaping vapors, cirrus clouds and lurid thunderheads, with ample room for hurricanes, or, peradventure, silent storms of light that beat the icebergs down; and after that, he limns the mountain ranges, smoothes them far above with snow, and silvers them low down with river-tributaries; and then he sets the seas to rocking;—"There's your world," he says; "built up and swung about, by everlasting Law. Do you approve the picture?"

"Yes, but where is home?" you ask. So on he paints and shows you cliff-built monasteries where men go barefoot and subdue the flesh; and, lower down, small caves for holy hermits, never seen by any; they wait behind the rocks till come the poor and leave them wheaten cakes,—and so they pray or praise the whole day through. (Who knows? Perhaps they curse!) And still he goes on painting: Nunneries where women waste their precious youth in telling beads or stitching scapulars; temples for gods, and palaces for princes; cities for thriving traders; mansions for the rich; attics for strivers; hovels for the destitute; cellars and under-cellars for the desperate; and, off at sea, great ships for sailors far from port, with countless voyagers. "All these are homes for human folk;—built up and roofed with Law. Now are you satisfied?"

"But no; the folk, before the homes!—show us the happy folk." And down he throws the brush: "Come, then, and live the Law!"

Even so Judge Evelyn showed us first the Laws magnificence, then stripped away the robe and proved its lowliness. He taught us how to walk the common world nor set our feet in traps; to get us earthly values—farms and factories and forges; to cut away, down every shaft, the ragged rocks of selfishness; to dig, and prune and buy and sell and give; each man an advocate of others' rights—no man a plunderer of any! So all should live the law!

At last he turned aside—or so I deemed—and talked of patents,—not inventions merely, but well-protected, marketable grants, designed to make inventors rich because of special merit. Night after night he talked of patents only; first, inventor's rights—sacred as

286

human life; then, people's rights,—since every value ought to count for all within its round and reach, not be engorged by any.

When he began, my ignorance was dense. I knew but two inventors—Levi Brown and William Livingston Browne, neither of whom had any capability for worldly enterprise. A Martian, sculling little boats along his broad canals, knows more of deep-sea navigation than I had ever learned of patent-management or patent-legislation. Under this stimulus, my faculties along that line were all ablaze with borrowed comprehension. Could all this clear instruction be meant for Mr. Browne alone,—who would not, could not—so it seemed to me—make any use of it? I wondered all the days; and never guessed the secret.

Now I confess this seemed so far away from what I most desired, I never dreamed that it was meant for me. Since I, in very truth, was no inventor. No flounce of mine had ever brushed a Patent Office door-jamb, or caught on courthouse palings. Perhaps the sole invention I had found of interest was Hargreaves' Spinning Jenny;—it was such fun, at eight years old, to watch three hundred spindles whirl and twist as many threads to Mother's one! What wonder if I grew a little restive, murmuring, about the break of every day: "But spirits, what about my mission work?

Why keep me here for this? I know that you are wise and have your purposes, but I have mine as well. Use me to educate this man, if that be thought worthwhile—but oh, my idle hands! I want my mission-work

Still, evenings found me placid—kindled me anew, and so the talks went on. One evening he who spoke to us caused me to turn and seem to look at Mrs. Browne. He broke off, saying gently: "Lady, you are very tired." Her husband answered: "She's been canning fruit all day."

"Friends, do you know there is a way of canning fruit without cooking it?"

"Tell us!" said Mr. Browne, with eagerness.

He answered in a voice of great severity: "When the right time comes, that shall be shown'

A tremor caught me: "Maybe I shall know."

I forced the thought away;—only next day I said confusedly: "Judge Evelyn taxes my credulity; to can and not to cook—that sounds preposterous. Not that I really doubt." And I am sure I never thought of that again, until the time had cornel

At last in early August—perhaps about the first, Judge Evelyn said that he desired to write. You know—or I have told you—that he had written once before; but let me say there had not been the least prevision on my part, that he would write again. There had not been a thought within my mind of any such necessity. A "mine," a "safety-cage," a "ragged rock of selfishness," a "cable" cut in twain, "two strong steel arms of Law," the perfect time,—all these, depicted when he first drew near and spoke to us, had faded out of sight. "Wise men, astrologers magicians"—even Daniel's self, unless inspired, could never have revealed the secret locked from sight among those five projected symbols. After they were shown some wrongful act was prophesied. And yet I had and could have had, no thought of this or of the safety-cage when—lifting up my yielding hand one quiet sunset hour (yet light enough for seeing)—Judge Evelyn took the pen and wrote out fair and large these unimagined, unimaginable words:

"THE CRUSADE DOCUMENTS."

This was years before the Women's "Temperance Crusade," and did not anyway prefigure it. Nothing was in my thoughts that could have taken shape and re-produced itself in but a single sentence out of all he wrote, which I transmit to you. I could no more have written thus, than built a tabernacle on Mount Tabor for you and me and Moses and Elias.

As to the manner of the writing, I choose to let another make report. His letter shall be fully verified.

Frank L. Browne, formerly of Shortsville, N. Y., to Amanda T. Jones: *Jan 15, 1909.*

"During a life that has now passed the half century milestone, many surprising and many pleasing events have transpired, among the latest being the receipt of letters from you........I feel that not a thousandth part of the warm affection which surges up from boy-hood recollection, will find expression or will—being put on paper—be expressed......The spirit within me harks back to boyhood's happy days and is filled with supreme gladness because of receiving a message from one so closely associated with those days. The joy within me seeks an outlet; the music within me seeks a listener; and I would fain share that joy and that music with the revered woman whose written words have produced them........I recall clearly much about

"THE CRUSADE DOCUMENTS."

"That yours was the hand that held the pen that indited these documents is perhaps a first and most important item. This I can affirm without hesitation or qualification. I was sixteen or just past sixteen—old enough to observe, remember, and know what transpired in my presence. To the best of my recollection I was present during the entire production of these documents—a process that occupied one hour or two nearly every evening for many weeks.—[About five.]

"It was the custom of the family to assemble in our homesitting room after twilight had faded into darkness and with no artificial light of any description, several pages would be written by your hand. As a mere boy, understanding but vaguely Psychic matters, I marvelled much at the clearness and perfect style of the writing, the accuracy with which the lines followed each other across the paper; the almost print-like contour of the letters—i e., their legibility; the fact that no blots or mis-strokes appeared (and you will remember this was before the day of the fountain pen—after each few words the pen had to be carried to the ink-bottle and back to the point where it was working); all this taking place in darkness dense enough to obscure everything except vague outlines of familiar objects......

"Even as I write now, after a lapse of thirty-six years, my mind questions: 'Was it really pen-work?' However, if but done with pencil, it would still be a strong demonstration of spirit control. But I am so sure. I know I had the written sheets in my hand each day following their production, and made copies therefrom, which, with boyish enthusiasm I filed away and treasured as something of extraordinary value. Surely all these impressions would not be so forcefully traced upon brain-records unless the facts were there to make them.

"We would sit quietly for a little time, and then in a resonant voice 'Judge Evelyn' would announce his presence, make some pertinent remarks, and the writing would commence. I recall clearly the fact that he once stated that the time would come when fruit would be preserved without the boiling process. And also my father's surmise that electricity would be the new element introduced to achieve that result. An idea, if I may digress for a moment, showing what a vague comprehension of electricity was in his mind, since the application of electricity almost invariably produces heat—even to degrees nearly beyond comprehension.

"The documents being finally completed, my father took charge of them, putting them away in a metal cylinder, made for the purpose, sealed closely and most carefully placed where they would not be disturbed. Why he did this was beyond my comprehension—but not beyond my investigating curiosity. Why it was done, I knew not, but how it was done was to me a wonderfully, interesting and clearly understood proceeding. My idea was that the extreme value of the documents inspired the action. The fact that he put the documents into print and had them copyrighted was also accounted for on similar lines.

"One more point; that is the date of the work, and I will pass to other matters. The documents were written at my boyhood's home in Shortsville, N. Y., through your hand, in the year 1872, I think in the late spring or early summer of that year. I place the date quite readily because in 1873, about a year later, I left home and made acquaintance with the outside world—its ways and customs in practical life being—up to that time—to me a sealed book.

"Recovery of the Original MSS. This I fear is doubtful. And before going into detail as to the why, I will state that if at any time the necessary expense can be met and it should seem advisable to make a search, I am willing to go and personally inspect the 'packed away' effects that Flora speaks of. I believe that I could do this with less trouble and more effectiveness than could anyone else. Should the time come when it seems wise or desirable or possible, I pledge you my honest service in this matter.

"Fred, in scraps of confidence, related of the sorting of father's and mother's papers and letters, and the numerous bonfires that received old treasured correspondence.......

Nothing was ever said of the 'Crusade Documents;' and while it may be possible that they are still in existence, there is also a strong probability that they shared the fate of other choice treasures.

"My recollections of 'The Crusade Documents' are written in more of a personal letter than a concise statement form. Use whatever meets your requirements, in form to suit yourself. I have simply stated facts as I recall them.......If, however, you wish to use my name and address in connection, I think it would be best to give Shortsville as the address. I will, however, keep you posted....

Remember that my recital comes from the heart rather than from the head, and is a tribute of affection, inspired by remembrance of days when you were a guide and counsellor to a 'timid' unsophisticated 'boy' who in the popular sense of the words, 'Never saw the inside of a schoolhouse.' "Ever Faithfully Yours,

"F. L. BROWNE."

From the same to the same, *Jan. 23, 1909.*

"Perhaps it would be well, if my written statement is to go on file as recorded evidence, for me to write and sign a letter devoted to that special subject.

"I recall the 'Safety-Cage' thought, or rather expression, but detail in regard to it does not come to mind. F. L. B."

From Miss Flora M. Browne, Shortsville, N. Y., April 19, 1908.

"I received your photograph. It looks just as I remember you when you were a guest of my father and mother and in delicate health.

"I was a large child but in the summer of '72 had not reached the age of eight by quite a little bit. The testimony you wish for would come more properly from my brother, Frank. I became quite familiar with the sight of the Crusade Documents in the old home, but you can readily understand that at that time I would not be likely to know from whence came your inspiration. The old home was sold soon after the death of my mother.......And the few things which were preserved have been packed in small quarters ever since. I don't remember that I ever saw the 'original writings' and am not able to say that there are any printed copies in existence or I would be glad to send them to you.

"Your friend,

"FLORA M. BROWNE."

I resume the story in *propria persona.* During the lectures there was never any artificial light—that being more or less disturbing to one in Psychic trance,—to me, at least, whose normal faculties were never put to sleep. We had our western windows—light in June will linger long; but when my well-sealed eyes were opened the room was always dark and all the outlines faint.

The writing was not done in Psychic trance; at least my eyes were always open after the spirit's introductory words. I saw, if there was light enough to see by, what was being written; or otherwise, I saw the outline of the paper, and was not troubled if I saw no more. What he said each time—mere words of greeting—was no way relevant to anything he was about to write. Not one of all his thoughts came fairly in advance of words. His mind, my brain, cooperated on the instant. Nothing was hurried, nothing was delayed. Not seeing well, I wondered: "Do the lines run true?" and that I did not know, or then or afterward, until the letter came that I have given you. At other times, I thought: "This is a complicated scheme;—do all its parts agree?" And I supposed they did. Once I said in mind: "He gives me 'Marshal,' would not General be better?" Having a certain superficial knowledge due to battle-studies, once I thought: "There were no Sergeants-General in the army. I wonder what he means."

These thoughts of mine were independent—stage-whispers you might call them. The writing went on steadily, without a break except to fill the pen, up to a certain limit—perhaps five hundred words,—then stopped, and Mr. Browne removed the sheets at once. I never asked to see them; all next day I moved about as in a dream thinking of that which had been written, wondering, but never guessing what was yet to be. I had a vivid consciousness of brain-illumination; much as the blind man knows there is a sun when out in August heats, I was aware of light.

Now, when we thought the work was done, Judge Evelyn said one afternoon: "I wish to copy all the pages. Please bring the writings here."

My host appeared displeased, yet brought the first few pages—taking them away together with the copies soon as they were made. Each time he brought me other pages—and took all leaves away. During this copying I read the former pages always as I wrote the new ones. I noted twice or thrice the substitution of a word, and once the alteration of a phrase. "Why not have written all correctly on the start?" said Mr. Browne, one morning. I could not answer then, but now I can. The spirit manifestly chose, by repetition, to print the whole of it upon my memory—knowing well that I was not to see the manuscript again—no, not one leaf of it! I do not mean that I could say it off by heart, just as I can my poems; but when I read it afterward in type, I recognized each separate word and every phrase and all the body of it perfectly. You have it unimpaired.

When the last word was written—still with my hand upon the page, Judge Evelyn chose to say:

"My friend has wondered why all this has come to her. She has a mission-work, wholly apart from this, she tells you,—needing to be done." He struck my hand upon the writing: "This is her mission-work! There is no way of getting funds for all she has to do, save through inventions. They will come. These documents are hers; and when the time is right, they shall be brought to light." He added: "Very soon my friend is going East. She has her work to do—she will not lack for friends." And so he said his final word "Farewell."

Then Mr. Browne arose and took the written pages—every one of them, and walked away. It proves that after Frank had copied them, his father sealed them up,—perhaps forever.

When, the next morning, I awoke, it seemed that I must leave at once. Announcing this to Mr. Browne, I had a sense of earthquake. I sat in utter silence while his underself came uppermost, denouncing me for leaving—demanding some addition to the documents. I had no right, he claimed, to leave them incomplete. Undoubtedly he felt that they belonged to him. Judge Evelyn, he said, should be allowed to finish them. By which he meant, as afterward appeared, the adding of a clause, approving him as organizer, owner—what you will.

We must not be severe. I think he was persuaded that they were truly his. A medium is not supposed to be the benefited one; and, I, myself, had not supposed them mine, till some few hours before, when they were so pronounced.

Besides—God help us! Where abide the saints? One did abide under the roof that had so sheltered me. I sought her out at once. We kissed each other tenderly and did not meet again for thirteen years. She visited me then, and hearts were satisfied.

This human Scripture, who can read it rightly? Who can interpret all its secret meanings? Or judge the errant wanderings of a soul?

> "But slowly the ineffable light comes up,
> And as it deepens drowns the written word."

THE CRUSADE DOCUMENTS

[Appropriated, by William Livingston Browne, printed and entered according to Act of Congress in the office of the Librarian at Washington in the year 1872, under the name of *The American Crusade*. Debarred from circulation and use by legal interference of Judge Edmonds, of New York, on behalf of the rightful owner, early in 1873.]

DECLARATION

WE believe in the sovereignty of the People. We claim for their Hosts all rights which are inseparable from the life of responsible beings; believing that culture of no available kind should be denied them, and no honorable means of gaining a subsistence placed beyond their reach, protest against all systems of labor and modes of conducting trade, which debar the laborer, inventor, seller or purchaser, from receiving a just payment for all labor, invention, time or investment; and we hereby pledge ourselves to endeavor faithfully to conduce to such an order of things as shall secure to each his or her just dues, and at the same time rob not the multitude nor enrich the drone.

So protesting, and so pledging our efforts, we declare ourselves to be Crusaders, enlisted in the worthy cause of rescuing the sacred land from selfish monopolies, and once more lifting up the standard of the chosen children of God, the Workers, that it may float from all the gateways, marts, temples, and palaces of the holiest of cities, the City of Good-will.

We therefore

CRUSADE CONSTITUTION

In accordance with the declaration of our sentiments, and in pursuance of the good which we believe may in time be attained through our united efforts, we, Crusaders, do approve of, and consent to abide by the following Constitution, with its accompanying laws and measures of organization.

ARTICLE FIRST.

The power of the Sovereign People composing the Host known as Crusaders, shall be vested in:

A BUREAU OF APPOINTMENT.

A BUREAU OF ADMINISTRATION.

A BUREAU OF INVESTIGATION.

To the Bureau of Appointment shall appertain the labors of ratifying all nominations to office, of defining the respective duties of officers, apportioning suitable payment for their services and sustaining them in the discharge of their obligations. It shall have authority in deciding all legal and judicial questions, constituting the final court of appeals in any or all cases of disagreement and confusion of purpose among workers for the commonwealth. It shall be composed of ten members, to wit: A judicial head, known as Chieftain of Battalions; his assistant justice, designated as Marshal of Battalions; two co-laborers, termed Squires; and a body-guard of six, called Aides-de-camp.

To the Bureau of Administration shall belong the responsibility of carrying out the designs of the organization of Crusaders, maintaining its laws, providing for its needs, and jealously protecting the rights of its members. It shall be empowered to preserve order and unity, in such ways and by such means as shall be pronounced in accordance with the true spirit of the Declaration, the Bureau of Appointment to be the adjudicator; and it shall be subject to that tribunal in all its relations with the Crusade Host. It shall consist of sixteen officers, to wit: A President of Councils, a Master of Finance, ten Gentlemen of the Council Chamber, two Scribes, a Bearer of Dispatches, and a Keeper of the Seals.

The Bureau of Investigation shall be empowered to sift the claims of all applicants for honors, examine the accounts of all Crusade recorders, discover any financial defaulter and report him or her to the Bureau of Administration, which shall examine into the demerit, and having pronounced its verdict, proceed to yield the case for adjudication to the Bureau of Appointment. All matters of business requiring official supervision shall first be tendered to the Bureau of Investigation, and, after suitable action, shall be given to the Bureau of Administration, which must conduct them, subject to the sanction of the Bureau of Appointment. The Bureau of Investigation shall be formed out of the Crusade ranks, and shall have a recognized head styled Sergeant-General of Crusade Forces. The number of his associate Investigators may be limited only by the number of enterprises which shall have received the authority of the Bureau of Appointment, and been incorporated into the Crusade body politic, each enterprise being represented by two Investigators.

These Bureaus shall be acknowledged as the outward wall and bulwark of defense for the Crusade Host. Through them its material interests will be secured and its masterly energy of purpose and labor directed. Their officers shall be selected from among those proven to have worthily borne the cross of sacrifice, and must be faithful to their high calling as gentlemen and Crusaders. They shall be annually confirmed in office, or others chosen by lot, out of the nominated numbers presented to the Bureau of Appointment, by the various captains of the banded soldiery, through their representatives, the Generals of the united battalions.

ARTICLE SECOND.

The Good-will of the Sovereign People known as Crusaders shall find expression in:

A BUREAU OF EDUCATION,

A BUREAU OF ASSISTANCE,

A BUREAU OF ATTRACTION.

To the Bureau of Education shall belong the privileges of receiving and entertaining all ideal projects of good, accepting or refusing them and bringing such as are judged feasible before the Crusade multitudes. It shall labor for the advancement of Art and Science, the progression of thought and truth, and the promulgation of benevolences among Crusaders. Its decisions shall be final in all cases requiring moral adjudication rather than legal, and it shall constitute the Supreme Court, where the higher equities shall be considered and pronounced upon. It shall be composed of ten members, to wit: A Mother of Sciences, A Mistress of Instruction, two Dames of Honor, and six Ladies in Waiting.

The Bureau of Assistance shall attend to all solicitations for comfort and material aid received through recognized Crusade channels, and shall make such responses as shall be deemed consistent with the highest requirements of the organization. It shall aim to promote the largest liberty of social life, compatible with unsullied purity and wisdom of behavior. To this end it shall consider and endeavor to supply the necessities of the various associations of Crusaders, pronouncing against all violations of propriety, and giving sanction to worthy efforts towards reform. It shall labor to help the young in acquiring such culture as may best fit them for the duties of life and employment, devoting a portion of the funds held for purposes of kindness to the children or orphans of poor Crusaders. It shall present its judgments in all matters to the Bureau of Education, deferring to its criticisms, decisions and commands. It shall be formed of sixteen ladies, to wit: A Dispenser of Benefits, a Bearer of the Purse, ten Almoners of Bounty, two Secretaries of the Bank, a Warder of the Gates and a Guardian of the Keys.

The Bureau of Attraction shall devise and promote recreations, organize classes, select instructors, suggest studies, and report progress of education to the Bureau of Assistance. It shall lend countenance to any laudable social movement, and support the leaders of approved Crusade pursuits. It shall discover disturbers of tranquility and such moral offenders as are amenable to Good-will tribunals, but not liable to legal arraignment. Such cases it shall refer to the Bureau of Assistance, which shall investigate each offence, presenting it, with any extenuations that may have been elicited from testimony, to the Bureau of Education for adjudication. The Bureau of Attraction shall have an acknowledged head, styled the Conductor of Harmonies. Her associate members shall be limited by the number of Crusade battalions, each battalion being represented by two ladies, who shall be denominated Sisters of the Choir.

These Bureaus shall be regarded as the inner citadel and stronghold of the Crusade Host, and it shall be the foremost thought among Crusaders how best to preserve this tower of Good-will from overthrow, and its hospitable board and hearth from defilement and desecration. Their officers shall be of those whom the people regard as blameless, and must be worthy of the lofty trust so reposed in them. They shall be annually confirmed in office, or their places filled by such as shall be chosen by lot, out of the nominated numbers forwarded to the Bureau of Appointment by the various Guides of the banded soldiery, through their representatives, the Governing Ladies of the united battalions.

ARTICLE THIRD.

Inasmuch as all elements should mingle and blend in harmonious and healthful interchange, the forces of the Crusade Army should acknowledge the influence of their inspirers, the ministering rulers of the mind and heart; and the Educators should, in their turn, revere and worthily regard the soldiers of the Host who stand without the temple, wresting from the material world the sustenance for all, which none can forego.

Therefore, the Bureau of Appointment and the Bureau of Education shall constantly communicate with each other, asking and receiving counsel, assisting to arrive at perfect conclusions, and in no wise holding such mutual exchanges in light esteem. Twice in each month these bureaus shall resolve themselves into one, deliberating upon the most important questions that have been presented to either body. Over such meetings the chief officers of both Bureaus shall preside in alternation and shall maintain order without respect to person or sex.

Also, the Bureau of Administration and the Bureau of Assistance shall at the same intervals unite in common deliberation, reporting the results of their conferences to the united Bureaus of Appointment and Education without delay.

Also, the Bureau of Investigation, comprising its chief and ten delegates from the body of its investigators, (annually chosen by lot) and the Bureau of Attraction, consisting of its chief and ten delegates from the Sisters of the Choir, (annually chosen by lot) shall unite semi-monthly with mutual interests, each giving its matters full unfolding before the resolved Bureau. The result of their combined deliberations shall be given without delay to the resolved Bureau of Administration and Assistance, which shall in its turn refer them, after suitable action, to the resolved Bureau of Appointment and Education.

In addition to these deliberative meetings, there shall be four gatherings in each year of all these Bureaus, resolved into one body for mutual suggestion and legislation. On such occasions the presiding officer shall be chosen by lot from among the six chiefs of the several Bureaus; and the chosen President shall preserve order without deference to rank or sex.

The people shall be at liberty to present for the consideration of this assembly, any petition or suggestion or general complaint, without resorting to official interposition; and no such petition, suggestion or complaint, accompanied by a considerable number of names, shall be lightly set aside without action.

All these deliberations of single or united Bureaus shall be open to the public whenever there is discussion of abstract principles or Crusade legislation. If, however, the matters under consideration relate to the misdoings of any Crusader, there shall be no publicity; nor shall the people be informed of any personal investigation, not formally demanded by them, unless it results in partial condemnation or expulsion from their ranks. If any woman shall be found guilty of unlawful dealing in any Crusade business, her fault shall be stated to the Bureau of Education, (after the usual formalities of trial) and her sentence pronounced by that tribunal, that she may be judged by her own sex. If any man shall be proven guilty of misdemeanor among Crusade Associations the Bureau of Education shall transfer his case to the Bureau of Appointment, that his sentence may be pronounced by his fellows. Nevertheless, where the fault or faults have transgressed both the civil law and the higher equity, the decision shall be rendered by the united Bureaus of Appointment and Education, and expulsion or deprivation of honor receive the sanction of the highest tribunal of the Crusade Host.

There shall be three additional responsible bodies, to wit:

A BUREAU OF PUBLICATION,

A BUREAU OF EMPLOYMENT,

A BUREAU OF REGNRATION.

To the Bureau of Publication shall attach the duty of fitly and in all cases truthfully, representing Crusade matters to the world whenever they shall have received official approval. It shall proclaim all news that should interest Crusaders, relative to the Host, shall place the issues at stake before them as clearly as possible, and uphold the highest conceivable standard of right, whether of earthly or divine law. To these ends it shall issue, at least once in every month, a printed sheet called "The American Crusader," and shall endeavor to place it before every member of the Host. It shall consist of not less than five men and five women, with a recognized head of either sex, who shall be styled Mentor of the staff. Whenever the business of the Bureau shall increase beyond the possibility of accomplishment by such a force, it shall be augmented sufficiently.

The Bureau of Employment shall have special charge of the working department of the organization, providing, as far as possible, all applying Crusaders with employment, and in no case allowing insufficient payment for labor well performed, of whatever sex, race or age the laborer may be. It shall connect itself directly with, all manufactories, stores, shops, or schools, which are the outgrowth of Crusade enterprise, and its authority shall not be gainsaid among them. Nevertheless it shall report its decisions to the Bureau of Publication, stating exactly what wages are received by operatives of every class, that it may so be held open to public censure or approval. It shall consist of an active corps of ten Advisers, headed by an officer styled Commander of Trades. These men shall execute the decisions of the Bureau. There shall be a reserve corps of ten women Advisers, having a chief lady, called Accorder of Justice. The reserve corps shall allow no matter designed for adjustment by the Bureau of Employment to pass unconsidered, and they shall guard the interests of the working class from all unrighteous encroachment. If the business operations of the

Host extend beyond possibility of diligent supervision by these numbers, assistants shall be granted them, who shall, however, have no voice in the Councils, nor vote in the decisions of the Bureau.

To the Bureau of Registration shall be conveyed promptly the name of every Crusader, of whatever age, race or sex, with such particulars as shall serve to identify said Crusader. Such registration shall then be certified to, and the recruit be duly supplied with a certificate of membership, and a legal recognition of his or her rights, acquired by virtue of enlistment in the Crusade Host.

The books of Registration shall be open to all necessary inspection, and a report of added recruits (in numbers, if not by name), shall be daily sent to the chief of the Bureau of Publication, to be summed up and published in each issue of "The American Crusader." In every instance where the Bureau of Employment shall provide a Crusader with work, the name of said Crusader shall be copied from the books of registration and preserved among the archives of the Bureau, that its effective operation for good may be readily ascertained, and frequently published to the people. This Bureau shall comprise a Janitor and as many assistants as he may require to perfectly transact the business appertaining to the office.

ARTICLE FOURTH.

The Crusade elements being recognized, and harmonious blending insured, these objects and only these shall be pronounced legitimate Crusade work, to wit:

The proper payment of labor, the equitable distribution of capital, the protection of manufacture and just liberty of trade, the education of the young, the improvement of the mature and the tender support of the infirm; the enhancing of innocent pleasures, the promotion of social security, the cultivation of the higher nature, and the deepening and broadening of the currents of human sympathy and love; the advancement of temperance, the increase of wisdom, and finally, the complete assenting of the human race to divine and beneficent law. To this end, we, as Crusaders, agree to embark heartily in such enterprises, material, benevolent or aesthetic, as promise to promote the objects above specified, and we subscribe willingly to the following rules and measures of action, believing them well worthy of examination and persistent trial.

RULES GOVERNING MATERIAL ENTERPRISES.

Every Inventor, Artist, Author, Manufacturer and Vender of Wares, may be placed, at his own solicitation, under the Protection of the Crusade Host, receiving the assistance and cordial co-operation of Crusade officers and people in circulating his or her inventions, works or wares, upon strict Crusade principles.

The inventor shall yield his right to the sale of territory, promising to abide by the Crusade Constitution. For this concession he shall be announced to the Bureau of Investigation as a candidate for the Honors of the Host. When said Bureau shall have decided upon the acceptance of his invention as a veritable means of assisting the work, increasing the wealth, or enhancing the legitimate enjoyment of the world, his case shall be reported forthwith to the Bureau of Administration, which shall induct him into his place as one of the leaders of the van, introducing him as such to the Bureau of Appointment. He shall then be formally announced to Crusaders under the sign and seal of the Crusade Host, kept by the Bureau of Appointment and the Bureau of Education alone; and his name shall be immediately transmitted to the Bureau of Publication. A careful account of his invention, divested of exaggerated praise, but wholly indicating its merits, shall be immediately published in "The American Crusader." Appended thereto shall appear as exact a statement as possible of the actual cost of the manufactured article, including material, oversight, labor and transportation, with the decision of the investigating committee as to its fair market value. To the actual cost shall be added one-fourth that sum as provision for all contingencies, modifications of prices current, losses by fire or other destructive agents, robberies or injuries of machinery used in its manufacture. The inventor, or any desirable number of agents, selected by the committee of investigation, or at least approved by them, may be employed in the active labor of soliciting purchasers; in which case to the above united sum shall be added ten per cent of the current price of the invented article, wherewith to meet all expenses incurred by travel of the solicitors. A similar percentage shall be paid to such agents as emolument for their time and efforts, and a percentage of not less than three nor more than five shall be paid to the inventor as his royalty. The sum remaining after these sums shall have been subtracted from the market price, shall be accounted as so much stock owned by the purchaser in the enterprise, constituting him or her a member of the Crusade Host, and an ultimate sharer of the divided spoils won by this most righteous warfare. When the invention shall be called for by the people, without the intervention of travelling solicitors, the percentages set aside for their travel and wages, shall be duly invested under the supervision of the Master of Finance and declared devoted to purposes of kindness. Also, whenever the cost of manufacture shall at the end of the year be found to have been less than the announced sum, the surplus monies shall be disposed of in the same manner. Also, when the time has legally expired, during which the inventor can claim his royalty, that amount shall still be paid in by the purchaser and be in like manner invested. The Good-will Fund so obtained shall be guarded by the Bureau of Administration, and at the proper time tendered to the Bureau of Assistance, for disbursements in benevolences.

These monies shall not, however, be given to any Crusade charity outside of the limits of the stock-holders in the enterprise which furnished them, that only purchasers and their heirs may reap the benefits accruing from such investments.

Nor shall any of the funds, devoted to kindness, be disbursed under ten years from the date of the acceptance of the invention, which forms the pivot of said enterprise, by the Bureau of Appointment. At the end of that time each company united in the manufacture or sale of such invention and all possessing stock in the enterprise, shall be at liberty to report all truly necessitous cases within its bounds, specifying the necessity, whether of widowhood, orphanage, sickness, physical disability or mental incompetency.

To these reports, properly substantiated and conveyed, the Bureau of Assistance shall not fail to make response, supplying each needy person with an exact and due proportion of the equitably divided funds. Each six months thereafter a similar distribution shall take place, adding to the list of applicants for benefits any that in the meantime may have been announced as worthy, and erasing all whose necessities have been removed. It shall be the business of the Investigators of the enterprise to discover any failure in the receipt of these Good-will monies, and to bring the defaulters promptly to justice. They shall moreover hold themselves responsible for the safe conduct of these received funds, which must be placed in the hands of the Master of Finance, subject to the control of the Bureau of Administration, until remitted to the Bureau of Assistance, and placed in the keeping of the Bearer of the Purse.

A full report of their matters shall be sent by the Investigators to the Bureau of Publication, as often as once in every month. A separate report of monies accounted for and received shall be forwarded to the same by the President of Councils; and a certificate as to the amount tendered for good-will purposes, furnished by the Dispenser of Benefits. If in the smallest fraction these three reports shall exhibit discrepancy, the most explicit examination shall be had and the error corrected. The Bearer of the Purse shall draw from the fund in her charge, no amount whatever upon any demand, without declaring such withdrawal to the Secretaries of the Bank, who shall not fail to record all particulars connected with such disbursement in the books of the Bureau.

The monies paid in by the purchasers, constituting their share in the stock of any enterprise, shall be received by the Master of Finance, or accounted for to him, and they shall only be expended under his approval and the sanction of the Inventor and the Investigators of the enterprise. They may be expended in the building of manufactories, store-houses, sales-rooms, or in purchasing any manner of real-estate as near the vicinity of the purchaser of the stock as possible. All such real-estate shall be held in the name of the Crusade Host, subject to Crusade oversight, and shall be sold on no consideration, whatever, (unless as an exchange for other real-estate equally as desirable) until the universal disbursement of property values, at the close of the term for which the patent is held. If, when the time for such disbursement shall come, the holders of stock shall prefer to leave their dividends for further increase, the business shall be carried on as before, except that any stock-owner shall be at liberty to call for his share after each half-yearly appraisal of properties.

At the expiration of the term covered by the patent-right, all real-estate held by the Crusade body politic in the interests of the stockholders of said patent, shall be justly appraised and the amount due each one announced, that it may be reclaimed, if so desired. All the purchasers of the first year of the term shall be entitled to a bonus of three per cent above those of the second year, those of the second year above those of the third and so on.

Great care shall be had in the purchase of real-estate with invested funds, that it may be of the full value of the amount expended in its purchase, and promise increase of value with each succeeding year. Such real-estate shall be under the Immediate care of the nearest band of Crusaders, who shall regard it as the representation of their interests and the interests of all stockholders. Taxes shall be paid thereupon out of the funds derived from rentals and other returns from real-estate connected with the same enterprise. All such returns shall be paid into the hands of the Investigators and be strictly accounted for by them, both to those remitting such returns and to the Bureau of Administration, through their chief, the Sergeant-General of Crusade Forces. When any purchaser of an article so patented and adopted by the Crusade Host, declines to be considered a member of the organization, and does not, therefore, claim his share in the common stock, said share shall be deposited in the Public Treasury as a portion of the Government Fund. If not required for the maintenance of the Crusade Government, it shall be distributed in pensions to such laborers as have been maimed or injured in the manufacture of said article, or to their widows, orphans or heirs immediately dependent on them for support.

Also, when any owner of shares shall have died without particularizing as to the disposal of his dues, they shall be paid, at the proper time, to his nearest heirs, unless such shall be no nearer than cousin-german, in which case the share or shares (which must in no case exceed five in any single enterprise) will revert, by virtue of his consent to the rules here given, to the Public Treasury. When the term of the patent-right shall have expired, the shares for which no owner can be discovered nor any heir entitled to them, shall be paid over to the Public Treasury, within a period of not less than six months from the time of general disbursement; and whenever thereafter any owner shall fail to attend to his claim for a period of five years, it shall be forfeited to the same fund, provided that he be semi-yearly invited to substantiate it until the expiration of that time. Any purchaser who is already a Crusader, and does not care for the value of his interests in any enterprise, may assign his share to any fund held for purposes of kindness, within the limits of said enterprise, or may present it to any individual, or may order it placed in the Public Treasury, he being afterward duly accredited, and informed of its acceptance and safe conduct.

There shall be a distinction between educational and material enterprises, inasmuch as the former must have passed the tribunal of the Bureau of Attraction, being accepted by the Bureau of Assistance and authorized by the Bureau of Education, before being placed in the care and under the government of the Crusade Host, to be conducted on strict Crusade principles.

Any author or artist desirous of obtaining Crusade authority as to the merits of any work or works, shall resign his right to public or private sales, or any exhibition of said work or works. For this resignation he shall receive official guarantee of the best assistance of the Crusade Government. From three to five per cent of all receipts from sales or exhibitions, or from lithographs or other copies of works of art, or from any method of circulation whatever, shall be paid to said author, or artist, for a term of twenty years from the date of his connection in that capacity with the Crusade body politic, or to his heirs. The Government of the organization shall have no right to dispose of any copyright or original work of art by direct sale to any person or body of persons, whatever, but shall use all diligence in bringing said book or work of art, as a veritable means of education, before the Crusade Host. No further percentages shall be paid to any but authorized agents, who must submit full accounts of sales or receipts from exhibition to the Sisters of the Choir in each Crusade district where such sales or receipts shall have taken place, and also to the author or artist concerned. These accounts must be tendered intact by the chief of the Bureau of Attraction to the Bureau of Assistance, and after their approval, be referred to the Bureau of Education. If they shall be found not to coincide with the accounts kept by the Investigators of each particular enterprise (to whom the agent must also be held accountable), an immediate investigation shall be had, and if a defaulter be found, he shall be punished according to Crusade legislation.

All monies collected through such enterprises, after the full expense of conducting them shall have been met, shall be expended under the supervision of both Investigators and Sisters of the Choir, in the purchase and fitting up of halls for meetings, lectures, etc., and in the procuring of libraries, paintings, statues or any educational appliances approved by the Bureau of Education. Such appliances shall be free to all Crusaders, but if enjoyed by any outside of the Host, shall be paid for at a moderate rate.

Any body of Crusaders may solicit the original of any work of art, so committed to the care of the administration, and may hold it on exhibition for a period of not more than five weeks (unless there should be no other demand for it). If the exhibition thereof shall be announced as a specialty, the funds gathered in by said exhibition shall be considered as belonging rightfully to that particular enterprise, though other works of art be on exhibition at the same time and place, so long as it be quite certain that said work is a special attraction, unless that time shall exceed four weeks. No Crusader shall be admitted free to such special exhibition, unless actively engaged in pushing the enterprise.

When art exhibitions are general in their scope, each work of art shall have accredited to it a due share of the receipts accruing from such general exhibition, accounting it to have a fixed money value, which shall have been previously determined by the decision of selected judges, and assented to by the artists.

If any work of art be not original, but a copy only of some original work, it may at the copyist's desire be sold outright at a fair price, and become the permanent property of any band of Crusaders so purchasing it; nor can such be placed in the list of works adopted by the Crusade Host, and subject to official oversight and legislation. The galleries of art, which consist entirely of works actually belonging to the Crusade camps, shall be open to all Crusaders; nor shall any work therein be disposed of, unless by voluntary desire of, at least, two-thirds of the band so owning it.

If, in any case, the artist, whose work has been legally accepted, shall desire its removal from one Crusade camp to another, the holders thereof shall be bound to comply with his demand, even though they have held such work but a portion of the time allotted, provided the expense of transfer, fitting up and announcement shall have been fully met and no public disappointment be likely to follow. The artist may accompany his work if he prefer, having his expenses paid out of its receipts, but receiving no further remuneration, unless his services shall have been pronounced a necessity, in which case he shall also be paid such a sum as shall equal that already allotted him for said expenses.

Nor shall he in any case receive further payment than the two equal sums specified and the percentage of receipts before agreed upon between himself and the Crusade Government. If his expenses happen to be lightened through hospitalities, however, he shall not, therefore, be mulcted in the payment therefor, but shall receive the full amount prescribed as sufficient to meet all contingencies. Any necessary agent of said artist shall be paid at similar rates, deducting the artist's percentage.

Any public singer, actor, reader, lecturer or teacher, having been approved of and accepted by the Bureau of Education, shall receive a Crusade welcome at every camp, where he or she may call, provided the leader of the camp shall have been notified of the call, and shall have signified a willingness to receive it. Any such friend having been received, shall be courteously attended to, and shall receive a sufficient amount of the monies gathered in through his efforts, to pay all expenses of board, travel, etc., (not allowing for hospitalities), and a sum equal to said amount as a return for his services. Added to this, when all expense attending such exhibitions, entertainments, lectures or instructions shall have been fully met, not less than one-half of the sum remaining out of the receipts (if there be such a sum) shall be paid to the visitor, unless such half shall be found to greatly exceed what might reasonably be exacted.

No person devoting himself or herself to the instruction and amusement of the Crusade people shall be allowed to receive such slight returns that he may not have any desirable means of self-cultivation open to him; nor, on the other hand, must useless extravagance of supply be demanded. The amount deemed necessary to enable every such person to live enjoyably and sociably with the world at large, retaining a sufficient fund for ordinary emergencies, shall therefore be fixed by the Bureau of Employment; and whatever monies he or she may receive above that sum, (as direct payment for labor) shall be refunded by him or her to said Bureau, and given in turn to such as shall have been underpaid. If receipts from such sources are found to be insufficient for that purpose, the Bureau shall levy taxes upon such Crusade camps as have a surplus of funds derived directly from the labors of such persons, and shall transmit the lacking monies to the underpaid laborers.

If any man or woman, so employed, shall be found to be unacceptable in his Crusade relations, the Bureau of Attraction shall report the case to the Bureau of Assistance, and after due investigation, it shall be referred to the Bureau of Education, which shall solicit formal withdrawal of the unacceptable person, or in extreme cases, resort to expulsion from the Crusade field.

Any manufacturer, importer, or vender of wares may throw his articles into Crusade markets, establishing or permitting to be established, depots of trade, subject entirely to Crusade jurisdiction. In such cases some Crusader shall be selected by the people to oversee all arrivals of goods, appraise them, and with competent assistance, fix their market value.

Said manufacturer, importer or trader, shall permit full investigation of the cost of his goods, including transportation and indispensable incidentals, receiving payment therefor and a bonus of ten per cent of that sum in addition. His goods shall then be sold at Crusade depots at the lowest market price, to all persons not connected with the Crusade Host, and to Crusaders themselves at actual cost, after all expenses of sale shall have been met. The profits derived from the sales of all goods at market value, shall be used in extending the facilities of trade, increasing warehouses, storerooms, etc. If such profits be not sufficient to meet the actual requirements of the business, the people may supply funds directly, or pay a certain established profit upon their purchases, until the necessity be removed.

Any manufacturer, importer or trader may employ agents or investigators at his own expense, and the people may have the same privilege; the Crusade Government to be the umpire in all cases of difficulty, having first given official sanction to the connection between its people and said trader, importer or manufacturer.

THE CRUSADE DOCUMENTS. II

RULES AND MEASURES OF ORGANIZATION.

ON the organization of the Host of Crusaders, three grand classes or orders shall be recognized, to wit:

AN ORDER OF HONOR:

AN ORDER OF BESTOWAL:

AN ORDER OF INHERITANCE.

The Order of Honor shall comprise all instigators to labor and thought among the people, approved and accepted by Crusade authorities; as Inventors, Authors, Artists, Teachers, Entertainers and projectors of Good.

No payment of monies shall be required to constitute such persons Crusaders, but each, upon adoption into the Host, shall receive his certificate of honorary connection therewith from the Bureau of Appointment or the Bureau of Education under their sign and seal. The holders of such certificates shall be entitled to a certain just share of the public funds set aside for purposes of kindness, after the expenses of Government shall have been met, provided their necessities are proven; or their heirs, dependent upon them for support, shall receive said share, upon their demise, premising that they are in actual want. If, however, there be no necessity, whatever, such a portion of the funds as shall have been collected through the agency of the members of the Order, shall, at the end of twenty years from the date of the opening of the Crusade Books of Registration, be equitably divided among them, or their immediate heirs; and thereafter half-yearly payments shall be made to the same persons (on demand only) from the same funds. Any member of the Order or any heir, may, if he choose, return his unneeded share to the Treasury for redistribution among the truly necessitous of the Order; or he may select some particular individual, whether he be a Crusader or not, to whom the amount must be given; constituting that individual his legal heir of that or any further benefits to be derived from such distributions.

Upon the demise of any member, a delegation of members from the nearest Crusade camp, shall ascertain the circumstances of his or her family, and afford relief, if such be required, by appeal to the Bureau of Assistance, through the Bureau of Attraction. The Bureau of Assistance shall at once inform the holders of the public funds and shall receive from them such monies as may righteously be given, without transgression of Crusade law, for transmission to the sufferers. Records of all such assistance shall be kept rigorously, and each transmitter of monies held personally responsible, so far as his trust extends.

To the Order of Bestowal shall belong all such as choose to present monies to the organization, provided the gift shall be not less than one dollar. Upon the presentation of such monies, each Bestower shall receive a certificate of connection with the Crusade Host, the amount of his gift being specified, both in his certificate and upon the books of registration. All such monies shall be added to the Crusade Public Treasury, subject to withdrawal to meet Government expenses and to distribution among Crusade benevolences. Each member of the Order shall be entitled to a share of said fund (proportionate to his gift) whenever he shall become disabled and poor; or said share shall be paid to his heirs, after his demise, if such shall have been, of necessity, dependent upon him for support. No monies shall be withdrawn, however, from the bestowed funds, except for government expenses, under five years from the date of the opening of the books of Registration belonging to the Crusade Host. At the end of that time, accounts shall be adjusted and the amount remaining, subject to calls from sufferers, published to the people.—At the end of every half year thereafter, a similar adjustment and distribution shall take place.

The Order of Inheritance shall comprise all such persons as have connected themselves with the Crusade Host, by the purchase of a share in the stock of any enterprise sustained by that body and used as a means for the accumulation of real estate, provided the sum so invested by the purchaser shall be not less than one dollar.

The members of this Order shall have no rights of inheritance outside of the enterprise or enterprises in which they may have invested; but there shall be no limit to the number of such enterprises, in which their interests may be represented. Inheritance secures for them a just and incontrovertible title to their share of all distributed funds arising from the schemes to which they have contributed by investment, and gives the same to their admitted heirs, after their demise. It gives them, also, or their heirs, a right to such a portion of the relief monies, as they may be rightfully entitled to, if they are known to be really necessitous.

The interests of all these Classes or Orders, shall be guarded on every hand, and immediate trial and expulsion follow any attempt, within the boundaries of the Host, to rob a single Crusader of his or her right to any monies, either as immediate or prospective payment.

The Bureau of Investigation shall guard the rights of all Inheritors, through its great body of Investigators.

The Bureau of Attraction shall secure the privileges of all Bestowers, through the vigilance of its Sisterhood.

The Bureaus of Appointment and Education shall see to it that the members of the Order of Honor are mulcted in none of their rights and privileges; calling upon all officers on guard, to advise them, through their respective Bureaus of Administration and Assistance, of all attempts to wrong said members, and promptly rebuking such as so offend.

The Bureau of Publication shall openly represent the interests of all, sifting carefully all matters presented by the People for publication in the Crusade organ, and rejecting none without sufficient examination of its sources and designs.

The Bureau of Employment shall faithfully guard the interests of all persons supplied with the means of subsistence through Crusade enterprises; and shall permit no Master of Manufactories or Director of Works of any kind, to lessen the salaries or wages, pronounced equitable by said Bureau. All its decisions respecting the sums earned by operatives of every class, shall be communicated to the Bureau of Publication, that there be no misunderstanding; and all laborers will be desired to appeal at once to the Bureau so guarding them, for redress, if robbed of any portion of their hardly-earned monies.

Immediate expulsion from the Crusade ranks shall follow the discovery of any Director of laborers, guilty of withholding even the smallest fraction of their salaries or wages.

All minor laws and observances shall be settled by the General Council of the six Bureaus designated as composing said Council, at their quarter-yearly assemblages, unless they are merely local or quite trivial in their nature.

Official salaries shall be paid out of the Public Treasury, and shall be sufficiently liberal to enable the Officers of the Host to maintain comfortable households, allowing for the increased expenditures due to their position, and indispensable to a proper fulfilment of Crusade duties and hospitalities. The amount of their salaries shall be fixed by the Bureau of Appointment, published in The American Crusader, and criticised at will by the People, who may, at any time, enter a formal protest at the General Council Chamber, against the doings and decisions of any or all of the Bureaus governing them as Crusaders. Any such protest shall be faithfully attended to by the assembled body of Councillors, whose verdict for or against such protest shall be immediately published in the Crusade organ.

The public funds shall be continually accounted for to the respective Bureaus. Each month a strict report shall be forwarded to each Bureau of all monies received, their source being indicated; and all such reports when accepted, shall be published in the Crusade organ. The reports of all the Bureaus shall be compared at the Bureau of Publication and if there be any discrepancy, the People shall have a right to demand an immediate investigation thereof.

Each fraction received by the holders of the public funds, shall be reported in its due time and place, and every fraction required for whatever purpose. The accounts of the public Treasury shall in this manner be laid open to the examination of the whole Crusade Host, each member of which is, in some measure, responsible for the safe-keeping and rightful conduct and expenditure of such monies.

A General Treasurer shall be annually appointed or confirmed in office, by the Bureau of Administration, subject to the assent of the General Council. He shall be empowered to employ as many assistants as he shall require, out of the numbers recommended to him by the leaders of the Crusade soldiery. The payment of such assistants, together with that of all employees of the Host not actually in office, shall be apportioned to them by the Bureau of Employment and paid out of the public monies.

All monies held in the public Treasury after the requirements of government shall have been met, shall be subject to calls of kindness, proceeding from recognized Crusade sources.

The General Treasurer may, however, decline to distribute so much as to leave the Treasury empty; retaining always an amount that shall be judged sufficient to meet the entire expenses of the Government for one year in advance; except in cases of great public distress, when he may deliver the whole reserve fund, at the demand of the General Council, whether such demand shall proceed from that body at its regular assemblage or at any special convention of its members.

The particular objects for which the public fund, in all its divisions, may be used, shall be specified by the General Council,

315

and announced to the People, with all other doings of that body, through the Crusade organ of publication.

Any monies, collected through the various enterprises of the Host, for purposes of kindness, shall be deposited for safe keeping in the public Treasury, and kept separate from all other monies, that no confusion of accounts may arise. Records of all such deposits shall be placed in the hands of the General Treasurer, and he shall be notified of any withdrawal of monies.

Immediately before opening the public Bank, each morning, dispatches shall be sent to the Chiefs of the Bureau of Administration and Assistance, stating the exact amount received the previous day, and the amount disbursed, together with an exact statement of the amounts remaining in the Treasury, whether such amounts belong to the public fund, or to the funds deposited by the Investigators of the various enterprises. Accompanying such dispatches shall be a correct account of the sources of all received monies, and of the purposes to which all disbursed sums were to be applied. Receipts shall be forwarded, at the same time, from every individual into whose hands disbursed monies shall have been delivered, and similar receipts shall be retained by the Bank.

If there be anything suspicious in said dispatches, the Chiefs of said Bureaus shall make diligent comparison between them and the accounts also received daily from the Bureau of Investigation, and cause to be sifted every evidence bearing upon the case, that the fault, if any, may fee discovered. Otherwise such reports shall be summed up, and referred to the upper Bureaus in their appropriate time and order.

That there may be less confusion of accounts, and to maintain the greatest possible simplicity of detail, there shall be no invention accepted by the Host, as a basis for the accumulation of joint stock real-estate, which cannot justly allow so large an investment by each purchaser thereof, as one dollar; but all smaller invented articles shall be accepted upon the definite terms hereinbefore stated, subject to Crusade oversight and jurisdiction; the inventor receiving his royalties therefor, and the agents their due percentages. The purchaser, however, shall yield his right to the surplus monies, which shall be regularly paid, and all the funds so collected, be deposited in the Treasury, through the proper channels of delivery, to be withdrawn only at the instance of the Bureau of Education and used for no purpose other than the establishment and maintenance of institutions for the aged, sick, blind, deaf, dumb, crippled, orphaned, insane, or idiotic.

The inventor of any such article so disposed of among Crusaders, may specify the particular benevolence to which such surplus funds shall be devoted. Monies paid by purchasers over the cost of the article (including all expense of sales and royalties), shall not be given into the hands of agents, but having been ascertained to agree with their accounts of sales, shall be tendered to the Sisters of the Choir, for safe conduct to the Treasury.

Definite reports from both Agents and Sisters shall thereafter be conveyed to the Bureau of Investigation and Attraction, and compared, that any discrepancy be detected.

The Bureau of Publication shall be accorded the assistance of a publishing board of three, (of either sex), whose duty it shall be to conduct the monetary affairs of the Bureau, continually keeping its accounts open to inspection, and rendering weekly reports to the authorized Investigators of the concern. Their work shall begin with the issuing of the Crusade Documents in any form deemed advisable; and the printing of certificates of Crusade Membership, and diplomas giving authority to Recruiting Officers. As soon as possible, "The American Crusader" shall appear, having been as widely announced as practicable.

Subscriptions thereto may be taken in advance, the subscription price being reasonably low. To aid in these matters, the monies derived from actual gift, shall be used first; those so giving, receiving their certificates as members of the Order of Bestowal. When the monetary affairs of the Bureau shall have become free and prosperous, all monies not required for the above-mentioned purposes, including payments of working persons and officials, shall be used in extending the facilities of publication, and issuing the best standard works, which shall be furnished to all Crusaders at the simple cost of manufacture, storage, transportation and incidental expenses, with the addition of ten per cent of said cost, to enable the Bureau to still further increase its business.

As often as ten members shall have been received into the ranks, by anyone official authorized to recruit, their names shall be transmitted, with all necessary adjunctive information, to the Bureau of Registration.

The Recruiting Officers shall place all monies paid in by the recruits as Bestowals or Investments, at the disposal of the Master of Finance, who shall be speedily informed by the Bureau of Investigation of the reports made to them by such officers, that there be no withholding of money received; and both accounts must be confirmed by inspection of the books of registration. When one hundred recruits shall have been obtained within a limit of five miles square, such recruits shall be formally organized into a Company, headed by a Captain, and an associate Lady styled a Guide. At the need of said Company, lesser officers may be selected to assist in transacting the business, or sustaining the meetings, of the membership.

All persons thereafter recruited within said limits, may attach themselves to the original Company, or remain in bands of one hundred, (more or less), each band electing Captain and Guide;— but all such bands recognizing some chosen Guide and Captain, of the Company of Crusaders inhabiting said circuit of five miles square, as seniors in office.

It shall require ten companies, each commanded by a senior Captain and Guide, to constitute a battalion.

Each battalion shall be officered by a Commandant and an associate Lady, styled a Warden. To these officers the senior Captains and Guides shall communicate all matters of interest essential to the well-being of their respective companies. As often as once in three months each company shall receive a visit from the Commandant or Warden, or both, and receive the encouragement of their suggestions and counsels. To said Commandant and Warden, the senior Captain and Guide shall represent the wishes of the bands under their charge, in the choice of public officers.

All instances of official corruption shall be reported and investigated, the result published to the people concerned and the corrupt officer formally expelled by them from his office. Any officer giving thorough satisfaction, will have the right to expect promotion in his office, when any suitable vacancy occurs.

It shall require ten Battalions to constitute an Army Corps. Said Corps shall be officered by a General and a Governing Lady. To them the various Commandants and Wardens shall deliver all necesssary information concerning their respective battalions, conveying the wishes of the

People with regard to public officers, and reporting the conduct of officials under their inspection.

The General and Governing Lady shall carefully guard against official corruption, watchfully regarding the conduct of those directly below them in rank, and promptly causing investigation under suspicious circumstances.

When the time approaches for the yearly nomination of Bureau officers, all Captains, Guides, and lesser officials shall be elected among the people by acclamation and immediately installed in office. They shall then be instructed in regard to the wishes of the people respecting the higher officers of battalion and corps, who are not to be displaced before the expiration of their allotted term of service, so long as they give thorough satisfaction. In case of displacement or promotion, offices will be given to those holding positions next below in rank, who have proved satisfying, unless such shall decline to serve.

All these officers will be considered as holding Offices of Honor, and will receive no payment for their services, unless obliged to render them at seasons when their soldiery are not convened for public exercise; in which case their labors shall be stated to the Bureau of Employment, and repaid, as shall seem just, out of the public funds.

So far as practicable, such officers as have been prompt and faithful in the discharge of their Crusade obligations, shall be selected by the respective Companies, according to the order of their rank, as candidates for their offices of trust. Any lesser officers of Corps or Battalions may be chosen as necessity shall require, in the same manner, and subject to the same rules of superior supervision.

When the complete Corps of Army Officers, holding Offices of Honor, shall have been elected or confirmed in Office, by the people, as indicated, there shall follow, among all the Companies, a general nomination of Bureau Officers. All men, women and youths over eighteen years of age, shall in each Company declare, by acclamation, what men and women they prefer should fill such offices of Trust, giving always precedence to those already installed, whose term of office shall not have fully expired; and after them, to those officers immediately below in rank. If any such shall not be deemed desirable, a lower rank may be elevated; or, in case of extraordinary benefits conferred upon the people by any member of the Order of Honor, he may be nominated to any vacant office, though not previously in official connection with the Host.

The companies having confirmed or renominated their candidates for all the offices of the Public Bureaus, shall deliver their votes, through their Captains and Guides, to the Commandants and Wardens, who shall communicate such results to the Generals and Governing Ladies, of the united battalions. Said Generals and Governing Ladies, throughout the entire Host, shall then proceed to confer with each other, and having selected all nominees who have received a vote of not less than one-fifth of the entire vote of the people, shall present them to the Bureau of Appointment. The names of such as shall have been nominated to any single office, shall be written down upon as many slips of paper as will signify their true proportion of votes, each slip answering to one-fifth of the entire vote, or the nearest approximation thereto. The lots shall then be put into the hands of the Chieftain of Battalions, who shall, in the presence of all the Bureau, proceed to draw. In doing this, he must be rigidly blind-folded, and the depository of names given to him, after each member of the Bureau shall have assisted in the fair disposal of them, preparatory to the final act.

The result shall then be returned officially to the people, who shall, by acclamation, declare their assent to the elections, or their disapproval of any candidate or candidates chosen. If one-third of the votes of the Captains and Guides thereafter sent in, representing the will of the people, should be against the election of any candidate, the lot shall be recast and others chosen from the remaining names.

When the Bureau of Appointment shall have finally ratified all nominations, the candidates shall be declared duly elected, and after assenting to the duties required of them, shall receive the insignia of their offices from the Chief of the Bureau of Education into whose hands each retiring officer shall deliver them.

All the offices of the public Bureaus and such offices as shall be left open to the appointment of the Bureau op Administration, (subject to the approval of the General Council) shall be considered as offices of trust, to be adequately supported out of the public funds.

Officers of Honor shall hold their position, as such, for a period of not less than three months, nor more than three years; receiving displacement or promotion therefrom at the will of the people, unless convicted of corruption, when they may be expelled by acclamation.

Officers of Trust shall hold their position, as such, for a period of not less than one year, nor more than five. If convicted of official corruption, their cases shall be brought under the jurisdiction of the General Council, which shall re-consider all testimonies against them, and if the previous conviction be found just, shall depose them from place and expel them from the Crusade ranks.

No Crusader so expelled, shall be again elected to any office in the gift of the people; but will forever remain outside of their counsels as unworthy of confidence. He shall not, however, therefore forfeit his promised rights, as Inheritor; and shall be still a subject for Crusade benevolence, if he become needy; or, his heirs, who have depended upon him for support, shall receive the full benefit accruing from his connection with the Crusade Host, if they be proven to be in want.

In order to carry out the design of establishing this organization of Crusaders, a body of not less than three men and three women, shall form themselves into a Provisional Bureau, accepting and judiciously using all bestowed monies, conducting all Crusade contracts, and giving certificates of membership, through such recruiting officers as shall have been authorized to extend invitations and receive recruits.

As soon as ten battalions shall have been formed, The Provisional Bureau shall call for a public election of Officers, which shall proceed in accordance with the Constitution; after which election, and the accompanying instalments, by said Bureau, of elected officers, the members thereof shall retire from public service, unless the people have signified their continuance in office, by electing them as members of the new Bureaus. Every year thereafter, the election of Officers shall take place in its regular order, at a date fixed by the people previous to their first nominations.

AERIAL BRIDGES

BUT of those fifteen weeks I have been telling of, through ten of them my days were occupied in writing things for pay, and reveling in sunshine out of doors. Save in a casual way, I spent no thought on "Social Jurisprudence" till evening lecture-time. But then my own poor personality dropped off;—another took its place. How long the lectures were—an hour or less or more—I only guessed; but I was unfatigued in any case. The being made to speak another's thoughts taxed neither brain nor body. To speak my own had been another matter;—there could have been no rush of eloquence. Up to that date and afterward till 1887, none ever heard me give discourses save when I had a spirit's aid. Having been used to halt in time of writing, and pick and choose and search for words—after the way of "Sentimental Tommy," I had no ready speech beyond the merest talk. Even yet, with many years to wear away the spell, it clings. Alas for oratory, should I essay to be an orator! Believe me, this is not to talk about myself—only to show my limitations!—Let them be reckoned up.

Sometimes the family drove for recreation. Once we went to Canandaigua Lake and stopped along the way for visiting. Then, for the first and only time, within my knowledge, the children had a play time. I rejoiced.

Moreover, now and then, crossing the village-line, we passed an ancient woolen factory, not quite unused it seemed. Such worn-out properties (made valueless by abolition of the woolen tariff) were nothing odd; and I had passed them otherwhere and scarcely taken notice. This was different. Each time we went that way I had what seemed a Psychometric consciousness of father. I do suppose that I was super-sensitive during those summer months, beyond my wont. One day, drawn by a singular force, I went alone and roamed among the tenter-frames. And there I met my father—not in flesh and not in exaltation, but as he used to be, or ever I drew breath. Not that I saw him. Nay, we need not see! It is enough to know.

Having a slight excuse, I went to see the owner,—an old, old man who oftentimes forgot. "What? Did I ever know a Henry Jones?" He started up with pleasure: "Wife! Wife! Come here! You've heard me talk so much of Henry Jones? Here's someone asks about him. Why he was like a son to me! He learned his trade of me! He lived with me five years till he was twenty-one. Then someone shot him with a ramrod; but he lived. They said he was so resolute he wouldn't die!"

"Oh, that was Father!—Father!"

"Your father? Now, look here: Go to the woolen factory, where he used to work. You'll find an old man there who worked with him."

So down the hill I went—heart beating high: "Tell me some little thing about my father, Henry Jones." He mused: "I knew him first fifty-eight years ago,—a handsome, red-cheeked boy, whom everybody liked. One day, when he was older, two burly Irishmen came in—both fighting-mad. They called for him: 'You've made complaint of us before the magistrate. You said we didn't half support our families;—our wives and children starve. We're under bonds to work and keep from drink. That's very well, but first we'll pay our debts; we've come to lick you, sir!'

"Your father laughed: 'Why, yes! I made complaint; lick me by all means. You'll find me in the weaving-room.' And then he walked away to tend his looms. They hung around for half a day, and finally went home ashamed. Their families fared the better.

"I saw your father last in 1832, just after cholera time. He left his work in Rochester to nurse the sick—people were so afraid. He never was afraid of anything, not even death. And that's the sort of man your father was."

O, wonderful Psychometry! Nothing through all that summer gave me such delight as that dear consciousness of him in early life. What you perceive without another's help, is altogether yours. It cannot be subtracted from the sum of you. Just take it, and be glad that you are Psychometric!

Come, spirits! use us if you will; inspire, speak, write; but never rob! Cut off no aptitude, deny no faculty. We'll yield to you, we'll work for you,—

"We'll die for you perhaps,—'tis probable;

324

But we'll not spare an inch of our full height;—We'll have our whole, just stature—five feet four."

Well, when the Documents began to be, sometime in early August, I ceased to write for pay. My mind was floating off in such a formless luminosity—an atmosphere above observable things—I could no more have written stories than could a butterfly creep back into the chrysalis, become a worm again, and breathe through spiracles. Moreover, as to planning schemes and framing rules of Government, I could as soon have mapped out Andromeda's nebula and named its hidden suns. This luminosity was not vacuity. I had no definite thoughts,—I had perceptions. Light, they say, attracts; I was aware of light that held me poised,—scarcely of gravitation.

This I know: Whoever framed "The Crusade Documents"—transmitted through myself—it verily was not I. Too well I know what composition costs, to dream that I—sub-consciously or otherwise—wrought out that piece of tapestry.

Frail Mrs. Browning tells us of a seraph-poet:

"He could enunciate and refrain From vibratory after-pain."

That may be true of seraphs. But no one resident in flesh can think or speak or write his larger thoughts without a tingling sense of effort, followed by recoil. I know that suffering well.

Not less you have the reader's right of judgment; but pray you understand, as to "The Crusade Documents" whatever be their worth or lack of worth, no thought or word of them had fallen into line within my mind before the time of writing. Foreign to all my moods and methods, strange to me as unknown birds of passage, sentence by sentence came to me in due succession—one might say with not a feather ruffled!—so you have the whole—complete, consistent, not a word crossed out and not a word supplied. 10,000 words perhaps, each after each in order; meant for you to read.

And note: Instead of "vibratory pain" I might as well have spent my time in plucking sweet verbena,—

"—which, being brushed against
Will hold the sense, hours after, by the smell."

325

Even so the "Safety Cage" was built and swung in place; and even so it waits.

What of the small, white tower, without a door for exit? In truth the very walls gave way and let me out wither was I to go?

Well, first, when "prisoners of poverty" desire to travel, needs must they count their dollars. Me—I had a few but lately earned, sixty or thereabouts; albeit I was made to understand that I must spend them on myself. And so I said to Rev and Mrs. Rawlinson: "I am going East about my mission-work. I need a little time for getting ready. Please let me board with you a month or so, while I am taking air-baths, furbishing my dresses—waiting on the Lord."

I really needed social consolation—having a wound or two that hurt; and verily these people were so dear, it seemed as though September's balms far out in woods and fields, were sending gales of perfume through the house. I breathed and slept and drove across the hills (after the ministerial pony) and lived like common folk. My precious coterie of friends believed in me, and in my work as well,—even in my veritable vision by the Yuh Heh Springs. For that I bless them all.

Miss Phillips sent for me one day: "You've charged us not to talk about your mission. Yesterday I disobeyed. I told a dear young lady all about it. She said: 'Oh, how I long to help! There's only one thing I can do. Ask her if she will share my ward-robe. That is mine to give.'"

What! Charity? But this was Love out-right!—No more to be refused than gushing water from the rock of Horeb,—one being in the desert, all athirst! Cloaks, dresses, bonnets, things to be desired, things needed urgently. Would I could give her name!

There was a gentleman who loved and visited my host.

We'll call him Mr. H—. Not very rich himself,—his brothers, multi-millionaires, were gathering him in among themselves. So he was all in line with wealth! He came and said: "My friend has told me that you wish to found a Rescue Home for women. Come to New York, and come to me."

There swung my first balloon! You'll hear of him again. But think of it; to float up high and far—a wondering crowd below! They say it's cold up there—please you, we'll go by land. Or no! we'll walk on air,—step out by faith, and feel a hand beneath press hard and hold us up.

I woke one noon out of my air-bath sleep, and caught this flying message,—half prevision: "Start for the East one week from Saturday; and what will come to you there in the East, you cannot possibly guess."

I counted off the days: "Why that's my birthday—thirty-seven years! I'll have a birthday gift; What will it be?"

I woke another day: "Write to Prof. L. C. Cooley. Say that you wish to stop in Albany and ask an interview." What for?—and even that I had no power to guess. Ah, well! I knew him somewhat, seventeen years before—my sister's husband's cousin. So, why not stop in Albany. I wrote; and frankly, had the spirit said: "Write now to Queen Victoria!" I should have dipped the pen, and if commanded, made the same request. But let me say—daring to own myself obedient—that spirits never asked of me a foolish thing! And if I walked on air, they set their props beneath. I did not fall nor fear.

Now, on the second morning after, at the breakfast table, I announced: "Just as I woke, before my eyes were open, I saw a blazing comet—starting from below—rush halfway to the zenith, stop, stand still, and seem to be a steadfast morning-star. That means that I shall know this very day what I must do about my mission-work. God has a gift for me—a wonderful, great gift. I shall not see the sun as yet;—the Eastern sky was dark; but I shall see the star that prophecies the sun."

Said Mr. Rawlinson, after his Methodist manner: "Sister, you seem to be a very Daniel for interpretation." What could we do but laugh.

Now, there was present Jane M. Kendall, a lovely friend of mine from Providence (sister of Henry Kendall, most revered). We had begun to love each other in 1859, at Clifton Water Cure. We never stopped; and I suppose, throughout eternity, we two shall call across as many worlds as Heaven may interpose, and answer each to each. But now (I stay so long!) we bide our time.

Waking that day out of my usual air-bath slumber—with not a memory in mind of what had once been told (note this!) and not a thought beyond, I said (these are the very words):

"I see how fruit can be canned without cooking it. The air must be exhausted from the cells and fluid made to take its place. The fluid must be airless also—a light syrup of sugar and water—that, or the juice of fruit."

Now, let me say at once, No spirit told me this. I have inventions—patentable—patented. They are as much my own as are my many poems—mostly studied out by slow and painful process, often at bitter cost. To every patent application I have taken oath, unperjured: "This is my invention.—This I claim."

Spirits may clear away the mists before us;—it is our eyes that see! Spirits may point the way; it is our feet that walk! Spirits may scatter thoughts like meadow-flowers; our hands must gather them. Whatever spirits know, they have no right to tell us—they have no power to tell us—unless we have the necessary mind and brain development, enabling us to fully apprehend. Then we can meet as equals—not before. And so this golden blossom dropped beside me,—so I picked it up.

Not less a spirit interposed a minute after: "That is the way to get your money. Go East and you shall be sustained." ... .Here was my rushing comet,—here my morning star; and all in God's good time would glow the rising sun.

Yet let us linger for a moment. I had perceived a principle, and nothing more. A principle is like a world—it swings upon itself; but also it must swing among the other worlds, subject to all their laws. You must allow for that; and give me many years to set my little orb to spinning—satellites and all. Moreover there are Jupiters, you know, that have a mighty pull; we'll swing as far away from them as possible.

Linger a moment longer: I did not know, I never yet had heard (down in my little valley) that "many men of many minds," in Europe and America, wishing to do what now meant to do, had toiled near thirty years to no avail. These men had lavished wealth—much wealth (one man in Baltimore had lavished half a million). And now they said: "The field has all been traveled over. We have been deluded. No such principle exists." Not one had ever thought of using fluid; not one had learned that fundamental lesson: "Nature abhors a vacuum." Curious!

Do you remember how a manufacturer in Sheffield, many years ago, chanced to escort a girl of sixteen years, with others, through his Works; and how he said, with sorrow?—"Wonderful to look at, but the air is full of flying particles of steel; my workmen breathe it in—they die. I've studied twenty years and found no remedy!" "But," said the girl: "Why not suspend a magnet near their mouths?" And so this man "invented" (after her) what saved innumerable lives. He won a deal of credit.

After this manner all those notable preservers, missed the simple thought that I, who had not canned a jar of fruit in all my life, discerned as in a dream. A thought, a principle not yet embodied—a law not yet expressed. Come, let us have a process! someone must collaborate. Why not Professor Cooley?—fine of mind and deft of hand—investigator, chemist, physicist—all that I was not. Moreover spirits had elected him; and that alone sufficed.

Said Brother Rawlinson: "This means, perhaps, far more than we imagine. I do believe God wants the world supplied with better food."

Said Jennie Kendall: "Prove that you are right in this, then come to Providence and let my brother know." (Item: He did not fly balloons.)

So, blest abundantly with human sympathy, inspired with singular faith, no more afraid than birds that cleave the wind, I started off that glad October day—as say the Methodists, with "glory in my soul;" and all the way along, I sang doxologies.

Even so, though I had wholly failed in sight of all the folk my failure would seem better than success, in clearer eyes than ours. Failure is but another name for loss that leads to gain. He cannot perish, who, beyond Belief, has caught the hand of Faith. I trusted,— that sufficed. Faith never fails; and that which fails must bear another name.

And so, when Dr. Cooley said that night: "These thoughts of yours are plausible; I'll try and prove them true," I felt no more elation than before. Only, when he had gone away, I fell upon my knees and asked for sacramental grace;—How else was I to serve? How else was I to suffer? There is no other way to serve except through suffering, till we are rid of bonds,—or bonds become delight.

But now we have to deal with open facts, with common life and labor. The laboratory-tests were promising; we saw the air escape— tearing the grapes apart, and knew of nothing more to do after the flasks were filled with fluid, only to seal them up (though that was difficult) and wait to prove results. There being nothing more for me to do—having provided means for further tests, I went, at last, to visit Mrs. Rathbone—the lady of the "pinks," you may remember. "This is the seventh day you've been in Albany and never called on me?" So I must needs explain.

She proved to be a Baptist lady, sweet and strict. Not less I told her of my vision and something of my inner history. Not recreant to any trust, nor recreant to any truth, from first to last,—against all prejudice, if any were, I dealt, and deal to-day, in open speech, whenever there is need. Folk say the orthodox, so called, are bigoted. I have not found them so. Those only sneer who have escaped from bonds— save such as they, themselves, have twisted hard! Let's hope they slip the knots. Love—love is what we need. That's always Orthodox.

I did not say to Mrs. Rathbone: "Hotel and laboratory-work have almost swallowed up my surplus funds." Ten dollars ought to be enough for toll, when one has but to pass the gate and walk along on air. Still, realizing need, her "woman's love" (plant full of pinks), led her to press upon me twenty-five dollars at the time, and after that she wrote: "My son willed me a sum of money, solely to give away,"—and sent a hundred more; also requiring me to make her house my home when I should come again.

Aside from that I had "One Night" at Scribner's, good for thirty dollars. That poem, written four years earlier, had been my last. Nine years from that to "Heart of Sorrows A—and not a "truly" poem in between! It's well to let your field lie fallow for a time; you get the better crop. Also there came a hundred dollars from father's cousin, Sarah Henry Beach—and may she walk on flowers!

"No, No!" I said to Mrs. Hester Poole: "You need not introduce me, even among the charitable. I have not come to beg. I've come to earn. Please recommend me to a boarding-house." No less I had a banquet with "Sorosis." That gave me keen delight: I listened, watched and wondered: "All these beautiful and able women—well equipped for service, together or alone, and I, a shrunken creature, made to stand up straight and carry on my head a greater weight than any!" Oh, not that I complained!

Who says that anything is due to chance?—Well then, it chanced I made my home awhile in Dr. Atwood's House—where people came for baths; and once (never again) Victoria Woodhull came, and, having heard my name, desired to see me. She said: "One W. Livingston Browne has sought me out, hoping to introduce a scheme founded on certain Documents. He says that they were written by your hand and in his house, but came undoubtedly from spirits. He thinks that they belong to him. It seems to me they should be yours instead. Has he your full authority?"

Being informed, she sent, with conscientious kindness, the copyrighted sheet wherein I read again the missing Documents and found them reproduced without a fault. My friend, the ardent boy who saw them written (howbeit lights were dim,) had proved himself a faithful copyist; but they, as written, had been sealed away from mortal sight. We hope they may be found. So far as I may know there is no other printed copy. None was furnished me by Mr. Browne, who did not let me know.

Having advised with that most honored judge and gentleman whose name I have already given you, I wrote by his command and in his name, forbidding further use. A certain "ragged rock" had rent the cable; "the strong, steel arms of law" struck out, and all was safe. But see how spirits make provision: One step, this way or that, taken by Mrs. Woodhull or myself—or even by Mrs. Poole who chose my boarding place—and all had been engulfed. I cannot choose but think that spirits intervened.

I beg to say that Mr. Browne was ignorant of law. He thought himself fairly entitled to the written word.—I being but a medium after all, a mere transmitter,—not responsible. And anyway, a medium, by common apprehension, is in a state of nonage. He made a good custodian. We have the service; let us render thanks.

Come, now, we'll forge ahead! And if you care to learn what may be done—even for general good—when spirits lend their aid; let me invite you all to listen just a little longer. Albeit nought begins or ends, yet this, my Psychic story, shall find a stopping place.

When I had been ten days established in New York, I heard from Doctor Cooley; and all our pretty flasks had come to nought. He wrote: "So far, I think of nothing else to do."

Did I appeal to spirits? No, not I! Some lady—thought to be a medium—had said unwisely: "Scald your fruit:—not boiling water—some degrees below." Well, what was that but cooking? Still it served to set me thinking. Warmth it seemed would aid expansion; let us have a little warmth; and this I wrote, advising Dr. Cooley.

There may have been telepathy abroad—from him to me, perchance from me to him; for when my letter reached him, he was trying warmth. This was but one of other instances; but let me say at once that he had frankly stated (when I had told of Psychic understanding): "I never had a vision." In truth he did not trust in mine, nor did I care to have him. Both believed that oxygen would ruin fruit, and both were bent on getting rid of it. We met on common grounds;—a tolerant Presbyterian, an ardent Spiritualist— what mattered some small difference of thought? We had a common purpose; and verily I think he had, no less than I, a great desire to help our common world.

332

So passed another week. And then—impelled, inspired or what you will—I went to Albany, this time the welcome guest of Mrs. Joel Rathbone.

"If this one flask should fail!" said Dr. Cooley: "I see no more to do." I answered him: "If there is nothing more to do, it will not fail; for God has promised me." Yet, when I reached the street, my heart went down like lead: "It will not keep, I know; it is already ruined."

What then was left to do but hide away within my upper room, and call and agonize and make demand? If you have ever read Charles Wesley's "Wrestling Jacob" (the greatest hymn a mortal ever wrote), or said to One Unseen: "I will not let Thee go except Thou bless me," you needs must understand. Oh, long I searched myself! If there but lurked the shadow of a doubt, the faint remembrance of a former doubt, God's light must burn it out.

Then, in a measure, I obliterated self. I thought of him whom I had left among his flasks, and begged: "Whatever else remains to do, show him and not myself. Reveal the secret now! Even this moment let him understand!". ... [And in that very time, he seized the thought!]

But after that I waited—still upon my knees. I waited .... then I saw! And will you share my vision?—guess the symbols out? Suppose, I let you try.

I saw a mighty mountain cleft almost in twain. I stood below and wondered: "Why do so many climb upon this nearer side, and no one cross the chasm?"—for on the further side no mortal shape was seen.

But then I saw that many neared the edge and looked across, while some essayed to leap; and all that leaped fell in. Whether they really perished, or would come in view and climb the hither side as once before, I paid no further heed.

But now I saw myself full half way up. The rift was narrow there; it seemed about to close. Easy to step across and take possession. So "Step across!" I called in spirit; and the one that seemed my very

333

self, strove to obey. The foot that should have passed was caught within the cleft—but presently withdrawn.

And now appeared a polished bridge of stone, set solidly in place to join this side with that,—a bridge so strong and heavy, neither flood nor earthquake could have done it harm; and just above the bridge, the rocks were all as one. I saw that seeming self move on and stand upon that bridge. I saw two shining spirits—tall women-spirits—angels if you choose to call them so—descend and come to me across the mountain from the further side. No words could tell how white and beautiful they were.

Now one of these two angels bore a sleeping babe. She held it out; she laid it in my arms. "The gift is yours," she said; "But look above; the path is long and steep, and at the very mountain-top there stands a cross." (I saw the snow-white cross.) "Let no one take the child. Bear it—a precious burden, till you have reached the cross. Then lay it down, close to the foot, and pass! Nothing shall hurt the child."

And did I hear these very words? I did—or so it seemed. So I have borne the burden all these years. I have not many steps to take before I reach the cross.

Well, the next evening, being at Dr. Cooley's house, he handed me the flask. I promise you it bubbled merrily! I knew no more of chemistry than I had known of law, before Judge Evelyn came; but this I knew: My foot was in the cleft—now I should see the bridge! I said; "If we could find some way of penetrating fruit with steam, and yet not cooking it—that would be the way.

"It is the way," said Dr. Cooley. "I discovered it after you left me yesterday. A cooking-heat is needed under atmospheric pressure; steam expels the air. But here we have a vacuum; our fluids boil at 80 Fahrenheit—and so we get the steam, but not the heat. I shall prolong the time and boil in vacuo till every trace of air is driven out."

See, what it is to be a Scientist. Up to that point the thoughts had been my own, of precedence and right. And yet, without his supplementing thought, this work of mine had ended then and there. I do not say he was inspired, but I had been inspired to visit him, and more than that to put my trust in him as one whom others trusted—souls released from earth! What matter though he saw them not? He served; and that sufficed.

"I cannot test this final thought," said Dr. Cooley, "before next week." Now, this was Friday evening. Sunday morning, I, being in New York, awoke: And there, beside my bed, close to the head thereof, stood up a tall white cross, wreathed down the center with a grape vine, bearing grapes. All day, and all the days thereafter, I rejoiced, until there came a letter: "On Saturday, I saw that you had left a box of grapes, and dropped my necessary work to make another test. Fifteen days have passed;—so far the fruit is keeping;— we may hope." Hope? I had sung doxologies two weeks because the grapes had kept! I had not been allowed to feel suspense. And when we broke the seal on Christmas morning, even to a doubtful Scientist, no further doubt was possible. The fruit had kept five weeks, three days and sixteen hours: "Delicious!" Rossa said.

And so I took away from Albany next day a pretty lot of samples; and it was evident that I must learn to be a business woman. Fifteen weeks that previous summer, one had instructed me in "Social Jurisprudence." I had a mind to make some use of all that I had learned—first for self-guidance, then for self-protection; after that, fulfilment.

Now, when a letter came from Washington: "We find the process patentable. Please send us twenty dollars," I had not twenty dollars left. It costs to live in cities, carry on experiments, and travel more or less. I had not laid the letter down, when Maggie knocked: "A gentleman to see Miss Jones."

I had an excellent friend who often called,—one of our "Nameless Club," not prosperous of late. So down I ran, and, throwing wide the door, held out my letter, crying:

"Read it, Mr. Cummings. I'm to have a patent!" The gentleman rose up and took the letter. Why this was John H. Keyser, who kept a hospital, a Stranger's Rest, and other "Good Will" places! He

335

plunged his hand at once into his pocket: "There's your twenty dollars; and now I see why I was made to come!"

Soon after that, his wife (a very lovely lady), came herself, and proffered kindnesses. So full of interest were both, so amply able to assist, one might have thought here was a happy opportunity. I put the chance aside—and if there was a chance!—because my guardian willed. And yet there came a time when I accepted something—not a money-gift. I wouldn't miss the telling for a lot of dollars,—if you will please to wait.

About that time—I haven't kept the date—right in a busy hour I was impelled to drop all else and call on Mrs. Collins' daughter (living in New York);—the very child who danced, and played for dancing, all unconsciously, way back in 1854, you may remember.

She said: "I think you'd better go, and come again. Mother is here,—shut up with Mr. Eighmie in the dining room, trying to settle up their business before she starts the Cure. He mustn't know you're here. He'd think it all contrived."

"Call out your mother; tell her I am sent." So "Take your choice," I said to Mrs. Collins: "Let him know or not."

Suspicious? Not at all. I hadn't seen him since we'd met at Yuh Heh Springs, when God's own hand had touched his heart, unsealed that sacred spring of charity, and made a desert bloom. He welcomed me with gladness. "Both of you come home with me. We'll give Judge Evelyn a chance." And off we went at once.

So the next day, after a cordial greeting, Judge Evelyn made me take the pen, and wrote, through me, in that old English script the Documents had shown, a full Agreement as between the two who had not yet agreed. When Mr. Eighmie would have signed his name, Judge Evelyn said: "I shall not let you sign till you have seen some very able lawyer. If he, on your account, should disapprove, withhold your name."

We went—all three of us: "Who wrote this Document?" the Lawyer asked. "A very perfect legal document! I could not change a word for either one of you." He added, full of admiration: "A pretty, pretty piece of work!" And so we signed the copies there and then, they as contracting parties, I (and I think the lawyer), witnessing for both.

The Articles released the lady, not from debts to Mr. Eighmie, but from the need of paying interest on debts; gave her the Cure for occupancy; left her free of him, in every sense, to carry on her work (throughout five years, I think) till she should have full chance to make the Springs remunerative. And yet his interests were protected,—mortgages, with interest, and finally a stated bonus (that "little usury" he had been promised, legally arranged!). In case of Mrs. Collins' death or failure, certain claims were his,—just claims that could not be denied.

Now, after Mrs. Collins passed away—there being none to take her place—the Springs, the Cure, and one small tract of land, became the property of Jeremiah Eighmie; and like the "Safety Cage,"—the work—well guarded—waits God's chosen time.

I take you into confidence: You cannot know how perilous have seemed my airy bridges. Walk with me along (you need not fear to fall), and I will show you, here and there, the setting of a pier on solid ground, to keep you well assured. But as for me, except by faith, I never saw the pier, what time I passed that way, until I stepped thereon. If ye have faith, "Say to this sycamine tree, 'Be thou plucked up and be thou planted in the sea,' it shall be done;" and though my faith, perhaps, was not so great, believe me it sufficed.

After the process-patent was allowed to me and Dr. Cooley, I visited that "very able lawyer" and had our contract drawn. It left me wholly free to act, and yet accorded Dr. Cooley what seemed a rightful share of possible results, without responsibility. So after that I went to Albany for mutual advisement. Let me state the case:

Here was a laboratory process, very beautiful, which after three hours' work, expertly done, would turn you out a little flask of fruit. Detaching that, you had an orifice exposed to air. Be quick as thought, and seal your orifice by any possible device—and lo, you have a sample! Worth—how many dollars? About as merchantable as a peacock's egg; or, let us say, a loon's.

337

Still, out of this "wee egg" must come (has come) a "muckle bird;"—wings great enough to cover—reckoning from tip to tip—a nest of crowding birds, well-pinioned for the flight. This may be spoken of hereafter; not to be dwelt upon, save through necessity. I mean to have you think of Psychic facts beyond all others; that is why I write.

And now was I suspended, high in air! With four more patents needed,—one for Dr. Cooley (a simple set of tubes), two for myself on fruit jars made to suit the tubes, another crowning one for Dr. Cooley, to take the place of vacuum-pumps—far more efficient, cheaper, not to be improved upon. This was his final contribution; all else that followed was, and is, my own.

Great was the need of dollars! "Daughter, why do you think so much of dollars? Trust and they will come." Mother would have me plant the "flower of patience,"—father, the flower of "trust." I held them both in honor; and yet.—what can a poor inventor do who needs five hundred dollars, and has but only five? Why, look around, of course, and try to get them! I sat me down to think.

Now there was Mr. H——. Had he not said: "Come to New York, and come to me?"—Himself not poor by any means, and now in partnership with elder brothers—multi-millionaires. I wrote to him after this manner:

"When you invited me to call on you concerning that proposed Reformatory, there seemed no other way of raising funds except by contribution. Since then, I have acquired some patent-rights believed to be of value. I have a way of canning fruit uncooked. Gordon and Dilworth, who have seen my samples, think the matter most important. Let me refer to them.

"Meantime I have to say, that since I lack the money for development, should it be furnished me by those in sympathy—not seeking personal gain—I should account to them, and hold myself amenable to guidance;—not giving up the patents, but pledging all their profits to the mission-work which you approve, and seemed disposed to aid."

There was a pretty scheme! And (not to be inordinately vain) I thought it out myself!

He answered very kindly: "Come to my Wall Street office. I shall be glad to see you."

Was he?—-Well, he took my samples—apples, plums and grapes with all their bloom upon them, showing through the fluid—looked them over, turned about, and said with cutting emphasis: "Why don't you sell your patents? No doubt preservers would be glad to get them. Take my advice and sell them. That's your only way."

"I cannot. They are mine to hold in trust. No price could purchase them. In any case they have no market value. That is why I need the use of money,—first to get them ready, then to prove their worth; and after that to gather profits year by year, for saving souls, according to my pledge."

He handed back the flasks: "Unless you choose to sell outright, there's nothing I can do;" and this he said with gentle dignity. (I thought he might have smiled!)

However, two days afterward, I got a letter: "I have changed my mind. I shall be glad to help. Come to my private residence on Thursday—ten o'clock."

Again I sat me down to think. "Is this good Methodist aware that I believe in spirit-intercourse?—that spirits visit me?....That I am led by them? Come now! There's time to reach him with a letter; let him understand."

I made him understand.

And how it rained on Thursday morning!—Rained and rained and rained. New York was all a-swimming. I waded round-a-bout from car to car—it took a lot of fares! The foot-man let me drain awhile; then took me in across the marble;—the very chair seemed all inhospitable!

My friend came in, and paused six feet away. I do believe he bowed! As for the rest, he stood up straight and tall and slender as an Arctic spruce; and wow!. ... but it was cold!

"It seems—you think—you have some special help about your business."

"That is what I think."

"Some very special help."

"Yes; very special help."

"A sort of inspiration."

"Certainly, why not! You, as a Methodist, believe in prayer. Faith comes with prayer, and inspiration follows. We all believe in that."

"But you believe in special inspiration."

"So I do."

"I never had such help about my business." (Tobacco— till he sold a sweeter product.) "We're quite at variance. There's nothing I can do."

"That doesn't change the fact that I shall have my 'special help'— and very speedily. I do not know of anyone on earth who would assist. God knows—and that's enough." Uprose my faith from lurking in the shadow; and I was glad that I had been denied.

I rose to go at once. He followed to the door:—"You'd better go and call on Mr. Black. I'll give you his address. He is rich and very generous. Doubtless your mission-work would interest him. True,— he's a Methodist—but—very—broad. Don't give my name."

"I needn't call. It won't be necessary."

"O, call! I think he'll help...........You'd better use my name. He's quite a friend of mine. I'm very sorry not to see the way myself. I wish you full success." Almost he smiled!

And so I shut the gate, and dripped away. '(That was a mighty rain!)

This Christian gentleman was right. He has my full respect. I was the one astray; and let me say: I didn't try again to fill that gaping purse without "some special help."

340

Trials of faith. Well, here is one of them. Aside from workshops (visited for study), I had a single calling place—the "Stranger's Rest." There, in a desolate upper story, dwelt a lady once esteemed in Journalism—assistant editor to—never mind his name!—now out of health and place— necessitous no doubt. Too proud to make complaint—she drew me strangely. So it chanced I spent an hour with her another day, after that well-deserved rebuff. I had a sense of some unusual trouble; and while we sat in silence, pondered if I could comfort her with words.

I wonder who stood near. But anyway this word came ringing in (set it to music if you can, it's awkward, but the element is there): "Can't you give this woman two dollars?"

Half I had, or more; but what of that? Five hundred other dollars were afloat, drifting my way from out the surf. "Now let me prove my faith." And so I rose and slipped the money in her hand and said: "Good-bye." Before I gained the door she burst out sobbing: "Wait!

You cannot guess what I have suffered for the past two weeks because I lacked two dollars,—just two dollars!" (When last I heard of her she was Director of another city's charities!)

Returning home I found a business proposition waiting me. A gentleman; not rich himself, but rich in friends because of unimpeachable integrity, could get for use some twenty-thousand dollars. So, by an equal partnership, he to bear every business burden, I to invent and have my will and way—we both could "bear out on the world" certain of all success. This would have been an upward flight indeed!—all in a well-inflated, fine, dirigible balloon!

I had been told that I must bear the child myself, till I should reach the summit where the cross was set; and that was very high, and very far away. Oh, evidently I must climb!—so I refused to soar.

Next day I thought it wise to stay at home; and now I had to ash. Are we not taught to ask with "importunity" as well as faith? What then was lacking but the clamoring voice that will not be denied? Faith passive is a tranquil morning-atmosphere, not wholly free from fogs. Faith active is a rushing wind that drives all fogs away.

Neutral or potential, faith exists in every soul—and not in mine alone.

And must we own that we are spiritual atoms—nothing more? Yet even so, they tell us now that every atom has its one electron. When that shall spring to action, mark the luminous effect! So, even I, one of the least of atoms, was fired with spirit-energy; and suddenly the miracle was wrought. Faith was no longer faith, but perfect knowledge; so the gift was mine. I rose from kneeling. I was like a flower whose petals lie all open to the sun,—as free from fear, as absolute in peace!

"Now, child, put on your bonnet. Go and visit Mr. Eighmie."

What common words these spirits utter! "Is this the way they prove themselves immortal?"—hear the doubter scoff. "Do they abide in light?—then let them shine." [I think this spirit shone!]

That man of old, who made the blind to see, used common clay. In all my thoughts I had not dreamed of bringing aught to bear on Jeremiah Eighmie. The very fact that he had yielded twice to Mrs. Collins all that a spirit asked, sufficed to set him far apart from me, their instrument.

But now he said, quite of his own accord: "I've wanted you to come. I want to know whether your faith holds out. You said that you would be sustained. How is it now? Are you in need of money?"

"Yes. I need five hundred dollars."

"What for?"

"To put fresh patent-applications in, get patterns, castings, fruit-jar molds and dies, perhaps experimental apparatus—pay my board, car-fare and ferriage. No doubt whoever shall advance the money will have to wait for payment very long. The difficulties are enormous—nothing can be hurried. That must be understood."

"Five hundred dollars! Have you prayed for it?" "Oh, yes; I have the evidence of faith. It's coming." "Well, if you get it, that will prove to me that God will answer prayer. That's what I want to know. I want to be convinced. I'm going to stand aside and watch."

So sweet and dear was Mrs. Jeremiah Eighmie, she would not let me go. She did not say: "Please stay till he is ready"; but that was what she meant in urging me. Her sympathies had been with Mrs. Collins; now they were with me. No man is ever at his best without a worthy wife— well loved. This may account for many a saintship; who can tell?

When I had been a guest two days my host appealed to me: "I want to hear Judge Evelyn again. I think he ought to come." And I suppose the spirit had been waiting for an invitation. Mark you, these spirits keep the straightest law of courtesy!—unless indeed they have not yet escaped the underself; and by that very test we find them out.

So first the spirit gave us cordial greeting, yet with a certain formal, English manner quite his own; and, after that, we had a jurist's talk concerning human needs. That failed to satisfy the needs of Mr. Eighmie. At close of it he urged: "Judge Evelyn, our friend has started out to do a mission-work—inspired by spirits. She ought to be sustained. Just now she needs five hundred dollars. Can't you get it for her? Haven't spirits power?"

"Sir; once I told you there should be a Home for fallen women. I said that if you chose it might be yours to lay the corner-stone! This is the corner-stone!"

When I was cloaked and bonneted for going after a happy stay, my host arose and crossed the room and laid his hand upon my arm:

"Don't you want to ask me?

And even so, was laid the "corner-stone."

WAS ever woman's life so revolutionized? Out in the open, haunting shops and factories planning manifold devices, solving mechanical puzzles,—what had become of all my pretty times? No more rhyming, story-telling, broidering, playing tunes, gossiping, sowing seeds and plucking lovely flowers! Oh, how I missed the flowers! I do suppose my soul had need of them; so let me tell you this: Close by St. Paul's (you always pass St. Paul's!), a boy stood selling little bunches—pansies, heliotropes and violets;—only ten cents. I used to hurry by. But once I stopped and opened purse, then shut it with a sense of shame: "I will not spend the Lord's money for flowers!— and so I sped along. At once—street-rattle in my ears (my common ears)—in came the Lord's own message! Who delivered it? No matter! Here it is:

"You shall have all the flowers you want upon your birthday

April—October; full six months to come! Let us admit a spirit might foretell a cataclysm, earthquake, avalanche or hurricane or even a Russian Revolution, by noting obvious laws. But seeing far away such tiny things as sprouting germs and growing slips, and positively knowing, half a year ahead, whose hand should grasp the flowers—why, that transcends belief!

I had a way of telling friends about these little Psychic messages; but now I said: "No one shall hear of this.

No friend shall have a right to say I brought the prophecy to pass myself by letting people know." Be good enough to wait. Some say that spirit-fabrics "will not wash"; we'll let this lie out in the rain and sun awhile, then look for faded colors. We'll wait six months for that.

I have no mind to dwell on so-called practical affairs, save as they illustrate or rather demonstrate my Psychic certainties. I said that "difficulties were enormous"; I might have said appalling, if I had ever been appalled. And now that I have conquered them, and many others after them, I realize that those who gave me work which seemed impossible to do, knew well that I should conquer finally, however long the time; else work had not been given.

Just a few moments then for better understanding. This initial process—canning without cooking (others were to follow) seemed to make imperative demands, that quite forbade all profitable use. "Preserve the fruit in glass," said my collaborator: "There is no other way. Give vacuum, send in fluids by gradation, furnish needed warmth, watch heedfully to hinder upward rush during the vacuum-boiling, detach the jars at close, and be expert and very swift in sealing—otherwise the air will enter through the orifice and goods will perish.—And oh, the three hours toil!

Not practicable for commercial work? Well, it devolved on me to make it so. Meanwhile most any housewife would be very glad to can her fruits uncooked, six jars at once (that seemed the uttermost) if she could only catch the trick. So first I tried to make it possible for family use—hoping, in time, to make it less exacting.

Ransacking three great cities, so far as I could learn, their "finished workmen" knew as much about hermetical sealing as great Jules Verne, the novelist. His wise astronomers (shut in a great retort with means for manufacturing air at need), were shot far into space, you recollect, by means of vast explosions. Off they went around the moon, observing it through plate-glass windows, with Nature's universal vacuum outside—and not the slightest leak!—not even through the slide at bottom, out of which they dropped thermometers for scientific test, and once a poor, dead dog! This is for illustration, not instruction; pray receive it so.

And yet in very truth men plan their "warranted airtight" retorts, then set the vacuum-pumps at work and keep them at it,—otherwise no vacuum because of leaks. Nothing insecure would answer. So I taught myself through many struggles, how to make an air-and-vacuum apparatus, valves and all, for very perfect work! Justice to Dr. Cooley requires that I should say he set the pace by giving me a practically perfect vacuum without the use of pumps. It had to be lived up to!

345

Just here, consulting my chronology, I find that I must show a branching road. It wound away and yet swerved back at times, belike to join at last and broaden all. That is to know about hereafter.

Hibbler & Dorrflinger were pressing fruit-jar caps for me; and so I hung about. One day the older partner swung away from writing: "Miss Jones, I see that you're a woman of ideas. I want to burn crude oil with safety under a glory-hole. Come out and see the furnace. I had a scientist at work four months at heavy cost. He couldn't do it; I believe you can. Anytime you'll undertake the task, I'll give you every chance." Very complimentary! I said: "I'll think about it."

Just then I dropped my work. I sprang up as a bough released and went a-visiting;—oh, much in need of cash! My friend Miss Kendall, had been urging me to visit Providence; and even sending funds. I went about the 10th of May, for I remember blue-eyed "innocence" was blossoming in fields (the first I ever saw) and lilies of the valley all around the house upon the southern side.

"I've wanted you to come and tell my brother all about your work. Why don't you speak of it?"

"Because he doesn't ask me. He's not the sort of man one can intrude upon."

At last he said: "Jane tells me that you have a Mission work. How did that come about?" I saw a curious twinkle in his eye and met the challenge: "Oh, I had a vision!" Why should I flinch from telling him the story—consecration, supplication, answered prayers and all? Being a business man of great affairs (not a chimerical scheme among them);—a Unitarian, like O. B. Frothing-ham, devout, clear-thoughted, no way credulous, I promise you he had a chance to scoff! And, last of all, I showed some certain samples all in flasks, because my jars were not yet operative—neither was my "family apparatus" more than half evolved.

To tell the truth he laughed. He—elderly, austere, a man who bore himself with majesty, and would have scorned the weak, save for a

346

certain tenderness—leaned back, and laughed and laughed. He rose and went to church, still laughing heartily.

"Jones," Miss Kendall said, all smiles: "You've done it now!" "What have I done?"—"No matter! you'll discover."

"And now," said Mr. Kendall in a graver moment: "I'll admit you have a fine invention. Let me tell you my experience. I took up something, easier to handle, worked for fourteen years and put in twenty thousand dollars, before I put it on the market. I estimate for you a longer time, and more expenditure. But will your faith hold out?"

"I've promised that it shall."

Another day (I was about to leave) he came to dinner early. I saw him smiling to himself, before I entered through the open door and somehow thought of Jeremiah Eighmie, just as he looked when yielding up that long acknowledged claim to Yuh Heh Springs; and just as happily this friend reached out his hand, and said: "Whether you succeed or fail, you have already done so much you ought to be assisted. Here are five hundred dollars for you."

"May it be a loan?"

"In case of great success." And so he laughed again. Perhaps you recollect he also laughed that time he found me in my sleep, after ten years had passed—declaring "God is law!"

And now I hid away in Brooklyn, partly for economy, partly to be with Julia Coleman (lecturer on temperance and dietetics—also editor), but also, just to hide. I knew that I must have five hundred dollars more within two months,—that half of what I had must go for fruit-jar dies, and nearly all the rest for glass, and patent-issues. I made a crucial test of spirit-power. No one should know I needed money. Not Mr. Eighmie—he had done his part; not Mr. Kendall—gifts must not be held repeatable. I walled myself about. I would not write to any possible assister, even by way of courtesy.

With all my workmen satisfied, I gave no further orders. I sought, instead, a business-college, bought a set of books, and paid for two weeks' lessons. When I handed out the money (all I had except enough for car-fares) I never thought of poverty. In fact I took no thought of anything till someone, close at hand—not clothed in flesh—spoke out vehemently: "O, Woman! Great is thy faith!"—Then I rejoiced!

All you who live by faith (I hope too many to be reckoned up) are well aware of this: Petition leads the way.

You understand God has a blessing for you; that understanding never hinders prayer. Sometimes you laugh for very joy of it, or weep for grief, knowing yourself unworthy. And yet you never cease to ask till you are all at peace. So day by day I asked, and day by day I waited for reply.

"Look at this granite cross", a spirit said to me one morning. "It wants a solid base before we set it up, and that is nearly ready." I saw the firm foundation being laid, and close beside, a cross, that, once in place, nor time nor tempest could avail to rock. Oh, I was well sustained with visions,—it was not meant that I should lose my faith."

Another day, Judge Evelyn, who had spoken much to others, now spoke to me alone. I had not risen from the act of prayer, when he approached and gave me utterance. There were no ears to hearken save my own or that of some chance robin in the green ailanthus by the open sash. How deep the Psychic trance, I cannot say; and yet I never lost a certain consciousness of earthly things. I doubt if spirits in their highest heaven lose thought of lower spheres.

Judge Evelyn said:—

"My friend, if we procure what now you need, success will be assured. But here we pause; we have no right to deal with you herein, till you have learned the cost. That being shown, we leave you wholly free to drop your work if that shall be your choice. Deeply consider this: Can you endure? If flesh and spirit prove too weak, if heart and strength must fail, if even in this hour you shrink from what must come,—resign your chosen work. Spirits will hold you blameless. From every promise you have made, we give you absolution. I shall myself pronounce you free from guilt."

And now indeed I saw. That future self of me was climbing mountain-paths, and they were always narrow. Sheer heights upon the right, sheer depths upon the left; the very chamois might have shunned the trail! Times when I passed from sight were many; times when a great stone rolled across and touched but did not crush; times when deep shadows fell and none would dare to move. I could not trace the track.

I waited long; it seemed that there was nothing more to see. Then finally I saw an open space—trees on the South and West, low shrubs along the East; and through the shrubs, I saw my future self-approach and cross the open space, and pause. And now appeared a little group of women standing very near to me. Then other women came in sight, but kept themselves aloof. They came from every quarter, following by ones and twos till there were thousands,—more than I could count. They seemed to look on me with favor; still they kept apart.

The little group stood still. They pressed so very close you might have thought them friends. So passed a certain time. But, now I looked upon the near-by faces, there were four or five among the group that scowled at me. The eyes were full of hatred. That was terrible! They would have murdered me it seemed, but had no weapons save their stabbing eyes. I had been used to woman's love. So far I had not realized a woman's power to hate. I saw my future self stand, all accused before these bitter ones, who had no cause for enmity, but seemed to think they had. Wherein was my defense, save that I meant no wrong? Misguided, false or treacherous— wherein was their defense? I could not understand. I saw them glide from sight. I faced alone the far-off multitude of women—silent as the dead; no stabbing eyes, no angry faces, one and all seemed waiting for the end.

It came: I saw my later self—my pallid, older self, move staggering toward the East;—move on, and pause, and start again with trembling limbs, till I had reached an altar. So I fell thereon. Now afterward there was a sound of weeping: "See how this woman loved us. She is dead! Would she were yet alive!"

349

The vision passed; but, still upon my knees, I said: "Accept my service even so; I want my work. Master, I want my work." But there was no response.

This was in 1873. My friends, after the mountain paths, the dangerous descents, the hidden ways, in 1889,'90 and '91, I drank that bitter cup of woman's hate down to the loathly dregs,—in sight of many thousand women capable of love. The final act is yet to be fulfilled.

Men say—who think themselves philosophers—that spirits in the flesh or those exalted high as Heaven, have not the gift and power of prophecy. It is not true. Down all the steeps of earth prophetic voices peal; in every vale prophetic echoes linger. God would have us know.

My father spoke of years when "peace was flowing as a river"; He had the gentler nature. Peace comes to me by hours—with many hours between. It came next day:—"The Peace that passeth understanding." And in the midst of it my guardian came again. "I did not show you all; there is a sweeter part I left untold. You ask for no reward; why should I promise one? There is a life beyond all human life; and what will come when you are one with us, I have no words to tell."

And, then a little after, came the simple message: "Child, put on your bonnet. Go to Mr. Eighmie."

The obvious thing to do?—Perhaps. I had not thought of him, save by a fleeting memory. Looking afar, through that ethereal space— how could I think of mortals? And it was all so simple! My patriarchal friend had been away from home three weeks, and he had just returned that morning, richer than he went away; for he had sold an iron mine; and to be richer meant, with him, to be a "better man"—a "ten years younger man." Pity wealth doesn't always have a like effect!

Sitting at ease upon his pleasant porch, he rose to welcome me both hands reached out. "I'm very glad to see you.

350

I want to know just what you're doing. Are you in need of money? I want to let you have five hundred dollars. It is an honor to be allowed to help your work. Wait; let me call my wife and son-in-law. And when they came, he said: "Amanda ought to have five hundred dollars right away. You are my heirs. Before I let her have it, I want your full consent." He did not lose a breath, but hurried on: "How will you have it? Shall I draw a single cheque or will you come when you have need of money?"

"A single cheque of course," his wife Naomi said: "Why should you bother her?" and let me add that twice again this Jeremiah Eighmie came of his own accord and said: "I ought to furnish more. Someone might offer it from selfish motives. You mustn't get entangled".......

Prepaid? Oh, not a doubt of it! Principal with interest and after that "a little usury"—we'll say a "bonus." All that in higher places!— down below, I think his heirs will get full value when the hour has come.

Now, in September 1873, having appliances, there was a very obvious need. I must devote myself to testing fruits and other goods, that many problems might be solved; and I must have a shop—a laboratory, a place for secret work; and that would cost perhaps a lot of money; no one could estimate the dollars. I counted in as debt all that had been so freely furnished; it being understood that payment must depend upon prosperity. So far, advances had been voluntary. So they must remain, unless I compromised the patents or nullified my necessary independence. I could not ask for loans; nor hope that charitable folk (like Mr. H.) would furnish means upon a woman's pledge, such as I had to offer.

Perhaps it isn't wise to be quite inconspicuous, if one has world-affairs. I went back to the city, almost to the heart of it, seeking a permanent home. I rather pride myself upon the fact that Alexander Hamilton, during his palmy days, had built the statelier portion of the double house wherein I lived, at whiles, from 1874 to 1877. Once said to be the handsomest residence in town—but now a little old and dingy. What of that? Wainscots, lintels, doors and banisters were all mahogany, mantels Italian marble; and a noble stairway let me pass along the quiet further hall to find my pleasant room—

351

curtained with century-old wisteria-vines flung over from the church yard. Everybody knows St. John's; not everybody knows the Laight Street House. It might have come in truth to be a shrine, save for a wanton bullet. Therein John Adams was regaled on melons at the breakfast table, and wondered at the luxury,—so wrote to Abigail advising melons; and let us hope that Massachusetts yielded an abundance, so that those twain might never murmur, after the manner of the Israelites? "For lack of them our souls are dried away!" We others were regaled on Graham-water-gems and grape-juice—that is, those of us who chose ambrosial diet. Maybe that conduced to Psychic apperception.

Anyway, about September 10th, one morning I awoke with all my outward senses not obliterated (mind you!), only in abeyance. This is what I saw, and partly understood. Myself upon a narrow mountain-path, a steep-set cliff above, sheer depths below,—one slight mis-step would send me down forever. Now there was dropped across the ledge above, suspended by a hempen rope, a bag of gold. Not that I saw the gold, shut in and wound about to keep the mouth from opening—only I fully realized that it was there, and that, if I should clutch and hold, strong hands above would draw me up to broader walking places. Just for a moment I was glad; but then a spirit said—not from above, but from the space between. "Is your courage great enough to step around this heavy bag of gold—not even touching it—and pass along, alone, upon the narrow path?"

"How can I step around it? The way is only wide enough for my two feet; I should be sure to fall."

"But have you courage?"

"Yes; although there seems no possible room, I'll take the step—if that is what you want."

"That is what we want." And so the vision passed.

Now this was Sunday morning: A gentleman at leisure came and introduced himself: "I've heard of you through

Mr. H——; and he has heard of you through Mr.

352

Rawlinson." "I come from Mr. H——-; I saw him yesterday, and I shall visit him again today. He says he has become convinced that God is with you. True, he doubted first, but he is ready now to furnish money,—all you need, I judge. What shall I say to him? He wants to know."

I had no thought of incivility. I said what I was bound to say: "God doesn't want his money. Tell him so." I saw no other way to carry on my work, only to clutch and hold that bag of gold; yet stepped around it, hardly with a dizziness, and did not fear to fall.

A few days after that came word from Jennie Kendall: "My brother wants to see the process. Please come without delay."

I packed my trunk. It held my "house-hold apparatus," vessels for preserving and all appurtenances. I left for Providence on Saturday afternoon. Times are "altered perfectly since then," no doubt; but there was being carried on a plundering scheme; and trunks were disappearing right and left; no one could trace them out. Mine also disappeared. I went to get my check exchanged; men said it wasn't there. I urged a search,—they "sassed" me, every one of them; and one cried out "Madam, you've just a minute. Go to the basement. There's a man will see to it." This other said: "I'll see to it. Give me your check and run. Cars start in thirty seconds." A good long run at that. I caught the moving train, and started off—trunk left, and not a check!

Arrived in Providence, I led Miss Kendall all along the platform thinking (as a woman thinks!); "Perhaps it had been sent ahead before I got there,—being labeled, 'Providence.'" A gentleman was tramping up and down: "What! Have you lost your trunk? You'll never get it in the world. I've waited here three days for my two trunks, and telegraphed to every point along the road. They're full of valuable things; they're worth a fortune. But they're lost! And so is yours."

All this we told to Mr. Kendall at the supper table. He said: "The man was right. You'll never get your trunk.

You haven't even a check to show for it. You'll have to be resigned."

353

"Look here!" I said in haste. "God has furnished means to me, because I prayed with faith. He sent me helpers so that I could do just what you ask of me;—prove that I have a beautiful new process for preserving fruits and whatsoever else we demonstrate. I have one working apparatus only; that is in my trunk. Be sure it isn't lost."

"It certainly is lost beyond recovery."

"Do you suppose that I have asked for Heavenly help to get so much accomplished, and had my prayers responded to in every case, only to be defrauded of results? Whatever else may happen, rest assured I shall not lose my trunk." "Suppose you do. Then what about your faith? Come now! Let's make a test of this! Not that I mean to be discouraging;—but let us pit your faith against my unbelief. Whoever loses makes acknowledgment. Will you consent to that?"

"I would; but candidly, it isn't faith with me,—its knowledge. I absolutely know God will not let me lose my trunk."

How could a sensible, straight-forward business man, who would not step, save on the solid ground, follow an ignis fatuus over such a swamp, however starred with flowers? He watched me furtively at Sunday dinner: "Confess; you're just a little worried. Oh you don't betray it, I admit! But come now! Are you absolutely sure?"

So sure, I only laughed.

On Monday morning someone, unseen, awakened me in evident haste: "Get up at once and you shall find your trunk." I heard the city clock strike out the hour, and it was five. The silver sound was no more clear to mortal sense than were those ringing words to Psychic understanding. Believe me they were heard, even by the ears that hear.

I dressed with speed; I tiptoed down the stairs, I softly drew the bolts, and turned the key, and gently closed the door. What then? There came no further message. I thought: "If I must find the depot, two miles off, I haven't strength to walk, nor do I know the way." And yet I walked along on Liberty for half a block, turned the first

354

corner, walked a half block further, looked up an alley, saw a waiting wagon, standing by an open door,—made for the door, went in and found a monstrous room containing many hundred trunks (all sent astray feloniously, no doubt), walked on, and laid my hand upon my trunk right in the center, evidently just brought in! The wagoner drove away.

Disgorgement isn't easy to an anaconda. We had an office scene at nine o'clock. "Madame, no check, no trunk." "I will identify the baggage. It has my name. I'll go and point it out." "That can't be done. Bring us a check;—there's nothing more to say." "Oh, yes, there is! Walk through that further door and I shall follow you and lay my hand upon my trunk. You dare not keep it back"....... Perhaps I hypnotized the fellow. I fear I

"fixed him with a glittering eye"; and he obeyed me "like a three years' child." Alas, for me, if only meekness may inherit Heaven! And yet, without an underself at times, what would a body do?

No man could be more sternly practical than Mr. Kendall—more averse to all that "willn't wash." But this small incident was such a vital fact, it touched him to the quick; and I had reason to be very glad I had not lost my trunk.

Straightway I set my "house-hold apparatus" up—good for six jars instead of that inevitable single laboratory flask. And, by the way, I opened one of those small flasks at supper-time (pine apple if you please—put up six months before, by Dr. Cooley's son, eleven years of age.)

So Mr. Kendall, busiest of men, took time to watch the process,— saw the escaping air burst open plums and grapes and breathe its way in beads through ruddy apple skins; saw fluid take its place and boil in vacuo; also he had the goods to keep for better proof.

But oh I had to travel long and far and wearily, ere I could plan a way to shut five times as many jars from sight and carry on all steps of that exacting process merely by turning valves, and, after that, to seal them perfectly and leisurely, nor let the air get in! But not by any means so long and far, to turn you out cooked meats and

355

novelties on which the vacuum had done its perfect work to give you perfect food! However, that's to show.

This is a Psychic story; but you and I and all, may walk on mountain-paths, beside the sheer abysses, on to eternal life, if we are true in heart, and firm of step, and not afraid to trust. Or say that we are lower down—lost in the wilderness—pillars of fire may lead, and never lead astray. But though the Psychic faculty with me became a columned flame, it did not melt confronting cliffs, nor burn one spiny shrub of all that rent my flesh. How can you know that spirits guided me, unless I show the road? I walked on solid earth and rock, through many perilous ways. These I must let you see by glimpses here and there—but always by mirage. They fade away in air; but light remains. I pray you see the light above the toilsome way.

Well then, to work! To work!—that is the primal need. Most happily for me, it was agreed at Mr. Kendall's instance, that I should have a private working-place at Watertown, aided at every need,— his brother Francis and his nephew John co-operants, and he to furnish means. To give me chance to work and yet not feel an absolute dependence, this was indicated: that should there ever come a time for bargaining, New England much desired a better green-corn process, and possibly the method might apply to oysters. "Should you succeed in canning these uncooked, we'll take New England, sharing profits equally. In any case we'll ask for nothing more."

Truly, success along these lines was hypothetical—hardly presumable. We had no written contract; none was needed. These were not birds of prey; they lacked the beaks and talons. I was the foremost one they chose to benefit. No doubt a certain Mr. H— had motives just as kind.

But having opened up for me a sack of gold, he would have backed himself against the door of Heaven, for fear of "special help."

And, by the way, there was a flask of green corn, even then, in Dr. Cooley's laboratory. He opened it, we ate of it in Dr. Wood's hotel on Laight St., New Year's Day;—"Sweet as a rose" was Francis Kendall's verdict. Moreover there had been a flask of uncooked beef,—not spoiled at all when opened. That argued for the oyster possibly.

I hope you've not forgotten what was promised me in

April: "All the flowers you want upon your birthday." Much I had thought of that the seasons through, but never dared to speak. That was to be my precious token—my one bouquet, flung from the galleries across the foot-lights, showing me approved. In all that time I had no flowers but once, and those were Michaelmas daisies, picked in open field beside the Sound. Thither had come my Clifton friends the Rawlinson's, with Susie Lane and glad Miss Phillips (air-uplifted from the couch I told you of and walking miles on any slight occasion); there I had welcomed them. No doubt they also cared for flowers; not even a marigold was in the gardens; and in October, frost had come and daisy seeds were flying all about.

Howbeit, my friends sent in a messenger: "Come out; we want to celebrate your birth-day, remembering how you left us just a year before—God being with you even to this hour. Come out and keep our feast!" That was the very spirit of the message. I had no right to purchase flowers for self, nor even for these whose chiefest luxury was common bread. I laughed in heart! "Now, spirits, find a way!" and did not doubt in heart but that they would.

October 17th, I spent the whole forenoon among the work-shops. Going home for dinner (due at two) I lifted up my hand and stopped a Broadway omnibus. "It seems to me this is the way I ought to go;" I said: and wondered why. Arrived on Union Square, I thought: "What am I doing here—all off the track?" And so I called a halt. Alighting, standing back as in a dream, I meditated: "There must be something that I ought to do. I can't imagine what!" No viewless friend suggested anything; nor did I stir at all, till all at once it came to me quite as a recollection: "I promised Mrs. Keyser, months ago, that I would visit her. Didn't she say they lived near Union Square? I've been uncivil; I shall go and make apologies." And so I looked them up.

A wagonette was at the door. Mr. and Mrs. Keyser met me in the hall, ready for journeying. What did they care about my incivility?

They greeted me as cordially as human heart could wish: "You're just in time. We're going to our country house to stay a week; and you are going with us."

"Oh, that's impossible."

"Not in the least. We'll take you off by force."

"You might; but certain friends of mine will celebrate my birthday Sunday. Today is Friday. I must go to them tomorrow afternoon. Nothing must keep me back." "Give me their address," Mr. Keyser said: "We'll help the celebration. We'll send you flowers."

I hardly dared to breathe—much less to tell my story. But anyway, next afternoon my friend the clergyman, saluted me: "A great white box has come to me for you."

"A great white box!"—And half that blessed Sunday, I spent arranging flowers. I had three little girls about me, they, as well as I, all wonder and delight. Oh, beautiful exotics; They made me think of those I saw when I was dreaming, yet a child myself. "These are the flowers that you are going to plant." I did not know the names of these, more than of those; nor could I count their numbers;—more hot-house beauties than I ever had all put together, both before and since; enough to bury me full deep—and if I could be buried!

What do you say to that?

Let me not triumph altogether; once I was rebuked. There came a mood upon me; half I thought it was induced by spirits. Now I know it was. I had a fault—I did not call it so, I carried it with pride; but it had risen up and rent me. None had done me wrong; instead I recognized my very underself, and would have hated it, but had not power. You know the way; and how you cling to that which must go over-board and yet belongs to you! What? Lose it in the sea? And after it you plunge!

Well, in the thick of that I walked along Broadway, near ,to St. Paul's; and there I saw, just balanced on the curb, about to cross right in the flare and glare, a hideous object—shocking to the sense, and shocking to the soul. A woman, quite erect and not so very old, clothed in the rags of utter poverty. Not altogether clothed; a little way above the gaping stogas, nearly to the knees, the limbs were bare and chapped with winter winds, though May was close at hand. I felt an instant's bleeding at the heart; my soul took time to say: "There is a woman isolated, desolate!

In all the world no human being loves her. Pitiful! Most pitiful!"

With that I took one of our whilom postal-scrips out of my purse, and reached around and put it in her hand. She whirled and clutched my arm: I would not look; I dragged myself away. "No, No!"—my underself protested: "I'm in too deep myself to draw another out."

And so I swept along, and certainly had quite forgotten her three seconds after that. For I was under billows! I could not lift the head, save for an instant's breath. How could I reach for her? So down I plunged again, I knew not how or why, nor yet how deep. Enough that I was under.

So home to dinner; or at least to shut myself away and have it out with Heaven. I locked my door, slipped off my wrap, and stood right in the center of my pleasant room in dreariness, even I, whom God had blessed beyond all thought or hope. What did I want? Nothing, I think, only to fling aside that underself as I had flung my coat. I said: "Now that I think of it, I haven't prayed for self alone since I began to pray for fallen women. That is not fair. I am God's daughter just as much as they. And that may be the very thing He wants,— that I should pray for me." I fell upon my knees. All personal desire, I spoke and dared to speak: "Thou Infinite, in whom I live and move"—then paused. If I had anything in mind to ask for self, it never found a voice, or then or afterward.

Two beautiful white arms—strong arms, angelic arms—swept into sight, and two white hands, no doubt well used to bearing burdens, set within my reach one I had seen before: A woman hideous to sight, erect not altogether old, hung around with filthy rags that could not cover all her nakedness; a woman isolated from her kind, unloved, unloving, desolate of grace, a high-way creature—one who knew the slough and made her bed therein. And clear to Psychic sense as any service bell, a voice rang out:

"Which needs to be prayed for most,—you or she?"

First I was all ashamed. And then my soul rose up from its abasement, so that I cried aloud: "Lord, not myself!

Oh, nothing for myself! Have I not always walked among the lilies? Clean ways and sweet for me! O, choose the clean for her!"

She passed from sight. My soul went out to find her,—whether in open road or ditch! went crying from afar: "My sister, here is one who loves you! Turn and hear and understand! You shall not be alone!"

Then for an hour I strove with God. I would not be denied: "O let her know that she is loved! Save her and save her speedily! Cleanse her. O, make her clean! O, leave her not alone!" And even so He answered me: "Daughter the hour is near. Her great salvation comes!" Friends, when the full eternal tides roll in, and turn again and bear my soul away, I shall not realize a sweeter ecstasy than this: To know the lost are saved!

CREVASSES AND CANONS

OLD fashioned folk averred that sunshine streaming through a window upon a blazing hearth deadened the fire;—they drew the curtains down. If they were right or wrong let chemists prove; but this I hold as truth: The Psychic light that floods the human brain puts out no fires of thought. It is not meant in Heaven that we should have no radiance on earth, save what our fagots give, though they be resinous and sweet in burning—cut from Lebanon's top. Nor is it meant to drive out natural warmth with supernatural glory. To put this plainly into words, many have thought the surest way of getting spiritual revelation, is by obliteration of the revelator—as in hypnotic sleep. They deeply err; but happily the deepest slumberer but plays, as children do, at "being dead"; and even so eternal life throbs on, and revelations come. No less, we'll keep awake and keep our mortal fires alive, nor draw one curtain down.

If then I write of common earth affairs, I cry you mercy. These will have significance I trust to you as well as me. They were the very roots that in the course of time would make it possible for me to hand you Psychic flowers—moulded from clay, yet steeped in cosmic light.

Now, by the river Charles in Watertown, almost within the sound of Boston bells, my friends, the Kendalls—sire and son—arranged my working room.

We well-conceived that problems must be solved, and theories confirmed or proved untenable, but I, at least—who saw a multitude of doubts appear, like specters of the Brocken—kept on my way and would not be afraid. It seems I had some natural aptitude for mechanism, or rather for adapting means to ends; so that in introducing novelties among my working men, I had not learned of them so much as they had learned of me. Nor did I think of needing further help from Dr. Cooley. He had done his part—being a very able physicist; but after all, the sole responsibility was mine. Still, when my friends proposed engaging him to come and start us off, I gave assent at once, on their account, and yielded up my place.

Most kindly Dr. Cooley came and took control—not as a mechanist but as a scientist. For my immediate part, so many of my jars were poorly tooled, with covers badly pressed, all thought it best that I should hurry off to Pittsburg for a better make. So, while I wandered off, three gentlemen went bravely on and did the things they would.

It chanced in traveling (I need to speak of this) that I foregathered with a bride and groom, returning home after a wedding trip to Boston. They would not be denied but I must visit them at Brady's Bend; so finding I must wait some days before my moulds were mended, I gladly sought them out. (Always you trust a Pennsylvanian for hospitality.)

One day we drove across the hills ten miles away, to see a stream of oil, just piped the night before, pour out from "caverns measureless to man." (Alas! for Kubla Khan, if such the odor of that "sacred river!") This was the first crude oil that I had seen, and it reminded me that I had promised Hibbler and Dorrflinger (glass manufacturers of Brooklyn) that I would "think about" their "glory hole," and how to heat it safely with petroleum instead of tar. Now was the time to think—at least, to learn. I questioned closely: "Is there any way of burning it with safety?"

It seemed that men had fed it to their furnaces by force of gravity, and under "rule of thumb," very disastrously; had soaked it up through wicks, had boxed it in with broken bricks, had floated it full breadth on water tanks, had sent it twisting in through red-hot serpent-pipes, had housed it close in separate generators—raging hot, gotten themselves blown up or maimed by various ingenuities, and last of all were steaming it and squirting it to keep their fires ablaze.

And, by the bye, their "steam jet" burners, "atomizers" and the like, have numbered many thousands, hard to count as mussels on a beach, washed in by every wave. And patented!—just change a thread, and swerve a line, and tip and turn and twist about though but a hair's breadth either way—you get a patent. All are serviceable, more or less; not one of them is mine.

So back to Watertown. Three weeks had passed and all had been at work—it seemed to little purpose. That which had been done but emphasized an uttermost necessity. What more remained to do must wholly rest with me, since Dr. Cooley's time was up and he was forced to leave. I cannot say my friends were very sanguine. Discouragement was in the atmosphere. No one declared it openly (how kind these Kendalls were!) but it was plain that should I fail to do what had not yet been done, I could not ask for further tolerance. Cast down in such a deep crevasse as that—my vaunted faith forevermore discredited—who then could rescue me?

Now I had used my "house-hold apparatus" only in Mr. Henry Kendall's kitchen. Dr. Cooley had not tried it till he came to Watertown, nor handled in the laboratory, more than one small flask at once—succeeding so by singular dexterity. There was a grievous fault, I had discovered, not quite prohibitive for canning fruits, as had been shown, but rendering even that too difficult for profitable use. This fault must be eliminated. But who eliminates a law of Physics? Well then, it must be dodged. And I have noticed this: Men, who are striving to invent, will take an obstacle as though it were a hurdle; leap it if they can, or otherwise declare the race impossible. But I had dodged a dozen obstacles already and slipped around them rather prettily—being a simple woman. Better to be adroit than risk a broken neck.

Please not to mind my "talking shop" a little—not for very long. This is to let you guess that even the greatest Physicist—Huxley himself—might profit now and then, right in the face of physical law, by some slight Psychic squint; as I did peradventure—leaving you to judge.

We had by Dr. Cooley's art, a vacuum-chamber far beyond a vacuum-pump for admirable work such as we had to do. That had to be our guarantee and proof of excellence for all the rest. We had his "transfer" one straight pipe with sidewise-branching tubes, permitting equal fluid-distribution. This had an upward pipe for vacuum connection, and, at the further end, a downward pipe for taking fluid up by atmospheric pressure, two stopcocks—nothing more. We had my jars, well-sealed save for a central orifice for tube

363

connection (sealed after work was done); I had devices for attaching jars to tubes, and, somewhat to my credit, let us say, we did not have a single leaking joint. Quite possible to get and hold secure a 29 inch vacuum, hour after hour. Why should we not succeed?

But even so, my "house-hold apparatus" (the only factory apparatus yet in sight), looked at without a square was but a dismal failure. This was the way of it: First thing we filled our jars with goods to be preserved, screwed them in place and turned the vacuum on to rend the cells and let the air escape. We gave abundant time; then sent our fluid in at intervals, preventing it from going all astray, by shutting off the vacuum-cylinder. It partly went astray in any case; finding a better vacuum in the pipes than in the jars, some of it hung suspended ready to be caught away on any slight pretense.

But did you ever see a water-spout? Suppose you boil in vacuo, and watch the up-take. Six water-spouts I used to see—boiling at 80 Fahrenheit, with all my fluid in. Or call them what you please, they took that fluid up by threads and skeins—you saw it spin away. There was a remedy, of course,—shut off the vacuum. But how about that last fine trace of oxygen so potent for destruction? Depend upon the pipes? There's no more vacuum there than in the jars for they are full of fluid.

I wrote to Dr. Cooley: "Unless there be a way devised for keeping safe our fluids, under the highest vacuum, there cannot be success. Can you devise a way?" He answered me: "Dexterity; there is no other way."

"Dexterity!" Well, in the work-shop, that had failed with him; and how could it suffice with me, or peradventure, housewives, factory girls, and all the common run of working folk? These friends, for all their trouble, asked the privilege of canning corn and oysters; and this they'd got to have if so they willed, though all the laws of Physics should array themselves against my vigilant will. My mother, at the age of four, was asked to lift the house. She thought it really moved. Of course, it did, for force is never wasted. Something of this I have inherited—not to be daunted whatsoever chance. And so I set myself to make that vacuum serve, as viewless Ariel did, with all docility, and bring my ship ashore whatever wind should blow.

Too late for green corn; so I called for oysters. They had been tried and shown to be unmanageable. Time after I found them so myself. A peaceable folk they are. They'll let themselves be eaten, you observe, with much tranquility; but to be canned is quite another matter. Up they rose under the vacuum; they magnified themselves! Rather than lose their air (if you'll excuse a rampant simile), they fought like bulls of Bashan. Add fluid—why, you maddened them. They blocked the orifice; they tore themselves; they went in fragments up along the pipes; they lost their air (almost) and lost themselves in vacuous space, from which they issued but to feed the eels.

Well, it was bad enough to lose my fluids; but when the solids took to flying after, something must be done and that right speedily. We'll say a change in process first of all. And so I let my oysters poise themselves on tip-toe for an hour or more and would not let them drink. The air within themselves was straining to escape through those distensible films, and yet they would not break. Astonishing the space one creature filled! Perhaps you've heard that should you chance to get an oyster in the windpipe he leaves you not one fighting chance for life! So you'll be glad to know, I brought him low and made him small again. I only made him just a little warm—90 degrees or thereabouts. Then having seen him shrink and drop all in a minute utterly cast down, I gave him water-floods to swell himself withal. I wish you could have seen that upward rush of air and vapor bubbles, silver white and beautiful. If you had brought me out of Italy, Queen Margharita's famous pearls, my faith, I wouldn't have exchanged one bubble for the whole of them.

Well, I had saved my solids anyway; and now to save my fluids. I woke, one happy dawn, aware of something strange. I realized an etching on my brain that had been traced in sleep,—by whom I did not guess. I only said: "Now this will rescue me." What I had seen, I sketched before the breakfast hour, and handing out the sketch to Mr. Kendall asked to have our apparatus taken down, at once and modified according to the plan. He said at supper time: "The work is done and everything in place." So down I went at six o'clock next morning to find my Psychic etching visualized, and made to serve my will.

Now this is what I saw: The "Transfer" still in place; its upward pipe connecting with a transverse one, and both, as one, connecting with the vacuum chamber—either or both detachable, at will; the downward pipe upon the underside, used for injecting fluid, taken out; another in its place, set horizontally and guarded with a stop-cock at the bend; a six quart cylinder, having a downward pipe for taking fluid in, an upward pipe, at top, that turned and led along to join the upper transfer pipe as I have said, and further on to enter the "Exhauster" both as one. Now you can see that, every stopcock being open save the one below for letting in the fluid, the vacuum draught was equal—jars and little cylinder all subject to the same exhausting power—the larger cylinder.

I looked upon it all, and knew no more than this: That I must set my jars in place, must send my fluid up into the little cylinder, and let the vacuum work. Fast as the air went up from out the goods to be preserved, so fast it bubbled up within the fluid-cylinder and fled in unison. Here then, would be an airless fluid for supply whenever needed, provided it should choose to flow along that horizontal pipe and down into the jars—you having turned the cock. And what should hinder? Gravity sufficed.

I nearly filled my jars. No drop had found its way along the upper pipes; even the body of the "transfer," above the curving tubes that met the jars, was void of fluid. In the "Feeder" as I named my little cylinder, lay all I needed for supply at last, when I should boil in vacuo and need to fill my jars top-full—still subject to a vacuum till all the work was done, and it was time to take away and seal. No fluid-column lurked above to snatch a whirling thread, lead off a water-spout and so denude my goods.

Yet there was one below: It lay in wait to pull the fluids back along the road they traveled going down. How should I keep them down? Ask any Physicist: He'll say: "They must obey the law. You cannot hold them back. He will not even whisper: "Try dexterity." Not so could Nature's will be contravened.

366

How then? I knew the law; no less I kept my faith. The Psychic part of me refused to be afraid. It made demand upon the obvious law that it should turn aside and let another take its place—some inner, physical law, concealed as yet, but having power to act. I said to one: "You shall not draw the fluids up; I choose they shall descend;" And to the other: "Bring the fluids down and while I boil, keep filling up the jars and feeding tubes, with still the vacuum on."

A great absurdity! No scientist alive but would have laughed at me! But please you understand!

Well, so I boiled in vacuo at 90 Fahrenheit—you know that never cooks. And when the time sufficed I shut the larger vacuum off, and utilized the lesser one—that is: the vacuum-space within the little cylinder above its fluid-space from which the jars must all be fed, if they were ever filled. I planned to make my feeder serve a double purpose—air and vapor entering at the top alone, and the cold fluid pushing down against the boiling fluid in the jars. The greater pressure yielding to the less?—Well, not in fact. I waited for that undiscovered law. I laid my hand upon the stop-cock of the horizontal pipe (choke-full of airless fluid sure to snatch and lift); I did not open it at once. I said: "I'll wait four minutes." No one told me I must wait four minutes. I knew no reason why. I only knew by Psychic sense, that I must keep the time. I watched the clock, and when the time expired, drew one deep breath, opened the cock and said: "If now the fluid come, I shall praise God." There was not time to draw another breath before it came. It trickled into every jar alike; it filled them brimming full. I shut away the emptied cylinder and fell upon my knees; for God was there, and I was filled with awe.

I rose to end the test. I boiled in vacuo till not the slightest trace of air could possible remain, and sent no fluid off. Not only had I magnified my process, I had redeemed it from an imminent death. Whatever food might be pre-servable by air exhaustion, coupled with fluid substitution, I need not set aside.

What would have happened if I had turned the valve upon the instant, not looking at the clock to let four minutes pass before the act? John Kendall tried that very thing; this is what came about. The little horizontal pipe, between the jars and feeder, caught at the dashed up spray, and made a central axis in the mouth of every jar that whirled the contents out. The empty feeder had the better vacuum; but being filled anew with vapor-yielding fluid, lost all governing power. For now the better vacuum was in the jars; so up and out along the horizontal upper pipe, and down again to fill six vessels underneath, the fluid came. Just keep the boiling up and back it rushed—a sort of reel—dance, wait awhile and dance again!

What did four minutes do? During that time the vapor from the boiling fluid (nothing more) stole up along the upper pipes—the main exhauster being shut away—and settled in the feeder. Now vapor has a pressure of its own. That's quite believable, for we have learned that even light exerts continuous pressure. This vapor lying on the fluid surface (not dissolving into dew) had quite sufficient power to send the fluid down. Or rather there was no more vacuum above than down below; and so we had the law of gravity in full control.

But now again; I thought, just for convenient work, it might be well to put the feeder at the other end; and though I caught the notion back and said it wouldn't do, we tried it so. There was no flow of fluid either way. This was the one result I had foreseen. The little pipe that should have filled the jars from underneath the transfer was eighteen inches long instead of three, and friction interfered,—it stopped the downward run. We set our feeder back in haste and all was well again. And I suppose that no inventor—physicist, or Psychist—could have accomplished that desired result by any other means.

This then you understand: Shut deep in that unclimbable crevasse, there fell close to my hand a rescuing rope.

"And if it came by some fortuitous chance,

We'll guess as much, too, for the universe."

Even so it came about that, after many years of futile effort and expenditure upon the part of others, that which they had sought so ardently was mine;—achieved with no more money-cost than might have served to build a laborer's cottage. Here was the basis of a mammoth pure-food Industry, a traffic in the very means of life.

Uncooked or cooked or desiccated, all destructive elements withdrawn, and none thrown in upon pretence of need for preservation—such was to be the work that I must plan for, pray for, toil for. How much might be involved I could not know. Meantime here was in hand one veritable process—verified, but far from ready for commercial use. I knew right well that other minds than those that dwell in flesh had made it possible for me to have and hold, by legal right, a very great, good gift for my behoof and people's use and profit.

A terminable right, you say? Assuredly so; and well it was and is that while I stumbled on, achieving point by point with long delays, I claimed no further rights for many years; and even now; with five controlling patents to the good, others are in reserve.

Once in my early life I had this dream: It seemed to me that I was walking on the strand in search of precious stones, and mother came and watched me till I said: "It seems to me that there are diamonds here." Therewith she came and knelt beside me, helping me to look. Now there were many pebbles, colored prettily, and some of them were glittering as bits of broken quartz; we picked them up and talked of them, but cast them all away.

At last we heard familiar voices calling: "Mother! Amanda! Come away. There's nothing by the sea worth looking at. Yonder there is a grave-yard that is full of flowers,—a lovely place to ramble in. Come, walk with us, for we are going there and mean to build a home among the graves, where all of us may live, and be at peace."

Then mother rose and said to me: "Maybe we'd better go." But I refused; and very slowly and reluctantly she moved away, but still kept looking back, long as she kept in sight. So I was left alone. But presently, I knew not how or why, I found myself far out among the waves. They tossed me high and dropped me low, they whirled me here and there; but I was not engulfed. After a breathless time, they flung me up against a spur of some deep rooted rock, round which I cast my arm. And clinging so, as one who knows that he must nevermore let go, I knew that I was safe whatever floods assailed.

Now while I brought my other hand out from among the waves, lo, there had lodged therein a wonderful blue glittering thing, that when I held it up on open palm, seemed a great diamond of the underworld, encolored as the sky. One called from over-head: "Truth: You have found it." Then I looked above and saw celestial forms with waving hands, where angels went and came. So even in my sleep I understood that they had suffered me almost to perish—otherwise I had not won their gift. I could not choose but cling about my rock and hold my diamond safe.

All this I held to mean that verity of spirit-intercourse that I was searching for through briny waves, while others walked in grave-yards beautified with flowers thinking about their dead. And oh, to keep that safe that I had won through stress, till sea and land should pass! And oh, to have it said of me in Heaven: "She was not recreant to any trust."

But dropping parables and dreams and tropes, here was a trust indeed! Here was my promised work made evident in part—made mine by very grace of God, who gave His ministers a charge concerning me that I should do his will. Do I affirm too much? I pray you bear with me. Not without ample warrant do I say that disembodied spirits wrought with me, and made me one with them for righteous purposes. It was not possible at any time that I should see the height and breadth of this my chosen work; they are not seen today, though strong foundations wait the builded edifice and there are "stones cast down upon the plain" to gather up again that men may there abide. So please you still read on an hour or two; hear the conclusion of the matter," far as it concludes. But nothing ever ends.

My faithful friends, father and son, had for a double season—half-a-year—put other plans aside, save those I had in hand. To still devote themselves would call for service and expenditure beyond their power to grant though not beyond their will. We halted, all of us, to see what might be done. Winter precluded work for me, and forced me back to semi-tropical New York. But ere I went, I had a great desire to be instructed from a higher source than speech of mortal lips, even as I had been before, and found the counsel sweet.

Truly, though I had seen the gold within my mining claim, there lacked the streams and sluices. How should I sift it out?

Before I left we rode a long way off to find a green corn canning place, whose owners paid two cents per can in royalties for privilege of cooking many hours. Discoverers of the method had become stout millionaires thereby, and dealers longed for patent expiration. Up to that date, none had conceived the wickedness of using chemicals, as afterward men did. We were assured that equal royalties upon a better process—no less economical—would joyfully be paid, and we too rank among the princes.

Well, what then? Reformatories, Homes for erring women, Households for the little ones, Cures for the richer invalids earning the means of maintenance for God's deserving poor—who needed healing not a whit the less; and all of these built round those Yuh Heh Springs spirits had found and claimed in equal partnership with mortals—share and share alike!

All this might be, if but a single product, thrown in honest hands, might have commercial swing in one small province—out of all the land. After this manner patentees are prone to reason, people say; but, for myself, I came of practical folk not given to speculation. Even that one who thought about perpetual motion, put all his bridges up without a swaying plank. Oh, yes! I had the framework of a mighty bridge in truth, but who would help me set it on the piers, and who would haul the planks?

Well, well! I waited for a Heavenly heliograph! What could I do besides? For I had pledged myself, you may remember,—nay, had been commanded of the angelhood and God—to bear this very burden safely on, till I should reach the cross set far and white among the snows of Death. So, using common speech, I could not sell, hypothecate nor put away from me in any way this first invention, made my own after that solemn hour! A beauteous babe, so heralded of Heaven, even the sword of Solomon must not divide.

Across the road from where the earliest Puritans were laid to rest in Watertown there stood a ruined manse—

"A residence for woman, child nor man,

371

A dwelling place and yet no habitation."

Because I had such need to be alone, I went there more than once, and had full liberty to cry aloud, with none to heed or hear. For when you strive with Heaven while yet on earth, not soul alone, but brain and heart and voice must bear a part. All—all of you shall feel the rocking wind—mayhap the earthquake and the breath of fire. Now afterward, at home, within my room, this time of strife passed by, and verily I heard the still small voice, and knew that God was there.

So being all at peace, illumination came. I have had many Psychic visions—none so bright as this that could but mean illimitable pain, yet filled me full of faith. Once more I saw myself upon a mountain-path, but now the way was widened, though it skirted still the precipice. I climbed within the shadow of a bluff, and I was free to climb—the hindering rocks were gone. Then, as it seemed, out of a cleft where he had stood in waiting, one stepped before, as any mortal would, and took me by the hands and held me fast. Now he was clad in golden mail that shone most gloriously. A battle-prince he seemed—one who would lead in war, defend, and guide, and hinder onward rush. Oh, I must wait, must wait! And I must war for life!

How could I fail of victory, so championed? I rose from kneeling, full of ecstasy, yet knew my prayer for haste had been denied.

The vision grew upon me hour by hour. Another day at earliest dawn—compelled to rise for passionate supplication, this is what I asked: "Bring me another gift; something to bargain with, to sell for gain, or hold for profit. This, that I have, it seems, is far too precious to be hawked about. It can't be sold or given up to other management than mine, and I have neither aptitude nor power. Show me a plainer way."

The answer came: "Before the day is done, it shall be shown." Faith took the promise up (oh, most incredible!) and while belief denied, no mist of doubt was in the golden atmosphere! Nothing took shape within my thoughts save this: No one would offer charity, no sudden rain of gold would fall. I should be shown another path in which to walk. It might be rough and long—but at the end would wait a golden gift worthy of all the toil. Now what this was to be I knew no more than you. I only said: "It shall be shown to-day!" Outlook was vacancy—all else was faith.

Having my long-loved Mrs. Manley as a guest, and she about to leave, I took a holiday. From eight o'clock to three we saw as many Boston sights as possible. Then, while we rested in the Public Gardens, out of the wide unseen, there came a prompting word. "Do you believe our promise? Have you still the faith?" My mind replied: "I have the faith. Before the sun has set a gift will come."

While we were thinking it was time to go—silent and sad because we had to part, no doubt for many years, there floated up to conscious thought a little phrase out of an old philosophy well-conned in childhood: "Fluid seeks its level." That and nothing more. Then in a flash it came to me: "Why, there's a principle to be applied—a means of feeding oil to furnaces with perfect safety; also with even distribution all along the furnace breadth. This involves a new invention—something for defence of what I have already. Here is my gift—better than charity." I carried home an automatic valve for keeping fluid-levels and very soon devised a gauge, a feeding cylinder and, after one experiment, an oil distributor—a sort of burning table capable of giving equal heat along the furnace width, by means of natural draft and well restrained supply.

Ideal—theoretical of course, as all inventions are till put to proof— certain to cost hard work and anxious thought; no less a gift of price. I so accepted it.

"When Ajax strives some rock's vast weight to throw," he dare not heed the shouting multitude. He plants firm feet, and takes deep breath with all his muscles tense, and so gets force to hurl. Deride me not for over-confidence in lifting weights. I stood between two worlds, and heard the higher voices rather than the lower. Beyond all inner doubt I had become aware of spirit-influence and spirit-aid. Whatever faith may be (I think its other name is knowledge) that I had for working capital, and that alone! And, strange to say, because of that I had the confidence of friends—sweeter than manna in the wilderness. I was not mocked.

373

Chiefest of all I had the confidence of Mr. Henry Kendall as a true inventor, certain to succeed if given time enough. "Wait for awhile," he said, "till Frank and John decide what they can do. You'll work the better for a time of rest." And either he or Jane provided means for rest. In any case they thought and felt alike.

While I was waiting in New York, to keep in touch with workmen pending further orders, whether from Watertown or other-where, there came a letter, no way heralded except by Psychic vision. (Nothing came unheralded that meant approach of work!) One whom I had known as advertizer on the Western Rural—a bright attractive fellow—wrote to this effect:

"I learn that you have patented a vacuum-preserving process? Will it apply to meats? If so, would like to form a partnership. Will pay for all experiments. Am Southern agent for the Wilson Canning Company. They much desire a better process. No doubt about financial backing. If you should favor this, please visit me at Baltimore."

This letter I referred to Mr. Kendall. He advised: "Accept, and let the other matters wait." And this I did. Why not consult the spirits? Well, Mr. Kendall was a spirit. So was I, and so are you. Please bear in mind that we are spirits all—able to give and take. Moreover if we wish to know the time of day why ask a ouija board? You turn—and there's the clock! You walk abroad and ask your way of men; but should you stray among the fierce coyotes and find yourself alone, you call for higher help. Be sure that when a danger came, I called, and I was heard.

Why be endangered? That's to show. But anyway I went to Baltimore. During a week of pleasant household visiting, I made my host aware on what a slender plank I walked, across how deep a chasm! That no way daunted him. Oh, certainly he heard the Psychic story!—I were nor honest else nor fair with him, who meant to spend a little money—"much" he said, "if necessary, to bring about results." But then he wanted much. His wants increased like Falstaf's men in buckram. Half and half, he wanted equal undissolvable partnership. Not patent ownership—he stopped at that—but mastership of business, sole and absolute by contract—I to

374

invent, and he to rule, so share and share alike. I let him state his wants:

"All kinds of meats uncooked, in glass or tin" (since I had made my feeder, tin was quite available). Curious I had never thought of purifying meats by vacuum and cooking afterwards; and that was well left out. "Green corn and oysters." "They are pledged," I said, "throughout New England."—"Well, for every other territory. Eggs, in the shell or out." Oh, he went far afield! He looked "before and after, and pined for what was not." And last of all, and most of all, he wanted fruits. I stopped him there. "The fruits are mine. No one on earth, but I, shall have the care of them."

"We might as well stop bargaining: I'll sign no document that doesn't give me fruits. And after all, where can you get the means to manage them?"

"Perhaps through something else. I mean to have a way of burning crude petroleum in furnaces. That would be something I could sell outright."

"That's the best of all. Grant me a partnership in that, and I'll give up the fruits."

"You can't believe in that! It isn't tested yet."

"Well, I believe in you at all events."

And so my "Automatic Safety Burner" proved a sure protector before it earned a name. A phantom, fiery blossom—out before its time!

"Now," said my host; "I'll draw the articles."

"Why not I?" In truth I thought about the Eighmie-Collins contract—a perfect document, accordant with the higher righteousness no less than common law. Would he submit to have a spirit lawyer? Would not Judge Evelyn adjudicate? It seemed I needed him; and yet he did not come.

I asked: "Why not employ a lawyer?"

"I'll pay no lawyer's fee. I can protect myself."

"And me, as well?"

"It's all one thing. We share and share alike."

"Will you insert a clause exacting justice to the factory-workers—women and children, equally with men?"

"With all my heart, and see it well enforced."

To pinch the poor would not have been a fault of his. In truth, I knew no fact to prove him capable of fraudulent intent. And yet a fact must be disclosed. This man had lately been the willing tool of swindlers, managing for them a certain "family paper." This was published as an advertizing vehicle for carrying on nefarious schemes and getting rich out of the common people. At last they dropped off, gorged! Moreover he had called on me to be its editor, because my name was known and meant respectability. That is what I missed because of spirit-guidance!

Yet here I was, by that same spirit-guidance about to touch a grimy palm, and so ally myself with one who might have stood behind the prison bars among his master-villains—had they been fairly caught. He had their gold about him yet. What! Tainted gold? Well, that is how you view it. I think that gold is good, however stamped;—well worthy to be scoured for sacred use! As for this man—obsessed and led astray—could any spirit guide him back to walk with honorable folk—enlist him as a raw recruit with honest soldiery? It seems that even Judge Evelyn, who wrote the righteous Crusade Documents and prophesied that I should have inventions, did not disdain to use, for godly purposes, ungodly gains. Whose is the image? Whose the superscription?—Lucifer's or God's?

My would-be partner spent two days and half a night preparing articles to bind me "fast in fate." That being done it proved, I woke at early dawn and found myself confronted with a Psychic vision. "Behold the lamb," one said, "prepared for sacrifice!" I saw the lamb. He stood before me, white and beautiful, and over him was flung a net of hempen rope lengthwise, across, tied fast at every intersection, never to be unwoven, clung the net,—and yet his feet were free. There was no master-knot to make the whole secure. And presently he walked away, the net slipped off, he disappeared, and not a priest of Baal could search him out.

Then said Judge Evelyn (mark me, I did not dream the words nor fancy them): "Sign what is brought to you without a protest."

So when my host that morning brought a lengthy document and read it out—not handing it to me for careful study—I took the pen and signed. "But wait," I said, "before you also sign; consider this; I am, as I have told you, guarded well. God gave me my inventions; none can plunder me of them. Severe as these agreements are for me, but keep them loyally and both of us will profit. Fail in honor, you will lose and I shall gain. Should that be so, do you consent to lose?"

"I do." And so he signed and so I waited orders: "Bring your appliances to Baltimore, and prove that you can put up oysters first, uncooked and well preserved." So I obeyed and spent two months about the work, nor failed to do it well. Meantime I visited the monstrous canneries that made a few (and these were men) inordinately rich, and kept nine thousand women-workers miserably poor;—alas! disreputable also, many people said, through lack of decent wage.

I promised God that I would wait His time, endure all labor, sacrifice all other hopes at need—oh, not to rescue fallen women only, but to prevent the fall. No doubt I swung too far away—"not by command, but by permission." I wanted none but women, first and last, to build all factories, to manage them with righteousness, to send out perfect foods, and reap the golden profits. A great monopoly? Well, not a "Safety Cage" by any means! How ran the Crusade Documents? Men were to be "the outward wall and bulwark of defense," women, "the ministering rulers of the mind and heart;" and both together, "asking and receiving counsel," were to work with "mutual interchange, not held in light esteem."

You see, these days I had to walk by lantern lights—just bright enough to serve for showing paths that ran along crevasses. Beware of avalanches when the sun is hot! Be slow and safe, even though you climb by night. So please you figure out my tropes as best you may.

My partner wanted avalanches—fortunes falling with a mighty rush no matter who went down. "And now," he said, "we'll test your scheme for burning oil. That may be something we can sell at once,—not wait for royalties."

It followed readily that, spite of recent Brooklyn laws forbidding oil as fuel, Hibbler and Dorrflinger contrived to let me use their designated furnace for a week—if I could keep it hot; and that without a possibility of profit to themselves. Let's make a note of it! And so when I had shaped my "fluid-level" apparatus hastily (a little feeding cylinder without, within a heavy perforated iron plate sunk in a shallow pan—oil entering underneath), I got the "Automatic Safety Burner" safe in place, one Sabbath day, and lighted up my fire. Five hundred men stood round agape, intent on learning how; and happily, when I arrived next day at seven o'clock, I found the furnace raging hot and all its fourteen glory holes in service; so throughout the week.

My partner sent his delegate, who walked about delightedly, and sent off telegrams: "Entire success!" "Still running splendidly and workmen satisfied!"

That's not to say that I was satisfied. Not even Tubal-Cain, I dare suppose, had kept his fires aglow without a smoke, nor Abraham at his altar—serving God with sacrifice! And as for mine—not being fitted out with any sort of blast—among the white-winged flames you saw the darker plumes that "didn't ought to be." But then the workmen claimed they wanted smoke—"it gave an oiliness and made the tools slip easier on the glass."

But all the same I understood that here was nothing to be bargained off as yet. My father always set his weights to make the best of cloth before the shuttles flew. If but my partner willed, I meant to have, before the selling time, a fire without a visible fume, and atomizing plates left clean as any lady's hand.

He telegraphed in haste: "Have brought preserving apparatus to Chicago. Bring your safety burner."

It seems a reasonable thing to say that any spirit, turning back to earth for worthy purposes, should seek out honest souls to further them; still, for comparison, a mountain stream must take the nearest channel. But then it has a blessed way of washing pebbles clean, and giving birds to drink, and feeding roots, and beautifying flowers. Be sure if spirits choose dishonest folk to help their plans, they know of some resultant good not otherwise to be.

Alas! My hope of rivaling Tubal-Cain! When I had fitted up a boiler—not without a blast-—and run the printing presses very well a week or two—but not without a smoke, my enterprising partner said: "It's time to advertise. They're wanting Burners everywhere. We'll manufacture them for sale at fifty dollars each—they'll cost no more than twenty. Thousands will send for them."

Something like this he talked, or made me understand; and much like this had been those other schemes of which I learned, that, years before, had brought in filthy script by sackfuls—used to found a Bank, to carry on a factory for canning beef, and, by an outside flicker it appeared, set fire to surfaces of crude petroleum tucked in among the bricks for furnace work. However, this one scheme was contravened by me, and laid aside.

Another took its place. I had my laboratory fitted up for tests on meat—uncooked. My partner interposed: "No use in canning meats uncooked; people don't want them so. The men I represent must have them cooked."

"Must have from us just what they've got already?—Besides, cooked meats are not included in the contract."

"What is the difference? They want another cooking process. They'll pay enormously."

"But why?"

"Because their patent isn't good for much. They had to compromise with Libby. He prosecuted them for putting up cooked meats, and they've agreed to help him prosecute infringers everywhere."

"Including me, perhaps?"

"But yours will be another process. Use your vacuum of course—that's covered by a patent; but give us what we want."

"Subject to prosecution? Our contract says that I'm to pay for all defense of patents. If none must cook but Libby and one other firm, how then shall I escape? My share would disappear—be swallowed up in law. I and my process both would be disgraced."

I took him in to see Judge Joshua Knickerbocker, to whom he made complaint: "You see, she isn't sharp. She doesn't understand that men in business must be sharp or fail." And yet he spoke with trepidation,—a generous man gone wrong, in need of pity!

"Let's see if we can find a better way"—so said the kindly judge. He turned to me: "Canned meats are very poor. Why not invent a better cooking process?"

Strange I had never thought of that! "A better cooking process;" and to be patented and made defensible? "I will!" and so we compromised.

Now this was done, and very speedily. My friend was back among his old associates, and I suppose they sharpened him the more—who sharpened him at first. But anyway, he caught the lines: "Your process? Where's your valid patent? Mine or anybody's!"

"Leave him with me," Judge Knickerbocker said: "Go home and rest."

So back I went to mother's little farm some eighty miles away (my oldest sister's, since my mother passed), and kept my "flower of Patience" well in bloom, through all the summer months. Then my advisor wrote: "Your partner grows ashamed. He gives the contract back and promises to make no further trouble." And even so the knotted ropes fell off; the lamb prepared for sacrifice escaped.

Don't be severe. He let me go. Let it be said that I have striven since then with one incalculably worse (may God assoilzie him!). But did I strive?—or did some angel, clad in golden mail, meet me and press me back and stand on guard, that none should murder me. That way it seemed.

What had my whilom partner lost? Five hundred dollars possibly. What had he gained? A sense of shame worth infinitely more. He, too, was bound with cords, and when the net slipped off, roamed into honest paths and showed the blush of shame.

What had I lost? Nothing at all; not even faith in human nature,—much less faith in spirit-guardianship. What had I gained? A wider range of thought—a firmer grasp, a clearer sense of world-necessities; and, if you like, a novel way of burning oil in furnaces—not very well nor altogether ill, but absolutely safe, and yet to be an art. What else? Far more than I could realize as yet;—what men have vainly sought. A perfect mode of canning vacuum-treated food, cooked none too much, and absolutely pure.

One thing I had not gained,—a better apparatus—much to be desired for factory work. The one I used was like a safe, not usable unless you knew the combination. Therein was my defense: Easy to say: "My process! Anybody's process!" Impossible to make the boast hold good! And well for me that God withheld his crowning gift through many years! He gives—but not too soon!

A farce I've read assumes a vacuum-space in every brain. Conscious of one in mine, I went a-wandering in Chicago streets, and knew not what to do, or where to go in search of further help; till came my mother's word—or so it seemed: "Go to Diana Howland!" Oh, spirit-guardians! However great you are in angelhood, stand back at need, and let our spirit-mothers guide—who better know the way!

What does Robert Browning say?—Something like this: "You're on the sea; you're caught in storm; the masts have snapped, life boats are torn away, the crew washed overboard, you, only, left on deck. Then floats along some 'exquisite she-creature.' Never fear; leap, clutch, hold fast, and lo, she swims away, to leave you on the very rock you saw from far, and had no power to reach!"

Well then, Diana Howland (mother's friend, and mine because of her), took me from off my wreck and left me on the rock. That is to say she gave me maintenance, sent out my sample meats for exhibition, helped me to put up more, and when a company was organized for work, wrote down her name the first. (See now! That partner left my apparatus all in place ready for instant use! I much approved of him.)

True, this was breaking ground for tillage after many days should pass, but then it broke the ground. And more; it brought me those, who, by perpetual favor, made my work secure, which but for them had gone the way of wrack.

Now when the time arrived for ceding rights, after three months' preparatory drill, our company needed more experienced men; and two of us, well-fortified with samples, went in search of them. We found "The noblest Roman of them all" (meaning the princely packers!). He, seeing that I had the better process, offered capital and promised leadership—that being what we needed most of all.

Just then from out the blue there came a thunderbolt, or let us say, under the feet of all who dealt in meats there ran an earth-quake tremor. Our convert, Mr. Culbertson (of Culbertson & Blair), had closed his packing house, foreseeing this, and called a two year's halt. But most the canners suffered. People averred their goods were undesirable; dealers abroad had sent them back in shiploads, marked "unsalable." There seemed no possibility of building factories to launch our better meats, till more propitious times. "But take your choice," said Mr. Culbertson; "go on alone or wait three years for me. I will not fail you then." No—of himself he would not fail, but Death put out a hand and palsied him before the time expired. There was no choice;—and oh, the waiting years! What should I do with them?

I hid away in woods as wounded creatures do. I spent myself in futile supplications, winning no response,—and that was hard! No word of comfort came; for God is often silent when we speak, till we have uttered all. And still I mourned: "Six years have passed since I was made to see a home for hapless women; five years since I took up the cross in hope of saving them; but none are saved through me. When Lord? and when? and when? It seemed that I must die without my work; and yet no answer came. Not even a mystic symbol flashed before my brain; not even a Bible text, as oftentimes before, was pointed out by chapter, verse and book, assuring me that spirits understood. Had God and they forsaken me?—I had not lost my faith!—Under the trees I spoke my final word: "Give me some other work to save my soul alive. I'll ask no more for this, but trust and wait."

I rose up trembling, went my way and ere I reached my sister's gate, said out of trouble's depth (and knew not why I said): "Her path breaks off."

But what had come to me? I reached my room, took up my pencil, wrote and wrote and could not stop! My soul caught up that one whom Christ forgave, and held her fast and would not let her go till all was said. So came my "Heart of Sorrows" (Scribner's Magazine I think for 1878)! Had I not asked a spirit once if I must sacrifice the poet? Had he not answered me:—"Not for a thousand worlds!"

But had I been a poet? Much I had doubted it; but now my heart rejoiced. Not to my hurt had been the long unsinging years, and there were nine of them—soul-searching years, enriching years! I sang and I was glad!

AND so I hid in canons two full years to sing my songs, and no one troubled me. Not even spirits interposed between my verse and me, with any work of theirs, which truly I was most incompetent to do without their leadership. Still, now and then I was aware of them. They came and dropped a word or two, so giving me a sense of being watched with friendly sympathy.

Once, I remember, halting on a line needing a word of weight, some spirit said: "similitudes"—which I had never used nor chanced to think about. And once when I had set myself to use archaic words and knew of none that signified a place for beasts unclean, one brought me "stigh," which gave the sense and forged the rhyme as well. Most like he flung a baited hook in some old castle-moat, six hundred years gone by, to catch that one particular thing alive, whose froggy croak should make the verse come right. Oh, afterward I fished it out myself! but verily, just then, it would have been as far beyond my mental reach as Aldebaran, brightest of the Hyades—or any star you please.

One little word—no more. But mark! Ten thousand words make up the "Crusade Documents." They came in rank and file, each in his rightful place,—all keeping well together—none of them a-limp. They came, a swift, invading host—took soul and sense by storm, and so encamped.

Who summoned them from out the "vasty deep?" Not I, in very truth. At best I deal in no prodigious arts. Ten thousand words in forty hours! I've spent as long a time in choosing eight that pleased me thoroughly. But these I did not choose. They stand out plainly on the page to be accounted for,

"Subconsciousness?"

"Unconscious Cerebration?"

"Hypnotism?" "Self-hypnotism?"

Oh, I know the lingo! Always remember I am not a sleeping medium. These words came pulsing through my brain with all my faculties alert,—not any sense was dulled of all the five.

"Telepathy?" Yes, the celestial kind. The other sort exists no doubt. "Illuminative?" Well, you see a light—something to guess about. Is it a glow-worm possibly? A star-backed beetle wandering at will? And if it be a thought transferred, what then? Prove me a hundred words that came that way, from conscious human mind to human mind! Meantime, one seems to say: "I am a disembodied spirit. Once I lived on earth. I turn again, and, out of all good will, I bring you something that you seem to need for social governance." And, speaking so, transmits to you, through me, if so you please, ten thousand words, not one of which comes lagging in all out of place. Moreover, not to practise mysteries, he tells you first and last: "My name on earth was Evelyn—I was a judge in Liverpool." Why should you say "He lies! He cheats! He tricks! He works by hypnotism; he sends his thoughts from far, and makes this woman write them out for him?"—he being yet on earth.

And, by the way, will any living man declare to you: "I thought these very thoughts and used these very substantives in 1872; and here's a manuscript to show for it?" And if indeed it happened so, before the year was out it all appeared in print—my host the publisher! Where then was this mysterious personage who should have claimed the whole?

Never suppose that during these two rhythmic years, I willingly forewent my mission-work. That was an underwave, a counter current—drift of sunken thoughts, whichever way I rowed. I never set a sail to catch the lightest wind, unmindful of the deeps wherein my soul had plunged, and yet must plunge again.

How could I choose but weep? For all this while, it had not yet been given me to point to any soul and say: "This one escaped from hell because of me."

"In England no one lives by verse that lives," so Mrs. Browning writes; and even in rich America to-day, who wholly lives by that? Did Lanier—even who sang: "Into the woods my Master came,"—the most heart-breaking, beautiful, unmortal lyric of the Christ that ever moved the lips of mortal man?

Did Whittier have a bank account before his sixtieth year?

Still, now and then, one finds a favoring editor as I in Dr. J. G. Holland—heart of gold, and counted friend as well. So having funds and, further still, a book to show for bargaining, I issued forth and dared the world again. This time I saw no way of climbing mountain-paths (and crossing dread crevasses possibly)! I took the lower road. That means that nothing seemed within my reach except to burn petroleum. This others did in other ways than mine; but that was not for me to stumble over. A "petroleuse" among the "petroleurs"—why not?' To tell the truth I had a pledge to keep. There was a psychic contract made in 1875 between my spirit-guardian and myself;—not written out but sanctioned, ratified and held by both to be inviolable! Suppose we dare to say a partnership. Mind you, I had not lighted yet the torch that fired my furnace of the glory-holes. That one of us who had the gift of prophecy as I had verified, thought best to futurize. And first he said: "The ground that you are standing on is very rich." I saw the gold beneath, but could not see a way of getting it. No less he added this: "When you achieve an excellent way of heating furnaces, that will be yours to sell. I ask for half the price. Reclaim for me 'The Crusade Documents' and organize a host for goodwill purposes. The other half be yours, to keep or give away at will. Do you consent?"

And then and there we entered into partnership—not yet dissolved. You know I cannot tell a part unless I tell the whole, if that be Psychic history; or otherwise you see but half the shield, and miss the true device.

I took the lower road. No one compelled and no one lured me on; but I was not alone. At every turn I felt a guiding touch, and I suppose my silent partner knew my whereabouts and all I planned to do. It came to me that I must write to Dr. Barr, of Titusville, where Drake first drilled for oil. He proffered hospitality at once, and spoke of introductions. That sufficed for promise. True, I was very sick at Margaret's. She grieved: "I see no hope but you must die; and yet you talk of leaving me; you even talk of work. I beg you

386

not to go." I held her in my heart of hearts and yet I would not yield. "Margaret," I said, "I do believe that God has called. As for my health; He knows how frail I am. He has His remedies. I trust in Him."

Now, out of all this world, one man in Titusville—an excellent "magnetic healer," if you please—had begged a tank, borrowed a boiler, guessed a way of using compressed air, and started up a Cure,—not knowing patents were prohibitive. And lo, you, on the second day I breathed again my double atmosphere, and laughed at threat of Death! This Cure was just about to fail disastrously. Some wanton enemy averred that whosoever took the novel baths was pretty sure to die—as witness many done to death in Buffalo! Moreover, Dr. Stone, of Rochester, who held the patent-right, had heard and written word that he was coming on to close the little place at once, and sue for damages.

Ah, well, the pen is mightier than the sword! Myself a Buffalo patient—who could nail the lies as well as I! and so I took the daily paper quite by storm, till sick folks hurried in. When Dr. Stone came on he made an advertising pamphlet of my articles for permanent use, allowed the Cure, and formed a partnership. The work went on.

And all within a month myself was saved—a dying baby brought to life, a crazed asthmatic kept from suicide, converted patients boasting better health, and furthermore (appreciate the climax), under the little boiler, safely bricked in place, an "Automatic Safety Burner" sent the gauge up to the highest point permissible, and no one saw a smoke! Safe? Part of the time I burned benzine to prove it so! And Economical?—Saved fuel by a third! Moreover Colonel Roberts—great authority!—declared that he had melted platinum with no more fervent fire.

That may have been; but take away your boiler (water lined) construct instead an arch of brick and melt—first thing of all—your burner plates! In that case what to do but keep your principle and change your apparatus,—get the full broad, upward-flying blaze by other means and fuse your metals happily? All that might happen after many years. Meantime I kept the plates. They warped in time— nothing to worry over, easy to exchange. But no "aerial bridges" could span the gap between a twelve-horse boiler and a smelting furnace! Piers were yet to build, ere any soul could cross.

What has all this to do with Psychic mysteries. I cry you mercy! Everything to me—who deal in them. To burn crude oil the better way, the way beyond all other ways, because a master-thought, because a master-mind was moving me (always with my consent), to pass beyond my sphere. Can you suppose I had proclivity to such pursuits? To crawl through furnace doors, devise my baffles, set my bricks and smear myself with clay, emerge and like a goblin of the underworld, stand close and feed the flames—rather than gather flowers? (The hills were sweet with them.)

At least, I loved my fire. By means of that I hoped to forge the swords my Captain-general needed for the host—Crusaders, all of them, equipped for holy war! Had not Judge Evelyn asked for half the price? Come! Let us toil and moil; or otherwise how can there be a price? And, by the way, if you are prone to skip the while you read, you'll often lose the sense and think it isn't there. Please don't!

Even before I got my smokeless fire, a man who hailed from Philadelphia, proposed a partnership. Not to decry the business enterprise of men within the oil-producing belts, before all other lures they heed the lure of oil. A burner meant to them something to use in drilling wells and pumping them—no more. This man had larger thoughts—too large it proved; but I accepted him for what he seemed—a generous gentleman whom one could trust. That is a way of mine.

I sat me down to study out agreements by myself, if possible. My spirit-partner had not interfered till now; but, in a breathing space, he came and just as he had written "Crusade Documents" and Collins-Eighmie contracts, so he held me thrall and wrote again, plain word by word, and not a phrase amiss.

A friend, not knowing all, adjured me: "Do not trust yourself. You need an able lawyer. Let me see to that." He took the document away to be revised or wholly changed perhaps; but came back wondering: "It can't be altered in the least. The lawyer says it's 'boss.'" To this my new associate agreed, and so we signed, and even so I set myself to be obedient,—his part to furnish funds and carry on exploiting, mine to do the furnace work and bide results.

And first he sent me off to Buffalo to study furnace-work; then wrote that I must go to Jamestown for the holidays and try a hundred horse-power boiler—just to see! And there I found my burners—much enlarged to furnish breadth, was told that I could have six days for installation, and experiment during their idle time. In fact they started up the Mills on my account—a mighty Corliss engine running many looms a day for perfect test. "Plenty of steam," "the heat intense"—"the Burner safe in all respects." So ran the testimonials—a lot of them.

But not for permanent use: Partly because so great a furnace needed study; but chiefly, as it seemed, because the transportation rates on oil were made prohibitive save to the Standard Company (which didn't care for anybody's needs except its own, as all the world has learned).

Still, here was evidence of weight. Moreover, Mr. Hall, the manager—son of the owner—seemed inspired with singular faith. He said that he had studied under Bunsen when in Heidelberg, and knew I had the quality of fire that might apply to metallurgical work. He charged me not to be content with limited success, however hard the task.

So much for that! But now my partner wrote that I must stay and hunt up capital, and that was rather queer. I halted long enough to have a fit of sickness due to overwork, then sent him on a helper. Back he came: "Your partner says that running furnaces is not a work for women anyway. So you can stay away; we'll manage it ourselves."

That message took me back to Titusville. Men stopped me in the streets: "What does this mean? Have you sold out? Your partner says he owns the Burner—drops your name and substitutes his own."

Well, so it was. And there was nothing left to do but take mine own again. "A perfect contract," so the lawyer said: "It leaves you wholly free."—And so my "courteous gentleman" slipped out—and well for me!

We had a Burners' tournament in March, at Eaton's Boiler Works (Oil City, near at hand),—the best and worst, in rivalry with mine; and since comparative evaporations by the hour, were sixty gallons only on their part to ninety on my own, a price was offered me;—not for the use alone but for the patent. Just about enough, I estimate, to send two good Crusaders off to Palestine. But what about the Host? Impossible to disregard my spirit-partner's rights; and I refused to sell.

So while Jarecki manufactured apparatus, I made myself a very small promoter,—putting burners in among the Bradford hills, and showing drillers how to manage them. So for a year perhaps; till certain men of worth proposed to organize a Company, getting Jarecki's leave as well as mine. "Wait patiently," they said; "We'll be a little slow, but take the time for rest."

"For rest?" God would not have it so. Look you! Eight thousand people lived in Bradford; thousands more who centered there, were drilling thereabouts; churches a-plenty; money in abundance; temperance lectures carried on four months all nights, at heavy cost; six thousand dollars at the close of them contributed for "Law and Order;" eloquent McCabe, who wanted churches built for mining men and gambling pioneers a long way off, took in eight thousand dollars with a single talk; two thousand followed for a Boot-black's Home (for there were twenty boot-blacks needing guardianship) and some proposed to raise twelve thousand more for a gymnasium. "Young men must be amused to keep them safe," they said.

Meantime eight hundred women walked the streets, and herded on the "Island." One had dared to ask for help; and certain lovely women—borrowing sixty dollars—had sent her to a Magdalen asylum. Only one!

They drew me in to help them earn it back by writing up the case;—someone sent in a dollar! Help for all—except for fallen women! Still we earned the sum another way. Moreover with a song sent out for sale on "Fireman's Day" I earned a further sum. We

390

organized for work, and took that money for a nucleus, if any other came. Before a day had passed I learned of one who wanted to escape; and so began my work!

About that time there was a general raid of evil haunts. Men walked away unchallenged;—women were marched to Court and fined. That made the city rich. It may have made the mayor popular; but one—not having funds to pay her fine, committed suicide.

Some four of us—one was a clergyman—offered to those who found the means for burial (poor sinners all of them!), a Christian funeral,—singing and talk and prayer. That pleased them well, and one of special note drew near to me and pleaded: "Come and visit us. We're bad; but not so bad as people think."

Now one who had a reputable home and thought herself a Christian said to me: "I'll help not one of them! They're where they chose to be, and let them stay." Ah, they—were "not so bad!" For if I led one out the others cheered her on: "You're doing right. You're very fortunate." Sometimes they wept; and always when they saw me, asked: "Is Jennie doing well?" "Is Effie happy?" "Where is Fannie, now?" Someway they loved each other—there was no treachery among them!—"Not so bad!"

God gave me twelve that year, and none of them went back. Five I took to Quaker Magdalen Asylums, where they were qualified to live; two went to hospitals, came out and earned their bread by honest toil; two were comfortably married; two went home rejoicing—welcomed happily; and one—the worst of all, grown murderous with drugs and alcohol, was taken by her father and myself (by her desire), to Kirkbride's Home for the Insane. "A hopeless case," he said. "We only take her in because of you"—and in a year doctors were training her to be a nurse! Not savable?

I think of all the sinners Christ forgave, the one most sweetly saved was Magdalen.

For these I had to beg—and that was hard. I could have saved two more with what the flowers had cost that made one church smell sweet on Sabbath days—as verily it ought, save at the cost of souls.

"Evil is wrought by want of thought As well as by want of heart."

And others would have come, could I have made a place for them. But these, at least, were mine, to have and hold throughout eternity!

But something more was done: I found that honest farmers' daughters drifting in to search for work, were often caught away! and so I moved to have a Working Woman's Home. And now I did not beg—the money came right easily. I merely entered offices, laid my subscription papers on the desk, conversed (since men preferred to talk) on—City government perhaps or nitro-glycerine, or, if they urged me, different ways of burning oil. (Most everyone had his particular way; and that explains in part, why mine was dragging so.) But by and bye, a hand would slip along, take up the pen, write down an honorable name: one hundred, fifty, twenty-five,—or, very seldom, ten.

And so some fifty women organized themselves for work. We got ourselves a charter and a house. I had to be the matron half-a-year; that was delight. Meantime the leaven spread. But as for me, I took the road again. A lady whom I never saw before, nor since, came with a gift: "You take no price for what you do, take this." With that and with my "Abigail Becker" for the "Century," I started east. For, after all the long delay where was my Company?

I walked in Boston—mortally alone—after one night of rest. Why seek a friend?—Why let the Kendalls know? I was aware of one who surely knew the way and I suppose he stopped me suddenly. He said—some spirit said: "Go up these stairs!" and I obeyed.

A gentleman who sat beside his desk, observed me through an open door, came out and asked me kindly: "Can I be of use?"—"Perhaps you can. I have a way of burning crude petroleum, and want it tried for iron work."

He wrote a name: "Go to my brother-in-law; he'll tell you what to do;" and that one said: "Go straight to Mr. Coffin."

I found a gentleman of seventy or more, I think a former iron-monger, long retired. He heard my story, looked me through and laughed: "You're very like those abolition women—friends of mine—

392

who faced the Boston mob when Harriet Martineau was here. No need to show your testimonials; I believe in you. I'd rather help than not; but understand I want no profit for myself. Just do your best; I'll ask for nothing more!"

He called an office boy: "Gogin went up the stairs awhile ago; tell him I wish to see him."

"Haven't you an idle furnace, Mr. Gogin? This lady has a way of burning oil. I want to see it tried. I'll bear the whole expense."

"Very well; we have an antiquated furnace, seldom fired, we'll let her use four weeks. No doubt our men will let her heat their iron—if she can. We can't attend to it. We're pledged to use the generating process."

Inwardly I laughed; and yet was sorry men could be so gulled. It cost them dear; but that is how we learn. At worst, they learned how not to burn petroleum, and that was much.

And so, all insignificance, I wound my way among the "generators," "super-heaters," oil-pumps, pipes and things, to take my place well out of sight, with privilege to do exactly as I pleased. Now this was at the Norway Rolling Mills. I had to bring wrought iron up to welding heat, and this I did, not stinting oil nor moderating blasts; and so in some few hours my burner plates began to melt. There was no remedy except to simulate a boiler surface, water-lined, just over them; no new device it seemed, and yet my own. That answered very well. I doubt if such a tempered heat had melted platinum. The heated iron welded perfectly.

Three things remained to do (not that I thought of doing them): First, throw away the burner-plates; then throw away the water arch; and then, still with my automatic feed (improved), contrive a better way of getting in the oil—with just the same effect of equal distribution. So get your furnace roofed aright and—melt your platinum! But that was but a dream as yet.

Well, anyway, a group of expert gentlemen—superintendents, furnace-builders and the like, came visiting, at Mr. Coffin's call, and they agreed that with a curving roof, a lower "velvetry" and smaller throat, I'd use a deal less oil and do a third more work. It followed that the Bay State Company asked for a conference, and, very fairly, undertook to carry on all further tests, maintaining me as well, -rind this, until three several superintendents—two from other mills, should say the trial had been fair and full. For this the Company was granted right and use "in any of its mills;" leaving all other rights to me. A very liberal contract, such as Judge Evelyn himself might well approve.

Robert H. Morrison, the Company's man of men through forty years, instructed me in furnace craft—greatly to my advantage afterward. But just as he and I set out to build—my part the burning chamber—his the shell—he sank and passed away. That stopped all work for many weeks. Then, unexpectedly, disasters came, so that the company failed.

Now I have told these happenings because they undeniably revert to Psychic facts. You will remember those;—the urgent prayer at dawn of day, the call for "something more," the answer, promising a gift before the day should end, the gift made evident in Boston Public Gardens; guidance here and there; till finally a spirit-voice directed me: That way I found the only man in Boston-town, no doubt, who would not fail to help. And I suppose that spirits knew of him long time before; nor doubt but he has met Judge Evelyn, and been repaid.

"But then," you ask, "why wait so long in Bradford?" I'll answer that among my happy twelve in Paradise.

And, after all, there is a Psychic part to every story,—yours no less than mine. Suppose you want a picture true to life;—well there's your negative! And dark is light and light is very dark. But bring your skilled photographer and all is clear. Why curtain off the sun?

Six years adrift: Once more you wonder why. God's ways are otherwise than ours.

"Deep in unfathomable mines,

Of never failing skill He treasures up His bright designs And works His sovereign will."

And what are we that we should make demands?—"Hasten our times and seasons! Give us all we need with little cost to us!" He will not have it so. Slow step by step we cross the deserts, creep through mountain fastnesses, climb rugged crags, and stand at gaze to see the great sun lifting up his head. He keeps God's time, not ours!

Six years and little done—or much! "Gather the waters of the lower pool," Isaiah saith. We'll gauge them afterward.

Something was done. I drifted west to Cleveland, where my brother William lived, for I was ill, and much in need of rest. Chancing to see an Iron Trade Review, I found my furnace work had been reported handsomely. Calling to render thanks, I found a gate of entrance open wide, and so I wrote (for pay) some general articles on burning oil—which had a circulation;—one was copied as authority in England. To tell the truth the matter was so little understood, most any word would be "authority"—and why not mine?

It followed that I puddled iron for a day, with very good results. This would have brought a partnership, only the mills were burned, and business crippled. It brought me calls from California, but I was much afraid of heavy oil—the only kind they had—and this I let them know; but still they urged. My burning plates were atomizers of themselves—give them sufficient heat, but had their limits—proved inadequate below a certain gravity. Something must be improved. This troubled me.

The woods are always like the gates of Heaven to me. I slipped away in search of them. Perhaps I feared, in spite of all, lest I should lose my faith. As one whose feet are planted in the sea, I felt the buffeting of waves, and cried aloud for help. I would not be denied.

With that, one came and spoke: Though what he said I need not wholly tell, I felt that I was "comforted with flagons"—still I taste the draught. At last the spirit spoke of earthly things; and I suppose no spirit is too great to know of them, if he but knows of us. Not to exalt unduly, this had been a business man on earth, and knew the way of it. And so to give me cheer he added this: "The time will come when you shall see a way to burn the heaviest oil that can be made to flow." I thought: "At worst, that isn't tar!"—and drew the line at that:—so pledged myself to try whatever ranked above.

The man who pledged himself came from Los Angeles and met me in Chicago,—rather incidentally, it proved. He had two burners of his own on which to form a Company, but wanted mine as well, on which to found another Company, belike, when time should serve. Not quite aware of all, I did my part, at his expense, in testing Lima Oil—the heaviest I had tried—succeeding fairly well. At least, I ran De Tamble's eighty horse-power boiler for a month with watered stuff just piped from out the wells, and used, by scientific test, two barrels and a half against a ton of coal, though not without some carbon on the plates. No doubt my partner would have kept his word but for the double load. He had to be released. But since I claim a Psychic origin for all this toil of mine, it seems permissible to say that for economy my own results have never been approached. At least they were not when the Navy "Liquid Fuel Board," at government expense—using the best among the atomizing burners, tested them for many months, one after one. I had its thanks for those reviews of its report I published in "Steam-Engineering" and "The Engineer;" so I am well-informed.

But now my furnace work had caught attention. By and bye I found myself upon the verge of getting rich. Merely to do again what I had done before, I should have had a company with half-a-million stock—I being given half, and, for a bonus, just five thousand dollars cash in hand. It wasn't I who framed that liberal contract be assured, nor yet my "silent partner." Alack! Just on the point of "firing up," my visible partner lost his all upon the Stock Exchange; and so the scheme fell through. But well it did! For "fuel oil" came into use,— sixteen degrees of gravity too low for me. It would have loaded well my burning plates with carbon. Down went my hands. I dropped the work forthwith. Till faith should yoke itself with circumstance, the hindered ark must wait!

"But how about that spirit-promise—'You shall see a way?'" Oh, I suppose the waters of the "lower pool" had not been "gathered up." The rains were not in season. My other work had waited very long, and why not this? All things must take their turn.

But now two hands caught mine; and Orrington and Mary Foster—marvelously kind, and not devoid of faith—said: I This is too hard for you. Come rest with us." Now these were part and parcel of the Canning Company, that sought to be ten years before, when came the business crash that stopped such work; and these were loyal—they believed in me. God sends me friends whenever there is need—incarnate or discarnate all is one; and if at last He sends me enemies, they serve who would have harmed! Dark threads with light, to make the lovely pattern evident; and not a shade too deep!

We'll say the King has need of tapestry. Make haste—He is the King! Set up your loom, stretch on your warp, spin out your many colored threads for woof;—But wait till Raphael comes to paint the picture clear for copying;—then ah, be slow! Set every stitch aright, (He is the King).

You who have watched my weaving cannot fail to know how all impossible it would have been, save that a master-weaver guided all. Do not forget that, only for a psychic vision—not to be effaced— there would have been no loom, no hope, no inspiration, no desire, no courage made invincible by faith. "So to be exercised therewith" makes great the soul for time and for eternity. God spare us idleness.

So, being loosed from bonds, and fortified by sympathy,—also not wholly destitute (My "Kansas Bird Songs" brought a tidy sum), I left the sunken road. Through all those years of valley-wandering, if I but lifted up my eyes, there stood my cross upon the mountain top! "Carry the burden till you reach the cross!" So one had said, and fain would I have climbed, save for the spirit-hands that held me fast. But now they let me go. What though the rocks were sharp and feet must bleed? What though the mountain lion lurked, and one must guard the steps from pit and sheer descent? Still one must climb, or die of grief and shame. The vision had its way with me! Always I sought the heights.

Facts that appeal to sense must have their place in every Psychic history; and some, I needs must tell about, were fearsome things. But, after all, nothing can be without divine consent; and though a

397

sword rise up from out the deep, behold a lifting arm. "Clothed in white samite, mystic, wonderful," and have no fear.

Lo, these be spirit-mysteries! Now let us drop to sordid facts—subject to transmutation, gold for lead—if any have the art.

And first: One of our whilom company for canning meats, not lacking faith, had kept my apparatus safe through all these years. True, patents all had lapsed, but better ones might be in lieu of them and all the work be saved. Meantime, three heads of packing houses, Pond and Underwood and Fowler much befriended me. And let me say that I have been in touch with all the greater firms, nor missed a courtesy nor heard a doubting word. True, none of them could drop their long-established ways, their great equipments costing many millions, even to get a better canning process; moreover, I was well aware that on my side that could not be allowed; but I may reckon them as friends (not enemies in any case) and give them thanks.

And now I had a room accorded me in Fowler's monster building (not a cannery); and did the things I would, aided by his advice, because he knew the market well and what was needed for the finer trade. He sent me to the chilling rooms, to make selection when and how I pleased.

The keeper roared at me: "Nobody puts up meats in such a state; you'll have them ruined in the cans." No less they kept. We had the experts in, who brought those other goods to make comparison. Mine answered for themselves. No one has ever yet disputed their superiority.

So much for education! Always something more to learn; but here was quite enough, so men averred, to found a business on and look for rich returns. At least I had my cooking-process well in hand.

Undoubtedly our worldly rush and roar affright the birds; at best, who hears them sing? And how was I—so wrapped about with noise—to hear a spirit voice proclaiming good or ill? Not given to tremors, prone to see the brighter side and live by faith; yet I arose one morning, all depressed: "Disaster comes!" And through the day I walked as in a cloud. "Disaster comes and there is no escape." Till suddenly I dropped upon my knees: "Lord, let disaster come to me—

myself, but let it aid my work!" Now notice: It was I who spoke of sacrifice; no one exacted it. At once the sky came clear. I rose up well content. "Let come what will, so I may do my work." And I suppose that spirits knew just what would come and might have hindered it! Nay, possibly they planned: "If this one thing be brought about, her work and ours may prosper finally, however, long the time. But let her first consent—nay, let her ask!"

Do you remember how Judge Evelyn said in 1873: "Can you endure? If flesh and spirit prove too weak.... resign your chosen work. I shall myself pronounce you free from guilt?" And how he showed me in a vision wonderful, my future self and what would happen many years thereafter? How I answered him: "Accept my service; even so, I want my work?" And praying to a higher One than he, implored again: "Master, I want my work?"

No need to ask again: "Can you endure?" The time was close at hand , and once again I said: "Accept all sacrifice, but let me keep my work."

Within an hour, I said to Lafa Jones (my nephew who assisted me in certain tests), "Lets go a-visiting." And I was moved to go where I had never been, nor ever dreamed of going. We climbed an outer stair—not quite so high as Jacob's ladder—spent a merry hour and said: "Goodnight."

Right from the top I fell! And Lafa picked me up a crippled creature—not "a thing of shreds and patches" happily, but sure to carry crutches quite two years—and be a spectacle! (You should have seen policemen follow me along the streets, when I emerged—frail as a cyclamen!)

"What was the use?" Why, don't you see! It took me to the Woman's Temperance Hospital, founded by banker Hobbes and wife; and there I met with Mary Allen West, the "Union Signal" editor (who died a martyr in a year or so). Within two months, because of her, in chief, and other women-souls, was brought about a Woman's Canning Company for which I long had prayed—not being worldly wise.

Sometimes God answers prayers

399

"And thrusts the thing we asked for in our face—

A Gauntlet with a gift in it."

Suppose the gauntlet buffet you,—what then? Be patient; take the gift; and render thanks for all in spite of buffetings.

This company was organized upon the basis of a newly granted process-patent-claim, indubitably mine;—we'll say, food-products vacuum-prepared and moderately cooked. The contract granted right of use, chiefly exclusive, save on heavy meats—not to be canned by lesser folk than slaughterers.

So with a hundred thousand capital stock and eighteen hundred dollars cash (myself as business manager) our Archer Avenue factory opened up. And now, in lieu of transfers (cast aside except for bottling juice of grapes) I studied out retorts for larger work and had for certainty my secret valves—not to be shown till patented, and safe for steam or air or vacuum, year after year. So we were well equipped for enterprise.

Nothing so good as tongues, by way of meat; nothing so hard to get. Yet, by the grace of E. F. Robins (manager at Underwood's), we were assured of them in quantity. To these I added novelties— desserts and puddings not to be preserved by other methods; meaning to follow on with many more. So far, we aimed to be monopolists. Who casts the stone?

But suddenly (please let me talk in tropes!)—our fragile boat, with a white sail or two, just putting out to sea, and not a cloud in sight, rocked in a little squall. You've heard of them; but how they start and how they die away, not even Captain Marryatt could guess. And through the pother, women's voices rose—

"And then unto a hoarser murmur grew."

"Stop now! Go back to shore; load in the heavy meats! Why not be slaughterers? This woman has defrauded us. We'll have our heavy meats with all the rest, or sink the boat."

There! Have I kept the metaphor intact?—

But anyway our President and Secretary held us with a grip week after week;—the factory deserted, Lafa and I out skirmishing for bread (to starve inventors—that's the good old way!). Till many lawyers said: "We can't compel; you have enormous interests already—be content. But organize anew, increase your stock tenfold and so get rich."

And that explains how very rich we came to be after a time—alas! Till all men heard of us! Would I could follow comedy with comedy; but seas are dangerous, skippers and mates not always competent, and winds blow high. To tell the truth I thought about "The Crusade Documents" and wished them lashed aboard,—for anchor possibly in case of wreck.

Now being "wise as wise," I voted in for President that one whom others chose (as I had done before); and made my humble self just one of seven directors—only a business manager, intent on running factories and selling goods. Pray what would you have done? Kept all the power?

You think that spirits should have guarded me? Why, let us say they did. Not shrieking out: "Avoid the hunter's pit!" "Keep to the chamois track!" "Escape the avalanche!" It seems I did them all—but not of human wit; for these, as mountain guides, went on before or followed me along my pre-determined way; and when my slender alpenstock was sure to break, and strength and skill might not avail, why there they were to save! I was the climber—they the rescuers. And always, understand, there was no other way but up the crags and all along the clefts!

Straightway, I charged our lady-officers: "This is to be a woman's industry. No man will vote our stock, transact our business, keep our books, pronounce on women's wages, supervise our factories. Give men whatever work is suitable, but keep the governing power. This is a business training school for working women—you with all the rest. Here is a mission; let it be fulfilled." All this they understood. They pledged themselves; they laughed for joy of it!

Now, being well at work, with orders coming in, I sent a box of tongues to Thurber-Whyland Company, New York—declared to be

401

the greatest jobbers on the continent. Straight came their most amazing order: "Twenty-four thousand cases wanted soon as possible"—almost six hundred thousand cans! And we, with two retorts, were putting up, say possibly four hundred cans a day, and selling them in haste to can the more. We had not advertised our stock, save in a casual way. I did not mean we should, till firmly placed beyond all peradventure. Women must never say that they had risked—and lost. So there was little in the Treasury.

Meantime, not three months well at work, we paid our bills, and throve, and won respect.

About those days our president came in with what she thought was very cheering news. A group of gentlemen would pledge themselves to put in eighty thousand dollars, manage our affairs without our help, enlarge our factories to meet demands, take every burden off, and give us half the profits. Moreover they were honest men of large affairs. What better could we do?

Was this disloyalty in her? I would not think it so. You thrust a rod in water—how it seems to bend! And yet you call it straight. I trusted her, and trusted all alike—chiefly because I loved.

"A little leaven leaveneth the lump." Fermenting elements, once brought in play, produced results. To get the help of men and not invalidate our contract—theirs and mine—became a moving motive. It may as well be owned that I was frozen out from counsel,—these were governing, and I was nought. Why, that was what myself had chosen! I to give the service, they to have the mastership;—too late to lift the voice!

At last, before the year was out, they found a way. It did not seem the way of wickedness to them, nor yet to me; and though I hated it, when all the others gave consent—rather than be a quarreler—I answered "Aye." So far I share the guilt.

I make the story short as possible. It must be told; for even so my Woman's Company, so long desired, so ardently beloved, met with untimely death. We'll talk with bated breath.

Two men were pledged to advertise our stock at heavy cost to them—and none to us: To sell at par, to give us half-returns until we had enough for honest enterprise, and then to drop away and leave all further benefits with us. It sounded fair—if one must deal in stocks. A woman's mind might take it in, and not be over-taxed,—unless indeed it chanced to effervesce and "work like madness in the brain." I pray you make excuse. Even a corporation meant to be an honest one may have its underself; and notice how a stream that had a mountain source, will flow discolored past your very door and find a stagnant marsh. The springs of God abound; but let us drain our bogs.

So drop to common talk. Now it was thought worthwhile to start a country factory far North, where people urged and furnished means. This was to give us what the City lacked—pure produce, poultry, eggs for puddings—whatsoever served; and having given assent to what our officers desired, I sped away to find the place and get the building planned.

When all was fitted up and work about to start, our governing directors came and stayed a week, not to report their acts, but supervise my own. Nothing they told of what was being done by way of advertising stock and selling it. Nothing I asked—and I was far away from guessing out the truth. Instead, I set myself to make them understand my part of it; for this was manufacture,—these must learn. I couldn't always hobble around and run retorts to teach our working girls; someone must be prepared to take my place. I would have put the three in pinafores to get my way. This is to let you know how dread a thing was I,—how all compact of tyranny.

Come, let us hurry on! Yet wait a moment! Months before this time when all was roseate enough to give these others cheer and give me happy thoughts (howbeit "A storm was coming but the woods were still"), a something stronger than myself got hold of me, and drew me unto shade. It seemed there was no sun! I should have been afraid, but fear and faith are grown from different soils. There in the dark alone, I leaned on faith.

And first I prayed for what I wanted first, because it seemed that all I most desired must follow after that,—Wealth for my Woman's

403

Company! Right in the ear of Heaven, I called for gold, much gold—and felt no shame! Why, honest gold, of course! I dreamed of nothing else.

One of an old religion (is there a young religion?), said to me one time: "God and the holy angels love the sight of gold." But then it must be gold thrice purified—right from the crucible! And that is hard to get.

And now I think that God would have us pray with faith, even out of ignorance,—He, out of wisdom, granting what we ask, to show a better way. Never suppose that we, who have our Psychic visions, always understand their ultimate significance. Such have their lights and shades; we have to study them,—to guess them out in part, albeit we somewhat see.

Now I was shown a hill but little clothed with verdure. "That," I thought, "is ours. It needs the rain." So far I understood. And then I saw—thrust up along the side to reach the crest, an iron pipe—not small—and out of it abundant water spouted, flooding all. And this was forced,

I knew, from far below; for how could water rise beyond its source by natural means.

Then when the flow had ceased, I looked for flowers, but there was nothing to be seen, save just a barren hill, the little verdure washed away—a sodden slope not worth a ploughman's hire.

One time—and that was very long before—my spirit-guardian, Dr. Andrews, gently chided me for want of trust. "You lack perception of your own perceptions." That puzzled me; and yet the man born blind, after the miracle saw men as trees, and we, with Psychic eyes half-opened, cannot claim to see inerrably. As to this vision of the hill and spouting pipe, it seems I should have fully understood; and yet my eyes were holden. When I looked for more and nothing came (remember, nothing comes because you will it so) I thought: "At least, the lower lands will be enriched,"—so made myself content. And after all, the lower lands must yield the heavy crops, and not the hills. Don't sow the seeds too high.

Mind you, our advertising agents scattered ours from sea to sea; good ground or fallow, marsh or stony places—still the sowers sowed!

After some weeks—two months or so—I chanced (but is there any chance?) to catch a paper up,—and so I read at last what took me hurrying home. Then by another chance—those governing directors being out of sight—one who was keeping books delivered me a letter, sent astray at first and sent astray again, not to the advertisers but to us.

"I think," she said, "it's time for you to know."

A letter headed by a single truth; unjoint the rest—you got the lies, all capable of propagation; lies, on lies! This was the style of it.

"A Woman's Company for working women—started by a woman. Twenty-five dollar shares, all owned and voted on by women only!" (Men had slithered in; their names were on the books!). "Make haste and buy before a total sale. Just fifteen hundred dollars builds a factory! Select a site and send the money on; we'll do the rest. We've set our mark; there'll be a thousand factories within a year." (Only one crippled woman capable of starting them.)

"No one so poor but she may buy a share and look for dividends! Immense returns!"

So widows, washer-women, working girls, were being tricked; and every lying letter (thousands on the wing) was made to bear our very signatures and seal!—my name indorsing all. Friends, this was horrible. Nothing in all the world for me to do but stop this mighty enginery—this windmill-force that drained the valley brooks to wash all growing things from off this hill of ours—our very place of shame.

And so I hurled my puny self against these whirling vans,

"For women are Knights-errant to the last;

And if Cervantes had been greater still,

He had made his Don a Donna."

I brought no accusation, called no conference, but sought a lawyer out: "You organized us, save us. Stop these plunderers." So Aldrich,

405

(then United States attorney-general) with him arrested them—stuffed with ungodly gains;—eight thousand dollars in a single mail—with more and more to come; for what could stop the flow?

I let complaisance go and called Directors' meeting. Therein I took my rightful place for governance (sustained by Mr. Aldrich): "Haste in restitution—humble confession to investors; death if that be willed, but death with honor left."

That might have been, save for the death which might be waived aside and none of us desired. There still was hope. But then "upstarted Urgan, hideous dwarf," and who should say him "nay?"

"She signed him once, she signed him twice,

That lady was so brave,

The fouler grew his goblin hue,

The darker grew the cave!"

Truly he had a fearsome way withal,—the nostril smoked. Come, let's not be objurgatory! This was a human lawyer's underself—no less (alas, no more!). And yet he went among us like a raging fire. All things were given up to be devoured. "This woman—who is she to order you about? She owns no stock, she never asked for it. I kept it back for you. She had inventions—what of that? She gave them up; they're yours, see that you hold them fast."

"But who will teach us how to manage them?"

"Command her to instruct. If she refuse, I'll make it hot for her!"— He did for half a year! Meantime I sent instructions in by folios, being locked outside and "no admittance" written on the doors.

"But who will be our business manager and sell our goods?"

"I've hired a man for that."

"What! Must we pay two hundred dollars every month, instead of forty-five?"

"Well, yes;—a man you know! And haven't I secured you all the million stock, instead of half? Go on and sell."

Even so they did. And still the cry went out: "A Woman's Industry... .No man employed.... Inventor philanthropic—gives her stock." And still the hill was being drenched—the brooks were being drained.

Incredible?—But true. Along this very way, with fears, faint protests, futile tears, they followed him down to his underworld, and got the soot of it.

Not all of them. One strove to hold them back,—one clear of judgment, incorruptible as spirits are who know the way to Heaven. Her name was Lois Celley; let her be extolled. As for the other names—once written plain—the time is long, the ink has faded out.

I think,—most truly think, that in beyond God's temple gates, one stands with sprinkling hyssop, naming us by other names than these we bear on earth. There Urgan's very self, redeemed through grace, shall stand as fair a Knight as ever trod the sward. So let it be.

Through all these months—hurt nigh to death with treachery—I used to think about my rescued twelve, and long for love again. Those would have died for me; and these—it seemed that I must die because of them. They too shall be forgiven. Do I forgive? God knows! I dare not say.

Darkness that might be felt! But in the thick of it Judge Evelyn came—a viewless spirit, not a voiceless one. He made me understand that he had found a man yet on the earth, to be my faithful friend. Not one whom I had ever seen, but one who would not fail through all my mortal life to stand on guard and save my work and me. He said: "A man of honesty." So I was cheered; nor had I long to wait. Through nineteen years, this man he chose and sent me out to find—this Charles C. Linthicum, Solicitor—• has been my counsellor, my aid, my sure defense. And if I stand today, with both hands full of patent values five-fold greater than at first, that is because of him. No need to scour his armor for the tournament. It shines—the KING may see.

As to the Woman's Company, so caught and harnessed in and whirled away, why tell the worst? I would not if I could. But being down at last among those trampling hoofs, strong hands got hold of me and dragged me out whether I chose or no;—clean hands of honorable men. Said one of them: "We will not see you killed." So I escaped. Alas! "On went the chariot;" even the downward way, spite of attempts to guide. Some two years after that the law reached out, flung wide the treasury door, and proved its emptiness. Widows and washer-women, working girls and men alike despoiled .... For these I well believe God has his coin of recompense.

For me, being released and safe, I took my work in hand, and would have staggered on—did stagger on until I knew of Death not far away. But while I mused: "Here is no room for him; God will not let me die;" a spirit came—God's harbinger of Life. He showed an open grave, myself upon the brink. He said: "Step in if so you choose,—none shall condemn; or turn aside and pass."

How turn aside, was past my power to guess; not past my power to will. For how could I be recreant who had so great a trust?

Now, all this while, four sisters would have cherished me; and one of these, just now, contrived a way to save. I let them have their will. Nine years—so low had sunk the springs of life—I lived because I would, and waited for the sun and wind and prairie-quietude to do their healing work. For Death, however strong, is not so strong as Faith—whose other name is Prophecy. I knew God's time would come.

No doubt His angels prophesied of us, or ever seas were gathered up and land went dry. His older angels prophesied of them, while yet the suns were mist. And do you scorn our faith? Let be! We also prophesy of lesser things. We follow on—we haste. "Much people" know of us "in Heaven," We need not be ashamed.

FOUNTAINS OF DESIRE

THROUGH all those idle years only to think about my vanished work would shake me to the heart. I dared not pray for it,—I kept my soul aloof. But now and then I said, and said no more: "Master, I trust!"—then turned and plucked my flowers and heard the birds, but never sang myself. Enough to live and wait!

One happy dawn I slipped from bonds of sleep and grew aware of unexampled bodily ease and mental equipoise. Then, on the instant, I began to see. Whether the things I saw were etchings traced upon the brain or pictured in the air by spirit-hands—my very own (the lower self-submerged from consciousness) or other spirit hands, is not for me to say. I saw no spirit, heard no voice, received no telepathic word; as thus: "We bring you gifts; do with them as you will." Instead of that, my quickened mind perceived the pictured things and gave them names; just as you name the children sent of God, and dare to call them yours. These are the things I saw:

First a retort—a quadrilateral "vacuum-chest" like those I had devised and used for canning air-exhausted goods by means of heat. I looked within and there was something never seen before in any vacuum. An underchamber, separate from all the rest,—a flattened shell of little depth, but wide and long, hermetically sealed, having two pipes that pierced the further wall. Outside of that were valves for entrance and escape.

Strange how I knew the office and the name! "That's my transmitter—meant to carry warmth, and not degrade the vacuum even by the lightest vapor-drift. This I shall fill with heated air or circulating water not too hot, or possibly with graduated steam. This does away with water-baths about my jars for raising temperatures—"to can, and not to cook."

What next? Slid in on narrow ribs, close to the roof, I saw a fluid-feeding pan, having a central orifice sealed from without. I saw a new device—the wheel that turned and let no air go in, a lengthened sealing stem, a seat, and on the other side a little feeding-pipe to fill

409

the pan. Just under all, I saw a trough to take the fluid out through branching arms and spill it in the jars.

Where were the jars? "They stood in rows upon the flattened shell, filled full of ruddy fruits, just plucked and ready for the process—everyone, its cap half set in place, dropped in a tightly fitting case, its mouth well out of sight. Easy to understand! Here is a way to seal without exposure to air; fill jars and cases full; reach in and tighten every cap in turn—sunk under fluid, safe from all the winds." I laughed for very joy! So simple, after all!

The door was shut; but still I seemed to see with Psychic eyes whatever passed within; the rending of the cells, the air-escape from fruits below and fluid over-head, the dripping down in unison, the filling of the jars brimful, the cases topping them. And under these the heated shell, transmitting gentle warmth by contact—all the space a-cold because of vacuum, and yet the vaporous boiling going on. I watched the little hurry, starting first low down, the upward drift, the downward flow, the rise again, the fall, the slow subsidence;—airless fruit and airless fluid waiting to be sealed. And then—the door flung wide;—nothing to do but lift the cased-in jars, their mouths submerged from sight, dip fingers down, make tight the caps, slip out and set aside for trade.

"Carry the child," said those angelic guests, long time before: "Nothing shall harm the child" And not a wicked hand of man or woman, all these years, had plucked the cloak away and snatched the babe! And now indeed the cross was not too far away, though on the mountain top!—nor I too weak to climb! Well had the babe been hidden! Well does God protect!

Now look you! Whether I, being myself a spirit, or whether any finite spirit in the universe, had done this thing to me, no need to ask. God had befriended me. We face His light, we breathe His blessed air, we plunge in healing springs, and have a right to all these gifts I tell you of, were His to give whatever way He chose; and other gifts as well. God has been good to me. I render thanks.

When in the course of time I had these new inventions legally in hand (five patents waiting issue—mechanism, food uncooked, or cooked, or desiccated), pending work to come, I sat me down to think:

"Well, how about those three distressful years I spent in burning oil? Spirits incited me—they prophesied success. Did not Judge Evelyn ask for partnership, with profit sharing, when the gain should come? Spirits are not infallible we'll say, but when they speak, at least they tell the truth; and one who never lied to me on earth, came back and promised me that I should find a way to burn "the heaviest oil that could be made to flow." That seems beyond all possibility; reason revolts; but faith accepts. I have not been betrayed, nor anyway deceived." And so, with not a doubt, I let the matter rest.

After my dinner hour, I fell asleep—no Psychic sleep at all, but just an old folks' drowse—you know the way of it; as little wonderful as any moving cloud that casts a shadow down. It passed, but out of it had leaped, as by a lightning flash that yet remained a steadfast luminant—a comprehensive, all-embracing knowledge. How to master "fuel-oil" for furnace work. No need to see or think or trepidate: I knew.

"A Burner?" No; a burning system. Fluid level certainly—that basic principle (though all beside had scoffed at gravity and utilized the "squirt.") Out went my shallow pans and vaporizing plates ("the best of friends must part"); in went the bricks in place of them to seal my furnace. And what was left? My jutting bridge; my sideling baffle-plates, the further bed, the arching roof friend Morrison had taught me how to shape, the lowered "velvetry," the lessened throat, the dip and rise to reach a narrowed stack, and carry little heat.

But for the System: First a flue in front for downward rush of air to feed the tuyers set low and used to complement the natural draft (for Nature knows the way); also to muffle noise and mitigate the heat for stifling men; above the tuyers a couch for "levelers"—fed from an outer "safety trap," an inward reaching cul-de-sac to hold distributors, and under them a perforated arch or checker-work protecting them from heat; beneath that massive arch, a raging flame to catch the falling drops and give no chance for gas-escape—to tear their hydro-carbons into finest atoms, burn them gas and all;

411

to drift the heat along—oh, not for melting furnace-walls by misdirected flames, but—platinum perhaps! And not alone for generating steam to run our mills, but possibly to drive those battle-ships not driven yet with oil. Smoke?—you need not stint your oil; keep open hearth; give blast for agitation;—then behold the flames along your furnace-front rise up and seek escape—turn back and heat the more! Why, there you get economy, efficiency and might!

Well, anyway, I have my liberal patent claims allowed. They do me ample grace.

They who are disenthralled from flesh, cannot escape the law that made and makes them one with human kind. What though they learn the speech of seraphim? The old, familiar words are theirs to use again and ours to hear, what time they make descent—as verily they may!

And when they come—not loving Heaven the less but us the more—they plan to do us good. They walk with us at need; they sit with us at meat; they break and bless our bread; and if we toil at night and get no fish, they stand on shore and call, as one of old: "Cast now the net upon the other side." We cast—the catch is great. How shall we drag it in? And when we come to land, be sure that we shall find the fire of coals—the Master near at hand.

And still you challenge me for proof of spirit-intercourse?

Now, I am prone to think that where you see a flower among the garden-beds, some hand has dropped the seed. And where you see a wide parterre, some gardener has been at weary work. Forethought and care—the little plants along the edge, the larger ones beyond, space for the sturdy bush, a trellis for the tender vine, the gentle showers for all, the glowing harmonies of hue, order and life and beauty plain to see—all these to come by chance?

Have you not watched with me the shaping of the beds, that pulverizing of the soil, and how the seeds were scattered here and there, and how the rains came down and frosts were fended off and how the blossoms grew? Have you not seen the print of feet along the paths where went the gardeners? What need to pull the plants, and pry about the roots in search of mysteries? Let be! The seeds are ripe. Come, let us sort them out!

When John, the Revelator, saw one sent from Heaven and would have worshipped him, the spirit answered: "See thou do it not; I am thy fellow servant—one of thy brethren, the prophets." Who shall say, that when the lesser ones descend, they do not come as earth-born souls and let us know their earthly names? For even Moses and Elias came that way,—howbeit we hear they shone.

Soon after I had "touched" my promised work in 1871-only the rim of it, the white periphery whose belted force should start so many wheels (for nothing moves alone;)—it came about that one who called himself Judge Evelyn, drew very near to me. Whether his raiment shone, I did not see; but this I know; he gave himself a voice and talked with me alone. Having the gift of prophecy, and knowing I should walk the way of suffering, he let me know, but cast a light before. He said: "I choose a text to comfort you now and hereafter—all your earthly life: Read Judges, first, fifteenth."

I turned the leaves and read: "She said to him: 'Give me a blessing; thou hast given me a Southland; give me also springs of water,' and Caleb gave her the upper springs and the nether springs."

Now, after that, "Judge Evelyn" named me "Friend;" and I was glad and proud. He asked for willing service—not for subjugation; spirits lead no slaves. And so I followed where he chose to lead, or high or low—to mountain tops that overlooked the earth or into caverns dank with spray of seas where none had been before.

And now, it seems that whatsoever path my feet must walk, even till the "cool of day" these prophet spirits traced; and whatsoever hands should reach to give me help they saw from far away; and whatsoever bird of prey should drop to clutch the lamb or snatch the creeping babe, for him their bows were bent, their arrows set to slay; and whatsoever God would have me bring for temple service—candlesticks and lamps with oil for light, incense and onyx stones, or altar brass, with leavened cakes and doves for sacrifice—they put within my reach. And yet the end is not!

Last year, that one who had been silent long, returned and spoke again: "Friend, you have not been recreant, and I rejoice. But write—the time draws near; fulfillment waits."

To write—why that was hard. I urged the while I wrote: "See! I am old and worn and hard-bested. Come, comfort me with words."

Then one drew near and named the Book of books! "Read Joshua—fifteenth chapter, nineteenth verse." Therewith I turned the leaves and read: "Give me a blessing; for thou hast given me a Southland; give me also springs of water." And he gave her the upper springs and the nether springs.

Behold my Fountains of Desire! Friends be at peace. Farewell.

THE END

Discover more lost history from BIG BYTE BOOKS

46333867R00255

Made in the USA
Lexington, KY
25 July 2019